BEGINNING ARCGIS®
FOR DESKTOP DEVELOPMENT USING

T0268973

BEGINNING

ArcGIS® for Desktop Development Using .NET

BEGINNING

ArcGIS® for Desktop Development Using .NET

Pouria Amirian

A Wiley Brand

To the best mother and father in the whole world, Nosratolah and Soghra

To the best wife in the solar system, Ana

To the best sister and brother in the Milky Way, Paria and Payam

ABOUT THE AUTHOR

 **POURIA AMIRIAN** holds a Ph.D. in Geospatial Information Systems (GIS). Dr. Amirian is a developer and GIS/IT lecturer with extensive experience developing and deploying small to large-scale Geospatial Information Systems. At the moment he is a research fellow of Strategic Research in Advanced Geotechnologies (www.StratAG.com) at the National University of Ireland in Maynooth, where he focuses on Geospatial Service Oriented Architecture and working with NoSQL databases to handle big geospatial data. When he is not coding, Pouria is often found reading aviation magazines or practicing Wing Tsun. Pouria welcomes feedback about this book by email at PouriaAmirian.ArcObjects@gmail.com.

CREDITS

ACKNOWLEDGMENTS

EVEN THOUGH THE AUTHOR'S NAME is the one that graces the cover of a book, no book is the result of one person's efforts, and I'd like to thank a few of the people involved in this one. First and foremost, thanks to John Wiley & Sons for giving me the opportunity to write and providing me such a brilliant team for publishing this book. They were the only people willing to take a risk on an unknown author for the first book on GIS published by Wrox, and for that I will be forever grateful. Thanks to the staff of John Wiley & Sons — specifically Tom Dinse, Debbye Butler, Daniel Scribner and Louise Watson, whose watchful eyes saved me from potentially embarrassing mistakes. Thanks also to Chris Webb for getting me started with the book and Ellie Scott for keeping me on track. All of them did a great job of dealing with the frequent changes I made to the book as I was writing.

I'd like to thank my technical editor, Alexy Treshenkov, whose efforts made this book far better than it would have been otherwise.

I'd also like to thank Dr. Adam Winstanley, head of the Department of Computer Science at the National University of Ireland, Maynooth (NUIM), Dr. Martin Charlton from the National Centre for Geocomputation (NCG) Ireland, and Dr. Jan Rigby, program manager of StratAG (Strategic Research in Advanced Geotechnologies).

My gratitude, also, to those who helped create the .NET Framework, ArcObjects, tools, APIs, libraries, standards, specifications and all the other fun stuff that helps bring the geospatial to the mainstream and make GIS development and programming exciting today.

I would like to thank everyone who bought this book! I sincerely hope you have as much fun reading it as I did writing it, and I hope that you find it to be worth your hard-earned money and that it proves to be an educational and eye-opening experience.

It is time for expressing my feelings that never can be told using words. I am the luckiest person in the whole world because I have the greatest parents. I want to thank them for countless reasons: for always listening patiently, for their constant support, and for always being by my side. Also, I am so grateful to my father- and mother-in-law for all they do for Ana and me. I owe my life to my wife; my unprecedented wife Dr. Anahid Basiri, who saved my life with her love, passion, and patience. In addition to being the first reader of the book, Ana also took the photograph that is on the cover of this book. This is an image of the International Neuroscience Institute (INI).

Last but most definitely not least, we both (Ana and I) appreciate the high level of care and support of all INI's staff, especially Prof. M. Samii, Dr. J. Pieper, Prof. B. Mohammadi, and Prof. A. Samii. The service I got there was more like inspiration rather than just a brain surgery. In fact, the idea of writing this book had been on my mind for several years, but when I was in INI, I promised myself I would write this book, and now I am so happy to make this promise come true. To be honest, I want to thank that brain tumor because after getting rid of it, I started truly living every single moment. My life is now so joyful that if I could go back and choose not to have such a problem, to continue my life as it was, I would definitely choose to have that brain tumor and successful surgery and to enjoy every single moment beside my family as I am doing now.

CONTENTS

PART III: ARCOBJECTS PROGRAMMING

INTRODUCTION

WELCOME TO *Beginning ArcGIS for Desktop Development Using .NET.* If you have always wanted to start your journey in the world of ArcObjects, this book is your perfect one-stop resource.

Whether you are a new ArcGIS user with no background in programming or a programmer with a little experience in the ArcGIS platform, this book helps you be more productive. This book starts with the basics and brings you thoroughly up to speed. You first discover all you need to know about .NET programming for developing ArcObjects: variables, flow control, object-oriented programming, and interface-based programming. Then the book helps you build skills for developing ArcObjects and creating Desktop Add-Ins; reading object model diagrams; querying data; working with symbology, the geometry of geospatial data, and geoprocessing; and finally, deploying code.

WHO THIS BOOK IS FOR

This book is for anyone who wants to learn how to customize and extend Esri's ArcGIS for Desktop applications using .NET. It is intended for anyone who wants to learn ArcObjects step by step. With the knowledge gained after reading this book, you will be able to build different kinds of add-ins and traditional ArcObjects developments in Visual Studio.

No prior background in programming is assumed, and anyone familiar with ArcGIS should be able to follow the examples. It does help, however, if you have a basic understanding of .NET and COM. The book starts with programming in .NET and ends by covering deployment topics. Each chapter is built on the knowledge gained in previous chapters.

This book is also for anyone who knows how to customize and develop ArcGIS using Visual Basic for Application (VBA) or Visual Basic 6. If this is your interest, you've gained a lot from the new capabilities of the 10.X versions of ArcGIS.

All example code in this book is presented in C#, which can be easily converted to Visual Basic.NET. If you are a hard-core fan of VB.NET don't worry. All the source code used in this book is available for download in both C# and VB.NET at www.wrox.com (for more information, see the "Source Code" section later in this introduction).

WHAT THIS BOOK COVERS

This book walks you through ArcGIS development from the very first steps to the deployment phase. You will learn that it is a simple task to customize and develop ArcGIS for Desktop applications — this process isn't as hard as it seems at first. In other words, *developing ArcObjects is not rocket science.*

This book uses the latest version of ArcGIS, which is ArcGIS 10.1. All the code examples are tested to work in version 10.0 as well. The focus of this book is on creating a new model of ArcGIS customization: the Desktop Add-In (or add-in for short). Unfortunately, the add-in model is not available for previous versions of ArcGIS (8.x and 9.x). However, if you have one of the older versions, you can still use this book to create traditional ArcObjects projects (Extending ArcObjects Template in Visual Studio).

HOW THIS BOOK IS STRUCTURED

This book is divided into three parts. The following explains each of these three parts in detail, and what each chapter covers.

Part I: The Basics

Throughout Chapters 1 and 2, you will see different approaches for customizing ArcGIS for Desktop applications.

➤ **Chapter 1, "Why Geospatial Is Special":** This chapter shows you some unique characteristics of geospatial data. Then it explains the different kinds of GIS software and provides a high-level survey of the ArcGIS platform. The chapter finishes with an overview of the major approaches for storing and managing geospatial data.

➤ **Chapter 2, "Introduction to ArcGIS for Desktop Applications Customization":** Chapter 2 looks at different approaches for customizing ArcGIS for Desktop applications. It introduces techniques for customizing the user interface, Python scripting, Desktop Add-Ins, and extending ArcObjects. For each approach, I present at least one Try It Out example to show you how the different approaches fit together.

Part II: .NET Programming Fundamentals

In Chapters 3 and 4, you gain the necessary knowledge of .NET programming to put ArcObjects to work.

➤ **Chapter 3, ".NET Programming Fundamentals, Part I":** Chapter 3 explains the basic elements of C# that are necessary for successful ArcObjects development. The chapter covers topics such as variables, arrays, operators, decision making, iteration, object manipulation, enumeration, and the basics of object-oriented programming. When you complete this chapter, you will have good knowledge of implementing properties, methods, and constructors for classes.

➤ **Chapter 4, "NET Programming Fundamentals, Part II":** This chapter is the second and final chapter on pure .NET programming. You complete the big picture of object-oriented programming in C# by exploring object-oriented principles and techniques. I explain the concept of types in .NET and how reference types differ from value types. The final topics in this chapter include accessing files and folders and creating a simple KMZ (Keyhole Markup Language Zipped) file.

Part III: ArcObjects Programming

Throughout the chapters in this part, you learn ArcObjects programming from the ground up.

➤ **Chapter 5, "Understanding ArcObjects Object Model Diagrams":** Part III starts with one of the first things you have to know in the ArcObjects world — object model diagrams. Chapter 5 shows you how to read and interpret the different symbols of object model diagrams that are part of ArcObjects developer help. In addition, this chapter describes the technique of interface-based programming.

➤ **Chapter 6, "Accessing Maps and Layers":** You put your knowledge of reading object model diagrams to work and use various classes in ArcObjects to access various properties of maps and layers. You also create your first add-in button to get basic information about existing Data Frames and layers in the main window of ArcMap.

➤ **Chapter 7, "Working with Tables and FeatureClasses":** Tables and FeatureClasses are the most common structures for storing geospatial data in the ArcGIS platform. You learn how to access existing tables and FeatureClasses inside a map and how to add and delete a field in a table. Finally, this chapter looks at the topic of creating tables and records.

➤ **Chapter 8, "Subsets of Records":** Querying geospatial data and working with selections are explored in this chapter. It also explores cursors and calculating simple statistics out of numeric fields.

➤ **Chapter 9, "Constructing and Using the Geometry of Features":** This chapter explains how to create different types of geometries for different types of features. As a related topic, this chapter explores the most common types of geoprocessing analysis, such as buffer, overlay, and union using the ArcObjects Geometry library.

➤ **Chapter 10, "Rendering Geospatial Data and Using Hyperlinks and MapTips":** This chapter presents an overview of setting symbology for vector and raster layers and explores some types needed when working with Renderer classes. The contents of this chapter can be divided into two parts: The first part discusses how to change the appearance of geospatial data, and the second part deals with how to make features to go beyond display through hotlinks, hyperlinks, and MapTips.

➤ **Chapter 11, "Labeling, Exporting ActiveView, and Working with Elements":** This chapter covers some topics related to creating softcopy output out of geospatial data. This chapter presents an overview of making different kinds of labels using the standard and Maplex labeling engines. Exporting an ActiveView is also covered in detail, and finally you learn about working with elements and getting prebuilt items from the Style Manager.

➤ **Chapter 12, "Geoprocessing with Tools and Models":** Chapter 12 focuses on the geoprocessing framework. Geoprocessing is a core and indispensable part of any GIS software. Users of ArcGIS perform geoprocessing via ArcToolbox. This chapter provides an overview of using the geoprocessing framework in code and shows you how to execute tools and models as well as background geoprocessing.

➤ **Chapter 13, "Feature Data Management":** This chapter provides an overview of the most widely needed topics in geospatial data management in ArcObjects for vector data. Topics such as spatial reference systems, exporting features, creating geodatabases, and assigning domains to fields are explained.

➤ **Chapter 14, "Some Advanced Topics in ArcObjects Programming and Deployment":** This chapter explains some advanced topics such as sharing state and functionality between components, creating application extensions, and wiring ArcObjects events. In addition this chapter illustrates how to create setup projects and configure them to make an easy-to-use installer package. A custom behavior is sometimes needed during the setup procedure, such as reading and writing registry keys. This chapter demonstrates how to create this custom behavior in order to perform appropriate actions.

The final part of the book is the Appendix:

➤ **Appendix, "Answers to Exercises":** Answers to all the questions asked at the end of each chapter are presented in this appendix.

WHAT YOU NEED TO USE THIS BOOK

To use the examples in this book, in addition to ArcGIS Desktop 10.0 or ArcGIS for Desktop 10.1, you need at least .NET 3.5 sp1 (service pack 1), which is installed with ArcGIS for Desktop 10.0 and 10.1. You also need an Integrated Development Environment (IDE) to be able to write code. You can use any IDE from Microsoft that supports .NET 3.5 sp1. The following is a list of available IDEs that can be used to develop add-ins for ArcGIS Desktop 10.0 and ArcGIS for Desktop 10.1:

➤ Supported IDEs for version 10.0:

   ➤ All editions of Visual Studio 2008 including Express

   ➤ All editions of Visual Studio 2010 except Express

➤ Supported IDEs for version 10.1:

   ➤ All editions of Visual Studio 2010

In addition to ArcGIS and an IDE, you need to install ArcObjects SDK for Microsoft .NET Framework, which comes with ArcGIS for Desktop. The following table provides a summary of all required software packages:

REQUIRED SOFTWARE PACKAGES FOR THIS BOOK

TITLE	PACKAGE
GIS software	ArcGIS for Desktop 10.1 or ArcGIS Desktop 10.0
Integrated Development Environment	For ArcGIS for Desktop 10.1: all versions of Visual Studio 2010 For ArcGIS Desktop 10.0: all versions of Visual Studio 2008 and all versions of Visual Studio 2010 except Visual Studio 2010 Express
Software Development Kit	ArcObjects SDK for .NET

CONVENTIONS

To help you get the most from the text and keep track of what's happening, I use a number of conventions throughout the book:

> **WARNING** Boxes like this one hold important, not-to-be-forgotten information directly relevant to the surrounding text.

> **NOTE** Boxes like this one indicate notes, tips, hints, tricks, and asides to the current discussion.

TRY IT OUT

The *Try It Out* is an exercise you should work through, following the text in the book.

1. They usually consist of a set of steps.
2. Each step has a number.
3. Follow the steps through with your copy of the source code.

How It Works

Following each *Try It Out*, I explain in detail the code you've typed.

As for styles in the text:

➤ I *italicize* important words when I introduce them.

➤ I show URLs and code within the text in a special monofont typeface, like this: `persistence.properties`.

I present code in two different ways:

```
I use a monofont type for most code examples.

I use bold to emphasize code that is particularly important in the present context
or to show changes from a previous code snippet.
```

SOURCE CODE

As you work through the examples in this book, you may choose either to type in all the code manually, or to use the source code files that accompany the book. All the source code used in this book is available for download at `www.wrox.com`. Specifically for this book, the code download is on the Download Code tab at:

```
www.wrox.com/remtitle.cgi?isbn=1118442547
```

You can also search for the book at `www.wrox.com` by ISBN (the ISBN for this book is 978-1-118-44254-8) to find the code. A complete list of code downloads for all current Wrox books is available at `www.wrox.com/dynamic/books/download.aspx`.

At the beginning of each chapter, I provide the name of the folder on Wrox.com that contains the code for that chapter. Throughout each chapter, you also find references to the names of code files as needed in listing titles and text.

Most of the code on `www.wrox.com` is compressed in a .ZIP, .RAR archive, or similar archive format appropriate to the platform. Once you download the code, decompress it with an appropriate compression tool.

> **NOTE** *Because many books have similar titles, you may find it easiest to search by ISBN; this book's ISBN is 978-1-118-44254-8.*

ERRATA

We make every effort to ensure that there are no errors in the text or in the code. However, no one is perfect, and mistakes do occur. If you find an error in one of our books, like a spelling mistake or faulty piece of code, we would be very grateful for your feedback. By sending in errata, you may save other readers hours of frustration, and at the same time, you will be helping us provide even higher quality information.

To find the errata page for this book, go to

```
www.wrox.com/remtitle.cgi?isbn=1118442547
```

Click the Errata link. On this page, you can view all errata that has been submitted for this book and posted by Wrox editors.

If you don't spot "your" error on the Book Errata page, go to `www.wrox.com/contact/ techsupport.shtml` and complete the form there to send us the error you have found. We'll check the information and, if appropriate, post a message to the book's errata page and fix the problem in subsequent editions of the book.

P2P.WROX.COM

For author and peer discussion, join the P2P forums at `http://p2p.wrox.com`. The forums are a web-based system for you to post messages relating to Wrox books and related technologies and interact with other readers and technology users. The forums offer a subscription feature to e-mail you topics of interest of your choosing when new posts are made to the forums. Wrox authors, editors, other industry experts, and your fellow readers participate in these forums.

At `http://p2p.wrox.com`, you will find a number of different forums that will help you, not only as you read this book, but also as you develop your own applications. To join the forums, just follow these steps:

1. Go to `http://p2p.wrox.com` and click the Register link.

2. Read the terms of use and click Agree.

3. Complete the required information to join, as well as any optional information you wish to provide, and click Submit.

4. You will receive an e-mail with information describing how to verify your account and complete the joining process.

> **NOTE** *You can read messages in the forums without joining P2P, but in order to post your own messages, you must join.*

Once you join, you can post new messages and respond to messages other users post. You can read messages at any time on the web. If you would like to have new messages from a particular forum e-mailed to you, click the Subscribe to this Forum icon by the forum name in the forum listing.

For more information about how to use the Wrox P2P, read the P2P FAQs for answers to questions about how the forum software works, as well as many common questions specific to P2P and Wrox books. To read the FAQs, click the FAQ link on any P2P page.

PART I
The Basics

1

Why Geospatial Is Special

WHAT YOU WILL LEARN IN THIS CHAPTER:

- ➤ Main reasons that geospatial data are special
- ➤ Some sources of errors in using and collecting geospatial data
- ➤ Major types of GIS software
- ➤ A brief description of the ArcGIS platform
- ➤ Various geospatial data storage models
- ➤ Different types of Esri geodatabases

WROX.COM CODE DOWNLOADS FOR THIS CHAPTER

The wrox.com code downloads for this chapter can be found at `www.wrox.com/remtitle .cgi?isbn=1118442547` on the Download Code tab. The code is in the Chapter01 folder and is individually named according to the names throughout the chapter.

Geospatial data have played a major role in human life for centuries. Almost all human activities and decisions contain geospatial components. Collecting, managing, processing, and representing various kinds of geospatial components are accomplished by various kinds of geotechnologies, including GIS (Geographical Information System), remote sensing, photogrammetry, cartography, surveying, and GPS (Global Positioning System), to name just a few. Many research organizations have identified geotechnology, nanotechnology, and biotechnology as the three most important emerging fields. There is no doubt that the need for geospatial data and use of geotechnologies will continue to grow for years to come.

GIS is the heart of geotechnologies and Esri's ArcGIS is the most widely used and powerful commercial GIS software. In this chapter, you will learn various categories of GIS software and see how the ArcGIS platform provides software products for each category. After reading this chapter, you will know what makes the ArcGIS platform compelling to users and developers alike.

> **NOTE** *Esri is the worldwide leading supplier of GIS software and services. The company was founded as Environmental Systems Research Institute in 1969 by Jack and Laura Dangermond. Today Esri products (particularly ArcGIS for Desktop applications) have more than 40 percent of the global market share.*

A TOUR OF GEOSPATIAL DATA

Nowadays, in order to create a map or collect geospatial data with a handheld GPS device, all the necessary steps are:

1. Turn on the GPS receiver.

2. Walk around and periodically click the button with the "Mark" label, or simply let the device collect data for you constantly.

3. Connect the GPS receiver to the computer and let the software draw a map for you. Even better, have the small screen of the device itself display the map.

Simple stuff, right? Collecting and using geospatial data like this is very common today. Millions of people explore the world on www.OpenStreetMap.org, which collects and updates most of its geospatial data in the mentioned fashion (called *crowdsourcing*). *Geocaching* is another fun example of using and collecting geospatial data. Geocaching is a low-cost sport in which a person (called a geocacher) uses a GPS device to find something that was hidden by other geocachers. Technically speaking, geocaching is fun outdoor navigation with GPS devices.

As a more recent simple example of using and collecting geospatial data, consider the W3C Geolocation Application Programming Interface (API) specification. This API provides the location of a device (desktop, handheld without GPS, handheld with GPS, etc.) through location information servers in standard and transparent fashion directly from the web browser. The Geolocation API is implemented in almost all modern web browsers, including Microsoft Internet Explorer, Mozilla Firefox, Google Chrome, Apple Safari, and Opera. The following Try It Out demonstrates the simplest example of using Geolocation API.

TRY IT OUT Using the Geolocation API to Get the Current Location (TheSimplestExample.htm)

1. Open the text editor of your choice (like Windows Notepad). You also can use any HTML editor, but for this example, a simple text editor suffices.

2. Enter the following statements:

```
<!DOCTYPE html>
<html lang="en">
<head>
    <title>Simple Usage of Geolocation API </title>
     <script type="text/javascript">
if (window.navigator.geolocation)
{       navigator.geolocation.getCurrentPosition(getLocationCallback,errorCallback);
```

```
      } else {
         alert('Unfortunately your web browser does not support Geolocation API.');
      }

      function getLocationCallback(location) {
         var geospatialMessage = '';
         geospatialMessage += "Your geographic location is:\n\n";
         geospatialMessage += 'Latitude: ' + location.coords.latitude + "\n";
         geospatialMessage += 'Longitude: ' + location.coords.longitude + "\n";
         alert(geospatialMessage);
      }

      function errorCallback(error) {
         alert("something wrong !");
      }
    </script>
</head>
<body></body>
</html>
```

3. Save the file with the name of "TheSimplestExample.htm". In Notepad, make sure that you enter the double quotation marks before and after the name of the file in order to save it as an .htm file.

4. Close your text editor. You are now ready to test the Geolocation API. Open the file with Internet Explorer 9.0, Firefox 3.5, or Opera 10.6 (or newer versions of these Web browsers). As Figure 1-1 shows, you are asked if you would like to share your location with the Web page.

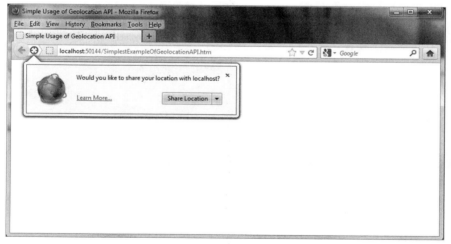

FIGURE 1-1

5. If you click the Share Location button, you will see the screen shown in Figure 1-2, which, strangely, shows a location even if you are sitting in front of your computer using a dial-up modem to connect to the Internet.

FIGURE 1-2

6. If you enter those numbers in an online mapping application like Microsoft Bing Maps (www.bing .com/maps), you will notice that it is the approximate location of the device that provides location information to your browser, GPS, or any other device. (See Figure 1-3.)

FIGURE 1-3

How It Works

To see the purpose and use of the Geolocation API, let's begin by examining the code. The code first checks for support of the Geolocation API in your browser with the following statements:

```
if (window.navigator.geolocation){
  navigator.geolocation.getCurrentPosition(getLocationCallback,errorCallback);
} else{
  alert('Unfortunately your web browser does not support Geolocation API.');
}
```

If the browser supports the Geolocation API, the script calls the getCurrentPosition function and passes the names of two other functions. If the browser does not support the Geolocation API, the script alerts the user.

The first function will be called if the Geolocation API successfully gets the current position of the browser and will report the current position:

```
function getLocationCallback(location) {
        var geospatialMessage = '';
        geospatialMessage += "Your geographic location is:\n\n";
        geospatialMessage += 'Latitude: ' + location.coords.latitude + "\n";
        geospatialMessage += 'Longitude: ' + location.coords.longitude + "\n";
        alert(geospatialMessage);
}
```

The second function is called if the Geolocation API fails to locate the current position of the browser.

> **NOTE** Instead of getting the position directly from the `getCurrentPosition` function, we have to pass the names of two functions as input. The reason for passing the names of two other functions is that behind the scenes, the Geolocation API makes use of many calls to other resources to get the browser's position. As a result, we have to use the Geolocation API in asynchronous fashion with the help of callback functions.

HOW THE GEOLOCATION API WORKS

How the Geolocation API works is out of the scope of this book, but briefly, consider that every device that is connected to any network can be located. Various methods exist for locating devices in many different kinds of networks. In fact, the Geolocation API is a very high-level API, and it doesn't provide the positional information itself. It uses the network infrastructure to get the position. If the device (for example, a smartphone or tablet) has a built-in GPS receiver, the Geolocation API gets the position using the device's GPS receiver. If the cellphone doesn't have a built-in GPS receiver, the Geolocation API uses the location information services of the mobile communication network to get the positional information (it could be as simple as cell-ID of the wireless network). Even if you use your desktop computer to connect to the Internet, your location is available to the Geolocation API using your IP address (or the IP address of your Internet service provider). As a developer, it doesn't matter how the positional information becomes available or how the Geolocation API finds the position. All that matters is that it provides positional information for any kind of device as long as it is connected to a network. Based on the device and network, it provides various levels of accuracy. Again, simple stuff, right?

If you understand how geospatial data are used today by the Geolocation API, GPS devices, Google Earth, and so on, you might ask yourself: if collecting and using geospatial data is so simple, why do the techniques, concepts, and sciences like the Geospatial Information Science (GISc), Location Based Services (LBS), and Spatial Decision Support Systems (SDSS) exist at all? In other words, is it all about software? If it is all about software, we can use and collect geospatial data just like any other kind of data. But geospatial data are different kinds of data and special methods and techniques have to be created and developed to handle them. The following sections briefly discuss what is special about geospatial data.

WHY GEOSPATIAL IS SPECIAL

Today, all human activities and decisions have a geospatial component, and maps are the most widely used type of geospatial component. Most of the time, we are exploring maps in many different kinds of media — such as TV channels, newspapers, mobile apps, websites, and even the small display of a car navigation system to find an address, a best route, a nearest facility, tomorrow's weather, and so on. In contrast to what they seem at first, using and collecting geospatial data are not so simple.

In its basic form, a geospatial component is a pair of geographic coordinates called *latitude* and *longitude*, which are used to represent the location of a point on the surface of the earth. The latitude and longitude belong to geographic coordinate system space, so they are called *geographic coordinates*.

As we already know, earth is not a perfect sphere. Mathematically speaking, among 3D shapes, spheroid provides the best approximation of earth. This approximation injects a variable amount of errors in all geospatial-related activities (from representation to processing) of geospatial data.

Spheroid is a 3D shape, so in order to represent it on the 2D plane of display screens (like a map or the screen of any device), the 3D spheroid has to be projected on a flat coordinate system. This is called *projection* or *map projection*. All map projections distort geospatial components in some way. If you take a look at Greenland (with an area of 2,166,086 km^2) as it is represented in Microsoft Bing Maps (www.bing.com/maps), you will notice that it is drawn a little larger than South America (with an area of 17,840,000 km^2; see Figure 1-4). This map has a map projection that distorts the area of geospatial features. In spite of this, most of the time we use and work with a projected coordinate system in which geospatial data are projected on the flat coordinate system.

Depending on the purpose of the map, some distortions are acceptable and others are not. Different map projections exist in order to preserve some properties of the spheroid (or any other 3D shape) at the expense of other properties. This is an additional source of error in using and collecting data. Moreover, the sources of geospatial data have their own errors too. For example, most handheld GPS devices provide accuracy for no more than several meters, which might not be acceptable in many engineering projects.

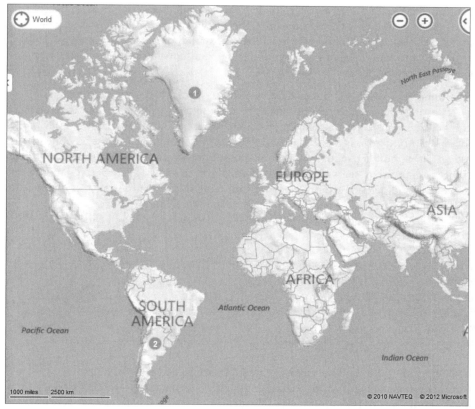

FIGURE 1-4

What about processing? Any kind of geospatial processing needs precise geospatial data with a known coordinate system. (As mentioned previously in this section, coordinate systems come in two flavors: projected and geographic.) Many processing methods of geospatial data can be applied to various spaces, like the human body, for example, as is done for analysis of the human body with medical images. There are also many processing methods that are specific to geospatial data, which in most cases are very complex and time consuming. Even with the horsepower of today's computers, most PCs and laptops aren't designed to handle the intense workload of geospatial processing. The simple reason for such a huge workload is the high volume and unstructured nature of geospatial data. For example, a polygon can have at least three and at most millions of points as its point collection.

So to manage geospatial data effectively, we have to resort to databases, in which case, each activity for querying, visualizing, editing, and geospatial processing includes interaction with the database. Besides the distinctive techniques needed for managing geospatial data inside databases (such as indexing geospatial data for quick retrieval), to make matters even more complicated, one of the unique aspects of geospatial data is the relationships that they can have. In addition to regular relational relationships (like parent-child relationships), geospatial data can have many topological relationships, which is the arrangement for how point, line, and polygon features share their geospatial components or geometry.

In addition to various kinds of errors, huge volumes of data, special types of relationships, complexity of processing, the need for coordinate systems, and various kinds of representation, editing geospatial data usually requires long transactions, which is rare in managing other kinds of data. Simply put, a *transaction* is a package of units of work on data that must be done in all-or-nothing mode. Editing non-geospatial data in most cases must be done in a fraction of a second (e.g., transactions in financial systems like banks). In contrast, any edit of geospatial data (inserting new features, updating and deleting existing features) might take a few minutes to several months to be completed. For this reason, geospatial data must be managed in quite different information systems. Those are the quick answers to the question asked at the beginning of this section: Why are geospatial data so special?

> **NOTE** *For in-depth exploration of why geospatial data are special, read* Geographic Information Systems and Science, *third edition, by Paul A. Longley, Michael F. Goodchild, David J. Maguire, and David W. Rhind (John Wiley & Sons, Inc., 2011).*

As I said at the beginning of this chapter, nearly all activities and decisions of humans contain geospatial components. Collecting, managing, processing, and representing various kinds of geospatial components are accomplished by geotechnologies, which include GIS, remote sensing, photogrammetry, cartography, surveying, and GPS, just to name a few. GIS is the heart of geotechnologies. I think of it this way: If geotechnologies were a human, GIS would be the brain.

> **NOTE** *There are a lot of good books on geotechnologies. Most of them focus on a specific geotechnology. But if you are more interested in a brief introduction to almost all geotechnologies, then read* Basics of Geomatics *by Mario A. Gomarasca (Springer, 2009).*

GIS consists of six components: hardware, software, people, data, methods, and network. The focus of this book is on the software component. The next section delves into the GIS software topic.

VARIOUS KINDS OF GIS SOFTWARE

GIS software is a collection of computer programs that store, retrieve, query, process, and visualize geospatial data. Based on functionality and type of users, the main categories of GIS software are server GIS, desktop GIS, developer GIS, and mobile GIS. To introduce these main categories of GIS software, this section focuses on the Esri ArcGIS platform.

Server GIS

As the name implies, server GIS is all about serving geospatial resources to its clients over networks (such as the Internet). It is fair to say that currently, the Web is used almost exclusively in server GIS to share geospatial resources. Geospatial resources could be maps (images of geospatial data), geospatial data, processing services, geospatial metadata, and so on. Based on who consumes the geospatial resources, this category has three subcategories: web GIS, GIS web services, and geospatial data access.

People use web GIS applications for many purposes. A web GIS application could be as simple as a website with a slippy map that provides search capability and navigation controls such as zoom in/out and pan (like most web mapping applications such as www.OpenStreetMap.org), or as sophisticated as a web application that provides processing and editing of geospatial data and contains tools for data management activities and workflows (such as http://gis.hudson.oh.us/HudsonSL/).

In contrast to web GIS applications, GIS web services are consumed by other applications. Other applications call GIS web services to get access to geospatial resources. Users of those applications may never know about this fact. The Open Geospatial Consortium (OGC) has played an important role in the evolution of GIS web services. Specifically, OGC has tried to provide interoperability between GIS software through the development of standards that facilitate sharing and accessing geospatial resources. Among the most widely used standards are Geography Markup Language (GML), Keyhole Markup Language (KML), Web Map Service (WMS), Web Feature Service (WFS), and Web Coverage Service (WCS). GML and KML are XML-based formats and are explained later in this chapter. WMS, WFS, and WCS are GIS web services that provide access to map data (an image of geospatial data), vector geospatial data, and raster geospatial data, respectively. If you enter the following URL into the address bar of your web browser, you will see the image shown in Figure 1-5:

```
http://webservices.nationalatlas.gov/wms?SERVICE=WMS&REQUEST=GetMap&VER
SION=1.1.1&FORMAT=PNG&WIDTH=600&HEIGHT=425&SRS=EPSG:4326&BBOX=-170,20,-
65,85&LAYERS=states,farm_1
```

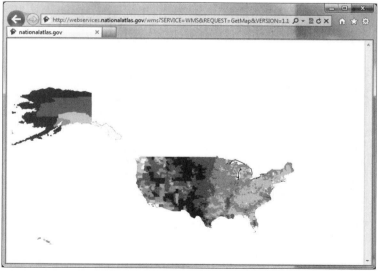

FIGURE 1-5

Yes, you are right: It is a map from the national atlas of the United States. The text preceding the question mark ("?") is the address of the WMS service of National Atlas. Everything after the question mark (called the *query string*) is a key-value pair in the form of `key=value`. You can see by looking at the query string that the web browser requests an image of geospatial data with the following characteristics:

➤ Format of the image, requested as Portable Network Graphics (`FORMAT=PNG`).

➤ Size in pixels with two keys — width and height (`WIDTH=600, HEIGHT=425`).

➤ Spatial Reference System (SRS) in European Petroleum Survey Group (EPSG) coding scheme (`SRS=EPSG:4326`). This SRS code is the other name for the World Geodetic System of 1984 (or WGS 84), which is a well-known geographic coordinate system. (Remember latitude and longitude?)

➤ Bounding box of the area in terms of minX, minY, maxX, and maxY (`BBOX=-170,20,-65,85`).

➤ Layers constituting the map (`LAYERS=states,farm_1`).

This usage of WMS isn't suitable for human users — quite the opposite — but other GIS software can use this method easily. GIS web services provide an interface for other GIS software instead of a user interface for human users. Did you notice what programming language or database is used to implement the WMS functionality? Again, it is transparent to users of WMS (both users are software applications). No matter what software infrastructure (operating system, middleware, programming language, and database) is used to implement the service, all that matters is that they can be used in platform-neutral fashion to provide valuable geospatial resources. Using GIS web services provides an efficient and simple way of sharing and accessing geospatial resources. Today, thousands of organizations all around the world provide GIS web services to make it easy to access and share very large amounts of data.

Various GIS software products can consume GIS web services. Consuming GIS web services is in most cases as simple as adding a geospatial layer to the GIS software. You see an example of this in the "Using a GIS Web Service Inside ArcMap" Try It Out, later in this chapter. Even GIS web services can use other GIS web services to build a composite GIS web service.

> **NOTE** *The ability to combine GIS web services brings a new opportunity to make GIS software a composite of autonomous, general purpose, and reusable GIS web services. This is where Service Oriented Architecture (SOA) and cloud computing (Software as a Service, or SaaS) come into play. In the ArcGIS platform, ArcGIS online provides huge geospatial resources that are ready to use over the Web inside Esri's secure cloud. Coverage of ArcGIS online is beyond the scope of this book.*

ArcGIS for Server (formerly known as ArcGIS Server) provides necessary tools and functionality to create web GIS and GIS web services easily. Thanks to ArcGIS for Server, by configuring some simple settings (mostly just selecting appropriate options from check boxes), you can build sophisticated web GIS applications and GIS web services without a single line of code. Although replaced by ArcGIS for Server, ArcIMS is worth mentioning. ArcIMS provided an easy way to create and develop web GIS software.

ArcGIS for Server has another subcategory. Let's call it geospatial data access, which provides access to geospatial data inside databases. Geospatial data access doesn't store data; rather, it provides the necessary tools and utilities to enable Database Management System (DBMS) software to manage geospatial data. In this case, it doesn't matter that a DBMS is able or not to handle geospatial data natively; all that matters is that geospatial data access software uses DBMS as a repository of geospatial data. Unlike web GIS and GIS web services, geospatial data access is not an independent product. In other words, it doesn't provide user interface for human users, and it does not provide an interoperable and public interface for other systems. Geospatial data access works with the other components or software in a GIS system to enable management of geospatial data inside a DBMS. In the ArcGIS platform, ArcSDE plays this role. It is part of ArcGIS for Server software.

> **NOTE** Spatial DBMS is another kind of server GIS explained in the section "Geospatial Data Inside Spatial DBMS," later in this chapter.

Desktop GIS

Desktop GIS is GIS software installed on the user's computer that provides a range of capabilities. Conventional desktop GIS provides users all the tools needed to perform geospatial-related activities. The desktop GIS is without a doubt the largest category of GIS software in the professional GIS community, and for this reason we divide it into viewer, virtual globe, and professional subcategories.

Desktop viewers provide simple display and query capabilities. Usually they provide no tools for data editing and processing. But desktop viewers in most cases are free, and they help to create de facto standards, terminology, and formats for specific vendors. ArcReader is free downloadable software from Esri that provides easy-to-use tools for working with geospatial data. Use of ArcReader is limited to geospatial data, which are packaged using ArcGIS for Desktop ArcPublisher extension. In other words, you can't add your local geospatial data to the map (there is no "add data" button!). ArcGIS Explorer is the other free desktop viewer software from Esri (which has add-data capability). In its latest version (Build 1750), it provides both a 2D and a 3D view of geospatial data as well as adding online geospatial resources such as geoprocessing models. Being able to represent and process data in 3D, ArcGIS Explorer belongs to both viewer and virtual globe subcategories.

As the name suggests, a desktop virtual globe is primarily used for viewing and analyzing 3D geospatial data. Google Earth is a successful example of a desktop virtual globe. Since they are low cost (and in most cases, free at the basic versions), desktop virtual globes have gained considerable traction in the GIS and non-GIS communities. ArcGlobe is desktop virtual globe, and ArcScene is desktop 3D modeling software in the ArcGIS platform. They can be used for visualization, analysis, and animation of 3D geospatial data. ArcGlobe uses a globe-shaped surface and just one map projection to visualize all 3D data, which makes it the best choice for visualizing geospatial data at global scales. In contrast, ArcScene usually uses planar projections and is best suited for regional scales.

Professional desktop GIS products are full-featured GIS software and usually contain tools for collecting, editing, and analyzing geospatial data. In addition, professional desktop GIS products provide many tools for making various kinds of visual output and reports from geospatial data. They often include necessary tools for geospatial data management and administration. ArcMap and ArcCatalog are two professional desktop applications included in the ArcGIS for Desktop applications package that provide a full range of geospatial capabilities. ArcMap is the main mapping application of the ArcGIS platform. It is used for collecting, editing, analyzing, visualizing, and publishing geospatial data. ArcCatalog is primarily used for geospatial data management and administration. In the following Try It Out, you learn how ArcMap uses a GIS web service.

TRY IT OUT   **Using a GIS Web Service inside ArcMap**

1. Ladies and gentleman, start your engines by running ArcMap, and be sure you are connected to the Internet (actually, the Web, the Internet's major application).

2. Click the Add Data button, shown in Figure 1-6, to open the Add Data dialog box.

FIGURE 1-6

3. Click the Up One Level arrow several times to get to the Home folder, as shown in Figure 1-7.

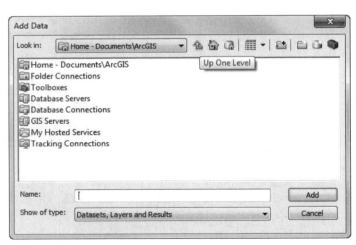

FIGURE 1-7

4. Double-click the GIS Servers folder to display its contents, as shown in Figure 1-8.

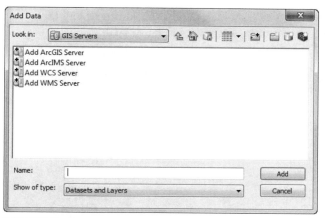

FIGURE 1-8

5. Double-click Add WMS Server to open the Add WMS Server window. Enter the address of the WMS service for the national atlas of the United States (`http://webservices.nationalatlas.gov/wms`) into the URL textbox and click the Get Layers button.

6. If there is no problem, you should see the list of layers shown in Figure 1-9. Click OK.

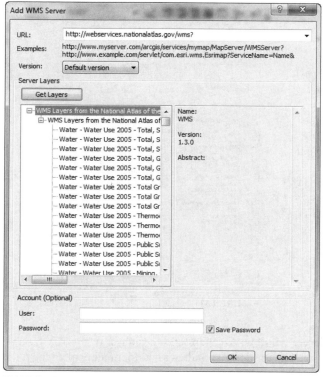

FIGURE 1-9

7. A new node for WMS is added to the GIS Servers folder. Double-click it to add all layers to the map. You will see lots of layers added to the map, as shown in Figure 1-10.

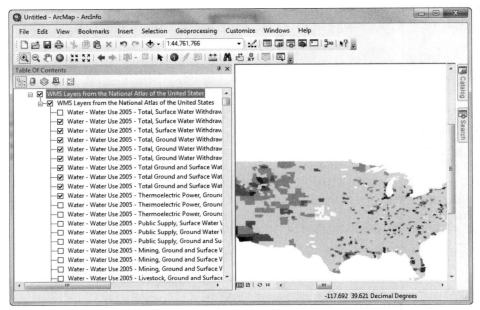

FIGURE 1-10

8. If you scroll down the layer list and turn on the layer with the name Agriculture-Farms 2007-Average Size of Farms in Acres, you will see the same layer that you saw in your browser in the "Using the Geolocation API to Get the Current Location" Try It Out, earlier in this chapter. Also, if you double-click the layer to open the Layer Properties window, you will notice that the name of the layer is "farm_1" (see Figure 1-11). Where have you seen this name before?

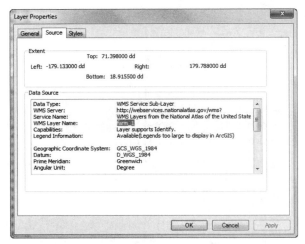

FIGURE 1-11

How It Works

As mentioned earlier, using the WMS service is as simple as adding a layer. When we enter the URL address of the WMS service and click the Get Layers button in the Add WMS Server window, ArcMap sends a request to the WMS service and asks about the capabilities of the service. The service responds with a document called a *capabilities document.* Using the capabilities document, ArcMap recognizes layers which can be served by the service. From this point, you can use layers from the WMS service as you would any map layers and let ArcMap take care of interaction with WMS.

> **NOTE** *As you can see, the capabilities document is intended to be used by software. But it is a human-readable XML document as well. If you want to retrieve the capabilities document of the mentioned WMS, enter the following URL into the address bar of your web browser:*
>
> `http://webservices.nationalatlas.gov/wms?request=getCapabilities`

Developer GIS

When you want to build specific-purpose and highly flexible GIS software, you have two options: build the software from the ground up, or alternatively, make use of ready-to-use components to build the software. As you now know, geospatial data are special, so in addition to the usual tasks for building any kind of software, there are many special techniques and methods to perform even simple tasks in GIS software. Remember that putting some pushpins or markers on Bing Maps or Google Maps, making mashups, or creating flashy layouts is not considered GIS software. When considering geospatial data from different sources with various errors and, most notably, different kinds of coordinate systems, even a simple distance measurement tool can become a nightmare for a team of knowledgeable developers. As a result, many organizations use ready-to-use tools and components to save money and time rather than implementing the software from the ground up. In general, tools and components, along with documentation and additional utility software, are packaged together in a *Software Development Kit* (SDK). Developer GIS products are SDKs that provide developers the tools they need to customize existing GIS packages or create new GIS applications. The main audiences of this kind of GIS software are brave developers like you and me. An SDK can be used to customize existing software or it can be used to create brand new software. All aspects of serious development of GIS software are considered developer GIS. Many flavors of GIS software exist, and in turn, there also are many kinds of developer GIS (or SDKs). The following list constitutes a brief explanation of development opportunities in the ArcGIS platform. (Chapter 2 introduces ArcGIS desktop application development.)

➤ In the Esri desktop GIS arena, there are ArcGIS desktop SDKs, an ArcGIS engine SDK, and an ArcGIS Explorer SDK.

➤ ArcGIS for Desktop provides two SDKs (.NET SDK and Java SDK) for customization of ArcGIS for Desktop applications (ArcMap, ArcCatalog, ArcGlobe, and ArcScene).

➤ In the ArcGIS platform, the ArcGIS Engine is considered the main developer GIS for building brand new GIS applications. It is, in almost all cases, used for creating high-end, specific-purpose, and flexible desktop GIS software.

➤ ArcGIS Explorer has its own SDK, which provides easy and neat ways to customize the look and feel of the user interface, as well as extend its functionality using .NET.

For exposing all kinds of web mapping functionality over the web, ArcGIS for Server provides GIS web services that can be used to create web GIS applications. This is the pattern to opt for when you're building web GIS applications. In other words, you first publish a GIS resource (e.g., an ArcMap map document) as a service and then build your web application, which consumes that service. In addition, GIS web services provided by ArcGIS for Server can be used by major web application development platforms and technologies such as JavaScript, .NET, Java, Microsoft SharePoint, Microsoft Silverlight/WPF, and Adobe Flex (generally Esri calls these APIs ArcGIS Web Mapping APIs).

There are also SDKs for using geospatial data on handheld devices that provide access to the device's hardware and services (like GPS). Esri provides SDKs for all major platforms of handheld devices such as Google Android, Apple iOS, and Microsoft Windows Phone. These SDKs can provide access to GIS web services that are published by ArcGIS for Server and other GIS web services that adhere to OGC standards (just like WMS).

Mobile GIS

Mobile or handheld GIS is simply GIS software that runs on handheld devices such as smartphones and tablet PCs. Mobile GIS software can work in connected and disconnected modes. This capability makes them the best choice for a full range of field-related activities like field data collection and validation. With the rapid progress of the hardware industry, wireless networks, and the popularity of handheld devices, mobile GIS software might become the dominant category of GIS software in the near future. ArcPad is the main mobile GIS of the ArcGIS platform. There is also ArcGIS for Smartphones and Tablets as well. These products provide many useful tools for navigation, querying, and analyzing geospatial data on a handheld device, and they can edit existing geospatial data.

Table 1-1 organizes the ArcGIS platform based on the main GIS software categories.

TABLE 1-1: The ArcGIS Platform Based on the Main Categories of GIS Software

CATEGORY	ARCGIS SOFTWARE
Desktop GIS: Professional	ArcCatalog and ArcMap
Desktop GIS: Viewer	ArcReader and ArcGIS Explorer
Desktop GIS: Virtual Globe	ArcGlobe, ArcScene, and ArcGIS Explorer
Server GIS: Geospatial data access	ArcSDE
Server GIS: Web GIS	ArcGIS Server and ArcIMS
Server GIS: GIS Web Services	ArcGIS Server
Developer GIS: Web GIS application development	Web APIs for ArcGIS Server (JavaScript, Flex, Silverlight/ WPF, Microsoft SharePoint, .NET, and Java)
Developer GIS: for customizing Desktop GIS	ArcObjects SDK for .NET and Java and ArcGIS Explorer SDK

Developer GIS: for Desktop GIS development	ArcGIS Engine
Developer GIS: for mobile device development	SDK for Android, iOS, and Windows Phone
Mobile GIS	ArcPad, ArcGIS for Smartphones and Tablets

GEOSPATIAL DATA MODELS AND STORAGE

The term *model* can get quite confusing, given its use in a number of different contexts. The term *geospatial data model* refers to how geospatial data are described and stored in the file or database and how data are represented in a computer system. Raster and vector data models are two of the most used methods of representing geospatial data on computers with many different storage models and formats. Note that geospatial data consist of both attribute and geometry elements. Positional data and all their related characteristics (such as coordinate system and accuracy) constitute the geometry element of geospatial data.

> **NOTE** *Other kinds of models are available for geospatial data. A* conceptual model *describes the elements of significance for a specific purpose (domains or applications like water management), including attribute characteristics and relationships between attributes. The* logical model *represents business requirements with definitions and examples that prioritize importance and how elements relate to each other. The* physical model *describes how the logical model is represented in files or a database with corresponding sets of constraints.*

Raster

In a raster model, space is usually divided into a 2D array of cells (picture elements, or *pixels* for short) and each cell is assigned a value. When geospatial data are represented in a raster model, all detail about variation of the data within each cell is lost, and instead, the cell is given a single value. That single value is almost always determined by the value that occupies most of the area of the cell. Additional values stored for each cell may be a discrete value, such as a land use code, a continuous value, such as pollution or elevation, or a null value if no data are available.

Two commonly used sources of raster data are satellite images and digital aerial photos. Raster data is stored in various formats, from a standard file-based structure of PNG, TIFF, JPEG, JPEG2000, and GeoTIFF to binary large object (BLOB) data stored directly in a relational database management system (RDBMS). In the ArcGIS platform, there are many file formats you can work with where raster data is concerned, and they can be stored outside the geodatabase model. But as you will see in the "Esri Geodatabase" section later in this chapter, a geodatabase provides a mechanism to store raster data beside other elements of a GIS system, such as vector data, toolboxes for processing geospatial data, and many more. For a complete list of supported raster formats, consult the ArcGIS Help.

Vector

In a vector model, a *point* is the basic structure with which all the other geometries can be created. Line and area features historically have been constructed using simple linear connections (straight connections) between their point collections. As a result, line and area objects in GIS are modeled as a collection of connecting line objects (called *segments*) and the terms *polyline* and *polygon* have been coined to describe this fact. Vector models represent more precise and efficient models for storing and representing geospatial data, but the analysis of this model can be more complicated than for raster models in terms of algorithms and computation resources needed. As with raster data, there are quite a lot of formats and structures for storing vector data. The following sections briefly explain the most widely used structures for storing geospatial data.

> **NOTE** *Technically speaking, in GIS the connecting line between two points is called a segment. Traditionally, segments were stored just as straight lines. But in most modern GIS systems like ArcGIS, segments can be parametric curves as well as straight lines (such as circular arcs, elliptical arcs, and Bézier curves). So the line or area feature in GIS is composed of an ordered set of points (a point collection) and the types of segments used between each pair of points in the point collection.*

Geospatial Data as Text or Binary File

Geospatial data can be stored simply in text files using comma-separated values (CSV) or similar structures. In fact, almost all GIS packages provide some import/export functionality based on simple text or spreadsheet files. In most cases, these structures provide the bare bones of geospatial data and are used only for point geospatial data.

Early GIS systems used a proprietary structure or file format for storing and processing geospatial data natively. Being proprietary, many early GIS systems didn't publish their own proprietary file format specifications. When there was a need to share geospatial data, they provided a textual format with limited capabilities compared to the native proprietary format, or a different proprietary format that had a published specification.

As an example of such proprietary formats, Autodesk's DXF (data exchange format) is a proprietary file format intended to provide data interoperability between the Autodesk AutoCAD platform and other software for vector data. Data in DXF can be saved as binary as well as ASCII encodings, which makes it a low-cost choice for import/export functionality for geometry elements of geospatial data. But limited support of spatial reference systems, attributes, and complex geometries makes it a less useful file format for storing and processing geospatial data.

Esri GRID is a raster file format that supports two distinct file formats. ARC/INFO GRID is a proprietary binary raster format for native storage and analysis of raster data in Esri products. ARC/INFO ASCII GRID is a textual format primarily used for exchange of raster data.

Geospatial Data in Georelational Models

The georelational model is one of the most widely used models for storage, processing, and sharing geospatial data. In this model, geospatial data is divided into two separate but related structures. The geometrical element of features is stored in a binary file or set of binary files, and corresponding attributes are stored in a RDBMS table. Association between the geometry elements and attribute elements is available using keys (unique keys in each set of features or feature class or identities). In other words, there is a one-to-one relationship between geometries in binary file(s) and the records of attribute data in the table.

The *Esri shapefile* (*shapefile* for short) is the most widely used georelational format for storing and sharing geospatial data. A shapefile actually consists of at least three files with the same name and with different extensions. These three files store core data of the georelational model, and other optional files can be used to provide further properties and metadata of the geospatial data in shapefile format. Mandatory files in shapefile are:

➤ **.shp:** geometry element of geospatial features

➤ **.dbf:** attribute element of geospatial features; a dBase (a RDBMS) native format

➤ **.shx:** geometry index of geospatial features to enable quick geospatial data retrieval

Each shapefile represents a single feature class of points, lines, or polygons. Over time, shapefile has become widely accepted as a de facto standard for storing geospatial data, and it is still widely used and deployed. Despite its popularity, the shapefile has serious limitations:

➤ Limited support for Unicode for field name and attribute values

➤ Restricted length of field name (10 characters)

➤ No support for topology

➤ Limited feature storage (2 gigabytes)

➤ Limited number of fields (255)

➤ No support for time data

➤ Rounding errors (because numeric attributes are stored in character format rather than in binary format)

Geospatial Data inside Spatial DBMS

With the increasing use of geospatial data, the previous models for storing, processing, and sharing geospatial data were rarely efficient. A spatial DBMS is simply a DBMS in which geospatial data can be stored and retrieved. In some cases, DBMS supports geospatial data natively. In the world of commercial DBMS products, Microsoft has commenced support of geospatial data in all editions of its flagship DBMS product from version 2008 onward, so Microsoft SQL Server 2008 and 2012 (even the free Express editions) support geospatial data natively. In some other cases, spatial DBMS is a database extension to a full-featured DBMS. A famous example of an open source database extension is PostGIS, which adds support for geospatial data to the PostgreSQL DBMS. Both SQL Server of the latest versions and PostgreSQL/PostGIS are examples of native spatial DBMS.

In yet other cases, geospatial data access — which is a package of components and services — enables use of geospatial data in RDBMS products. In this case, it doesn't matter whether those relational DBMS products are able to handle geospatial data natively; all that matters is that geospatial data access software uses them as a repository of geospatial data. In this case, the geospatial data access component, in conjunction with DBMS, comprises the spatial DBMS (a *spatially enabled DBMS*). The old SQL Server 2000 plus ArcSDE is an example of a spatially enabled DBMS.

In this book, when I refer to the term *spatial DBMS*, I mean native spatial DBMS as well as spatially enabled DBMS. As you have seen earlier, spatial DBMS is an indispensible part of server GIS. The spatial DBMS provides a central solution to store the geometry and attribute elements of geospatial data in seamless fashion. In addition, it provides the necessary tools to store vector and raster data efficiently. When one or more of the following conditions exist, resorting to spatial DBMS is inevitable:

➤ **Simultaneous users:** In corporate environments, when geospatial data is of interest to more than one group of users or departments, the DBMS should be used to handle geospatial data sharing efficiently and without any data duplication. Also, tracking users' activities, saving the lineage of geospatial data, and ensuring geospatial data consistency are much simpler using a central solution like a DBMS.

➤ **The need for long transactions:** When long transactions are needed, there must be a flexible and efficient mechanism to handle them. Long transactions are common in enterprise workflows; they occur when simultaneous users edit the same geospatial dataset. In this situation, each user must see his or her own changes with respect to shared geospatial data without directly changing the shared geospatial data (until it is approved).

➤ **High volume of geospatial data:** Most previous models have limitations in handling geospatial data. For example, shapefile and most file-based formats cannot handle geospatial data when it reaches the 2GB limit. In addition, because geospatial processing is complex in nature, the higher the size of geospatial data, the higher the risk of crashing the whole GIS software system.

➤ **Storing dynamic geospatial data or historical archiving of geospatial data:** Today storing and analyzing spatio-temporal data is a common practice in many sciences and businesses. Besides the many advantages of managing dynamic and historical geospatial data in databases, analyzing changes of spatial data over time reveals many facts and patterns (and it can be used in geospatial data mining applications).

➤ **Integration of GIS with other information systems:** For obvious reasons, almost all large information systems make use of DBMS. It is the exception to have GIS as the only information system in any enterprise. With spatial DBMS, it is possible to use the same data in different information systems.

Today, many commercial and open source DBMS products can be called spatial DBMS. In fact, in recent years, spatial capabilities have become trendy, must-have capabilities in the IT world. All major players in DBMS software have made their main products spatial DBMS. As another example of standardization, OGC and the International Organization for Standardization (ISO) provide the Simple Features specification, which extends the Structured Query Language (SQL) for spatial types. In this regard, the good news for developers is that the familiar SQL statements can be used to retrieve geospatial data. The other good news is that all major DBMSs implement the standard Simple Features specification.

Geospatial Data in XML Structures

Today, XML technologies play a major role in many aspects of computing, from designing the user interface of an Android mobile application to defining the web service interface of a component and from saving a Word document in Microsoft Office to saving vector graphics in Scalable Vector Graphics (SVG). It is fair to say that we all use one or more XML technologies nearly every day. XML has become the de facto standard for data exchange, and it is the most common tool for data transmission between all sorts of data processing systems. In this regard, there are some dominant XML-based formats that are used for storing, modeling, and visualizing geospatial data. The most important XML-based formats in the geospatial community are KML, GML, and GeoRSS.

> **NOTE** Simply put, XML technologies are all formats, languages, grammars, tools, and so on describing, modeling, storing, manipulating, querying, transforming, transmitting, and linking data in XML-based formats and structures. Because there are quite a lot of elements in XML technologies, there are XML integrated development environment (IDE) software products to help you work with them. If you are interested in XML technologies and IDEs, www.w3schools.com provides a good starting point.

Creating KML Files

KML is an XML-based file format designed to store and display geospatial data in Internet-based maps such as Google Maps, and virtual earth applications such as Google Earth or NASA World Wind. KML was originally developed by Keyhole, Inc., which Google acquired in 2004. The huge number of Google Maps and Google Earth users makes KML one of the most widely used interchange formats for exchanging, sharing, and viewing geospatial data. In fact, Google submitted the KML 2.2 specification to the OGC to ensure that KML remained an open standard. This was very good news for us. It became an official OGC standard in 2008. Geospatial features are modeled as placemarks, descriptions, ground overlays, paths, and polygons in textual files with extensions of .kml or .kmz (the zipped version of a .kml file).

The following code is the simplest example of a point described in KML. It can be viewed as geospatial data that have a name and description as their attribute and a point as their geometry. If you save the file with the .kml extension, you will be able to see the actual feature on the surface of the terrain with any virtual globe application like Google Earth, NASA World Wind, or ArcGIS Explorer. In the following Try It Out, you are going to see the placemark in ArcMap using the KML To Layer tool. So open your favorite text editor, enter the following code into it, and save it as KishIsland.kml.

```xml
<?xml version="1.0" encoding="UTF-8"?>
<kml xmlns="http://www.opengis.net/kml/2.2">
  <Document>
    <name>Kish Island</name>
    <Placemark>
      <name>Kish Island</name>
      <description>Kish island in Beautiful Persian Gulf</description>
      <Point>
        <coordinates>53.96575016905689,26.50243592677882,0</coordinates>
      </Point>
    </Placemark>
  </Document>
</kml>
```

TRY IT OUT   **Using KML in ArcMap**

1. Start ArcMap and make sure that your ArcToolbox window is displayed. If it is not, click the button with the toolbox icon on ArcMap's standard toolbar (see Figure 1-12).

FIGURE 1-12

2. Expand the Conversion Tools toolbox, and then expand the From KML toolset to see the KML To Layer tool, as shown in Figure 1-13.

3. Double-click the KML To Layer tool. This tool creates a file geodatabase containing a feature class within a feature dataset. As shown in Figure 1-14, you have to provide an input .kml file, address, and the name of the output geodatabase. Since .kml files contain styles as well as geospatial data, the path of the file geodatabase will be the path of the layer file. Set the input parameters and click the OK button.

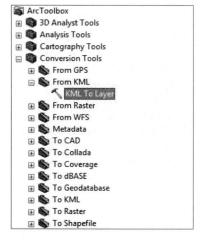

FIGURE 1-13

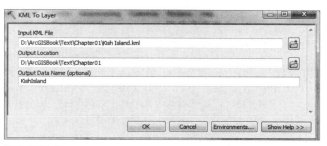

FIGURE 1-14

4. A layer that visualizes a point feature should have been added to your map; if that isn't the case, click the Add Data button (refer to Figure 1-6) and select the point feature class inside the Placemarks feature dataset of the output geodatabase, as shown in Figure 1-15.

5. As you see in Figure 1-16, a point feature is added to the map. To make your map more meaningful, add the National Geographic Basemap to the main window of ArcMap. You can do this by clicking the drop-down list button right beside the Add Data button and selecting Add Basemap.

FIGURE 1-15

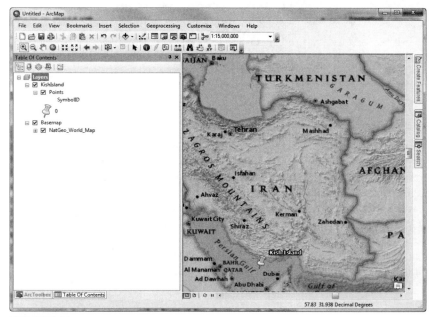

FIGURE 1-16

How It Works

KML is a simple but powerful format for storing and sharing geospatial data in simple structures. In contrast with most other formats of geospatial data, it contains instructions on how to draw geospatial data in addition to the geospatial data itself. A Point Placemark is the only way to draw an icon and label in the 3D Viewer of Google Earth. By default, the icon is the memorable yellow pushpin. In KML, a <Placemark> can contain one or more geometry elements, such as a LineString and Polygon. But only a <Placemark> with a Point can have an icon and label, as shown in Figure 1-17.

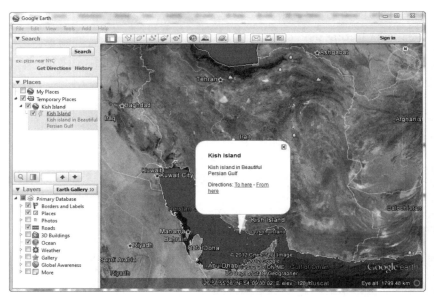

FIGURE 1-17

Retrieving Geospatial Data as GML

GML is the successful effort of OGC to provide an integrated means for storing, sharing, and modeling all forms of geospatial data. Generally, GML can be used for two different purposes. First, the GML standard provides basic structures and tools (similar to basic data types in all programming languages through which we can create the full range of structures and classes) for defining schema or data models of geospatial data (which is called a *GML application schema*). Another purpose of GML is to store and share geospatial data. In this case, GML instances or GML documents (which are geospatial data based on schema defined by a GML application schema) are used as an interchange format for transactions over the Web. GML can model vector and raster data as well as sensor data (spatio-temporal observations and measurements).

GML is focused on the description of geospatial data, and there is no style information (such as thickness or color) inside GML documents. As a result, GML, like most geospatial data formats, relies on other languages and approaches like KML and SVG for graphical representation.

GML is also important for another reason. Web Feature Service (WFS), another standard specification from OGC, is a web service for retrieving geospatial data as GML. In contrast to WMS, which provides images of geospatial data, WFS provides full access to geospatial data. WMS, WFS, and GML can be used extensively in ArcGIS for Desktop applications like any other native source of geospatial data. The only requirement for using GML data is to install and enable the ArcGIS Data Interoperability extension. The following Try It Out reveals how to use a WFS service to retrieve geospatial data as GML.

> **WARNING** *Make sure to install and enable the ArcGIS Data Interoperability extension. Otherwise you can't follow the next Try It Out. To enable the ArcGIS Data Interoperability extension use the Extensions...item in the Customize menu.*

TRY IT OUT Using WFS in ArcMap

1. In the Catalog window inside ArcMap, double-click the Add Interoperability Connection item, as shown in Figure 1-18, to add a new connection.

2. Click the Ellipsis button to open the FME Reader Gallery. Almost at the end of the list, select WFS as shown in Figure 1-19 and click the OK button.

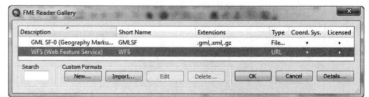

FIGURE 1-18 **FIGURE 1-19**

3. In the Dataset textbox, enter the following URL: `http://ogi.state.ok.us/geoserver/wfs?VERSION=1.1.0&REQUEST=GetFeature&TYPENAME=okcounties`. Click OK to see a new connection beneath Add Data Interoperability Connections.

4. Add another interoperability connection using the following URL: `http://ogi.state.ok.us/geoserver/wfs?VERSION=1.1.0&REQUEST=GetFeature&TYPENAME=firestations`.

5. Drag and drop both datasets from the Catalog window to the Table Of Contents window (see Figure 1-20).

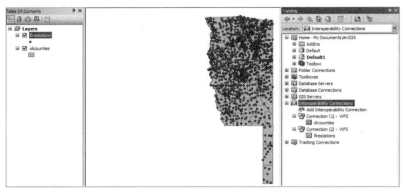

FIGURE 1-20

How It Works

As mentioned previously, it is possible to use GML as a native source of geospatial data in ArcGIS after installing and enabling the ArcGIS Data Interoperability extension. Rather than adding a GML dataset directly, in this Try It Out, we used a WFS service to retrieve counties and fire stations in Oklahoma. You can simply open the attribute table of those layers. Unlike WMS, which provides only an image of geospatial data, you can query geospatial data provided by WFS.

Using GeoRSS

GeoRSS is a relatively new specification to provide locations as part of web feeds. The prominent standard for web feeds is RSS, which stands for RDF Site Summary (often nicknamed Really Simple Syndication). Web feeds are in most cases used for frequently changing data or headlines of news in websites and are aggregated automatically using feed readers like Google Reader and Feed Demon.

> ### RELATIONSHIP BETWEEN XSD, GML, AND KUNG FU PANDA
>
> RDF, or Resource Description Framework, is a set of standards served as general tools for describing and modeling web resources (every resource that can be served on the web is called a web resource). GML was first designed and implemented based on RDF; subsequent versions of GML use core XML technologies (especially XSD) to make development easier and more manageable.
>
> At this time if somebody asks me, "What is XSD?" I remember when Po (the fat panda in *Kung Fu Panda II* who was assigned as dragon warrior) asked his father, "Where did I come from?" his father (who was, strangely, a goose) told him that baby geese come from eggs (much like my explanation about where GML comes from) and added, "Don't ask me where the egg comes from" (like my lack of explanation about XSD). If you're serious about learning GML, I recommend you read *Geography Mark-Up Language: Foundation for the Geo-Web,* by Ron Lake, David Burggraf, Milan Trninic, and Laurie Rae (John Wiley & Sons, Inc., 2004). If you want to read about XSD, I recommend *XML Schema Essentials,* by R. Allen Wyke and Andrew Watt (John Wiley & Sons, Inc., 2002).

GeoRSS location is attached to web feeds, a very efficient and simple mechanism for building distributed geo-enabled sensor networks or services for notification and early warning with devices like smartphones.

There are currently two encodings of GeoRSS: Simple and GML.

➤ GeoRSS-Simple is a very lightweight format that developers can easily add to their existing feeds with little effort. It supports basic geometries (point, line, box, polygon, and circle). Coordinates in this encoding should be based on the geographic coordinate system (latitude and longitude).

➤ GeoRSS GML is a formal GML application schema, and supports a greater range of features, particularly coordinate reference systems other than WGS-84 latitude/longitude and topological relationships between features.

In ArcGIS GeoRSS, feeds with an .rss or .xml extension can be easily added to ArcMap using the ArcGIS Data Interoperability extension. Because GeoRSS services provide feeds on frequently changed data, in most cases we use the URL of the GeoRSS service instead of downloading the feed file.

As an example of using GeoRSS, many organizations, such as NASA, USGS, and British Geological Survey, provide GeoRSS feeds about earthquakes (see Figure 1-21). If you want to see the latest worldwide earthquakes, add another data interoperability connection, set the format to GeoRSS, and provide the following address as the dataset when establishing a new interoperability connection in ArcMap: `http://www.bgs.ac.uk/feeds/School Seismology.xml`.

FIGURE 1-21

ESRI GEODATABASE

The Esri geodatabase is the native format for geospatial data in the ArcGIS platform. Throughout this book, the term *geodatabase* always refers to the Esri geodatabase. In its basic form, the geodatabase is a collection of geospatial data stored in an RDBMS or file system. Geospatial data inside the geodatabase are called *datasets*. Many kinds of datasets can be managed in a geodatabase (e.g., raster, vector, network, terrain, and so on).

Rather than being a container for geospatial data, the geodatabase provides a model for managing all aspects of geospatial data in an integrated manner. All forms of geospatial data can be modeled in the geodatabase. In addition to geospatial data, geospatial analysis toolboxes, relationships, specific behavior, and rules and constraints (for geospatial data consistency) can be stored in the geodatabase.

In addition to modeling and storing geospatial data as you see in this book, the geodatabase model provides straightforward and common sets of classes and interfaces for working with geospatial data whether they are stored as geodatabases or not. So when you are working with geospatial data through code, in most cases you won't care about the physical storage of geospatial data.

These capabilities of a geodatabase (and many more which are included in the ArcGIS platform) make the geodatabase a distinct storage model for geospatial data (or at least an advanced spatial DBMS model).

There are three geodatabase types in ArcGIS 10 and 10.1, each of which provides core geodatabase functionality but a distinct set of physical storage and additional functionality. They are personal, file, and ArcSDE geodatabases. The following sections begin with the simplest type, the personal database.

Personal Geodatabase

A personal geodatabase uses the Microsoft Access engine (which is called Microsoft Jet) to store and manage core geodatabase functionality. Personal geodatabases are stored as .mdb files in the Windows operating system (the only supported operating system). Being Microsoft Access database files, personal geodatabases are limited to 2GB size. Generally speaking, personal geodatabases are slower than file geodatabases or even shapefiles. Another limitation is that personal geodatabases are not geared toward a workgroup environment. The number of users for a personal geodatabase is limited to only one editor and a few readers.

The nice facet of personal geodatabases is that you can open them with Microsoft Access and perform all sorts of operations (such as editing text values, making calculations, and linking data to Microsoft Excel) with the tools provided by the familiar Microsoft Office products or by using SQL statements inside Microsoft Access.

File Geodatabase

File geodatabases are the preferred type of geodatabase for small workgroups. In addition to all the functionality that a personal geodatabase can provide, file geodatabases provide more storage, high performance, and a platform-independent solution to handle geospatial data without requiring the use of an RDBMS. A file geodatabase is an encrypted file folder that contains different datasets as separate child folders. The default size limit for a dataset inside a file geodatabase is 1TB, which can be increased up to 256TB. Each file geodatabase can contain many datasets, so there can be huge amounts of geospatial data managed by a file geodatabase.

File geodatabases outperform shapefiles in terms of performance, and at the same time require less disk space. File geodatabases need about one-third of the feature geometry storage in comparison with shapefiles and personal geodatabases. In addition to geospatial data, file geodatabases can be compressed to enable users even faster read-only access as well as use less disk space.

As is true of a personal geodatabase, file geodatabases have limitations in multi-user environments. For each dataset, it is possible to have one editor and a few readers. But unlike personal geodatabases, file geodatabases can have more than one editor at the same time for the whole geodatabase (but they have to edit different datasets). This means that file geodatabases are suitable for small workgroups. In addition to small workgroups, file geodatabases can be used in enterprises with simple, predefined, and non-overlapping workflows for editing geospatial data.

A useful feature of a file geodatabase is that Esri published a C++-based open API for working with file geodatabases. Using this API, you can make use of file geodatabases to manage geospatial data right from your .NET code; there is no need to have a license or ArcGIS software on your machine to do that.

ArcSDE Geodatabase

Both personal and file geodatabases are freely available for all ArcGIS for Desktop applications at ArcEditor and ArcInfo license levels. As mentioned in the previous sections, for truly multi-user environments, neither the file geodatabase nor the personal geodatabase provides adequate tools and mechanisms for handling complex workflows and simultaneous editors. This is where ArcSDE comes into play. As mentioned earlier in this chapter, ArcSDE is Esri's technology for managing geospatial data in major DBMSs. Since ArcGIS 9.2, Esri stopped selling ArcSDE as a stand-alone product and began bundling it with ArcGIS for Desktop and ArcGIS for Server products. Because ArcGIS for Server has two levels of capacity (Workgroup and Enterprise), in general there are three types of ArcSDE geodatabases (the first two types can also be considered the same type with a different number of users):

> **ArcSDE for SQL Server Express without ArcGIS for Server:** ArcGIS for Desktop applications (basic and advanced levels formerly known as ArcEditor and ArcInfo respectively) are shipped with Microsoft SQL Server Express, which is the lightweight and free edition of Microsoft SQL Server DBMS software. Through the use of ArcGIS for Desktop applications, it is possible to create and manage this kind of geodatabase easily. Up to three simultaneous users (ArcGIS for Desktop application users) can use this kind of geodatabase. This type of ArcSDE geodatabase is well suited for low-cost deployment of a GIS system along with other kinds of information systems.

> **ArcSDE for SQL Server Express with ArcGIS for Server Workgroup:** ArcGIS for Server Workgroup edition is needed for this kind of ArcSDE geodatabase. Similar to the preceding ArcSDE geodatabase, it requires Microsoft SQL Server Express, which only runs on a single machine. But unlike the preceding ArcSDE geodatabase, it is not free, and a workgroup level license of ArcGIS for Server has to be purchased. Up to 10 simultaneous users of

ArcGIS for Desktop application users plus any number of web clients can use this kind of geodatabase. This type of ArcSDE is best fitted for deploying web GIS applications.

➤ **ArcSDE with ArcGIS for Server Enterprise level:** As the name suggests, this kind of geodatabase provides the complete features of a geodatabase without limits on the number of simultaneous and concurrent users or the size of the geodatabase, and it handles complex workflows. It can work with five major DBMS products: Microsoft SQL Server, Oracle, IBM DB2 Informix, and PostgreSQL. This type of geodatabase can be installed on more than one server machine.

A powerful feature of an ArcSDE geodatabase is that it supports standards such as OGC's Simple Features specifications and ISO's spatial types standard. The good news for developers is that because ArcSDE geodatabases make use of one (or more, in some situations) of our favorite DBMS products, we can use our knowledge of that DBMS product and SQL language to manage ArcSDE geodatabases.

SUMMARY

This chapter provided a brief overview of geospatial data and the reasons they are special. Then it explained the ArcGIS platform based on the main categories of GIS software. In addition to the ArcGIS platform, some major standard GIS services and formats such as WMS, WFS, KML, GML, and GeoRSS were described in brief. At the end of this chapter, three types of Esri geodatabases were explained. Chapter 2 deals with various approaches for customizing ArcGIS for Desktop applications.

EXERCISES

1. What is the difference between WMS and WFS?

2. Which of the following formats provides the fastest performance: personal geodatabase, file geodatabase, or shapefile?

3. What are the main categories of desktop GIS software?

You will find the answers to these exercises in this book's appendix.

► **WHAT YOU LEARNED IN THIS CHAPTER**

TOPIC	KEY CONCEPTS
Geotechnologies	Collection of sciences and technologies for collecting, managing, analyzing, and visualizing geospatial data. Geotechnologies include sciences and technologies such as GIS, Remote Sensing (RS), Cartography, Photogrammetry, GPS, and Surveying.
Types of GIS software	Server GIS, Desktop GIS, Developer GIS, and Mobile GIS
Types of geodatabases	Personal geodatabase, File geodatabase, and ArcSDE geodatabase
OGC WMS	A standard GIS web service for retrieving an image of geospatial data over the Web
OGC WFS	A standard GIS web service for retrieving geospatial data as GML over the Web
KML	An XML-based file format for storing and displaying geospatial data in web-based applications such as Google Maps and virtual earth applications such as ArcGIS Explorer and Google Earth. Since 2008, it has been managed by OGC.
GML	An XML-based language for storing, sharing, and modeling all forms of geospatial data in an interoperable fashion. GML can play two roles: 1. As modeling language to define a data model of geospatial data for a specific application domain (schema of geospatial data for specific purpose) 2. As file format for storing and sharing geospatial data
GeoRSS	An XML-based format for associating positional information with web feeds. There are two encodings for GeoRSS: simple and GML.

Introduction to ArcGIS for Desktop Applications Customization

WHAT YOU WILL LEARN IN THIS CHAPTER:

➤   The different ways to customize ArcGIS for Desktop applications

➤   How to create an add-in for ArcGIS Desktop

➤   How to build custom components for ArcGIS Desktop

➤   How to use Python in ArcGIS Desktop

WROX.COM CODE DOWNLOADS FOR THIS CHAPTER

The wrox.com code downloads for this chapter can be found at `www.wrox.com/remtitle`
`.cgi?isbn=1118442547` on the Download Code tab. The code is in the Chapter02 folder and
is individually named according to the names throughout the chapter.

Esri has been providing customization in almost all its products since its inception in the
1970s. In some cases, Esri developed specific scripting languages and programming interfaces
(API) for its own products in order to allow users to customize their use of the products.

The ArcGIS platform is a complete system for performing all sorts of geospatial-related activities.
Also this platform is flexible enough to provide almost all its functionality to GIS professionals
and developers as development kits for customization and extension. In other words, there are lots
of opportunities for customizing the ArcGIS platform. The "Developer GIS" section of Chapter
1 mentions some of the opportunities that exist for developing an ArcGIS-based solution for all
major computing platforms such as desktop, web, and mobile. Since the focus of this book is on
ArcGIS for Desktop applications, in this chapter you are going to look at different opportunities
for customizing and developing upon ArcGIS for Desktop applications.

FOUR WAYS TO CUSTOMIZE ARCGIS FOR DESKTOP

When the first version of ArcGIS released in late 1999, Esri changed its strategy from using its own specific scripting languages to standard programming languages. Since then, GIS professionals and developers have happily customized and developed their own customization in familiar and well-known programming languages such as Visual Basic. Until version 10.0 of ArcGIS, desktop applications shipped with an embedded programming language called Microsoft Visual Basic for Applications (VBA). In addition to ArcGIS, VBA is embedded in many other software products, such as the Microsoft Office package. Microsoft decided to stop supporting VBA or offering a VBA distribution license. As a result, version 10.0 of ArcGIS is the last version in which VBA can be used for development.

> **NOTE** *In ArcGIS 10.0 and 10.1 there is no ArcObjects VBA SDK. For backward compatibility with previous developments in VBA, Esri offers an optional separate setup that needs an additional license.*

That was very bad news for the ArcGIS community.

Most ArcGIS users learned customizing ArcGIS for Desktop applications through VBA. But there is good news as well; Python is the preferred scripting language in versions 10.0 and 10.1. To be specific, Python was in the ArcGIS platform for many years. But Python recently gained major growth in terms of capabilities and user communities. It is open source, and many open source projects use this programming language to develop and implement geospatial-related concepts and techniques. Python will be supported in the next versions of ArcGIS and is the best choice for writing geoprocessing scripts in ArcGIS for Desktop applications.

> **NOTE** *As mentioned in the previous note, VBA is not supported in versions 10.0 and 10.1 natively. But you can use map documents (.mxd files) containing VBA code after enabling the use of VBA in ArcMap. In order to enable use of VBA in ArcGIS 10.0 or 10.1, you have to follow these steps:*
>
> *1. Install ArcGIS Desktop VBA Resources for Developers.*
>
> *2. Get an authorization file for VBA from Esri.*

ArcGIS for Desktop applications are the flagship professional GIS products for performing all geospatial-related activities. There are quite a lot of opportunities for customization in almost every aspect of ArcGIS for Desktop. ArcGIS for Desktop applications 10.0 and 10.1 have four options for customization and development, listed below and sorted from least to most complex.

➤ User Interface (UI) customization

➤ Scripting

> ➤ Desktop add-ins

> ➤ Developing custom components using ArcObjects SDK (Extending ArcObjects)

In the upcoming sections, you look at each method to understand when and how to use each approach.

CUSTOMIZING THE USER INTERFACE

The user interface (UI) of a software product is where users of the system interact with an application in order to perform their intended activities. Software developers should provide users with all the required toolbars, tools, and commands. Also, users appreciate having all needed toolbars and tools in tidy and easy-to-reach locations in the main window of software products. It is an excellent idea to provide UI customization options to avoid crowding the main window of the software when there are lots of toolbars, tools, and commands that can be used. Users want the flexibility to arrange UI components based on their personal preferences. This is why all software producers provide some sort of customization capabilities in their own products.

> **NOTE** *Microsoft Word provides lots of tools to work with. Even advanced users of Microsoft Word may not be completely aware of what can be done with this masterpiece word processor software. When I want to let audiences know that there are lots of things they can do with UI customization, I often ask them, "How can you do a simple calculation in Microsoft Word?" Don't think about Microsoft Excel or even Calculator; surprisingly, it can be done inside Word. All you need to do is to add the Calculate button to the main window of Microsoft Word!*

Sometimes, with a little UI customization you can give users all that they need without a single line of code. Four applications of ArcGIS for Desktop (ArcMap, ArcCatalog, ArcGlobe, and ArcScene) are shipped with dozens of built-in toolbars, tools, and commands. In this case, you can save all the UI customization in a document (such as an ArcMap map document [.mxd file]) and put this document in a public folder in a shared network place where all users have access. Next, you see how to customize the UI and what you can do with this kind of customization. In the following Try it Out, you create a new toolbar and populate it with some handy tools.

TRY IT OUT   Adding a New Toolbar and Menu to ArcMap

1. Run ArcMap.

2. Point to the Customize menu and select Customize Mode, as shown in Figure 2-1. Also note that you can open the Customize Mode window by double-clicking the empty gray area in ArcMap where all the toolbars are located.

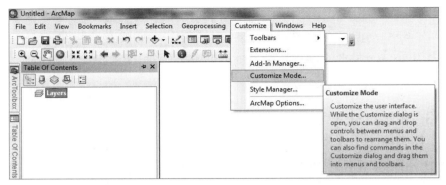

FIGURE 2-1

3. From the Customize window, click on the New button (as shown in Figure 2-2) to create a new toolbar.

4. The New Toolbar window pops up. As shown in Figure 2-3, enter **Useful Analysis** as the toolbar name and then click on OK. The Useful Analysis toolbar should be added to the end of the toolbars list in the Customize window. You can switch it on or off by checking or unchecking the checkbox in front of the name of the toolbar. As the name suggests, you use this toolbar for placing frequently used geoprocessing tools such as Buffer, Overlay, Clip, and Spatial Join.

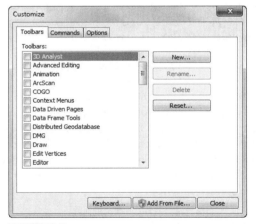

FIGURE 2-2

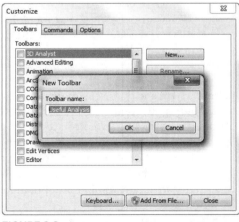

FIGURE 2-3

5. Check the checkbox in front of the new Useful Analysis toolbar to display it. Click on the Commands tab and wait for the lists of Categories and Commands to be populated (see Figure 2-4). Several commands can be used in ArcMap. Most of them are provided as tools and commands on the toolbars. Some other commands are provided as tools in ArcToolbox. There are also commands and tools that you can't see on toolbars or in ArcToolbox. You can put all commands on your newly added toolbar as well as on all existing toolbars that come with ArcMap by default.

6. As shown in Figure 2-5, scroll down the Categories list to find Analysis Tools. These are the same tools that you can find in the Analysis Tools toolbox inside the ArcToolbox window.

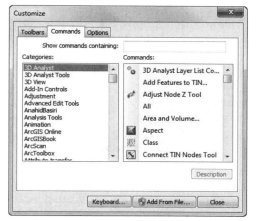

FIGURE 2-4

FIGURE 2-5

7. Select the Buffer tool from the Commands list and drag and drop it onto your newly created toolbar. Notice that while dragging the Buffer tool, the mouse cursor is a small "x" indicating that the cursor's current position is not a valid place to drop the tool. When the mouse cursor is over a valid command container (such as any toolbar or menu), the small "x" changes to a small "+" indicating that you can drop the tool or command to add it. After you drop the Buffer tool on the newly created toolbar, you see a small hammer icon on the toolbar. You are going to change its image. So right-click on the image of the newly added Buffer tool to see its context menu, shown in Figure 2-6.

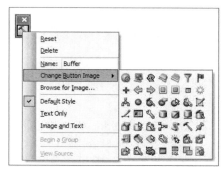

FIGURE 2-6

8. In the context menu, select the Name option and enter any helpful text such as Buffer the Features in the Name textbox, as shown in Figure 2-7. Then select an appropriate image from available images or select the Browse for Image option to select an image on your local drive. The image should be in .png or .bmp format and usually 16 × 16 pixels. In addition, select Image and Text as the display option. As you will see, the title of the toolbar is displayed together with the tool's image.

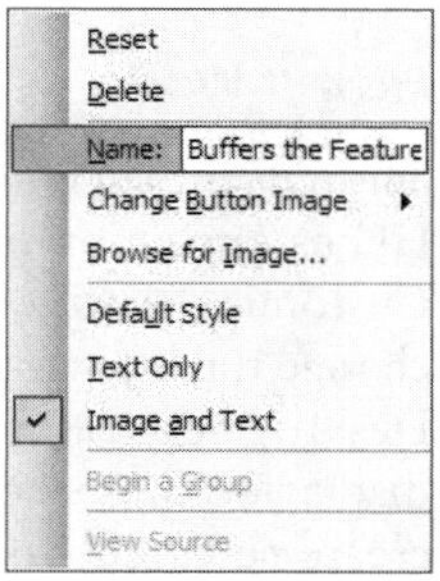

FIGURE 2-7

9. At this point, you have a new toolbar with only one tool. Add the Intersect, Clip, and Spatial Join tools from the Analysis Tools category to the toolbar. Change their images and set a helpful name for them (see Figure 2-8). Right-click on the Intersect tool, and from the context menu select the Begin a Group option to add a vertical bar (separator) between the Buffer and Intersect tools.

FIGURE 2-8

10. There are some other useful geoprocessing tools that are less frequently used than Buffer or Overlay that you are going to add as menu items. Scroll down the Categories list to find the New Menu item, as shown in Figure 2-9. When New Menu is selected in the Categories list, there is always a New Menu item in the Commands list. Just drag and drop the New Menu command in the Commands list to the Useful Analysis toolbar.

11. Rename New Menu to Other Analysis, select the Begin a Group option, and then add the Multiple Ring Buffer, Identity, and Erase tools from the Analysis Tools category to the menu in the same way that you added Buffer to the Useful Analysis toolbar. Close the Customize window. The toolbar should now look like Figure 2-10.

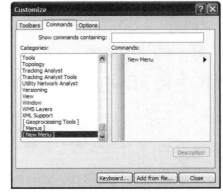

FIGURE 2-9

FIGURE 2-10

12. Save the map document using the Save command in the File menu. Name the map document `CustomToolbar.mxd`. If you close ArcMap and then open it, you will notice that the UI customization you just completed (the Useful Analysis toolbar) is missing. But if you open the Custom Toolbar map document (`CustomToolbar.mxd`), you will find the Useful Analysis toolbar.

How It Works

The Customize window is the central controller of any UI customization in ArcMap. When you see and use the Customize window, you are in Customize mode. You can change the look and feel of the standard UI of the ArcGIS for Desktop applications by changing the images, names, and display options of existing tools and commands. You can also create new toolbars and menus and add existing tools and commands to them. By default, all the newly added toolbars and menus are saved only in the current map document. But you can change this behavior by using the Options tab. If you uncheck Create New Toolbars and Menus in the document checkbox, your newly added toolbars and menus will be available whenever you open ArcMap (see Figure 2-11).

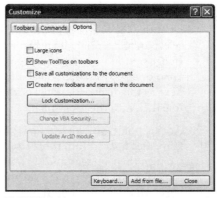

FIGURE 2-11

Because you can share your customization with other people by sharing the map document that includes customization, in most cases the default behavior of ArcMap (to save newly added toolbars and menus in a specific document) makes perfect sense. Also you can lock your customization in order to avoid others tampering with what you have customized in the ArcMap environment.

You have to be in Customize mode in order to remove commands or tools from any built-in or newly created toolbar. All you have to do is drag and drop any tools or commands to somewhere in the main window of ArcMap where there is no other toolbar or menu.

NOTE *When you change anything in the UI of ArcGIS for Desktop applications, by default all the changes (except newly added toolbars and menus) are saved in a special template file (such as the* Normal.mxt *file in the case of ArcMap). Examples of these changes are switching on or off any built-in toolbars of ArcMap, docking a catalog window, and adding or removing any tools or commands to built-in toolbars or menus. This special template, which is generally called the application configuration template, is read each time the application is started. All the newly added toolbars and menus are saved in the current document by default. You can find all the application configuration files in your profile folder in the Windows installation drive. For example, if you use ArcGIS 10.0 or 10.1 on Microsoft Windows, your application configuration templates are in the following folders:*

➤ *Windows XP:*

```
<Windows Installation Drive>:\Documents and Settings\<Your user
name>\Application Data\ESRI\Desktop10.x\
```

➤ *Windows Vista or 7:*

```
<Windows Installation Drive>:\Users\<Your user name>\App Data\
Roaming\ESRI\Desktop10.x\
```

Remember that ArcCatalog doesn't use map documents, so all the customizations are always saved in the Normal.gxt *file (the ArcCatalog application configuration file).*

NOTE *In addition to existing toolbars and menus, context menus can be customized easily. (A context menu is the menu displayed when you right-click somewhere in the software product.) Based on where the right-click event happened, or more precisely what object is right-clicked, different context menus should be displayed. I don't discuss customization of context menus in this book.*

SCRIPTING

Knowledge of scripting is vital for ArcGIS professionals interested in promoting their automation and analysis skills. Python is used as the scripting language in the ArcGIS platform. Python is an open source, cross-platform, and general-purpose programming language that can be used in many applications, ranging from financial to pure scientific applications. Python is a modular programming language. In most cases, you can use (import) many modules for your applications free of charge. It is a very high level programming language and easy to learn. In contrast to its simplicity, Python is a very powerful programming language.

Inside ArcGIS, Python allows users and developers to create tools and scripts ranging from single functions to complex multifunction workflows which can be easily reused, shared, and executed. In ArcGIS 10.0 and 10.1, the Python scripting language is the primary scripting language and nearly completely replaces the unsupported VBA. So what can you do with Python? The simple answer is you can do many things with Python in ArcGIS for Desktop.

You can use Python to populate field values based on simple calculations in Field Calculator when working with attribute tables in ArcMap. This capability was first added to ArcGIS 10.0. Another welcome addition to all ArcGIS for Desktop applications is a new Python window. Previous versions of ArcGIS had the Command window.) In the next Try It Out, you learn about some opportunities for using the Python window.

TRY IT OUT **Using the Python Window to Execute Simple Select by Attribute**

1. Start ArcMap and add states, cities, and `intrstat` feature classes from the `TemplateData.gdb` geodatabase file that is shipped with ArcGIS. If you install ArcGIS using its default settings, you can find the geodatabase file in the `<ArcGIS installation folder>\ArcGIS\Desktop10.0\ TemplateData` for ArcGIS 10.0 or `<ArcGIS installation folder>\ArcGIS\Desktop10.1\ TemplateData` for ArcGIS 10.1 folders. You need these feature classes in order to perform your scripting.

2. Click on the Python window button (shown in Figure 2-12) to display the Python window.

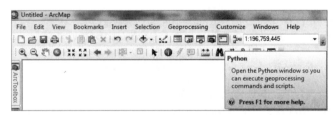

FIGURE 2-12

As you can see in Figure 2-13, the Python window is a two-part window. The upper part of the Python window is used for coding and the other part provides help as you type the code.

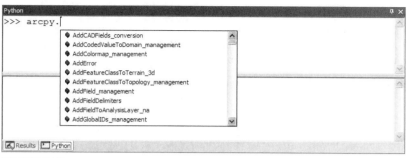

FIGURE 2-13

3. Type **arcpy** into the upper (code) window. Be careful of the case of your text because Python is a case-sensitive programming language. Notice that as you type the text an autocomplete list is shown. The autocomplete list provides suggestions that you can select from based on what you have typed, and as you type further it filters the list of suggestions.

Like almost all other object-oriented programming languages, Python uses a period or dot (.) to provide access to members of a parent object or module. So a huge list of functions, modules, and classes appears as you type a dot after arcpy.

4. Continue your statement with select and you will see a list of six autocomplete suggestions, all of which start with the text you entered, as shown in Figure 2-14. Using the arrow keys on your keyboard, pick SelectLayerByAttribute_management from the list, then press the tab or Enter key to insert the selected item in the code window. At this point, your Python window should contain the following line of code:

FIGURE 2-14

```
arcpy.SelectLayerByAttribute_management
```

5. Continue your coding by entering an opening parenthesis character, "(". As shown in Figure 2-15, another list is displayed that suggests input layers for the SelectLayer ByAttribute analysis tool. As you can see in Figure 2-15, the help window provides (1) general syntax, and (2) a short description. You will also find detailed information about each input and output for the specified analysis. Use the arrow keys to select the last layer in the list: U.S. States (Generalized). Then press the tab or Enter key. You have now provided the first input.

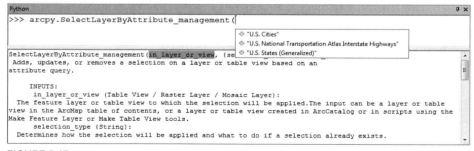

FIGURE 2-15

6. For providing the second input, `selection_type`, you have to enter the comma character (,). Look at the syntax of the analysis, which requires this character for separating arguments. You can see that a list of available types for selection displays, as shown in Figure 2-16. Select `NEW_SELECTION` from the list and enter a comma character.

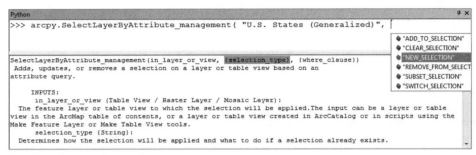

FIGURE 2-16

7. The last argument is a `where_clause`, which is a conditional statement for selecting a subset of data. The syntax for this argument has to be based on Structured Query Language (SQL). Enter the following text for this argument. Remember that you have to be careful about case sensitivity and quotes. Then enter a closing parenthesis to finish your first Python scripting.

```
"STATE_NAME = 'California'"
```

Your Python window should resemble Figure 2-17.

```
Python                                                          ₽ ×
>>> arcpy.SelectLayerByAttribute_management("U.S. States (Generalized)",
 "NEW_SELECTION","STATE_NAME = 'California'")

 Results   Python
```

FIGURE 2-17

8. Press Enter to run the code. You will notice that a progress bar in ArcMap indicates that the tool is running. After finishing the whole process, a beautiful blue message box pops up and tells you the task is finished successfully. You will notice that the California state feature is selected on the map.

How It Works

Python was used for executing the Select Layer By Attribute geoprocessing tool, which you can find in ArcToolbox. In fact, this Try It Out was a simple geoprocessing task composed of a single function. So inside ArcGIS, Python is really a scripting language to execute geoprocessing tasks. You likely have noticed that `arcpy` is a gateway to all Python functions, tools, and classes that can be used in ArcGIS. When you use the Python window, execution is done in background mode. This means that when you execute the tool you can do other things, like interact with a map, print a map document, or even perform another geoprocessing task. This is a new feature introduced in ArcGIS 10.0.

Geoprocessing in ArcGIS is performed through the ArcPy site package (or ArcPy for short). In Python terminology, a *site package* is a library or module that extends the Python programming language. All geoprocessing tools can be accessed through ArcPy. In addition, ArcPy provides several functions, classes, and modules that provide extended functionality as well as simple coding. More access to geospatial data is provided with ArcPy in comparison with previous scripting experience, known as ArcGIS scripting, in previous versions of ArcGIS. As an example, ArcPy provides access to map documents and layers using a mapping module. For example, you can use Python scripting and mapping modules to remove all layers of a Data Frame. You see this in action in the following Try It Out.

TRY IT OUT **Removing All Layers of a Data Frame Using Python (RemoveAllLayerPY.zip)**

1. Add some layers to your map. Click the Python window button to display the Python window. You are going to use the mapping module of ArcPy.

2. Enter the following script to access the current map document (the map document in which you are coding), then press Enter to execute the code.

```
mxd = arcpy.mapping.MapDocument('Current')
```

3. Type the next line of code to get the first Data Frame inside the current map document.

```
df = arcpy.mapping.ListDataFrames(mxd)[0]
```

4. Enter the following line of code to get a list of all layers inside the current map document.

```
lyrs = arcpy.mapping.ListLayers(mxd)
```

5. You want Python to remove a layer from the first Data Frame of the current map document and iterate through all layers in that Data Frame one by one. So you have to resort to a `for` statement. Enter the following line of code. Note that you have to provide a colon (:) after the `for` statement, then press Enter.

```
for lyr in lyrs :
```

6. In Python, you have to indent all lines of code that are intended to be considered as execution code inside a `for` block. So press the Tab key and then enter the following line of code, then press the Enter key to execute the script.

```
arcpy.mapping.RemoveLayer(df, lyr)
```

If you type everything correctly (remember Python is case sensitive), all layers of your map should be removed.

7. You can save this script by right-clicking the code window and selecting Save As.

How It Works

ArcPy and Python are a powerful couple that are able to perform geoprocessing tasks inside ArcGIS. ArcPy is not all about geoprocessing. As mentioned previously, in addition to geoprocessing it provides special classes, functions, and modules to enhance and extend the capabilities of Python to work with geospatial data. You have seen a mapping module in this Try It Out. The `arcpy.mapping` module is a library of functions and classes that allows you to automate mapping tasks such as opening and manipulating map documents and layer files. There are also other modules inside ArcPy, such as the Spatial Analyst module (`arcpy.sa`), that can perform powerful spatial analysis operations like map algebra and image classification, to name a couple.

In addition to running a single geoprocessing analysis, you can perform a sequence of geoprocessing tasks using ArcPy and Python. Suppose that you have many feature classes and want all of them to be clipped to a certain extent. You can do this easily using ArcPy. In the next Try It Out, you clip all feature classes inside the USA feature dataset inside the `TemplateData.gdb` file geodatabase to the extent of New York State.

TRY IT OUT   **Clip All Feature Classes in a Feature Dataset (ClipNewYorkPY.zip)**

1. Start ArcMap and add the `states` feature class from `TemplateData.gdb` (see the "Using the Python Window to Execute Simple Select by Attribute" Try It Out earlier in this chapter for how to find `TemplateData.gdb`).

2. As a best practice, you are going to make a copy of the whole `TemplateData.gdb` file geodatabase and work with that copy. So enter the following line of code, and then press Enter on your keyboard to execute the code. Please pay attention to the backward slashes as you enter the path and name of the copy of the geodatabase.

```
arcpy.Copy_management("C:\Program Files\ArcGIS\Desktop10.1\TemplateData\
    TemplateData.gdb","C:\ClippedGDB.gdb")
```

3. You are going to use the newly created geodatabase in your code. So it is good idea to set it as your default workspace. You can do this using the following code snippet:

```
arcpy.env.workspace="c:\ClippedGDB.gdb"
```

4. Select New York State and create a new feature class for it using the code below:

```
arcpy.Select_analysis("states", "NewYork", "STATE_NAME = 'New York'")
```

5. Now you want to get all feature classes inside the USA feature dataset. So you have to use one of the special functions provided by ArcPy. Use the `ListFeatureClasses` function to create a list of all (* wildcard) feature classes of all geometry types (All) in the USA feature dataset:

```
fcs= arcpy.ListFeatureClasses("*", "All", "USA")
```

6. As the final step, you need to clip all feature classes in the list by the New York feature class. Remember to include the colon (:) after the for statement and to add the indentation before the second line of code as shown here:

```
for fc in fcs:
    arcpy.Clip_analysis(fc,"NewYork", fc + "ClippedByNewYork")
```

7. If everything goes correctly, you will see all clipped feature classes added to your map.

How It Works

In this Try It Out, you first made a copy of the TemplateData.gdb file geodatabase. Then you used the Select_analysis function to extract the feature class needed as a clip feature class. Finally you clipped all feature classes inside a feature dataset by the clip feature class. All the results from the Python window are added to the map. This way, you create a simple geoprocessing workflow inside ArcMap. You could do the same task outside of ArcMap using any Python editor, such as IDLE, which comes with ArcGIS. All you need to do is import the ArcPy module.

As you have seen, it takes little effort to write a script containing several geoprocessing tools to create a simple workflow. In addition, because the workflow is performed in the background you can work with other tasks at the same time. More importantly, you automatically and without setting anything manually perform the workflow. This is why using Python is far superior to working with ModelBuilder or executing tools in ArcToolbox in batch mode. Also you can use the Results window (shown in Figure 2-18 and available from the geoprocessing menu in ArcMap or ArcCatalog) to watch the progress of the workflow and much useful information about each individual geoprocessing operation. You see the ModelBuilder and Results windows in action in Chapter 12.

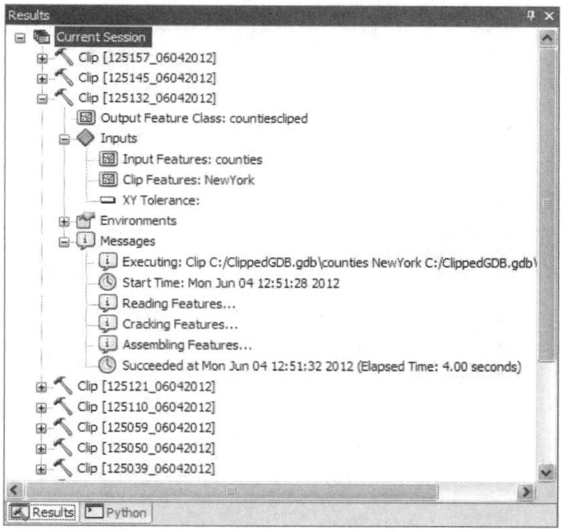

FIGURE 2-18

As you have seen in this section, you can run a single tool or sequence of tools to create geoprocessing workflows. But the real strength and power of using Python and ArcPy is not limited to that. You can execute long and advanced workflows. With Python, you can create and execute scripts without any ArcMap session. This means that there is no need to open or run ArcMap to execute scripts, and scripts can be executed at certain points in time based on defined schedules. You also can make your scripts more generic to be shared with other users as script tools that can be run like any other geoprocessing tool.

Version 10.1 added even more capabilities to Python. Creating desktop add-ins, faster cursors, and Python geoprocessing tools are just a few of them. Further discussion about Python is outside the scope of this book. You can find thousands of samples and code snippets of using Python in the ArcGIS Desktop Help and online ArcGIS Resource Center, especially in the ArcGIS Geoprocessing Resource Center.

DESKTOP ADD-INS

ArcGIS Desktop Add-Ins is the newest way to customize and extend ArcGIS for Desktop applications. For many years, using Microsoft Visual Basic 6.0 or Microsoft .NET platform to create custom components was the only way to develop and customize ArcGIS Desktop applications. Add-ins provide some advantages when compared with other methods of developing and extending ArcGIS for Desktop applications. In particular, they provide a tidier model for development that focuses on business logic. In comparison, when you are developing or extending the ArcGIS for Desktop applications using the alternative approach, you have to provide many details for components. Components used to build the ArcGIS platform are called ArcObjects. ArcObjects are at the heart of the ArcGIS platform. All the ArcObjects can be accessed by using add-ins. This means that everything that a user can do through the user interface can be done through code. Another advantage of desktop add-ins (or add-ins for short) is that they provide an easier deployment model, which makes them a perfect choice for sharing functionality. Sharing add-ins is performed by simply copying and pasting add-in files. So what exactly is an add-in file?

An add-in file with an extension of `.esriaddin` is a zipped folder containing an XML metadata file, assembly file(s), and resources. The XML metadata file or `config.esriaddin` holds the static and descriptive data about an add-in, such as the captions of buttons. Programming aspects of an add-in are specified in compiled .NET assemblies (`.dll` files). All the required resources for an add-in are in the resources folder. You will see this structure in the next Try It Out.

How can you install an add-in file? Add-in files are automatically discovered in well-known local folders and plugged into the desktop applications at runtime. What qualifies as a local well-known folder depends on your operating system, and can be one of the following paths:

➤ **Windows 7 and Vista:** `<Windows Installation Drive>:\Users\<your user name>\My Documents\ArcGIS\AddIns\Desktop10.0 or Desktop 10.1`

➤ **Windows XP:** `<Windows Installation Drive>:\Document and Settings\<your user name>\My Documents\ArcGIS\AddIns\Desktop10.0 or Desktop10.1`

In addition to a local well-known folder, you can introduce any shared folder in a network as a shared well-known folder. By doing this, the add-in shared well-known folder can be used by anyone who has access to that folder through the network.

One nice feature of add-ins is that there is no need to make a setup or installation package for them. When you want to share your add-in, all you need to do is copy it to media like a USB flash disk, e-mail it, or even upload it to a website. In order to install an add-in, all you need is to double-click the add-in file. Esri provides an installation utility associated with add-in files (files with the `.esriaddin` extension) that copies the add-in file into the well-known folder. You can also copy and paste the add-in file to a local well-known folder manually to install it.

So far you have learned that add-ins are useful, but you might be wondering how you can create add-ins.

In version 10.0 of ArcGIS, add-ins can be created using VB.NET, C#, or Java. In version 10.1, in addition to those languages, you can use Python to create add-ins.

> **NOTE** *Because this book focuses on developing and extending ArcGIS for Desktop applications using .NET, from this point, you won't see anything unrelated to the .NET platform. In addition, all code examples in this book are based on C#. If you are a VB.NET programmer, it is easy to understand what C# code does. In fact, VB.NET and C# have similar syntax and capabilities, and in most cases, the difference between similar pieces of code in those two languages is a single semi colon.*

In order to create add-ins, you need at least .NET 3.5 sp1 (service pack 1), which is installed with ArcGIS Desktop 10.0 and 10.1. Secondly, you need an Integrated Development Environment (IDE) to be able to write code. You can use any IDE from Microsoft that supports .NET 3.5 sp1. The following is a list of available IDEs that can be used to develop add-ins for ArcGIS Desktop 10.0 and 10.1.

➤ Supported IDEs for version 10.0:

  ➤ All editions of Visual Studio 2008 including Express

  ➤ All editions of Visual Studio 2010 except Express

➤ Supported IDEs for version 10.1:

  ➤ All editions of Visual Studio 2010 including Express

You need to install the ArcObjects SDK for Microsoft .NET framework. You can find the ArcObjects SDK for Microsoft .NET on the same media from which you installed ArcGIS for Desktop. When you install the ArcObjects SDK, it adds useful templates, wizards, and utilities to Visual Studio. To summarize, you have to install the appropriate IDE, and then ArcObjects SDK, for .NET to be able to execute the code in this book. In the next Try It Out, the journey begins!

TRY IT OUT   Creating the Simplest Add-In (FirstAddIn.zip)

1. Start your IDE. In this book I use the Visual Studio 2010 Ultimate and Professional editions, which may be slightly different from your IDE. You are going to create a new project, so click on the New Project link on the Start Page or select New Project from the File menu.

2. Expand the ArcGIS node under Visual C# in the Installed Templates section. You should see three child nodes. Select Desktop Add-Ins to display four different templates for four desktop applications. If you don't see the ArcGIS node under Visual C# or Visual Basic, you have to install the ArcObjects SDK. If you have installed the software, but the four templates shown on Figure 2-19 are still not available, you might have to select .NET Framework 3.5 as your platform. Select the ArcMap Add-in, provide a name for your project and solution, and specify where the project should be saved. Then click the OK button.

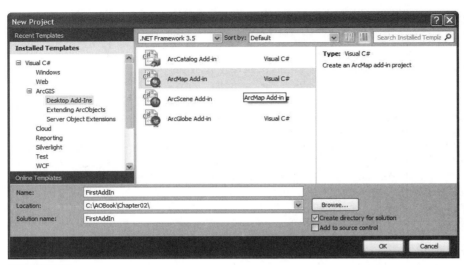

FIGURE 2-19

3. The ArcGIS Add-Ins Wizard will be displayed. Provide some information on name, author, publisher, and a short description for your add-in in the Welcome section of the wizard. Name it **FirstAddIn,** then click on Add-in Types to see a list of available items that can be created as add-ins. Select Button and enter the information shown in Figure 2-20. (In particular, be sure to enter ShowTime as the Class Name. I refer to this file in the next steps.) Then click Finish.

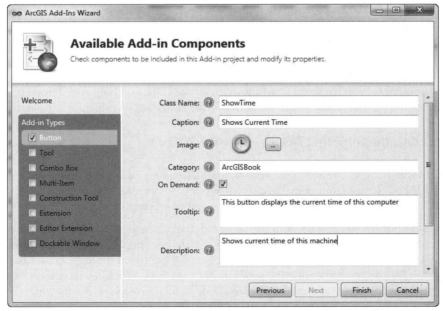

FIGURE 2-20

4. After a few seconds, Visual Studio creates the necessary files. If you open the `Config` `.esriaddinx` file, you will notice that everything that you have provided resides in this configuration file. You can change them whenever necessary. There is a class file with the name of `ShowTime.cs`. You are going to add functionality for your button in this file. Double-click the class file in Solution Explorer. Several skeleton pieces of code are written by the wizard. Find the `OnClick()` method in the middle of the file, then delete the comments (lines of code that start with `//`). Type the following lines of code in the `ShowTime` class body:

```
ArcMap.Application.Caption = DateTime.Now.ToLongTimeString();
```

Your whole code should be similar to the following:

```
using System;
using System.Collections.Generic;
using System.Text;
using System.IO;
namespace FirstAddIn
{
    public class ShowTime : ESRI.ArcGIS.Desktop.AddIns.Button
    {
        public ShowTime()
        {
        }
        protected override void OnClick()
        {
            ArcMap.Application.Caption = DateTime.Now.ToLongTimeString();
        }
        protected override void OnUpdate()
        {
            Enabled = ArcMap.Application != null;
        }
    }
}
```

5. Run the code by pressing F5 or click the Start Debugging button (▶). Because you have the ArcMap Add-in template, Visual Studio starts an ArcMap session for testing and debugging the written code. In ArcMap, select the Add-In Manager from the Customize menu to see a list of installed add-ins. Select the add-in you have created (`FirstAddIn`). You will see that there is only one button in this add-in, which shows current time (see Figure 2-21). Click on the Customize button.

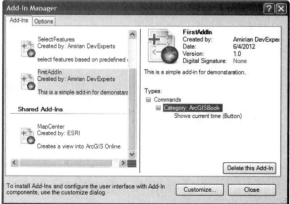

FIGURE 2-21

6. The familiar Customize window appears, as shown in Figure 2-22. Your first add-in is in the ArcGISBook Commands category because you entered ArcGISBook in the Category textbox in the Welcome section of the Add-In Wizard in Visual Studio when creating the add-in from the template). If you are not sure about the category of your add-in, open the configuration file and find the category attribute. Place the Shows Current Time button wherever you want, such as on the Tools toolbar. After dragging and dropping the button on an appropriate place, close the Customize window by pressing the Close button.

FIGURE 2-22

7. Test the functionality of the button by hovering the mouse on the button to see if the tooltip works correctly. Finally, click the button to change the title of the ArcMap map document from "Untitled" to the current time.

How It Works

You start creating add-ins by choosing an add-in template based on the desktop application where you want to use the add-in. All the templates and wizards are integrated into Visual Studio, so you can easily and quickly provide the necessary information. This simple add-in just changed the title of an ArcMap map document. Surprisingly, there is no tool or option to change the whole title of an ArcMap map document through the user interface of it (you can change the title of the ArcMap map document by saving it, but some text, such as ArcMap-ArcInfo, will remain. Using this add-in you can change the whole title of the ArcMap map document). So this simple Try It Out reveals that add-ins can do many things that cannot be done with the user interface.

Add-ins are managed using the Add-In Manager window. You can delete an add-in by using the Add-In Manager or simply delete the add-in file from the well-known folder. When you delete an add-in using the Add-In Manager, the add-in goes to the Recycle Bin of your operating system so you can restore it if you deleted it accidentally. You need to use the Customize window to use add-ins. The add-ins framework can be used to create different kinds of controls, windows, extensions, and toolbars, to name a few. Next you see how to create a toolbar using an add-in. In the following Try It Out, you will first create a button to remove all layers of the active Data Frame and then put your two buttons on a toolbar.

TRY IT OUT Creating a Toolbar Using an Add-In (FirstAddIn.zip)

1. If you are in debug mode from the previous Try It Out, close ArcMap or click on Stop Debugging (■) inside Visual Studio. (You can also use the Stop Debugging command from the Debug menu in Visual Studio.) Select the FirstAddIn project.

In Visual Studio terminology, a *solution* can contain one or more projects and a *project* can contain multiple files and folders. Because your solution just contains one project, you can find the FirstAddIn project beneath the solution and the project displayed as a parent node for all the other files and folders. Right-click on the FirstAddIn project and choose New Item from the context menu. From the Installed Templates list, choose Visual C# Items ⇨ ArcGIS ⇨ Desktop Add-Ins and select Add-in Component. Name it **RemoveAllLayers**. Note that if you don't see the Solution Explorer in Visual Studio, you can turn it on using the View menu.

2. In the ArcGIS Add-Ins Wizard, select Button as your add-in type and set its properties to match those shown in Figure 2-23. Then click the Finish button.

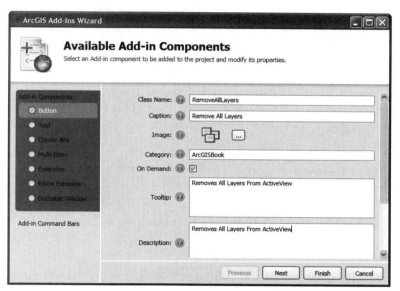

FIGURE 2-23

3. Because you are going to work with maps and layers, you have to add an appropriate reference to your project. You can think of a *reference* as a call to a particular software library. In Solution Explorer, right-click the References folder and choose Add ArcGIS Reference from the context menu. Under Desktop ArcMap, select ESRI .ArcGIS.Carto and click the Add button, then click Finish (see Figure 2-24).

4. Double-click the RemoveLayers.cs file in the Solution Explorer and add the following lines of code at the very first line of the code window:

```
using ESRI.ArcGIS.ArcMapUI;
using ESRI.ArcGIS.Carto;
```

FIGURE 2-24

5. Change your `OnClick()` method to be similar to the following code listing:

```
protected override void OnClick()
        {
            IMxDocument mxdoc = ArcMap.Application.Document as IMxDocument;
            IMap map = mxdoc.FocusMap;
            map.ClearLayers();
            IActiveView activeView = map as IActiveView;
            activeView.Refresh();
            mxdoc.UpdateContents();
        }
```

6. The second add-in button is ready. You can test it by pressing the Start Debugging button (F5) and use the Customize window to put it on a toolbar inside ArcMap. Add a couple of map layers to ArcMap from the `TemplateData.gdb` geodatabase like you did in the previous Try It Outs in this chapter. Click the newly added add-in button in ArcMap to test if all the layers in your map document will be removed. After that, you can click the Stop Debugging button in Visual Studio. Next, you are going to add a toolbar to your add-in. Right-click the project inside the Solution Explorer and select Add New Item from the Add menu. Then select in the Installed Templates section by selecting Visual C# Items ➪ ArcGIS ➪ Desktop Add-Ins.

Adding a toolbar is slightly different in versions 10.0 and 10.1.

➤ For version 10.0, choose Add-in Component, name it **FirstToolbar**, and then click the Add button. The ArcGIS Add-Ins Wizard pops up. Click the Add-in Command Bars link and from the list of available Command Bars select the Toolbar item.

➤ For version 10.1, choose Add-in Command Container, name it **FirstToolbar**, and then click the Add button. The ArcGIS Add-Ins Wizard pops up. From the list of available Command Bars, select the Toolbar item.

7 In the Items grid, you can add both of your add-in buttons (the add-in for showing the current time and the add-in for removing all map layers). Set the property of the toolbar to match Figure 2-25 and click Finish.

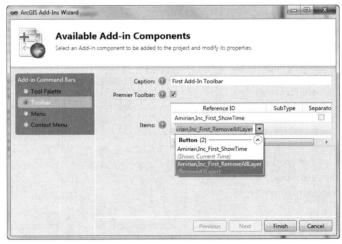

FIGURE 2-25

8. Press F5 (Start Debugging) to see the toolbar with two buttons. This time there is no need to resort to the Customize window since the toolbar will be already available to use.

How It Works

In this Try It Out, you first create another more useful button and provide functionality to remove all layers from the active Data Frame (FocusMap in terms of ArcObjects) in ArcMap. If you don't understand the code, don't worry. Throughout this book, you will learn the necessary skills to create add-ins. add-in framework toolbars are added declaratively. This means that unlike buttons, they don't have an associated class file. In fact, because toolbars don't contain any logic (like responding to the `OnClick()` event), in the add-ins framework you work with toolbars through the `config.esriaddinx` file. If you look at the configuration file, you will easily find the toolbar.

Add-ins provide a simple, declarative model for development for ArcGIS Desktop. But this simplicity has its expense. You explore more about add-ins in upcoming chapters. For now just consider that all the ArcObjects and therefore all the capabilities of the ArcGIS platform can be accessed using the add-in framework, and in order to create an add-in you need to be familiar with one .NET programming language (VB.NET or C#).

ARCOBJECTS SDK

Developing ArcGIS for Desktop applications using ArcObjects SDK (or ArcObjects API) has been available for more than 10 years. All the ArcObjects can be accessed through this method of development (just like add-ins). By using ArcObjects SDK, you have more flexibility than with the add-ins model, but the cost of flexibility is complexity. A comparison of these two models of development shows that most of what you can do with ArcObjects SDK is exposed to the add-ins model (such as creating buttons, toolbars, dockable windows, and context menus).
Add-ins provide a declarative model for configuration, and there is no need to build an installation or setup package. Just copy and paste your add-in file and you will have the add-in in your ArcGIS for Desktop applications. In contrast, when you use the ArcObjects SDK you have to be imperative. This simply means that you have to write code for all aspects of your customization, such as putting buttons on a toolbar. In order to publish anything created with the ArcObjects SDK, you have to build an installation or setup package. To install any type of software, you need operating system administrator privileges. These are some of the advantages and disadvantages of development for ArcGIS for Desktop applications using add-ins and ArcObjects SDK. The good news is that the code for both methods of development is similar and often is identical. Just remember that add-ins provide an easier, tidier, and more high-level model for creating new functionalities. But this fact doesn't mean that you don't need to be familiar with .NET and ArcObjects for creating add-ins. Quite the opposite: You have to be familiar with .NET and ArcObjects to be productive enough to implement your ideas in either model of development (add-ins or ArcObjects SDK models). Now try the ArcObjects SDK to create a button for zooming into the full extent of an active layer. (An *active layer* is the selected layer in the Table of Contents inside an ArcMap application.)

TRY IT OUT **Using the ArcObjects SDK (UsingAOSDK.zip)**

1. Create a new project in Visual Studio and, as shown in Figure 2-26, select the Extending ArcObjects category in the Installed Templates section under the ArcGIS node. Then select the Class Library (ArcMap) template. You have to select .NET Framework 3.5 as the development platform. Provide a meaningful name for the project and solution, and set an appropriate location for saving your first ArcObjects SDK project files. Click OK.

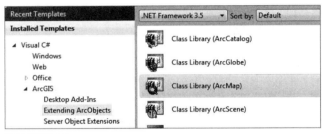

FIGURE 2-26

2. The ArcGIS Project Wizard displays in which you have to provide references for your project. Note that adding references can be done later using the Add ArcGIS Reference command from the context menu of the References folder. For this Try It Out just add two references for ESRI.ArcGIS.ArcMapUI and ESRI.ArcGIS.Carto (you can find them under the Desktop ArcMap list as shown in Figure 2-27). After adding the references click Finish.

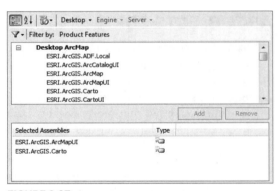

3. You don't need the `class1.cs` file, so delete it (right-click the file in the Solution Explorer

FIGURE 2-27

and choose Delete). Then right-click on the project and select Add New Item from the Add menu. From the list of available items, select the Base Command template from the Installed Templates section under Visual C# Items ➪ ArcGIS ➪ Extending ArcObjects (see Figure 2-28). Name it **ZoomToActiveLayer** and click the Add button. As you can read in the right part of the Add New Item window, Base Command is used when you want to create a button (or more precisely a command) in ArcGIS for Desktop applications.

FIGURE 2-28

4. You have to determine the type of command. You are going to create a command to be used in ArcMap, so select Desktop ArcMap Command as shown in Figure 2-29 and click OK.

5. After a few seconds, multiple lines of code appear in Visual Studio, which has nothing to do with the code that you have seen for the add-in in the previous Try It Out. But don't fret. Most of the code is for component registration. You are going to use a nice feature that you can use inside Visual Studio called code snippets, or snippets for short. *Code snippets* are blocks of reusable pieces of code which can be easily incorporated into your code. Point your cursor outside of any method and right-click. (You can simply right-click before two "}" at the end of the class file.) Select ArcGIS Snippet Finder

FIGURE 2-29

from the context menu. As the name suggests, ArcGIS Snippet Finder is used to find and insert ready-to-use code snippets for ArcGIS development inside Visual Studio. Type **Active Layer** in the keyword textbox as shown in Figure 2-30, and then click the Search button. One snippet appears in the upper pane and when you select it, the entire code for that snippet will be shown in the lower textbox. Then click the Insert Code button. If your cursor was inside any method, a warning pops up. In that case, change your cursor position and try again.

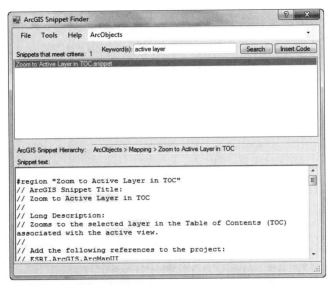

FIGURE 2-30

6. The `ZoomToActiveLayerInTOC` method is added to your code. With a little attention, you notice the intention and required argument for this method. Find the `OnClick()` method, which is executed when your command is clicked in runtime. Inside the `OnClick()` method, enter the following two lines of code.

```
Public override void OnClick()
{
    IMxDocument mxdoc = m_application.Document as IMxDocument;
    ZoomToActiveLayerInTOC(mxdoc);
}
```

7. You are almost finished. You just have to provide some information about the command itself. So find the `ZoomToActiveLayer()` method and change all the code shown in bold.

```
Public ZoomToActiveLayer()
    {
        base.m_category = "ArcGISBook";
        base.m_caption = "Zooms To Active Layer";
        base.m_message = "Zooms To Active Layer inside TOC";
        base.m_toolTip = "Zooms To Active Layer inside TOC";
        base.m_name = "ZoomToActiveLayer";

        try
        {
            string bitmapResourceName = GetType().Name + ".bmp";
            base.m_bitmap = new Bitmap(GetType(), bitmapResourceName);
        }
```

```
            catch (Exception ex)
            {
                System.Diagnostics.Trace.WriteLine(ex.Message, "Invalid Bitmap");
            }
        }
```

8. That is it. Press F5 to test your first ArcObjects SDK development. When you press F5, Visual Studio runs ArcMap. In ArcMap, find the ArcGISBook Command category inside the Customize window on the Commands tab. You will see your command. Put it wherever appropriate and close the Customize window. Add some layers to ArcMap, then select one of them inside the Table of Contents window and test your command. Hope you enjoy it.

How It Works

In this Try It Out, you used the ArcGIS Snippet Finder to insert a reusable block of code. Snippets make life far easier for developers. Most of the time, snippets provide a great starting point. But in order to get the most out of snippets, you have to be familiar with finding appropriate classes and interfaces and reading Object Model Diagrams of ArcObjects. Throughout this book, you will become familiar with most of them.

SUMMARY

In this chapter, you have explored all the models for customizing and developing ArcGIS for Desktop 10.0 and 10.1 applications. Through add-ins or by extending ArcObjects, the ultimate in customization and development in ArcGIS for Desktop applications can be done using .NET. In both models, you need to write .NET code in VB.NET or C# to make use of ArcObjects. Also, ArcGIS code snippets are available for both models; like any other ready-to-use piece of software, they just provide a good starting point but in almost all cases you need to write your own business logic. Also, ArcGIS code snippets are very good for learning ArcObjects programming. So as you step into the specific topic of ArcObjects programming, feel free to explore ArcGIS snippets. In the next two chapters, you are going to learn the basic and necessary parts of .NET programming to be able to put ArcObjects to work.

EXERCISES

1. What is the best way for creating and executing geoprocessing workflows?

2. Which model of development provides declarative configuration?

3. Which model of development of ArcGIS for Desktop applications provides more flexibility?

4. Which models of development of ArcGIS for Desktop applications don't need operating system administrator privileges?

You will find the answers to these exercises in this book's appendix.

▶ **WHAT YOU LEARNED IN THIS CHAPTER**

TOPIC	KEY CONCEPTS
Programming languages used for ArcGIS development	C#.NET, VB.NET, Java, and Python
ArcPy module	`arcpy` is a gateway to all Python functions, tools, and classes that can be used in ArcGIS.
	Python geoprocessing in ArcGIS is performed through an ArcPy site package (or ArcPy for short). All geoprocessing tools can be accessed through ArcPy. In addition, ArcPy provides several functions, classes, and modules that provide us with extended functionality as well as simple coding patterns.
Models of ArcGIS customization	1. User Interface (UI) customization
	2. Scripting
	3. Desktop add-ins
	4. Developing custom components using ArcObjects SDK (Extending ArcObjects)
Tools required for ArcGIS Desktop development	1. Visual Studio (support for .NET 3.5 is necessary)
	2. ArcObjects SDK for Microsoft .NET
VBA support in current and next versions of ArcGIS	Until version 10.0 of ArcGIS, desktop applications shipped with an embedded programming language called Microsoft Visual Basic for Applications (VBA). Microsoft decided to stop supporting VBA or offering a VBA distribution license; as a result, by default VBA is not directly installed with ArcGIS for Desktop applications.

PART II
.NET Programming Fundamentals

3

.NET Programming Fundamentals, Part I

WHAT YOU WILL LEARN IN THIS CHAPTER:

➤ Microsoft .NET framework and its relationship to C#

➤ General features of C# programming language

➤ Major data types in C# and corresponding data types in .NET

➤ Object-based manipulation

➤ Introduction to object-oriented programming in C#

WROX.COM CODE DOWNLOADS FOR THIS CHAPTER

The wrox.com code downloads for this chapter are found at `www.wrox.com/remtitle`
`.cgi?isbn=1118442547` on the Download Code tab. The code is in the Chapter03 folder and
is individually named according to the names throughout the chapter.

This chapter presents an overview of programming in the official language of .NET: C#. You
learn about the fundamental aspects of this programming language. Topics such as data types,
operators, loops, and conditional statements are explained. This chapter assumes you are
familiar with these concepts and only teaches how to implement them in C#.

THE .NET FRAMEWORK

The .NET Framework is a collection of fundamental technologies designed to provide the
common services needed to run applications. Microsoft designed the .NET Framework with
certain goals in mind, such as support of industry standards, extensibility, unified programming model, improved memory management, and so forth. Following is a brief explanation of
.NET Framework technologies.

➤ **.NET programming languages:** Include C#.NET (or C# for short), VB.NET (or VB for short), F#, and managed C++. The main programming languages inside the .NET Framework are C# and VB. C# and VB are similar in terms of syntax as well as performance of code execution. Though the syntax is a bit different, both use the .NET class library and are supported by the Common Language Runtime (CLR). Microsoft recently has stated that it will now aim to ensure that VB and C# contain the same functionality. According to Microsoft, choosing to program in C# or VB is just a lifestyle choice. If you are a hard-core fan of VB don't worry. All code samples in this book are in both C# and VB. Dozens of other languages are ported into the .NET Framework, but the main languages are the mentioned ones. The unified programming model provided by .NET enables you to develop a class written in C#, which can extend the class written in VB.

➤ **.NET Framework Base Class Libraries (BCL):** The giant repository of classes that provide prebuilt functionality for everything from reading a text file to drawing graphics and textures in an online game. The class library collects thousands of pieces of prebuilt functionalities that you can use in your applications. Sometimes parts of BCL are organized into a technology set such as ADO.NET (the technology for working with databases), ASP .NET (technology for creating web applications), Windows Forms (technology for creating traditional Windows applications), and WPF (technology for creating modern Windows applications), to name just a few.

➤ **CLR (Common Language Runtime):** The fundamental component of the .NET Framework is the CLR. This is the engine that executes all .NET programs and provides an environment for managed execution of .NET applications. It manages the execution of .NET applications by providing services such as memory management, security checking, and code optimization. For this reason, .NET code which executes inside CLR is called *managed code*. In short, the CLR provides a layer of abstraction between the code and operating system.

➤ **Visual Studio:** This is not really part of the .NET Framework, but because Visual Studio is always used in .NET development it is considered a part of the .NET platform. Originally written in C#, Visual Studio provides one of the most complete and fully fledged (if not the best and most complete) integrated development environments, or IDEs, for development of all kinds of software. Visual Studio contains a complete .NET Framework, so in order to prepare your necessary tools for .NET development all you need is to install Visual Studio.

THE C# LANGUAGE

The official language of the .NET Framework is C#. Learning C# is quite simple, and you get a lot of help from Visual Studio's coding tips and built-in IntelliSense (the code autocompletion feature of Visual Studio). The following sections provide an overview of programming in C#.

A Brief History of C#

C# is a simple, modern, general-purpose, object-oriented programming (OOP) language. During the development of the .NET Framework, the BCL were originally written using a managed code compiler system called Simple Managed C (SMC). Anders Hejlsberg (father of C#) formed a team to build a new language at the time called C-like Object Oriented Language (COOL). Microsoft has the habit of choosing sexy names for its products: ActiveX, XNA, Xbox, and so forth. For trademark reasons and maybe because COOL is not cool and sexy enough, Microsoft changed the name of the language to C#.

Basic Concepts

Like all the programming languages, C# has its own syntax. C# generally follows the syntax of the C and C++ programming languages.

Case Sensitivity

C# is case sensitive. This means whenever you define a variable, method, and so forth, you have to refer to them using the exact name and case for them. In addition, you have to write all the keywords of the language in lowercase. For example, if you want to declare an integer variable you have to type *int* instead of all other variations, such as Int, INT, and iNT.

Comments

Comments are valuable descriptive text that are ignored during execution and enhance the readability of the code for developers. In C#, you can comment out a single line of text using a double forward slash (//). For multiline comments, you can insert a forward slash plus asterisk (/*) at the beginning of the first line and an asterisk plus a forward slash (*/) at the end of the last line. Using multiline comments, you can comment out a block of code for test purposes. This way, you still have that block of code in your source code, which is not considered by a compiler for execution.

```
//this is a single line comment
// feel free to write anything descriptive
//even in your mother tongue
/*this is a multiline comment
* always use comments to explain your code
* it makes it easier and faster
* to understand
* the code when it has some comments
*/
```

When you insert the */ in a multiline comment, note that all subsequent new lines automatically get an asterisk. However, you can remove the asterisk at the beginning of lines between /* and */ because they are unnecessary.

```
/*this is a multiline comment
always use comments to explain your code
it makes it easier and faster
to understand
the code when it has some comments
*/
```

C# has some other options for commenting code. You look at one of them later in this chapter in the "Methods" section.

Block Structure

In C#, blocks of code are composed of code that is grouped together for execution in loops, conditional execution, defining methods, and so forth. In all these cases (and more that you will see throughout this book), blocks of code are defined using curly braces ({ }).

The following is the syntax for a code block:

```
{
    // Code in a block
}
```

Statement Termination Character

The C# compiler recognizes a semicolon (;) to denote the end of an executable line of code. Every statement in C# must end with a semicolon except when you are defining block structure and comments. Remember that comments are not executable code; thus, they don't need a semicolon. All the code inside the block must have a semicolon (;); however, because the definition of a block requires a curly bracket ({) at the beginning of the block and a curly bracket (}) at the end of the block, there is no need for a semicolon (;) at the end of a block definition.

```
//block of code (Method definition)
void CalculatingSummationAndAverage()
{
    // executable code inside a block (method)
    int summation = 0;
    int count = 0;
    //block of code (for block)
    for (int iteratorVariable = 0; iteratorVariable < 10; iteratorVariable++)
    {
        //executable code inside a block
        summation = summation + iteratorVariable;
        count = count + 1;
    }
    //executable code inside block
    double average = summation / count;
}
```

Because the C# compiler considers one line of code as a statement with one semicolon (;), you can break your code into multiple lines to enhance readability. The following two lines of code show various ways to write the same statement. You can write either

```
summation = summation + iteratorVariable;
```

or

```
summation = summation +
            iteratorVariable;
```

Variables and Data Types

Like any modern programming language, C# uses variables to store all kinds of data: numbers, text, and objects. A variable is a named location in memory. Using variables, your program can read or alter values stored in memory. Before you use a variable in your program, you must declare it. You have to provide a name and data type for the variable when declaring the variable in C#. Generally when you want to declare a variable you start with the data type followed by the name you want to use as the name of the variable.

```
int summation;
```

Specifying the data type is referred to as *strong typing*. Strong typing results in more efficient memory management, faster execution, and compiler type checking, all of which reduce runtime errors.

Once you declare a variable, you can assign it an initial value, either in a separate statement or within the declaration statement itself. For instance, the following code

```
int counter = 1;
```

is equivalent to this

```
int counter;
counter = 1;
```

C# safeguards you from errors by restricting you from using uninitialized variables. For example, the following code causes an error when you attempt to compile it:

```
int myNumber;
// myNumber is uninitialized
// The following line of code causes an error
myNumber = myNumber + 1;
```

So it is good idea to declare and initialize a variable in the same line of code. For this reason, always assign default values for your code (for example, 0 for numeric variables). Once you've declared your variables, you can freely assign values to them, as long as these values have the correct data type.

```
//declaring and initializing myNumber variable
int myNumber=0;
// since myNumber has a value it can be used freely
// The following line of code doesn't cause an error
myNumber = myNumber + 1;
//asssigning new value to your variable
myNumber = anotherVariable * 5;
```

All .NET programming languages make use of the same data types with somewhat different names. For example, the Integer data type in VB is the same as int in C#. In spite of the different names, the CLR considers those data types as two different names for the same .NET data type: System .Int32. This feature provides unlimited opportunities for language integration. Because languages share the same core data types, you can easily use and even extend objects written in one .NET language in an application written in another .NET language. In the following sections, you learn about the intrinsic data types in C# and .NET, which are numeric, character, and date.

Numeric Data Types

Numeric data types can be integral or fractional. Table 3-1 summarizes the most important integral data types of C# and the equivalents in .NET.

TABLE 3-1: Integral Data Types

C# DATA TYPE	.NET DATA TYPE	STORAGE SIZE	VALUE RANGE
byte	Byte	8 bit	0–255
short	Int16	16 bit	-32,768–32,767
int	Int32	32 bit	-2,147,483,648–2,147,483,647
long	Int64	64 bit	-9,223,272,036,854,775,808– 9,223,272,036,854,775,807

You have to use fractional data types when a variable should store numbers that include decimal parts. Table 3-2 briefly explains all fractional numeric data types available in .NET.

TABLE 3-2: Fractional Data Types

C# DATA TYPE	.NET DATA TYPE	STORAGE SIZE	VALUE RANGE
float	Single	32 bit	−3.4028235E+38 through −1.401298E−45 for negative values; 1.401298E−45 through 3.4028235E+38 for positive values
double	Double	64 bit	−1.79769313486231570E+308 through −4.94065645841246544E−324 for negative values; 4.94065645841246544E−324 through 1.79769313486231570E+308 for positive values
decimal	Decimal	128 bit	0 through +/−79,228,162,514,264,337,593,543,950,3 35 with no decimal point; 0 through +/−7.92281625142 64337593543950335 with 28 places to the right of the decimal

The default data type for integral numbers is the int data type and for fractional numbers it is double. This means the C# compiler considers each integral number as an integer and each fractional number as a double even if you declare a variable as another type and assign a number to that variable. In the following code, 123.123 is a fractional number and as a result is considered as a double to the C# compiler. If you try to assign 123.123 to a variable of type decimal or float, you get a compiler error that tells you it cannot convert double to float or decimal implicitly.

```
//both of the following lines of code
//cause errors
decimal myDecimal = 123.123;
float myFloat = 123.123;
```

For this reason, you have to append a special character to your numbers to explicitly tell the compiler that "I know you consider every fractional number a double, but I want you to consider this number a float and assign it to the `myFloat` variable." These characters, which are called type indicators, are as follows:

➤ M or m for decimal

➤ D or d for double

➤ F or f for float

➤ L or l for long

Using this special character, you can rewrite your code as follows:

```
    //no errors
decimal myDecimal = 123.123d;
float myFloat = 123.123f;
```

> **NOTE** Type indicators are one of the few features that aren't case sensitive in C#. The storage sizes along with the required range of values are the most important parameters when choosing a data type for a variable. An obvious reason for this fact is that the smaller the storage size, the faster the compiler can work with that data type. However, there is an exception. The C# compiler performs arithmetic operations with integers (the `Int32` base .NET data type) faster and more efficiently than the other numeric data types such as `byte` or `short`. For this reason, it's better to use integers as counter variables even though a `byte` or `short` type could easily manage the maximum range of values.

Fractional data types provide another point of consideration. The `float` and `double` data types always have rounding errors, but in most cases those errors are negligible. For example, consider the following code, which results in a really small number.

```
float floatPI = 3.14f;
double doublePI = 3.14d;
double result = floatPI - doublePI;
//the result will be a small number
//1.04904174680343E-07
```

The `decimal` data type holds a larger number of significant digits than either the `float` or the `double` data types, and it is not subject to rounding errors. The `decimal` data type is usually reserved for financial and scientific calculations that require a high degree of precision.

Other numeric data types also can be used in .NET, such as BigInteger and ulong (which are not covered in this book). If you are interested in other numeric data types in .NET, consult the .NET Framework documentation.

Character Data Types

In this category, C# has `char` and `string` data types for holding single characters and strings of characters, respectively. Both data types support Unicode, which means that you can easily represent and work with every language from Persian to Mandarin Chinese. The `char` data type can store just single unicode characters, such as "p" or "a," and every `char` variable occupies 16 bits of memory. Any `string` variable stores a sequence of unicode characters that can include zero to about two billion characters.

```
string firstName = "Pouria";
string lastName = "Amirian";
//string concatenation using + operator
string fullName = firstName + lastName;
//value of fullName is "PouriaAmirian"
```

C# treats any embedded backslash (\) as the start of a special escape character that specifies how the character should be printed in the output. Each escape character starts with "\" followed by a specific token. The most useful character literals are as follows:

- ➤ \' for single quote
- ➤ \" for double quote
- ➤ \n for new line
- ➤ \t for horizontal tab
- ➤ \\ for backward slash

Note that specifying the actual backslash character (for example, in an address of a file) requires two backslashes. Here's an example:

```
// A string variable holding the
// D:\ESRI\ArcGIS\TemplateData.gdb
string path ="";
path = "D:\\ESRI\\ArcGIS\\TemplateData.gdb";
```

Alternatively, you can use a so-called *verbatim string* by prefixing string literal with the @ symbol.

```
path = @" D:\ESRI\ArcGIS\TemplateData.gdb ";
```

Boolean Data Type

The boolean data type (`bool` in C#) holds a 16-bit value that is interpreted as `true` or `false`. It's used for variables that can be one of only two values, such as yes or no, on or off, or up or down (for this reason, they are often called *flag variables*).

```
bool isActive = false;
```

Date Data Type

Dates are held as 64-bit integers. C# has no keyword for the date data type, but the .NET Framework defines a few useful data types for working with date and time: the `DateTime` and `TimeSpan` structures.

Nullable Data Types

By default, no intrinsic data types (except `string`) can be assigned a null value. This can become problematic when retrieving data from data structures such as a database that does allow nulls. Since the release of .NET 2.0, it has been possible to create *nullable data types*. Simply put, a nullable type can hold all the values of its underlying type, plus the value *null*. Thus, if you declare a nullable boolean, it could be assigned `true` or `false` or `null`. When declaring a value type variable that may be assigned a null, you make it a nullable type by placing a question mark symbol (?) after the type name.

```
// compiler error
double employeeSalary = null;
//OK, no error
double? salary = null;
```

Operations on Variables

You can use all the standard types of variable operations in C#. When working with numbers, you use various math symbols, as listed in Table 3-3. C# follows the conventional order of operations, performing exponentiation first, followed by multiplication and division, and then addition and subtraction. You can also control order by grouping sub-expressions with parentheses.

TABLE 3-3: Math Operators

OPERATOR	MEANING
+	Addition
–	Subtraction
*	Multiplication
/	Division
%	Reminder

If you divide one integer by another integer, the C# compiler performs integer division. That means it automatically discards the fractional part of the answer and returns the whole part as an integer. For example, if you divide 15 by 2, you end up with 7 instead of 7.5. The solution is to explicitly indicate that one of your numbers has a fractional data type. For example, if you replace 15 with 15d, C# will treat the 15 as a double. Also you can reach the same result by replacing 15 with 15.0, which C# will treat as a double. Either way, the division will return the expected value of 7.5. Of course, this problem doesn't occur very often in real-world code, because then you're usually dividing one variable by another. As long as your variables aren't integers, it doesn't matter what number they contain.

C# also enables you to use the addition operator (+) to join two strings, which is referred to as *string concatenation*.

```
string firstName = "Anahid";
string lastName = "Basiri";
//string concatenation
string fullName = firstName + " " + lastName;
//value of fullName is "Anahid Basiri"
```

C# also provides special shorthand assignment operators. Here are a few examples:

```
// Add 15 to summation
// This is the same as summation = summation + 15;
summation += 15;

// Multiply mySalary by 3
// This is the same as mySalary = mySalary * 3;
mySalary *= 3;
```

For other math functions, you can use .NET's Math class. The Math class provides many useful functions for performing arithmetic and trigonometric calculations. The methods in this class are static, which means they are always available and ready to use, so there is no need to create a variable of type Math to be able to use them. Feel free to explore this handy class. The following code snippets present some examples of using the Math class.

```
Double myVar=0.0;
myVar = Math.Sqrt(49);          // myVar = 7.0
myVar = Math.Round(8.881, 1);   // myVar = 8.8
myVar = Math.Abs(-1388);        // myVar = 1388
myVar = Math.PI;                // myVar = 3.141…
myVar = Math.Sin(Math.PI / 2)   // myVar =1.0
```

In the following Try It Out, you see some of these features in action.

> **NOTE** *There are some other features for using complex numbers inside the .NET Framework. If you are serious about math in .NET, consult the .NET documentation.*

TRY IT OUT   **Simple Application for Calculation (FirstWPFApp.zip)**

1. Start Visual Studio. From the Start page, select New Project to open the New Project window. Because you are going to build this code as a Windows application, select the Windows node under Visual C#, and then select WPF Application. Provide a meaningful name for the project and solution (such as firstWPFApp), specify the location where all the files of the solution will be saved, and then click OK.

2. Shortly after you click OK, the Visual Studio designer appears. The designer is used to create the user interface of your WPF applications. Using the designer, click the Button control in the Toolbox dockable window, and then drag and drop it on the main window of your application, as shown in Figure 3-1. If you cannot see the Toolbox window, you can use the View menu to turn it on.

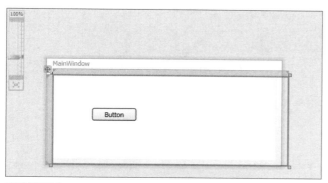

FIGURE 3-1

3. Add two Textbox controls and three Label controls to the main window by double-clicking each control type in the Toolbox or using the drag-and-drop technique. Change the position of the controls to look like Figure 3-2.

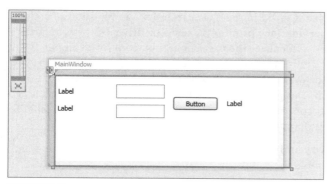

FIGURE 3-2

4. Now you are going to set some properties for the controls you added. In Visual Studio, the Properties window is used for accessing and changing the properties of everything. Generally, in order to use this window you have to select the intended object (control, window, component, and so forth) and then find the property you want to change. Click the Button control, and in the Properties window change the Name of the button to "btnAddition" and Content to "Add," as shown in Figure 3-3. You can use the View menu to turn on the Properties window (and every other window) if it is turned off.

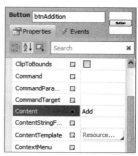

5. Changing the name of all controls to meaningful names is good programming practice. For this Try It Out, change the names of two textboxes to "txtFirstNum" and "txtSecondNum." Clear the content of the last label and change the content of two other labels to "First Number" and "Second Number." Your main window should be similar to Figure 3-4.

FIGURE 3-3

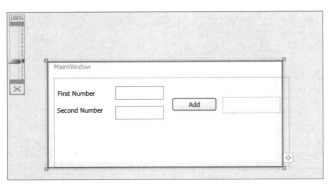

FIGURE 3-4

6. Now the user interface is ready. Press F5 to see how it looks in runtime. Because the main window contains no logic or code, nothing happens if you click the Add button. Stop debugging by pressing Shift + F5 or the Stop button inside the Visual Studio.

7. Now you add functionality to the Add button. Double-click the button to get to the code window. As you can see, the user interface is saved in the `MainWindow.xaml` file and the code in `MainWindow.xaml.cs`. Windows user interface programs are event-driven. *Events* are actions initiated by either a user or the system, whenever the user clicks a button, for example. Event-driven applications respond to the various events that occur by executing code that you specify. To respond to an event, you define the event handler to execute when a particular event occurs. When you double-click any control in Designer, Visual Studio creates the skeleton or stub code for handling the default event of that control. Because you double-click the button, Visual Studio adds skeleton code for the Click event handler for you.

8. Add code to perform addition on two numbers inside the two textboxes you created in Step 3. The Click event handler should resemble the following code:

```
private void btnAddition_Click(object sender, RoutedEventArgs e)
{
    //since the inputs (entered by user) are string
    //we have to convert them to double
    //get the first num
    double firstNum = 0;
    firstNum = double.Parse(txtFirstNum.Text);
    //get the second num
    double secondNum = double.Parse(txtSecondNum.Text);
    // + operator for string concatenate them
    label3.Content = firstNum.ToString() + " + " + secondNum.ToString()
    + " = " + firstNum + secondNum;
}
```

9. Test the functionality of the application by pressing F5 on your keyboard. As you can see, you implement a simple application that adds two numeric inputs provided by the user. As an exercise, add three additional buttons for performing subtraction, multiplication, and division.

How It Works

Programming in Windows is event-driven. You have to create some user interface controls for users and provide event handlers for those controls. When a user or the system initiates events, code inside the event handler will be executed. ArcGIS for Desktop applications follow the same model of development. Usually you create commands, toolbars, and other user interface controls, and then provide functionality for them using the event-driven model of programming; however, there are other events, like change, open, or close events, that are initiated by the system when a map document is changed, opened, or closed.

In this Try It Out, you created a WPF application. WPF (Windows Presentation Foundation) is a modern model and a more efficient way of developing desktop applications for the Windows operating system. Perhaps one of the most compelling advantages of WPF is that it offers a way to cleanly separate the user interface from the programming logic that drives it. Using XAML (Extensible Application Markup Language), it is possible to define the UI of an application via XML markup using the designer of Visual Studio or Microsoft Expression Blend and then connect that user interface to .NET code to provide the program's functionality. Usually (as you have seen in this Try It Out) the development lifecycle of WPF applications starts with designing the user interface and continues with coding the functionality needed for the application.

Another important point in this Try It Out was the use of the `double.Parse` method, which is discussed later in this chapter. You also will see how .NET provides several other ways to convert different data types.

Arrays

Arrays are the basic structures used to store data in all programming languages. They are often used to organize and work with groups of the same data type. In C#, you declare an array by suffixing an appropriate data type with brackets ([]) and then the name of your array:

```
string[] layerNames;
```

Each individual value in the array is set and accessed using its index inside the array. All arrays start at a fixed lower bound of 0. This rule has no exceptions. When you create an array in C#, you specify the number of elements. Because counting starts at 0, the highest index is actually one less than the number of elements. (In other words, if you have five elements, the highest index is four.) The `new` operator is used to create the array and initialize its elements to their default values. The default value for all numeric data is zero and for string is an empty string. Because the elements of the array are referenced by a zero-based index, the following array holds two elements:

```
// layerNames array will contain two elements
string[] layerNames = new string[1];
layerNames[0]="cities";
layerNames[1]="states";
```

To initialize the elements of an array when the array is declared, you can use curly brackets ({}) to list the values. Because the size of the array can be inferred, you do not have to state it,

```
//layerNames contains four elements
string[] layerNames = {"cities","roads","railway","states"};
```

C# supports multidimensional arrays. When you declare the array, you separate the size of the dimensions by commas. The following declaration creates a two-dimensional array of integers with three rows and two columns:

```
string[,] layerDescriptions = new string[2,1];
```

In this case you use curly brackets inside curly brackets to initialize the array.

```
string[,] layerDescription = {{"cities","cities of the world"},
                              {"roads","major road network'},
                              {"states","states of the US"}};
// Access the value in
//first row and second column
string desc = layerDescription[0, 1];
//desc is now set to "cities of the world"
```

> **NOTE** All intrinsic data types support what is known as a default constructor (you will see what a constructor is later in this chapter). This feature allows you to create a variable using the new keyword, which automatically sets the variable to its default value. This way the C# compiler assigns numeric variables to 0, boolean variables to false, character data types to empty (" "), date data types to 1/1/0001, and object data types to null (which is an empty reference pointer).
>
> ```
> //since the variable assigned to its default value
> //the following line of code doesn't cause errors
> int myInt = new int();
> myInt = myInt +1;
> ```

Decision-Making

From many viewpoints, decision-making is the core of programming. All decision-making in all programming languages starts with an expression (called a *condition*) that can be evaluated to true or false. Based on the result of the evaluation of the condition, different blocks of code are executed. To build a condition, you need at least a comparison operator (shown in Table 3-4) and two literals or variables.

TABLE 3-4: Comparison Operators

COMPARISON OPERATOR	MEANING	EXAMPLE	RESULT OF EVALUATION
==	Equal to	(20/5) == 4	true
!=	Not equal to	2 != 3	true
>	Greater than	2 > 3	false

>=	Greater than or equal to	3 >= 4	false
<	Less than	3 < 4	true
<=	Less than or equal to	3 <= 3	true

In the examples shown in Table 3-4, you can replace literals with variables. You also can create composite conditions using logical operators. Logical operators combine the results of conditional operators. The three most commonly used logical operators are the And, Or, and Not operators, shown in Table 3-5.

TABLE 3-5: Logical Operators

LOGICAL OPERATOR	MEANING	EXAMPLE	RESULT
&&	And	(2 > 3) && (3 > 2)	false
||	Or	(2 > 3) || (3 > 2)	true
!	Not	! (3 > 2)	false

The And operator (&&) combines two expressions and returns `true` if both expressions are true. The Or operator (||) combines two expressions and returns `true` if either one is true. The Not operator (!) switches the result of the comparison: a value of `true` returns false and a value of `false` returns true. In the case of the And operator (&&), if the first expression is false, the second expression is not evaluated. Quite the opposite is the case with the Or operator: If the first expression is evaluated to true, the second expression is not evaluated. This behavior is called *short circuit*.

The `if` statement is the heart of decision-making in any programming language. The `if` statement in C# is able to evaluate any combination of conditions and deal with various data types. The following code snippet demonstrates the use of the `if` statement,

```
if (layerName =="states")
{
    // do something with the states layer
}
else if (layerName == "roads" || layerName == "rails")
{
    // do something with both the roads and the rails layers
}
else
{
    // do something with the rest of the layers
}
```

The `if` block can have any number of conditions. If you test only a single condition, you don't need to include any `else` blocks. Keep in mind that the `if` statement matches one condition at most. For example, if `layerName` is equal to `"roads"` the second condition is met and no other conditions will be evaluated.

C# also provides a switch statement that you can use to evaluate a single variable or expression for multiple possible values. The only limitation is that the variable you're evaluating must be an integral numeric (int, short, long, and so forth), a boolean (bool), a character (char), a string (string), or a value from an enumeration. Other data types cannot be evaluated in a switch statement. In the following code snippet, each case examines the myLayer variable and tests whether it's equal to a specific layer name:

```
switch (layername)
{
    case "states":
        //do something with states Layer
        break;
    case "rails":
    case "roads":
        // do something with both the rails
        //and the roads layer
        break;
    default:
        // // do something with other layers
        break;
}
```

Every branch in a switch statement must end with the break keyword. If you forget this keyword, the compiler will alert you and refuse to build your solution. The only exception is if you choose to stack multiple case statements directly on top of each other with no intervening code. This allows you to mimic the logical Or operator in switch statements and hence write one segment of code that handles more than one case.

Unlike the if statement, in C# the switch statement is limited to evaluating equality conditions. (Maybe this handy feature will be implemented in future versions of this powerful programming language.) However, the switch statement provides clearer syntax than the if statement for situations in which you want to test a single variable.

Iteration

All programming languages provide several ways to repeat blocks of code until a condition has been met. C# provides the following four iteration statements:

- ➤ for
- ➤ for/each
- ➤ while
- ➤ do/while

The for and foreach loops are ideal for iterating through sets of known and fixed sized data like arrays and collections (you will see some of them in the next chapter). The while and do/while statements are ideal when the number of iterations is not known until runtime or the number of iterations depends on input from the user.

The for loop is a basic statement in many programs. It allows you to execute a block of code a defined number of times using a built-in counter. To create a for loop, you need to specify a starting value, an ending condition, and the amount of increment with each iteration. The following code snippet shows a simple `for` block for calculating the summation of 1 to 9.

```
//whenever we use the new keyword with intrinsic data types
//they initialize to their default values
//which is 0 for numeric and "" for string and char
int sum = new int();
for (int i = 0; i < 10; i++)
{
    sum += i;
}
```

Notice that the `for` loop starts with parentheses that indicate three important pieces of information. The first portion, `int i = 0`, creates the counter variable i and sets its initial value to 0. The second part, `i < 10`, specifies the condition that must be met for the loop to continue. This condition is tested at the start of every pass through the block. If for each iteration i is greater than or equal to 10, the condition will evaluate to `false`, and the loop will end. The third portion, `i++`, increments the counter variable. In this example, the counter is incremented by 1 in each iteration. That means i will be equal to 0 for the first iteration, equal to 1 for the second iteration, and so on. However, you could adjust this statement so that it decrements the counter (or performs any other operation you want, such as `i+=2` for setting the increment as 2).

The C# `foreach` keyword allows you to iterate over all items within an array (or a collection object). In this case, you just provide the counter like a variable; there is no need to introduce condition and increment values.

```
int sum = 0;
int[] numbers = { 1, 3, 5, 7, 8 };
foreach (int i in numbers)
{
    //do something with numbers
    sum += i;
}
```

The `foreach` loop has one key limitation: It's read-only. In other words, you cannot change any value inside the `foreach` loop. For example, if you want to iterate an array and change the values in that array at the same time, as shown in the following code snippet, the compiler will raise an error saying that the `foreach` iteration variable cannot be assigned to a new value.

```
int sum = 0;
int[] numbers = { 1, 3, 5, 7, 8 };
foreach (int i in numbers)
{
    //compiler error for the following line of code
    i+=2;
    //do something with numbers
    sum += i;
}
```

In this case, you have to resort to a `for` loop.

C# supports `while` and `do/while` loops that test a specific condition before or after each iteration of the loop. When the condition of the loop evaluates to `false`, the loop is exited. The following code snippet executes 10 times using a `while` loop. In this code, when the loop is exited, the code inside the loop was executed 10 times and the counter is equal to 10.

```
int i = 0;
while (i < 10)
{
    //following line of code executes ten times
    i += 1;
}
//here i is equal to 10
```

You can also place the condition at the end of the loop using the do/while syntax. In this case, the condition is tested at the end of each iteration through the loop.

```
int i = 0;
do
{
    //following line of code executes ten times
    i += 1;
}
while (i < 10);
//here i is equal to 10
```

Both of these examples are alike, unless you evaluate a condition which is false from the beginning. In this case, since the `while` loop evaluates the condition at first, the code inside the `while` loop won't execute. The do/while loop, on the other hand, will always execute the code at least once, because it doesn't evaluate the condition until the end.

> **NOTE** Use the `break` statement to exit any type of loop. It's common programming practice to evaluate a condition (using an `if` statement in a loop) and if the condition has been satisfied then exit the loop, as shown in the following code snippet:
>
> ```
> string[] layerNames = { "cities", "roads", "railway", "states" };
> foreach (string layer in layerNames)
> {
>     if (layer == "roads")
>     {
>         //you have found your layer object and
>         //there is no need to go on the iteration
>         break;
>     }
> }
> ```
>
> Also you can use the `continue` statement when you want to skip the execution of the current iteration and go to the next iteration.
>
> ```
> string[] layerNames = { "cities", "roads", "railway", "states" };
> string listOfLayers = "";
> foreach (string layer in layerNames)
> ```

```
    {
        if (layer == "railway")
        {
            continue;
        }
        // + operator on string data type concatenate the strings
        listOfLayers += layer + "";
    }
```

Object Manipulation

It is fair to say that everything in .NET is designed with object-oriented concepts in mind. Even a simple literal string like pouria is a full object. You can test this behavior simply by putting a dot or period symbol (.) at the end of the string value. In fact, even ordinary variables are really fully fledged objects in .NET. This means that everything, such as common data types, has the built-in intelligence to handle basic operations (such as counting the number of characters in a string). For example, in the previous Try It Out you learned about how to use the double class's Parse() method to convert the string representation of a number to its corresponding double precision floating point number. In addition, all data types in .NET include a ToString() method. In variables of intrinsic data types (like int and double), the result of the ToString() method is the string representation of the given variable. The following code snippet demonstrates how to use the ToString() method with a double variable:

```
// + operator for string concatenating strings them
label3.Content = firstNum.ToString() + " + " + secondNum.ToString() + " = " +
    firstNum + secondNum;
```

> **NOTE** The ToString() method is provided by the System.Object class, which is the ultimate base class of all classes (types) in the .NET Framework. Because all classes are derived from the System.Object class, the ToString() method is available to all classes in .NET.

This behavior is part of the object-oriented nature of .NET. Put simply, an *object* is something that has properties and methods and can fire events. You have already used some objects, such as buttons and textboxes. In the preceding Try It Out, to set the name for the button on your main window ("btnAddition") you set the Name property of the button object. You used the Click event of the btnAddition object to respond to users' clicks. The methods, properties, and events of an object are *members* of that object. You can access all the members of an object by putting a dot or period after the name of an object (this notation is called *object notation syntax*).

You use the arithmetic operators of .NET or the methods of the Math class for numeric data types. In contrast, the other data types use their members to perform primarily nonarithmetic activities. The following sections look at some of the more interesting (for our purposes) members of the data types and structures that have been discussed so far.

Useful Members of the String Data Type

The string data type is almost always used in all types of applications. For this reason, it is good to spend some time to master all its useful methods and properties. The following code snippet shows some of the methods of the string data type:

```
string GIS = "  Geographical Information System ";
GIS = GIS.TrimStart();
//  "Geographical Information System "
GIS = GIS.ToUpper();
// "GEOGRAPHICAL INFORMATION SYSTEM"
GIS = GIS.Replace("GEOGRAPHICAL", "Geospatial");
//Geospatial INFORMATION SYSTEM
bool IsGeospatial = GIS.Contains("Geospatial");
// true
int length = GIS.Length;
//32

char[] GISCharArray = GIS.ToCharArray();
// 32 elements are in array
char myInitial = GISCharArray[4]; //p

string[] sep= {" "};
string[] GISStringArray = GIS.Split(sep,
      StringSplitOptions.RemoveEmptyEntries);

//GISStringArray[0]="Geospatial", GISStringArray[2]="Systems"
string g = "Geospatial";
string i = "Information";
string s = "Systems";
string gis = string.Format("GIS is stand for {0} {1} {2}", g,i,s );
gis = "GIS is stand for " + g + " " + i + " " + s;
```

Methods such as `Trim()`, `ToUpper()`, and `Replace()` generate new strings, and each of them substitutes the current value of the `GIS` variable with a new string value. The `Length` property of any `string` variable returns the number of characters inside the `string` variable. As the name suggests, the `ToCharArray()` method returns a `char` array. One of the more useful methods in this code snippet is the `Split()` method. Look at the `GIS.Split()` method in the preceding code. Notice that this method can be used in several ways based on the input that it expects, which is controlled by the arguments in the parentheses. This is called method overloading. Most of the prebuilt methods in .NET provide this feature. The preceding code snippet uses the `Split()` method to split the `string` variable based on the `separator` array, explained earlier in this chapter. The plus operator (+) is used to concatenate string values. As is true of many things in .NET, string concatenation can be done using other approaches too. One of those approaches is the "`Format()`" method of the `string` class. Simply put, when you define a string literal that contains segments of data whose value is contained in other variables, you can specify a placeholder within the string literal using one curly bracket per variable. At runtime, the value(s) passed into `string.Format()` are substituted for each placeholder. In fact, this method is used to format any intrinsic data type. The following code snippet demonstrates some of its usage:

```
double num = 88.1388;
string output = "";
//you can use format characters in the Format method
```

```
output = string.Format("{0:c}",num);
//$88.14  . The c character is used for currency
output = string.Format("{0:f1}", num);
//88.1   - The f is for floating point and
//the 1 is for the minimum number of digits
output = string.Format("{0:###,###.000000}", num);
//88.138800
output = string.Format("{0:000,###.000###}", num);
//000,088.1388
```

The following code provides a way to create an acronym out of a `string` variable by combining some other useful members of the `string` class:

```
string GIS = "  Geographical Information System ";
//Creating an acronym
//get rid of spaces at the beginning and the end of string
GIS = GIS.Trim();

string acronym = GIS[0].ToString();
//GIS[0] is char so you need to convert it to a string

while (GIS.Contains(" "))
  {
    GIS = GIS.Substring(GIS.IndexOf(" ")+1);
    acronym += GIS.Trim()[0].ToString();
  }
```

Useful Members of the Array Type

Arrays also behave like objects in the world of .NET. (Technically, like other classes in .NET, they are derived from the `System.Object` class). So you can use the familiar object notation syntax to access the members of an array. Take a look at useful members of the array class in action:

```
int[,] intArray = { {1,100}, {2,200}, {3,300}, {4,400}};

int lengthOfArray = intArray.Length;
//result=8 . Total number of elements

lengthOfArray = intArray.GetLength(0);
//result=4 . Number of elements in specified dimension

int rows = intArray.GetUpperBound(0);
//result=3 . Number of rows = 4 (since it is zero based)

int cols = intArray.GetUpperBound(1);
//reslt=1 . Number of columns= 2 (since it is zero based)
```

Data Type Conversion

Converting data from one data type to another (*casting*) is a common programming task. For example, in the first Try It Out in this chapter, you retrieved text input (string data) from a user that contains a number you want to use for a calculation. You might also need to take a calculated value and transform it into text; to show it to the user, you have to convert the calculated value to a string. Conversions are of two types: widening and narrowing. *Widening* is the term used to specify an implicit upward cast that does not result in a loss of data. For example, you can always convert a

32-bit integer (int data type) into a 64-bit integer (long data type). You won't need any special code to perform widening. Narrowing is the opposite of widening, in that a larger data type is stored within a smaller data type variable. It is important to know that all narrowing conversions result in a compiler error, even when you are sure that the narrowing conversion should indeed succeed. For example, the following code always results in a compiler error:

```
int intAge = 120;
byte byteAge = intAge;
```

Here, the value of the int variable (intAge) is safely within the range of a byte variable; therefore, you would expect the narrowing operation to not result in a runtime error. However, C# is a language built with type safety in mind, so you receive a compiler error. For this reason, you have to explicitly tell the compiler that you wish to do the conversion even if it results in loss of data. You do this using the explicit casting operator, which is ().

```
int intAge = 120;
byte byteAge = (byte)intAge;
```

Even if you use explicit casting to perform a narrowing conversion, there is a risk of loss of data. For example, consider the code shown here, which results in an overflow:

```
int intNum = int.MaxValue;
long lngNum = intNum + 1L;
//lngNum is equal to 2147483648

intNum = (int)lngNum;
//at this point intNum is exactly equal to int.MinValue (-2147783648)
```

This code uses the MaxValue property of the int class to access the maximum number that can be stored in an int variable. Then the long variable adds 1 to that number. Notice that you have to use the L character to define 1 as long; otherwise, the compiler treats 1 as an integer and performs integer addition, which results in loss of data and then assigns that value to the long variable.

In C#, you will simply end up with incorrect data in intNum. To avoid this problem, either check that your data is not too large before attempting a narrowing conversion or use a *checked block*, as shown in the following code snippet. The checked block enables overflow checking for a portion of code. If an overflow occurs, you'll automatically receive an error.

```
// the following block of code results in a runtime error
//Arithmetic operation resulted in an overflow
checked
{
    int intNum = int.MaxValue;
    long lngNum = intNum + 1L;
    //lngNum is equal to 2147483648
    intNum = (int)lngNum;
    //intNum is exactly equals to int.MinValue (-2147783648)
}
```

In addition to casting operators, you can always use the methods of the Convert class to perform widening or narrowing conversions. This class provides methods for conversion among intrinsic data types. For example, the preceding code can be written using a method of the Convert class, as shown in the following code snippet:

```
byte byteAge =Convert.ToByte(intAge);
```

Enumerations

You often will need to assign the value of a variable to one of several related, predefined constants. In these cases, you can create an enumeration type to group together the values. *Enumerations* (or enum types in C#) associate a set of integer constants to names that can be used in code. For example, the following code creates an enum type used to define three different kinds of feature classes: point, line, and polygon.

```
enum FeatureType
{
    point,
    line,
    polygon
}
```

You can use the FeatureType enumeration as a special data type that is restricted to one of three possible values. You assign or compare the enumerated value using the dot notation, as represented in the following example:

```
// Create a new variable of enum type
// and set it equal to the FeatureType.point constant.
FeatureType myGPSdata = FeatureType.point;
```

> **NOTE** *Enumerations are used widely in .NET and ArcObjects. You won't need to create your own enumerations to use in ArcObjects or .NET unless you're designing your own components. However, the concept of enumerated values is extremely important, because the .NET class library as well as ArcObjects uses it extensively. For example, when you want to add a new field (programmatically or through the UI of ArcMap) to the attribute table of a feature class, you have to provide the data type of the field. In that case, you have to use one of the values in the esriField-Type enumeration inside the geodatabase model. The following table lists some of the more frequently used elements in the esriFieldType enumeration.*
>
> **ESRIFIELDTYPE ENUMERATION**
>
> | VALUE | NAME | MEANING IN C# |
> |-------|------|----------------|
> | 0 | esriFieldTypeSmallInteger | short |
> | 1 | esriFieldTypeInteger | int |
> | 2 | esriFieldTypeSingle | float |
> | 3 | esriFieldTypeDouble | double |
> | 4 | esriFieldTypeString | string |
>
> *Internally, enumerations are maintained as numbers. Clearly, enumerations create more readable code. They also simplify coding, because once you type in the enumeration type name and add the dot (.), Visual Studio will display a list of possible values using IntelliSense.*

> **WARNING** *Programmers often talk about the process of enumerating, which means to loop, or iterate, over a collection. As you have learned, enums or enumerations are sets of constant values. In ArcObjects, you have both of these concepts but usually enums refer to looping objects and enumerations refer to a set of constant values.*

TRY IT OUT   Creating a Simple Calculator (SimpleCalculator.zip)

1. Start Visual Studio and create new project using either the File menu or the New Project link in the Start Page. Select WPF Application under Visual C# ⇨ Windows, provide **SimpleCalculator** as the name of the project, and click OK.

2. Add 16 buttons and 2 labels to the MainWindow of your application from the Toolbox dockable window. Provide appropriate names for them (use **lblResult** and **lblSummary** for the two labels). Change the content property of the buttons to match Figure 3-5, and make sure that the labels have empty content, because their content will be used later in the calculations.

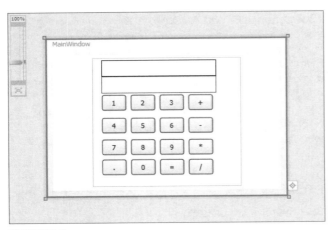

FIGURE 3-5

3. You want the user to click on the number buttons to specify the first operand, then click on one of four operator buttons, and after that again use the number buttons to enter the second operand, and finally, press on the equal sign to see the result and summary of its calculation. One way to do this procedure is to insert each number (the content property of each number button) into the label control and convert a whole string to a double variable when the user clicks on operators

and equal buttons. For this reason, you need to define three double variables and an enumeration for operators. Somewhere in the `MainWindow.xaml.cs` class block, which is not inside any other block of code, insert the required code for declaring those variables. Your code should look like the following code snippet:

```
public partial class MainWindow : Window
{
    double firstNum, secondNum, result;
    enum Operator
    {
        Addition,
        Subtraction,
        Multiplication,
        Division
    }
    Operator SelectedOperator;
    public MainWindow()
    {
        InitializeComponent();
    }
}
```

4. Now you are going to write code to handle the numeric buttons' Click event. As you've probably guessed, you can do this by clicking each button and appending the number of that button to the text inside the label. For example, for the button with "1" as its content the event handler should be something like the following code:

```
private void button1_Click(object sender, RoutedEventArgs e)
{
    lblResult.Content += "1";
}
```

Instead of writing code for the event handler of each button, you can write general event handler code that can be used by all the number buttons. Double-click one of the numeric buttons (such as the button with 1 as its content) and Visual Studio will create an empty event handler for the button's Click event. Rename the event handler to NumberClick.

In `NumberClick()` you need to cast the sender parameter of the event to the `Button` class and then use its content. The following code shows the `NumberClick` event handler:

```
private void NumberClick(object sender, RoutedEventArgs e)
{
    string enteredNum = "";
    Button clickedButton = (Button)sender;
    enteredNum = clickedButton.Content.ToString();
    lblResult.Content += enteredNum;
}
```

5. At this moment, if you look at the event of the button with "1" as its content (the double-clicked button), you will notice that in the list of events NumberClick is entered as the handler for the Click event. You can access the events by clicking the Events tab inside the Properties window, as shown in Figure 3-6.

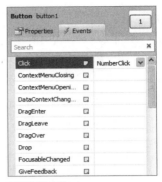

6. Set NumberClick as the handler for the Click event for all number buttons (from 0 to 9). Notice that as you set any property or event in the Properties window, the XAML code for that control reflects the changes.

7. Double-click on the dot button (.) and write the following lines of code as the event handler:

FIGURE 3-6

```
private void buttonPoint_Click(object sender, RoutedEventArgs e)
{
    if (!lblResult.Content.ToString().Contains("."))
    {
        lblResult.Content += ".";
    }
}
```

8. Double-click on one of the operator buttons (such as +). You are going to write general code for handling the Click event of four operators in one event handler.

```
private void btnAdd_Click(object sender, RoutedEventArgs e)
{
    //get the first number
    firstNum = double.Parse(lblResult.Content.ToString());
    //determine the operator
    string strOperator = ((Button)sender).Content.ToString();
    switch (strOperator)
    {
        case "+":
            SelectedOperator = Operator.Addition;
            break;
        case "-":
            SelectedOperator = Operator.Subtraction;
            break;
        case "*":
            SelectedOperator = Operator.Multiplication;
            break;
        case "/":
            SelectedOperator = Operator.Division;
            break;
    }

    //clear the lblResult to make it ready for second number
    lblResult.Content="";
}
```

9. Use the Events tab of the Properties window to set the preceding block of code as the event handler for the Click event of four operator buttons (+, -, *, /).

10. Double-click the equal (=) button and change its event handler to match the following code:

```
private void buttonEqual_Click(object sender, RoutedEventArgs e)
    {
        secondNum = double.Parse(lblResult.Content.ToString());

        switch (SelectedOperator)
        {
            case Operator.Addition:
                result = firstNum + secondNum;
                lblSummary.Content = string.Format("{0} + {1}", firstNum, secondNum);
                break;
            case Operator.Subtraction:
                result = firstNum - secondNum;
                lblSummary.Content = string.Format("{0} - {1}", firstNum, secondNum);
                break;
            case Operator.Multiplication:
                result = firstNum * secondNum;
                lblSummary.Content = string.Format("{0} * {1}", firstNum, secondNum);
                break;
            case Operator.Division:
                result = firstNum / secondNum;
                lblSummary.Content = string.Format("{0} / {1}", firstNum, secondNum);
                break;
        }

        lblResult.Content = result;
    }
```

11. Press F5 to run the application and test its functionality.

How It Works

In this Try It Out, you added some functionalities in an efficient manner. You wrote general code for handling the Click event issued by many objects (controls). You could write code more simply for each of the controls, but this approach results in less maintainable code. Suppose you wish to add some other functionality to your simple calculator or you want to include other logics in your handlers. In both cases, you have to change all event handlers, which is a tedious task. But using the method you used in this Try It Out, you wrote code in one position and wired many controls to it. Also you used the "sender" argument of the event handler block, which is added automatically by Visual Studio when it creates skeleton code for event handlers. Put simply, a "sender" object conveys information about the initializer of the event. Because the "sender" is of type Object, you need to cast it to "Button" to make use of it. At this point, your simple calculator is ready but it still doesn't contain the necessary code to handle the exceptions. For example, if a user enters 0 as divisor, this simple calculator crashes. You return to this topic in the next chapter, which introduces the concept of exception handling.

Methods

Methods are the most basic building blocks used to organize your code. Fundamentally, a method is a named group of one or more lines of code that are grouped together for the purpose of reusability.

In essence, each method performs a distinct logical task. Breaking your code down into methods helps you more easily manage your application.

When you declare a method in C#, the first part of the declaration specifies the data type of the return value and the second part indicates the method name. If your method doesn't return any data, you have to use the void keyword. Notice that the method name should always be followed by parentheses so the C# compiler will recognize it as a method. The following code shows two methods:

```
private int AddTwoNumbers()
{
    int firstNum = 10;
    int secondNum = 100;
    //you have to use the return keyword
    return firstNum + secondNum;
}
public void doSomething()
{
    //code goes here
    //no return keyword
}
```

In the preceding example, neither method specifies its accessibility. This is a common C# convention. By default, if you omit the accessibility keywords (such as private and public) for methods or variables, the C# compiler regards them as private. Private methods or variables are available only locally. On the other hand, public methods or variables can be called and accessed by all the other classes in your application.

```
private int AddTwoNumbers()
{
    int firstNum = 10;
    int secondNum = 100;
    //you have to use the return keyword
    return firstNum + secondNum;
}

public void doSomething()
{
    //code goes here
    //no return keyword
}
```

Calling or invoking any method is a simple task: Type the name of the method, followed by parentheses. If your method returns data, you have the option of using the data it returns or ignoring it.

```
int intAddition = AddTwoNumbers();
```

As you can see, AddTwoNumbers() just adds two hard-coded values. Using parameters, you can pass any int number to the method.

```
private int AddTwoNumber(int firstNum, int secondNum)
{
    return firstNum + secondNum;
}
```

Notice that you declare parameters in a similar way to variables. When you wish to call methods that accept parameters, you have to provide them with what they expect to receive.

```
int intAddition = AddTwoNumbers(10,100);
```

C# supports method overloading. You overload methods by defining multiple methods that have the same name with different signatures. A *method signature* is a combination of the name of the method and the number and data type of its parameters. If you change the number and data type of parameters for a method, you create a different method signature.

When you call the method, the CLR automatically chooses the correct version by examining the parameters you supply. The following code shows the AddTwoNumbers() method with different signatures:

```
private double AddTwoNumbers(int a, int b)
{
        return a + b;
}

private double AddTwoNumbers(float a, float b)
{
        return a + b;
}

private double AddTwoNumbers(byte a, byte b)
{
        return a + b;
}
```

.NET heavily uses method overloading in most of its classes. The best thing about method overloading is that it enables you to use a flexible range of parameters while centralizing functionality under common names.

C# 4.0 supports optional parameters. As the name implies, optional parameters are the parameters which have a default value. The default value of the optional parameter is used when the caller of the method doesn't provide the value for that parameter.

```
private string Multiplication(double a, double b, bool format = false)
{
    if (format == true)
    {
        return string.Format("{0:f4}", a * b);
    }
    else
    {
        return string.Format("{0}", a * b);
    }
}
```

In the preceding example, the caller can call the method with or without providing the optional parameter. The following code illustrates using the preceding method:

```
string testMultiplication = "";
testMultiplication = Multiplication(1388.0, 8.8);
```

```
//12214.4

testMultiplication = Multiplication(1388.0, 8.8, true);
//12214.4000
```

Notice that when you want to use the optional parameters you have to place them at the end of the parameter list. Sometimes you need to create a method with multiple optional parameters. For example, if you wish to make your "Multiplication" method more flexible you can use the following code:

```
private string FlexibleMultiplication(double a, double b, bool formatNumber =
    false, bool useCurrencySign = false)
        {
            string result = "";

            if (formatNumber == true)
            {
                if (useCurrencySign == true)
                {
                    result = "$" + string.Format("{0:f4}", a * b);
                }
                else
                {
                    result = string.Format("{0:f4}", a * b);
                }
            }
            else
            {
                if (useCurrencySign == true)
                {
                    result = "$" + Math.Round(a*b,2);
                }
                else
                {
                    result = string.Format("{0}", a * b);
                }
            }

            return result;
        }
```

In this case, you have lot more flexibility with optional parameters, as shown in the following code snippet:

```
testMultiplication = FlexibleMultiplication(28.10, 20.09);
//564.529

testMultiplication = FlexibleMultiplication(28.10, 20.09, true);
//564.5290

testMultiplication = FlexibleMultiplication(28.10, 20.09, false, true);
//$564.53

testMultiplication = FlexibleMultiplication(28.10, 20.09, true, true);
//$546.5290
```

Notice that as the number of optional parameters grows, providing optional parameters in the order defined by the method signature will be cumbersome. In this situation, you can use named parameters, a new feature in C# 4.0. Using named parameters you select the parameters you want to set by name. To use this feature, all that is needed is a colon (:) after the name of the parameter.

```
testMultiplication = FlexibleMultiplication(b: 20.09, a: 28.10, useCurrencySign:
    true);
```

Named parameters are not restricted to optional parameters; you can use this feature with mandatory parameters as well.

Related to the concept of methods in C# are XML comments, or documentation comments. You may notice that the autocomplete list for the methods of .NET provides descriptive help about the purpose, parameters, and return value (if any) of methods. But your methods don't provide such a feature. You can use XML comments for making your methods self-describing using XML tags. Type three slashes (///) before the method declaration to insert XML tags for any methods and provide a description for every tag. The following code shows this for the AddTwoNumber() method:

```
/// <summary>
/// Adds two input numbers
/// </summary>
/// <param name="firstNum">first integer number for addition</param>
/// <param name="secondNum">second integer number for addition</param>
/// <returns>summation of the first and second input</returns>
private int AddTwoNumber(int firstNum, int secondNum)
{
return firstNum + secondNum;
}
```

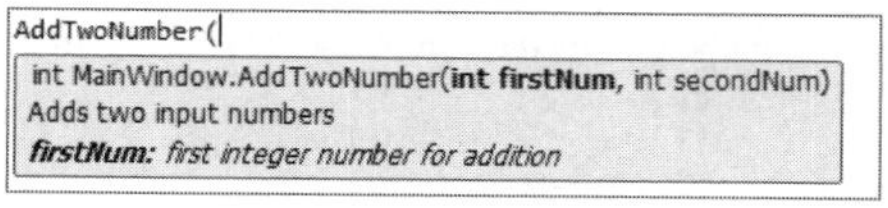

When you try to call this method in Visual Studio, the autocomplete list will show all the required information for calling the method in an elegant fashion, as shown in Figure 3-7.

```
AddTwoNumber(|
int MainWindow.AddTwoNumber(int firstNum, int secondNum)
Adds two input numbers
firstNum: first integer number for addition
```

FIGURE 3-7

You can find the source code for all the discussed methods in the Methods.zip file in the downloads for this book on Wrox.com.

INTRODUCTION TO OBJECT-ORIENTED PROGRAMMING IN C#

Object-oriented programming (OOP) is an approach to software development in which the organization of the software is based on objects that interact with each other to accomplish a task. This interaction takes the form of messages passing back and forth between the objects. In response to a message, an object can perform an action. Classes are the code definitions for the objects and provide a template for the many objects that can be instantiated from them. From a class, you can create as many objects as you need. For example, you might have a class that represents a geographical feature that can be used to store data about the attributes and geometry of real-world objects. You can store many geographical features by creating several instances of that class. These instances are called objects. Classes define the template for the objects using three key features:

➤ **Properties:** Enable you to access object state data. Some properties are read-only, which means they cannot be modified, while others can be easily changed. For example, int.MaxValue is a read-only property of the int class.

➤ **Methods:** Methods define the behavior or actions of an object. Unlike properties, methods are used for actions that perform a distinct task or may change the object's state (property of an object) significantly. The previous section of this chapter covered this feature. `AddTwoNumber()` is an example of a method or behavior that can be performed by an object.

➤ **Events:** Events provide notification that something has happened. You saw this in action when you coded the event handler for the click events of the button controls in the simple calculator. The button object fires a click event, which your code can react to using an event handler. Events often convey information about the initializer of the event through event arguments.

In addition to properties, methods, and events, classes contain their own code and internal set of private data and constructors. Classes behave like black boxes, which means when you use an object, you don't care about how the class works or what low-level details (such as algorithms) it's using. Instead, you care about the properties, methods, and events that are publicly available. Together these public properties, methods, and events are called members of a class. The members of a class define what is called the *public interface* of that class.

Object-Oriented Programming in Action

It is fair to say that everything in OOP is about using and creating classes and objects. In order to create a class in C# you use a special `class` block. In its simplest form, you use the accessibility keywords followed by the class name, as shown in the following code snippet:

```
public class GeographicFeature()
{
}
```

You can define as many classes needed in the same class file. However, good coding practices suggest that in most cases you make use of a single file for each class. Classes exist in many flavors. They may represent an actual thing in the real world (such as city and road), they may represent some programming abstraction (such as an application's window), or they may be just a convenient way to group related functionality (as with the `Math` class). Deciding what a class should represent and breaking down your code into a group of interrelated classes are part of the art of programming. A short example will help you grasp the nuts and bolts of OOP.

1. Create a new project and select WPF Application as the template. Name it OOP.

2. After Visual Studio creates the necessary files for your project, right-click the project in Visual Studio's Solution Explorer window and choose Add ➪ New Item from the context menu, then select Class Item as the new Item. Name it City and click OK. For the time being, ignore the `namespace` and `using` keywords and just pay attention to the definition of your class.

    As the name suggests, this class will represent city objects for a fictional GIS system. The `City` class is an abstraction of a real-world city, which means you are not going to include all the details of the city in your simple `City` class. As with other things in the real world, you cannot create fully detailed computer models of a city — but the main reason for the abstraction is that you simply don't need all the details.

3.   Once you have defined your class code, you need to add some basic pieces of data for it. The following code snippet defines three private member variables that store information about the name, country, population, and area of the city:

```
public class City
{
    private string name;
    private string country;
    private long population;
    private decimal area;
}
```

A local variable inside a method can be accessed only locally (in the place where it is declared). Also, its lifetime is limited to the execution time of the containing method. This means the local variable exists only until the current method ends. On the other hand, a local member variable inside a class (which is called a *field*) is available to all the methods in the class, and it lives as long as the containing object lives.

When you create a member variable, you set its accessibility using access modifier keywords. The accessibility determines the visibility of a member. In other words, it determines whether other parts of your code are able to read and alter this member or not. For example, all the fields in your City class are private, which means all the other classes in your project will not be able to read or modify any of them. Only the code in the City class will have that capability. If you defined the area field as public, you would be able to make it accessible for other classes.

Local variables don't support any accessibility keywords, because they are never available to any code beyond the current containing method. Generally, when you wish to reuse your code between multiple classes or when you start to create multiple classes, accessibility becomes much more important. C# provides the following accessibility keywords:

➤ public: Any member decorated with the public keyword can be accessed by any class.

➤ private: This keyword means the member can be accessed only inside the containing class. In other words, you can use private members only in the class which declares them.

➤ internal: Members that have internal accessibility can be accessed in any classes in the current assembly. The assembly is the compiled file of the code, such as a .dll file.

➤ protected: Members that have this keyword can be accessed by the members in the current class as well as in any inherited class.

➤ protected internal: This keyword is used for members that can be accessed by members in the current assembly (as with internal) and by members in any class that inherits from this class (as with protected).

The accessibility keywords don't apply only to fields. They also apply to methods, properties, and events.

When creating an object, you need to use the new keyword. The new keyword instantiates the object, which means it allocates a piece of memory and creates the object there. You use a variable to point to that piece of memory (remember that a variable is just a memory address which has an identifier). If you declare a variable for your object without using the new keyword, you'll receive the infamous "null reference" error when you try to use your object (the variable which points to that object). That's because the object you are attempting to use doesn't actually exist, and your variable doesn't point to anything at all. The following code snippet instantiates a `City` object:

```
City shiraz = new City();
//Also you could instantiate an object in two steps
City paris;
paris = new City();

//releasing memory which was allocated to this object
paris = null;
```

In .NET, you almost never use the last line. That's because CLR uses a garbage collection service. The garbage collection service runs periodically and releases objects when the variables pointing to them go out of scope. Objects are also released when your application ends.

In some cases, you might want to assign an instance that already exists to your object variable or you might receive a live object as a return value from a method. In this case, you don't need to use the `new` keyword. See the following example.

```
City dublin = getCityByName("Dublin");
```

Defining Properties

At the moment, the simple `City` class is useless because it has no public interface. All its information is private and unreachable from the outside world and other classes won't be able to set or get its information. To overcome this shortcoming, you could simply use the `public` keyword and make the member variables accessible to the outside world. Unfortunately, this approach is considered bad programming practice because it could cause many problems. Generally speaking, making fields of a class accessible would give other objects open and free access to alter every piece of information, even allowing them to apply invalid or inconsistent data. To avoid this, you can add a *property block* through which your code can manipulate `City` objects in a safe and logical fashion.

The property block has two parts. The `get` part allows data to be read, and the `set` part is for writing data in a memory location. In some cases, you might omit one of these parts, such as when you want to create a property that can be read but not modified. In this case, you omit the `set` part to make it a read-only property. In the following code, the `Name` property is just a gateway for reading and writing the `name` local field. Notice that in the `set` part of the property, you access the value that's being supplied through the `value` keyword.

```
public string Name
{
    get
    {
        return name;
    }
    set
    {
        name = value;
    }
}
```

The `set` and `get` parts of a property are similar to any other type of method in that you can write as much code as you need. For example, the property could raise an error to alert the client code of invalid data and prevent the change from being applied. Or, it could check any data supplied for the property, and if it encounters invalid data it sets the local field to a default value. The following code does this in a simple way for the `Population` property:

```
private long population;
public long Population
{
    get
    {
        return population;
    }
    set
    {
        if (value > 0)
        {
            population = value;
        }
        else
        {
            population = 0;
        }
    }
}
```

The client can now instantiate and configure the object by using its properties and the familiar object notation syntax. See the following example.

```
City hannover = new City();
hannover.Name = "Hannover";
hannover.Population = 600000;
```

If you have properties that do nothing except `set` or `get` the value of a private member variable, you can simplify your code using a C# language feature called *automatic properties*. Automatic properties are properties without any code and without any corresponding private member. When you use an automatic property, you declare it, but you don't provide the code for the `get` and `set` parts and also you don't declare the matching private variable. The C# compiler behind the scene adds the necessary details.

```
public string Name
{
get;
set;
}

public string Country
{ get; set; }
```

At this point, the final `City` class should be similar to the following code:

```
class City
{
    public string Name
    { get; set; }
    public string Country
    { get; set; }
    public decimal Area
    {
        get;
        set;
    }
    private long population;
    public long Population
    {
        get
        {
            return population;
        }
        set
        {
            if (value > 0)
            {
                population = value;
            }
            else
            {
                population = 0;
            }
        }
    }
}
```

Defining Methods

The current City class only represents a package of data. This type of class is often useful for sending packages of data to and from other classes or between methods. However, it's more common to add functionality to your classes along with the data. You use methods to provide functionality to your classes. The following code demonstrates how to define a method for the City class.

```
public decimal getPopulationDensity()
{
    return this.Population / this.Area;
}
```

Note that you use the this keyword to refer to the current object so this.Population means the Population property of the current object.

Defining Constructors

Currently, the City class has an issue. Ideally, classes should ensure that their instances are always in a valid and consistent state. In other words, they must be sure about the existence of all the required properties for their instances. For the City class, if you try to use the getPopulationDensity method you will cause an error for an object that doesn't have value for its Area property. To resolve this issue, you need to furnish your class with one or more constructors.

As the name implies, a *constructor* is a method inside a class that executes when an instance of a class is created. In C#, the constructor is always a method with the same name as the class. Unlike a normal method, the constructor doesn't define any return type (not even `void`). The following code example is a constructor of the `City` class:

```csharp
public City(string name, decimal area, long population)
{
    // you could use Name but using this.Name makes
    //your code more readable
    this.Name = name;
    this.Area = area;
    this.Population = population;
}
```

And here is an example of the defined constructor:

```csharp
City shiraz = new City("Shiraz", 179, 1600000);
City paris = new City("Paris", 105, 2300000);
```

The preceding code example is much lighter than the code required to create and configure the previous version of the `City` class. With the help of this constructor, you can create a `City` object and provide its necessary properties in a single line of code. If you don't create a constructor, .NET creates a default public constructor for you. If you create at least one constructor, .NET will not create the default constructor. Because of this, you cannot use the following code to instantiate a `City` object.

```csharp
City london = new City();
```

Using a constructor, you force the client code to provide the minimum number of properties for the object being created.

As with normal methods, constructors can be overloaded. The following code provides three constructors for the `City` class.

```csharp
public City(string name, string country, decimal area, long population)
{
    this.Name = name;
    this.Country = country;
    this.Area = area;
    this.Population = population;
}
public City(string name, decimal area, long population)
{
    this.Name = name;
    this.Area = area;
    this.Population = population;
}
public City()
{
    //default constructor
}
```

Note that in the preceding code, when you have more than one constructor for any class (as with the `City` class) you will have redundant code. In this case, you can use a technique called *constructor chaining*. In this technique, you create a constructor that takes the maximum number of parameters (called a *master constructor*), then you use that master constructor in all other constructors. The following code demonstrates how this technique can work for the `City` class.

Using this technique results in more maintainable code and also simplifies the procedure for class definition.

```
// master constructor
 public City(string name, string country, decimal area, long population)
 {
     this.Name = name;
     this.Country = country;
     this.Area = area;
     this.Population = population;
 }

 public City(string name, decimal area, long population)
     : this(name, "", area, population)
 {
     //there is no need for any code here
     //notice how "this" keyword is used in chaining constructors
 }

 public City(string name, decimal area)
     : this(name, "", area, 0)
 { }
```

Source code for the OOP solution can be found in the OOP.zip file in the downloads for this book on Wrox.com.

SUMMARY

In this chapter, you explored the basics of C# programming necessary for successful ArcObjects development. At this point, you have a good knowledge of implementing properties, methods, and constructors for classes. Because ArcObjects is organized in a hierarchy of classes, you should be familiar with object-oriented programming (OOP). You begin your object-oriented journey in this chapter, and in the next chapter you focus on more advanced object-oriented concepts.

EXERCISES

1. What is the best data type for scientific calculation in C#?

2. What numeric data type provides the fastest possible performance?

3. What is the purpose of XAML in WPF applications?

4. What should you do to provide descriptive text for your methods?

You will find the answers to these exercises in this book's appendix.

▶ WHAT YOU LEARNED IN THIS CHAPTER

TOPIC	KEY CONCEPTS
Properties	Properties represent data that an object contains. You define properties using property blocks in C#. Property blocks have `get` and `set` parts, which provide more control over how values are set or returned.
Methods	In general, a method is a named group of one or more lines of code that are grouped together for the purpose of reusability. In object-oriented programming, a method is an action that an object can perform.
Method overloading	You can overload methods by defining multiple methods that have the same name with different signatures. A method signature is a combination of the name of the method and its number of parameters as well as the data type of its parameters. If you change the number and data type of parameters for a method, you create a different method signature.
Events	Events provide notification that something has happened. For example, the `Button` object fires a Click event, which your code can react to using an event handler. Events often convey information about the initializer of the event through `event` arguments.
Enumeration	Enumerations (or `enum` types in C#) associate a set of integer constants to names that can be used in code.

.NET Programming Fundamentals, Part II

WHAT YOU WILL LEARN IN THIS CHAPTER:

➤ Object-oriented concepts

➤ Reference types vs. value types

➤ Structured exception handling

➤ Using collection objects to provide aggregation

➤ Reading and writing files using the System.IO namespace

WROX.COM CODE DOWNLOADS FOR THIS CHAPTER

Code downloads for this chapter are found at `www.wrox.com/remtitle`
`.cgi?isbn=1118442547` on the Download Code tab. The code is in the Chapter04 folder and individually named according to the names throughout the chapter.

This chapter covers aspects of basic programming in C# that Chapter 3 does not cover. You will learn about reference and value types in the .NET Framework and explore their behavior in various situations. Because working with files is a common programming task, this chapter provides useful examples of working with files with a focus on text files. More specifically, you read a text file into a manageable list of objects. Then you write the content of a list object and create a Keyhole Markup Language (KML) file. At the end of this chapter, you import an external component to create a KMZ (Keyhole Markup Language, Zipped) file.

OVERVIEW OF OBJECT-ORIENTED PROGRAMMING CONCEPTS

This section provides an overview of some fundamental concepts and terms common to all object-oriented programming languages. Chapter 3 covered concepts such as classes, objects, properties, and methods. In this section, you look at how those concepts work together to build object-oriented principles. The main principles of object-oriented programming are *abstraction*, *encapsulation*, *polymorphism*, and *inheritance*. This chapter starts with abstraction.

> **NOTE** *An in-depth explanation of all object-oriented concepts in C# is beyond the scope of this book. This book only covers topics that are necessary for beginning ArcObjects development. If you are interested in more in-depth explanation of the object-oriented programming, good reference books include* Pro C# 5.0 and the .NET 4.5 Platform *by Andrew Troelsen (Apress, 2012) and* Professional C# 4.0 and .NET 4 *by Christian Nagel, Bill Evjen, Jay Glynn, Karli Watson, and Morgan Skinner (Wrox, 2010). If you need a practical book that describes concepts using real-world applications,* Beginning C# Object-Oriented Programming *by Dan Clark (Apress, 2011) is for you.*

Abstraction

When you interact with objects in the real world, you are often concerned with a subset of their state and behavior. In other words, you make use of an abstracted version of the real object in your code. This way, you ensure that you just deal with the task at hand — you don't care about other characteristics of the object that have nothing to do with the task. When constructing objects in object-oriented applications, it is important to incorporate the concept of abstraction. For example, if you were designing a spatial database you would construct a `City` class with geometry and attributes such as a collection of points, name, and population. The cartographic aspects of the `City` objects such as color and size of point symbol would be irrelevant information and should be filtered out. On the other hand, if you were constructing a mapping application (which represents geographic features to users) the cartographic aspects of `City` objects could be important and would be included as the state or behavior of the `City` object.

Encapsulation

Encapsulation, or information hiding, is the term used for referring to the fact that no direct access must be granted to the state of an object. Only the object is allowed to change its own data. If you want to gain access to the data of any object, you have to interact with the object responsible for that data. You have seen this in action when you wanted to access the `Name` property of a `City` object. You use one instance of the `City` class to set or get the `Name` property of that instance. You use properties to encapsulate data inside the objects. In addition, using methods, you define which operations or actions can be performed by objects of a class.

In object-oriented programming, the encapsulation is mainly achieved by creating public methods and properties within a class. The class is kind of a container or capsule that encapsulates the set of methods (behaviors) and properties (states) to provide its indented functionalities to other classes. In this regard, encapsulation also allows a class to change its internal implementation without harming the other classes that use that class. In summary, the idea of encapsulation is to allow using a class and at the same time hide how a class does its functionality.

Inheritance

Inheritance describes the process of creating a new class from an existing class by extending it. You use inheritance in object-oriented programming to classify the objects in your applications based on common characteristics and functionalities. This makes programming easier because it enables you to combine general characteristics and functionalities into a base (parent) class and inherit these characteristics and functionalities in the child classes. With inheritance, you can easily extend the characteristics and functionality of the base class. Put simply, with inheritance, all the public members of the base class are inherited by child classes. So inheritance can be considered a form of code reuse. Figure 4-1 shows the inheritance concept.

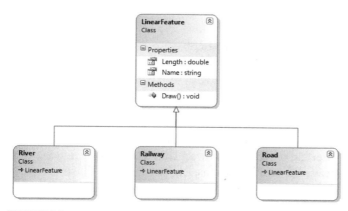

FIGURE 4-1

As you can see in this hierarchy, all the properties and methods of the base class (LinearFeature) are inherited to child classes. In this situation, you can say River is "of type" LinearFeature or similarly Railway is "of type" LinearFeature. Similarly, you can say that River is a specialized kind of LinearFeature. This kind of relationship between classes is called *specialization*. Inheritance is the best way to implement "of type" (specialization) relationships. You see some other kinds of relationships between classes throughout this book.

To create a derived class in C#, enter the name of the class, followed by a colon (:) and the name of the base class. The following code snippet demonstrates how to create a Road class that derives from a LinearFeature class:

```
public class LinearFeature
{
    public string Name
    { get; set; }

    public double Length
    { get; set; }

    public void Draw()
    {
        //implementation for draw method goes here
    }
}
public class Road : LinearFeature
{
}
```

At this point, when you instantiate a Road object you get all the public members of
its base class. As you can see, there is also another set of methods which you don't
create for either the Road class or LinearFeature class (see Figure 4-2). These
methods (such as the ToString() and GetType() methods) are provided by the
System.Object class, which is ultimately the base class of all the types in .NET.

FIGURE 4-2

Polymorphism

Polymorphism is a generic term that means "many shapes." In object-oriented programming,
polymorphism means the capability to request the same operations to be performed by a wide range
of different types of objects. More precisely, it is the capability of different objects to respond to the
same request message in their own unique way of implementation. If you look at the class hierarchy
of LinearFeature, you will notice that the Draw() method is inherited by all three child classes.
You can assume that this method has been implemented to draw all the linear features in the same
way. But what if you want the specific implementation of this method in some child classes? In this
case, you can use *method overriding*. Method overriding allows a child class to override a specific
implementation of a method that is already provided by its base class. Figure 4-3 illustrates the
concept of method overriding.

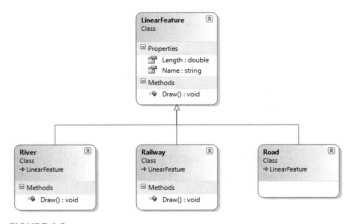

FIGURE 4-3

All the `Road`, `Railway`, and `River` instances are `LinearFeature` instances, so you can call the `Draw()` method of all of them in the same fashion. In this situation, all `Road` instances will be drawn using the implementation provided by the base class (`LinearFeature`). On the other hand, drawing of the `Railway` and `River` instances is based on their specific implementations. The following code snippet demonstrates how method overriding can be implemented in the previous hierarchy.

```
public class LinearFeature
    {
        public string Name
        { get; set; }

        public double Length
        { get; set; }

        public void Draw()
        {
            //implementation for General Drawing of linear features
        }
    }
public class Road : LinearFeature
{
}

public class River : LinearFeature
{
    public override void Draw()
    {
        //implementation for Drawing of Rivers
    }
}

public class Railway : LinearFeature
{
    public override void Draw()
    {
        //implementation for Drawing of Railways
    }

    public override string ToString()
    {
        return "Railway";
    }
}
```

Note that the `Railway` class overrides the `ToString()` method of its ancestor base class (`System.Object`) in the same way it overrides the `Draw()` method of its direct parent class.

Method overriding is one aspect of polymorphism. The other familiar facet of polymorphism is method overloading, which is discussed in Chapter 3.

REFERENCE TYPES AND VALUE TYPES

In Chapter 3, you learned that basic and intrinsic data types such as integers are actually objects created from the Base Class Libraries (BCL) in the same way that you instantiate instances from your classes. However, most intrinsic data types differ from classes in one important characteristic: The intrinsic data types are value types, while any class (such as the City class you developed in this chapter) is a reference type. This means that a variable for an intrinsic data type contains the actual information you put in it (such as the number 30). On the other hand, class variables actually store a reference that points to a location in memory where the full object is stored. In most cases, .NET hides this fact. You won't notice the difference in many programming tasks. However, in three important cases, you will notice that object variables act a little differently than ordinary data types: in assignment operations, in comparison operations, and when passing parameters between methods. Because this topic is the source of many mistakes in programming, make sure you have lots of active and unoccupied memory in your brain for concentration when reading this section.

Assignment Operations

When you assign a simple data variable to another simple data variable, the contents of the variable are copied.

```
int i, j;
i = 1388;

j = i;
//content of j is 1388
//there are two integers in memory
```

Reference types work in a totally different manner. Since in most cases reference types deal with larger amounts of data and complex structures, copying the entire content of a reference type object could degrade the performance of the application. For this reason, when you assign a reference type using an assignment operator you copy the reference that points to the object, not the full object content.

```
//create first instance
City BigApple = new City("New York");

//create second instance
City newYork = BigApple;
//at this point there is one instance of the City class
//with two different names
newYork.Name = "New York City";
//this statement change the Name property of the instance
//so if you check BigApple.Name you will get "New York City"
```

In the above example, two variables point to the same object instance, so changing the property of one variable results in changing the property of the in memory object.

If you really want to copy the object content and not just its reference, you need to create a new object and clone each piece of data of the source object. Some objects provide a Clone() method for this purpose. In addition, you can implement the ICloneable interface for implementing your

`Clone` method. (Interfaces are covered in Chapter 5.) The following code provides a simple method for cloning `City` instances.

```
public City Clone()
{
    return new City(this.Name, this.Population, this.Area);
}
```

When you use this method, you get two instances with the same state. Because you end up with two distinct objects, modifying the property of one of them doesn't cascade to the other object.

```
//creating a first instance
City BigApple = new City("New York");
City NewYorkCity = BigApple.Clone();
//at this point you have two instances with same properties
//these two instances point to two different
//memory addresses

NewYorkCity.Name="Gotham";
//the above code doesn't affect the BigApple.Name property
```

Comparison Operations

A similar difference between reference types and value types comes into play when you compare two variables. In comparison operations, only the content of value type variables is checked. But for reference type variables, references to the live objects are tested. Consider the following code snippet:

```
City BigApple = new City("New York");
City NewYork = new City("New York");

if (BigApple == NewYork)
{
//this is false, there are two distinct instances
}

City shiraz = new City("Shiraz");

City cityOfRoses = shiraz;
cityOfRoses.Name = "City of Flower and Nightingale";

if (shiraz == cityOfRoses)
{
//this is true, there are two variables for a live object
}
```

Passing Parameters between Method Calls

As you have seen in Chapter 3, defining a method is an easy task. In all the examples to this point you used the default parameter passing behavior in C#. There are two keywords (called *parameter modifiers*) which you can use to change that default behavior. You generally use two parameter passing behaviors, but there is no harm in knowing about all of them, starting with the default behavior.

The default fashion of passing a parameter in C# is *passing by value*. You use no keyword to denote this behavior. Using this behavior, a copy of the content of the parameter is passed into the called method. In other words, when the caller of the method passes parameters, the called method receives a copy of the content of the variable. On the other hand, when the caller uses the *passing by reference* behavior, its reference to the memory address is received by the called method. The following code snippet demonstrates both approaches. The `ref` keyword defines the passing by reference behavior.

```
private void changeNumberByValue(int x)
    {
        x *= 100;
    }

private void changeNumberByRef(ref int x)
    {
        x *= 100;
    }
```

You have to use the `ref` keyword when you decide to use the second method. When passing by reference, if you don't include the `ref` keyword, you'll get a compiler error.

```
int i = 10;

changeNumberByValue(i);
// i equals 10 because only the content of i
//is passed into the called method

changeNumberByRef(ref i);
//i equals 1000 because the reference to
//the memory location
// is copied and passed into the called method
```

This is a simple concept for integers and most intrinsic data types. But this concept can show its complicated face when you use more complex data types such as arrays and classes. For example, if you pass an array to a method, the called method can modify the input array whether you use the pass by value (default behavior) or pass by reference (using the `ref` keyword) behavior. The reason for this complicated behavior is simple: The entire array isn't passed in the parameter — only the reference to the array is transmitted. This behavior is much more efficient for large and complex objects and it saves having to copy a large block of memory, but it doesn't always lead to the behavior you expect.

C# also supports the use of the `out` keyword for returning multiple pieces of data from a single method. Just like using the `ref` keyword, you have to provide the `out` keyword in the method signature. You also have to adorn the parameter with this keyword when you want to use the method. When you use this type of parameter, you can provide an uninitialized variable as an output parameter.

```
private int testOutKeyword(int number, out DateTime timeOfProcess)
    {
        timeOfProcess = DateTime.Now;
        return number * 100;
    }
```

Using this method is represented in the following code snippet:

```
int i = 1;
DateTime t;
i = testOutKeyword(i, out t);
//at this point i is equal to 100
//and t shows the time of execution
```

As you can see, the only action that the called method can do with the parameter decorated with the out keyword is to set the output parameter.

BRIEF EXPLANATION OF ALL .NET TYPES

So far you have seen intrinsic data types such as integers and doubles. You have also learned how to define enumerations and how to encapsulate your desired functionality in classes. But there are also other types in the .NET world. To be precise, types in .NET means the members of the following set: enumerations, classes, structures, interfaces, and delegates. All these types can be categorized as value types or reference types.

➤ An *enumeration* defines a set of named integers. Enumerations are extensively used in both the .NET Framework and Esri's ArcObjects. Because integers are value types, enumerations are value types too.

➤ *Classes* are the most common type in the .NET Framework. Usually you create classes to be used in your applications as a package of data and functionality. Strings and arrays are examples of .NET classes (although as you have seen in Chapter 3, you can build your classes easily). All classes are reference types.

➤ *Structures*, like classes, may include properties, methods, and even events, and they are generally smaller and simpler than classes. Unlike classes, they are value types. The most important difference between value types and reference types is the way that they are managed in the memory. Structures also lack some of the more advanced features of classes, such as inheritance and extension. All the intrinsic data types (numerical, char, boolean, and date) except the string data type are structures.

➤ *Delegates* are the foundation for event handling in .NET. The delegate is a function pointer that allows you to invoke a method indirectly. Delegates are useful when you wish to provide a way for one class to forward a call to another class asynchronously. Also delegates have intrinsic support for forwarding a request to multiple recipients (multicasting). You see examples of using delegation for handling ArcObjects events in Chapter 14 of this book. Delegates are reference types.

➤ *Interfaces* define contracts or protocols to which a class or structure must adhere. An interface is a named set of abstract members. The abstract members do not provide an implementation. Interfaces are an advanced technique of object-oriented programming, and they are useful when standardizing how objects interact. You see them in action throughout this book. When you develop ArcObjects applications (such as ArcGIS Desktop Add-Ins), you usually work with types inside ArcObjects via interfaces. You see the concept of interfaces in Chapter 5.

> **NOTE** *The* `String` *type is a full-featured class and not a simple value type. But this data type overrides its equality (==) operator and assignment (=) operations. This means equality and assignment operations work like those of value types. Strings can contain various amounts of data, so this overriding makes them more efficient. Operator overriding is another facet of polymorphism.*

NAMESPACES AND ASSEMBLIES

The .NET Framework consists of thousands of types which reside logically in various namespaces and physically in assembly files. To make the .NET Framework more manageable, Microsoft has organized it in a hierarchical structure. This hierarchical structure is arranged into what are referred to as *namespaces*. Organizing the framework into namespaces greatly reduces the risks of naming collisions. Organizing related functionality of the framework into namespaces also greatly enhances its usability for developers.

All the .NET Framework types reside in the `System` namespace. The `System` namespace is further subdivided by functionality. For example, the functionality required to work with files and folders is contained in the `System.IO` namespace. Namespaces can contain several namespaces. For example, the functionality used to compress streams of data is contained in the `System.IO.Compression` namespace.

As mentioned in the first paragraph of this section, the actual code for .NET types is stored in assembly files that have `.dll` or `.exe` extensions. Assemblies and namespaces have a many-to-many relationship. In other words, an assembly can contain multiple namespaces (such as `system.data.dll`, which contains the `System.Data.Sql` and `System.Data.SqlClient` namespaces), and a namespace can be contained by multiple assemblies (such as the `System.IO` namespace, which is mainly contained by `mscorelib.dll` and `system.dll`).

To gain access to the types in the .NET Framework, you need to reference in your code the assembly that contains the namespace. Then you can access types in the assembly by providing their fully qualified names. In order to add a reference to assemblies in Visual Studio, you can right-click on the References folder in Solution Explorer and select the Add Reference item. Some assemblies are referenced by default. For example, you can get the size of a file using the `FileInfo` class, which resides in the `System.IO` namespace. The following code snippet demonstrates the use of a fully qualified name for the `FileInfo` class:

```
private void lengthOfFile()
{
    //since the System.IO resides in system.dll
    //and system.dll is referenced by default for all .NET projects
    //there is no need to add a reference to the system.dll file
    System.IO.FileInfo fileInfo = new System.IO.FileInfo(@"c:\testfile.txt");
    if (fileInfo.Exists)
```

```
        {
            //do something like get its size
            long fileLength = fileInfo.Length;
        }
    }
```

You can import namespaces to avoid using the fully qualified names of types. It is standard programming practice to import the namespaces to make your code cleaner and more readable. You import namespaces with the help of `using` directives. The `using` directives must reside in the very beginning of the class file.

```
using System.IO;
............ . .
............ . .
. . . . . . .

        private void lengthOfFile()
        {
            //since the System.IO resides in system.dll
            //and system.dll is referenced by default for all .NET projects
            //there is no need to add a reference to the system.dll file
            FileInfo fileInfo = new FileInfo(@"c:\testfile.txt");
            if (fileInfo.Exists)
            {
                //do something like get its size
                long fileLength = fileInfo.Length;
            }
        }
```

DEBUGGING USING VISUAL STUDIO

Visual Studio provides many features for making life easier for brave developers like you and me. In addition to providing an easier coding experience, it provides required tools and utilities for making us more productive. One of the brilliant facilities in Visual Studio is extensive support for debugging. The following Try It Out shows you debugging in action.

TRY IT OUT Debugging Using Visual Studio (Simple CalculatorFirstLineOfDefense.zip)

1. Open the Simple Calculator project that you developed in Chapter 3 by double-clicking on its solution file (`SimpleCalculator.sln`).

2. In the Solution Explorer window, click on `MainWindow.xaml`. Then press F7 to go to `MainWindow.xaml.cs`. Right-click on the declaration line of the `NumberClick` event handler; from the Breakpoint menu, choose Insert Breakpoint. A red dot will appear in the left margin to indicate that a breakpoint has been set. Alternatively, you can click on the left margin of any line of code to set a breakpoint on that line. (See Figure 4-4.)

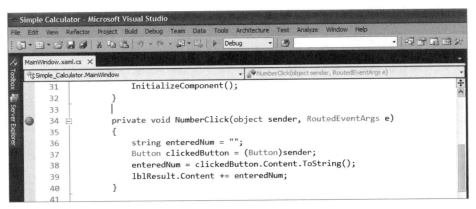

FIGURE 4-4

3. Set a breakpoint on the `btnAdd_click` event handler as shown in Figure 4-5 using the approach explained in the preceding step.

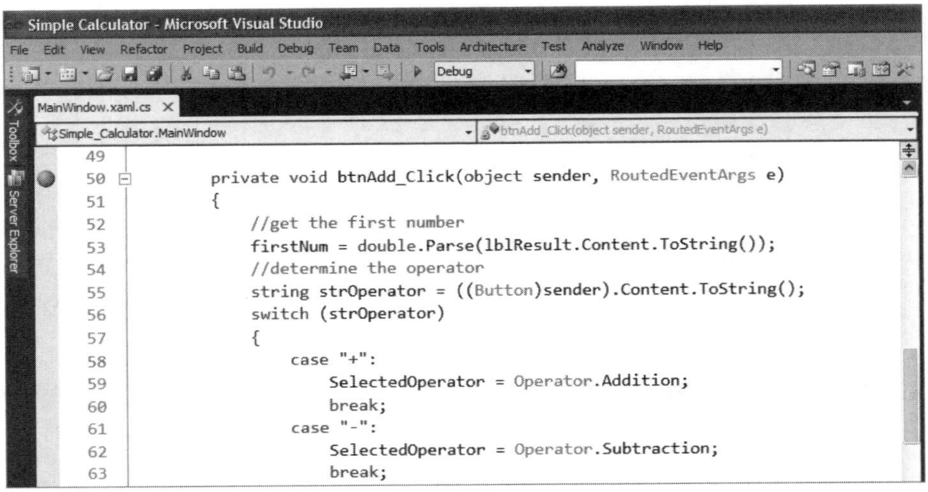

FIGURE 4-5

4. Make sure that the Debug toolbar is visible. If it is not, use the Toolbars item of the View menu to turn it on. Press F5 to start debugging. Try to press any numeric buttons. As you can see, program execution will pause at the breakpoint. A yellow color indicates the next line of code that will be executed.

5. To step through the code one line at a time, click the Step Into button on the Debug toolbar (see Figure 4-6). Alternatively, you can press F11 to step into code.

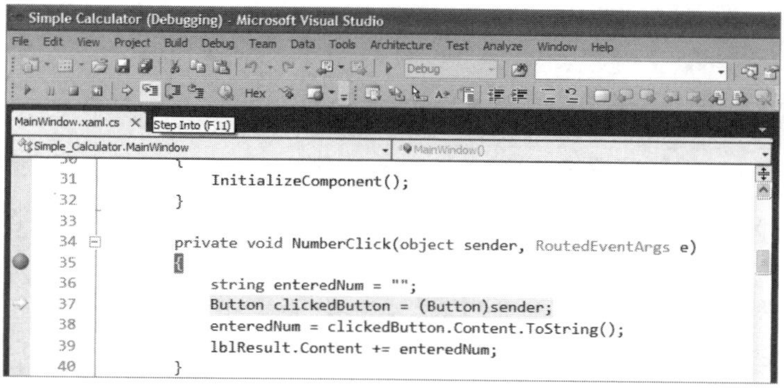

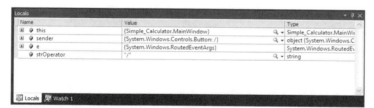

FIGURE 4-6

6. Click the Step Out button to exit from the current method execution. Click the Division button on the MainWindow. From the Debug menu, select Windows and then choose Locals. The Locals window (shown in Figure 4-7) shows local variables of the current method. Press F11 to see the changes in the Locals window. Also, as long as you are in debug mode you can see the content of a variable by simply hovering your mouse on that variable.

FIGURE 4-7

7. Input **0** as the denominator and then press the Equal button. Since you are in debug mode, the code executes one line at a time. Press F11 several times to get to the line of code which performs the division. The result of the division is "Infinity." The result is correct, but what if the user wants to continue playing with your calculator? From this point forward, every calculation with this simple calculator results in Infinity or NaN (Not a Number). You can simply add a Clear button to clear the contents of the lblResult label. Create a button, name it Clear, and enter code to clear the contents of lblResult. The following is the event handler for the Clear button:

```
private void btnClear_Click(object sender, RoutedEventArgs e)
    {
        lblResult.Content = "";
        lblSummary.Content = "";
}
```

8. Test the Simple Calculator. With this little button, your simple calculator application behaves more like a standard Windows calculator. But there is still a problem. If there is nothing in a label control (such as when the application starts or when the user clicks the Clear button) and a user presses one of the operator buttons, an exception is trapped by the integrated debugger of Visual Studio as shown in Figure 4-8; at the same time, the application stops working.

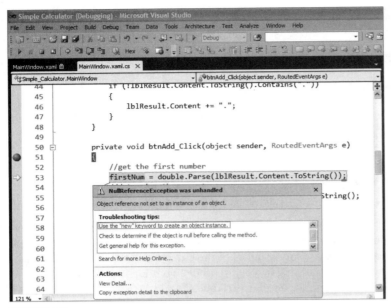

FIGURE 4-8

9. To fix this problem, comment out the first line of code in the btnAdd_Click event handler and enter the following code snippet:

```
////get the first number
//firstNum = double.Parse(lblResult.Content.ToString());
//using first line of defense
if (lblResult.Content == null || string.IsNullOrEmpty(lblResult.Content.ToString()))
{
    firstNum = 0.0;
}
else
{
    //get the first number
    firstNum = double.Parse(lblResult.Content.ToString());
}
```

How It Works

In this Try It Out, you saw some debugging facilities in Visual Studio. *Debugging* is the process of finding exceptions and bugs in code and altering the code to gracefully remedy them. Sometimes with checking values and providing logic in your code, bugs can be removed successfully. Developers are responsible for developing error-free applications. Use extreme cases for finding bugs in your code. Or better, provide your application to some testers to use and ask them to report any bugs they find in your application.

Because exceptions are unpredictable in most cases, you have to handle them in a way that doesn't crash the application. The next section is devoted to exception handling in .NET.

STRUCTURED EXCEPTION HANDLING

In general, three sources can prevent your application from working properly: bugs, user errors, and exceptions. *Bugs* are errors made by the developer that can be fixed by debugging. The divide by zero problem which you saw in the preceding Try It Out was an example of a bug. Developers typically use testing approaches to ensure that there are no bugs in their applications, but there is almost always at least one bug that shows up just as an application is about to be released.

User errors are typically caused by an application's end users. For example, an end user who enters a negative number in a Print form to indicate the number of copies he wants could very well crash the application. It is still the fault of the programmer, whose responsibility it is to anticipate all actions by end users. A part of good programming is to consider extreme situations and use the various debugging tools available in an integrated development environment such as Visual Studio.

Exceptions are typically things that are not expected to occur during normal processing. Trying to read a file that doesn't exist and attempting to connect to an offline database are two examples of exceptions. Programmers have little control over these exceptional situations. But it is the programmer's responsibility to imagine all possible exceptions and handle them in code.

When creating code that could end up causing an exception, you should place it in an exception handling block. Use an exception block to change the strategy for handling division by zero. Comment out the `if` block, which you added in the last step of the preceding Try It Out, and enter the following code snippet:

```
////using first line of defense
//if (lblResult.Content == null || string.IsNullOrEmpty
(lblResult.Content.ToString()))
//{
//    firstNum = 0.0;
//}
//else
//{
//    //get the first number
//    firstNum = double.Parse(lblResult.Content.ToString());
//}

//using exception handling
try
{
    //getting the first number
    firstNum = double.Parse(lblResult.Content.ToString());
}
catch (Exception ex)
{
    //an exception has been detected
    // reporting exception to the user
    lblSummary.Content = ex.Message;
    firstNum = 0.0;
    Console.Beep();
}
```

> **NOTE** *You can find the source code for this version of the Simple Calculator application in the StructuredExHandling.zip file in the downloads for this book on Wrox.com.*

Code placed inside the `try` block is protected code. If an exception occurs while the protected code is executing, code processing is transferred to the `catch` block, where it is handled. The optional `finally` block of the code can be added to the `try` block. The `finally` block is executed whether an exception occurs or not. This allows you to perform some basic cleanup, such as closing a database connection or releasing unmanaged resources.

Catching an exception makes application execution safe. If all you want to do is display a neat and user-friendly warning to the end user, you don't even need to add any code to the `catch` block other than the code needed to display the user-friendly message. For a more advanced implementation, you can show a user-friendly message to the end users and log the details of exceptions in a log file or database. You can also create a new exception object with additional information and *throw* that. You throw exceptions using the `throw` keyword. All you need to do is create a new exception instance and throw it. The following code snippet demonstrates throwing an exception:

```
void CallerMethod()
{
    try
    {
        int result = Divide(0, 0);
    }
    catch (Exception ex)
    {
        //reporting message to end users
        string message = ex.Message;
MessageBox.Show(message);
    }
}

int Divide(int i, int j)
{
    try
    {
        return i / j;
    }
    catch
    {
        Exception myEx = new Exception("divide by zero results in
infinity");
        throw myEx;
    }
}
```

In the preceding code, the caller method receives a newly created exception object which contains the user-friendly message.

You can use the `catch` block to catch all exceptions that may occur in the `try` block, or you can use it to perform different actions for different exceptions based on the type of exception. The following code demonstrates filtering exceptions based on the different exceptions that could occur when trying to read a text file:

```
public string readATextFile()
        {
            string data = "";
            try
            {
                data = File.ReadAllText(@"c:\test.txt");
                return data;
            }
            catch (DirectoryNotFoundException ex)
            {
                throw new Exception("Directory does not exist");
            }
            catch (FileNotFoundException ex)
            {
                throw new Exception("File Not Found");
            }
            catch (Exception ex)
            {
                //executed when none of the above exceptions occurs
                throw new Exception("Something is wrong!");
            }
        }
```

> **NOTE** *To execute the preceding code, you need to import the* System.IO *namespace. To do so, enter the following line of code at the very beginning of your code file:*
>
> ```
> using System.IO;
> ```

When you catch an exception in your code, it won't be directly an instance of the generic System.Exception class. Instead, it will be a direct instance of many specific types of exceptions. In other words, System.Exception is the ultimate parent class of all exceptions in the .NET Framework. Visual Studio provides a useful tool to browse through the exceptions in the .NET class library. Simply choose the Exceptions item from the Debug menu. The Exceptions dialog box will appear. Expand the Common Language Runtime Exceptions group, which shows a hierarchical tree of .NET exceptions arranged by namespace, and then expand the System.IO group, as shown in Figure 4-9.

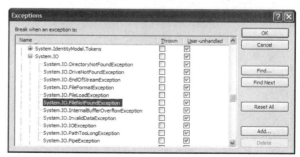

FIGURE 4-9

You can also use the Object Browser window to explore any type in Visual Studio. Just select Object Browser from the View menu to display it and enter the name of a type to display its members, base class, and other useful information, as shown in Figure 4-10.

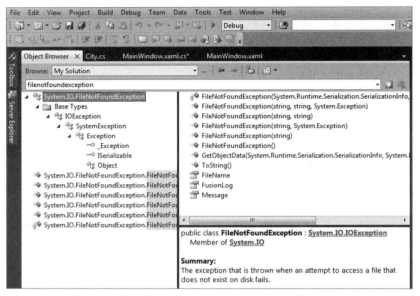

FIGURE 4-10

CASTING OBJECTS

As you know, all object variables point to the place in memory where the actual object exists. All objects can be converted with the same syntax that is used for intrinsic data types. This process is called *casting*. When you perform casting, you don't actually change anything about an object. In fact, it remains the exact same object in the same location in memory. What you change is the variable that points to the object. In other words, the way your code sees the object is changed.

The way your code sees an object specifies what you can do with that object. An object variable can be cast into one of three things: itself, an interface that it supports, or a direct or indirect base class. You have already used casting in the Simple Calculator solution:

```
private void NumberClick(object sender, RoutedEventArgs e)
        {
            string enteredNum = "";
            Button clickedButton = (Button)sender;
            enteredNum = clickedButton.Content.ToString();
            lblResult.Content += enteredNum;
        }
```

In this code, you cast the sender object variable (which you know is a Button) to the Button class. When you perform this casting, you don't lose any information. There is still one object in memory with two variables pointing to it. Here the ClickedButton variable really is a Button instance. However, the sender or ClickedButton variables specify what properties and methods should be available to the outside world. This means the following code causes a compiler error. Even though sender actually points to a Button and even though the Button has a Content property, you can't access the Content property through the sender object.

```
enteredNum = sender.Content.ToString();
```

You can validate the cast process using the is keyword. In other words, you check whether or not the object variable is of a specific type via the is keyword.

```
if (sender is Button)
{
    //here is a safe place to cast
    Button clickedButton = (Button)sender;
    enteredNum = clickedButton.Content.ToString();
    lblResult.Content += enteredNum;
}
```

You can also use the as keyword to perform the casting. Here the only difference is that the as keyword returns a null reference if it fails to cast the object to a specified type. In other words, when you use the as keyword you are able to find out compatibility between the object variable and a type by checking against a null return value.

```
Button clickedButton = sender as Button;

//check to see if the cast was successful or not
if (clickedButton != null)
{
    enteredNum = clickedButton.Content.ToString();
    lblResult.Content += enteredNum;
}
```

You learn about interfaces in Chapter 5, but all the casting operations that have been explained in this section can be applied to them as well.

AGGREGATION USING COLLECTIONS

In the "Inheritance" section earlier in this chapter, you learned that inheritance is used for modeling *specialization relationships* between types. Another more common relationship between types is containment or aggregation. In *aggregation*, an instance of the containing type contains one or more instances of the contained types. You see many examples of this type of relationship in real life. A state contains many counties, a county contains many cities, a car contains three or four wheels and one or more engines (hybrid cars usually contain two engines), and so forth. All you need to do in order to define an aggregation relationship is create an appropriate property in the containing type to indicate a set of contained type instances. The following code snippet demonstrates a simple approach to represent the relationship between City and County classes:

```
public class County
    {
        public string Name
        { get; set; }

        //array of City in County class
        public City[] Cities;
    }
```

The .NET Framework has some special classes that have no purpose other than to group various objects and provide them as a collection. Because C# arrays do not support re-dimensioning, using these collection classes, aggregation relationships can be modeled efficiently. In addition, some of these collection classes provide sorting and name-based retrieval for containing objects. This section confines the discussion about collections to two widely used types: the ArrayList class and generics.

The ArrayList

C# arrays do not support re-dimensioning. This means that after you create an array, you can't resize it to provide additional elements. Instead, you have to create a new array with the new size and copy values from the old array to the new, which would be a tedious and inefficient process. However, if you need a dynamic arraylike list, you can use one of the collection classes provided to all .NET languages through the System.Collections namespace.

When you work with collections, you often do not know the number of items it contains until runtime. This is where the ArrayList class comes into play. The capacity of an ArrayList automatically grows as required, with memory reallocation and copying of elements achieved dynamically. The ArrayList class also provides some methods and properties for working with its elements that the Array class does not provide. In order to use the ArrayList class, you have to import the System.Collections namespace. The following code snippet demonstrates the ArrayList class:

```
using System.Collections;

namespace OOP
{
    class test
    {
        void usingArrayList()
        {
            ArrayList myArrayList = new ArrayList();
            //ArrayList contains objects (everything in an ArrayList is
            //considered to be an object)
            //adding a string to ArrayList
            myArrayList.Add("Pouria");
            //adding a City object to ArrayList
            myArrayList.Add(new City("London"));
            //adding a DateTime object
            myArrayList.Add(DateTime.Now);

            //you have to cast the object inside the ArrayList to a specific type
            City London = myArrayList[1] as City;
        }
    }
}
```

ArrayList objects are not strongly typed, meaning that you can add any data type to a single ArrayList object. The flexible nature of the ArrayList class causes many issues when you want to retrieve data from an ArrayList object. When data is added to the ArrayList, it is cast to a generic System.Object type. In order to use items inside an ArrayList, you have to cast elements inside the ArrayList to their proper data types. In the preceding code snippet, you used the as keyword to do the cast operation.

An `ArrayList` can have only one dimension. In addition, an array of a specific type offers better performance than an `ArrayList` object. But it is easier to work with an `ArrayList` than an array. `ArrayList` objects also provide re-dimensioning and memory reallocation efficiently. This is why Microsoft provides the `ArrayList` class in the .NET Framework from its beginning. Developers used to work happily with the `ArrayList` and other classes in `System.Collections` namespaces.

However, Microsoft provides a new enhancement for collections in .NET 2.0. With this new enhancement, a brand new namespace was added to collections and provides strongly typed collections to the arsenal of developers. This new enhancement is called *generics* and use of it is highly recommended in the ever-changing world of .NET.

Generics

The .NET Framework supports generics to overcome the performance and maintenance issues associated with the weakly typed collections. Generics let you define a class without specifying its type. The type is specified when the class is instantiated. Using a generic collection provides the advantages of type safety and the performance of a strongly typed collection while also providing all the benefits of weakly typed collections. The following code shows the `List` class, one of the most widely used generic collections, in action:

```
//create a list for storing City objects
List<City> cities = new List<City>();
//adding some City objects
cities.Add(new City("London"));
cities.Add(new City("Paris"));
cities.Add(new City("Munich"));
//following code causes a compile error
//cities.Add("city of flower and nightingale");
```

The `List` class is easy to use. For example, you can use a `foreach` block to iterate through the individual members in the `List` object:

```
foreach (City cityObject in cities)
{
// do something with each City object
}
```

You see the `List` class in a real-world application in the next Try It Out. Remember that in addition to the `List` class, there are several other classes in the `System.Collections.Generic` namespace. Because the `List` class allows you to resize its contents dynamically (like `ArrayList` but far more efficient), it is the most frequently used type in the `System.Collections.Generic` namespace.

READING AND WRITING FILES

Files have always been an important aspect of programming, and it is necessary to work with multiple files in most programming tasks. In the .NET Framework, the `System.IO` namespace is devoted to file-based operations such as reading, writing, copying, and deleting, just to name a few. Like any other namespace, `System.IO` defines several types to work with files, folders, and also memory-based input and output. But in this section, you only explore the classes for accessing (reading and writing) files. Most types in the `System.IO` namespace are easy to understand, so don't be afraid to explore this useful namespace.

When you want to access a file, it is convenient to treat it as either a text file or a binary file. Text files contain plain text characters. They are usually read line by line or, alternatively, read completely, and then the result is put into a string variable. On the other hand, binary files do not contain plain text. Instead they contain text that is not human readable. Binary files must be read according to the structure used to write them. For example, a simple bitmap image file (a binary file) must be read one byte at a time to get the red, green, or blue value of a pixel. Then you combine the red, green, and blue (RGB) values to reconstruct the true color of that pixel. In short, you have to know the structure and organization of binary files before you can access them.

There are several ways to access files in .NET. The most widely accepted approach is by using `Stream` objects. The `Stream` object represents a sequence of bytes that can be accessed from local files, the memory of a local machine, the shared memory of a network, and so forth.

.NET concentrates on `Stream` objects rather than the source or destination for the data. This means you can write binary data to any type of stream (such as `FileStream`, `MemoryStream`, and `NetworkStream`), whether it represents a file or some other type of storage location, using the same code. In addition, writing to a binary file is almost the same as writing to a text file. The following code demonstrates creation of a `FileStream` object in its simplest form for creating a new file:

```
FileStream fs = new FileStream(@"c:\test.dat", FileMode.Create);
```

The `FileMode` enumeration contains other members to request (to the operating system) the required process on the specified file. Table 4-1 explains all the members of the `FileMode` enumeration.

TABLE 4-1: FileMode Enumeration Members

MEMBER	MEANING IN LIFE
`Append`	Opens the file in write mode and appends all the data to the existing contents of the file. If the file doesn't exist, it creates a new file.
`Create`	Creates a new file in write mode and overwrites the existing file if it finds another file with the same name in the specified address.
`CreateNew`	Creates a new file in write mode, and if it finds an existing file it throws an exception.
`Open`	Opens a file in read mode. It throws an exception if the file doesn't exist.
`OpenOrCreate`	Opens an existing file or creates a new file in both read and write modes.
`Truncate`	Opens a file in write mode and resets its size to zero bytes.

Once you access a file you can use the `StreamReader` and `StreamWriter` classes to read or write data on top of a channel that is provided by the `FileStream` object. The following code snippet demonstrates the `Write()` method of the `StreamWriter` class:

```
//for creating new files
FileStream fs = new FileStream(@"c:\test.dat", FileMode.Create);
StreamWriter sw = new StreamWriter(fs);
sw.WriteLine("this is content of a test.dat file");
```

```
//release the file resource
sw.Close();
fs.Close();
```

It is always good programming practice to use the exception handling mechanism when you work with files. In the next Try It Out, you create a simple text file.

TRY IT OUT Creating a Text File (CreatingTxt.zip)

1. Create a new project in Visual Studio, select the WPF application template, and name it **KML**.

2. Right-click your project in the Solution Explorer window and select Class from the Add submenu. In the Add New Item window, name the class file `city.cs` and press Add. In the `City` class, provide members to store data about the name, population, area, and x and y of each instance. Your code should be similar to the following code snippet:

```
namespace KML
{
    class City
    {
        //properties
        public string Name
        { get; set; }

        public long Population
        { get; set; }

        public decimal Area
        { get; set; }

        public decimal X
        { get; set; }

        public decimal Y
        { get; set; }
    }
}
```

3. Add required constructors for the `City` class. Use the constructor chaining technique you learned about in Chapter 3.

```
        //constructors
        //master constructor
        public City(string name, long population, decimal area, decimal x, decimal y)
        {
            this.Name = name;
            this.Population = population;
            this.Area = area;
            this.X = x;
            this.Y = y;
        }
        //second constructor
        public City(string name, long population, decimal x, decimal y)
            : this(name, population, 0, x, y) { }
```

```
//third constructor
public City(string name, decimal x, decimal y)
    : this(name, 0, 0, x, y) { }
//fourth (empty) constructor
public City() : this("", 0, 0) { }
```

4. Override the `ToString()` method to report the name, population, and area of an instance. Add the following code snippet in the `City.cs` class file:

```
public override string ToString()
{
    //
    return string.Format("{0}, {1}, {2}, {3}, {4}", this.Name, this.
Population, this.Area, this.X, this.Y);
}
```

5. Select the `MainWindow.xaml` file in the Solution Explorer and press F7 to go to the code window. Import the `System.IO` namespace in the `MainWindow.xaml.cs` file and then add a button to the `MainWindow` of your application. Change its name to **btnWriteTextFile** and its content to **Write Text File**, as shown in Figure 4-11.

FIGURE 4-11

6. Double-click the button to create the skeleton code for the `click` event handler. Add code to create some instances of the `City` class and populate a list of `City` objects.

```
List<City> cities = new List<City>();
cities.Add(new City("New York", 16500000, 1210, -74.0999m, 40.7500m));
cities.Add(new City("Tokyo", 23650000, 2187, 139.8092m, 35.6830m));
cities.Add(new City("Berlin", 5100000, 892, 13.3276m, 52.5163M));
cities.Add(new City("Paris", 10000000, 105, 2.4328M, 48.8815m));
```

7. Add the following code snippet to the preceding code to write the content of the list to a text file using the `FileStream` and `StreamWriter` classes.

```
//writing text file
            string fileAddress = @"C:\test.txt";
            FileStream fs = new FileStream(fileAddress, FileMode.Create);
            StreamWriter sw = new StreamWriter(fs);
            try
            {
                foreach (City ct in cities)
                {
                    sw.WriteLine(ct.ToString());
                }
            }
            catch (Exception ex)
            {
                MessageBox.Show(ex.Message, ex.Source);
            }
            finally
            {
                //cleanup
                sw.Close();
                fs.Close();
            }
```

8. At this point, the event handler for `btnWriteTextFile` should resemble the following code:

```
private void btnWriteTextFile_Click(object sender, RoutedEventArgs e)
        {
            List<City> cities = new List<City>();
            cities.Add(new City("New York", 16500000, 1210, -74.0999m, 40.7500m));
            cities.Add(new City("Tokyo", 23650000, 2187, 139.8092m, 35.6830m));
            cities.Add(new City("Berlin", 5100000, 892, 13.3276m, 52.5163M));
            cities.Add(new City("Paris", 10000000, 105, 2.4328M, 48.8815m));

            //writing text file
            string fileAddress = @"C:\test.txt";
            FileStream fs = new FileStream(fileAddress, FileMode.Create);
            StreamWriter sw = new StreamWriter(fs);
            try
            {
                foreach (City ct in cities)
                {
                    sw.WriteLine(ct.ToString());
                }
            }
            catch (Exception ex)
            {
                MessageBox.Show(ex.Message, ex.Source);
            }
            finally
            {
                //cleanup
                sw.Close();
                fs.Close();
            }
        }
```

9. Run the application by pressing F5. A file named `test.txt` should be created and when you open it in Notepad you should see Figure 4-12.

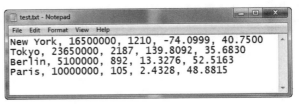

FIGURE 4-12

How It Works

In this Try It Out, you created a Comma Separated Values (CSV) file even though it has a .txt extension. You used the list of `City` objects to store your data in memory and then you utilized two classes of the `System.IO` namespace (`FileStream` and `StreamWriter`) to write the list of `City` objects to a text file. It is always a good idea to use defensive code strategies. One of the most widely accepted defensive code strategies in the .NET world is to use exception handling whenever your code deals with unmanaged resources like files and databases. Also, you used the `Close()` method to release resources that were occupied during the process of writing data to files. Again, you must always perform this kind of cleanup task whenever you are working with unmanaged resources like files and databases. This way your limited resources can be allocated to other users in multi-user environments.

For reading a file, you can use the `StreamReader` class in the same way in which you used the `StreamWriter` class. The following code reads the content of a text file completely into a string variable:

```
//for reading an existing file
FileStream fs = new FileStream(@"c:\test.dat", FileMode.Open);
StreamReader sr = new StreamReader(fs);
//reading content of file as a whole
string data = sr.ReadToEnd();
//cleanup
sr.Close();
fs.Close();
```

You can also use the `ReadLine()` method of the `StreamReader` class to read the content of a text file line by line. The mentioned method returns a null reference when there is no more data in the file.

```
FileStream fs = new FileStream(@"c:\test.dat", FileMode.Open);
StreamReader sr = new StreamReader(fs);
string oneLineOfData = sr.ReadLine();
while (oneLineOfData != null)
{
    //code to process a line of data goes here
    oneLineOfData = sr.ReadLine();
}
sr.Close();
fs.Close();
```

In the next Try It Out, you read the text file you created in the preceding Try It Out. Then you populate a `List` of `City` objects and use some simple magic to create a KML file.

TRY IT OUT   Creating a KML File (KML.zip)

1. Open your KML project if it is not already open. Add another button to the `MainWindow` of your application. Change the name of the new button to **btnCreateKMLFile** and the content of it to **Convert txt to KML**, as illustrated in Figure 4-13.

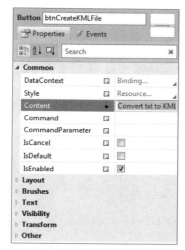

FIGURE 4-13

2. Double-click the button to create a `click` event handler. Add the following code to the `click` event handler of the newly added button:

```
//Read the text file
            //and populate the list of City objects
            FileStream fs = new FileStream(@"c:\test.txt", FileMode.Open);
            StreamReader sr = new StreamReader(fs);

            List<City> cities = new List<City>();
            try
            {
                string line = sr.ReadLine();

                while (line != null)
                {
                    string[] content = line.Split(",".ToCharArray());
                    City ct = new City();
                    ct.Name = content[0];
                    ct.Population = long.Parse(content[1]);
                    ct.Area = decimal.Parse(content[2]);
                    ct.X = decimal.Parse(content[3]);
```

```
                        ct.Y = decimal.Parse(content[4]);

                        cities.Add(ct);
                        line = sr.ReadLine();
                    }
                }
                catch (Exception ex)
                { MessageBox.Show(ex.Message); }
                finally
                {
                    sr.Close();
                    fs.Close();
                }
```

3. At this point, you have populated the list of `City` objects. As you can see by looking at the structure of a simple KML file (discussed in Chapter 1), all you need to create a KML file is to enclose `City` objects with some XML tags. A simple KML file has the following structure:

```xml
<?xml version="1.0" encoding="UTF-8"?>
<kml xmlns="http://www.opengis.net/kml/2.2">
  <Document>
    <name>Kish Island</name>
    <Placemark>
      <name>Kish Island</name>
      <description>Kish island in Beautiful Persian Gulf</description>
      <Point>
        <coordinates>53.96575016905689,26.50243592677882,0</coordinates>
      </Point>
    </Placemark>
  </Document>
</kml>
```

4. To make life more interesting you are going to use some HTML tags to make up the description of `City` objects inside the KML file. Enter the following code into the `City` class:

```csharp
        private string CreateKMLDescription()
        {
            string description="";
            description += string.Format("<i>Name: </i>{0}<br />",this.Name);
                description += string.Format("<i>Population: </i>{0} <br/>",
                this.Population);
                description += string.Format("<i>Area: </i>{0} Square
                Kilometre",this.Area);

            return description;
        }
```

5. Add another method in the `City` class to create the rest of the tags for each `City` object:

```csharp
        public string WriteKMLFragment()
        {
            string kmlFragment = "";
            kmlFragment += string.Format("<Placemark id='{0}'>", this.Name);
```

```
kmlFragment += string.Format("<name>The City of {0}</name>", this.Name);
kmlFragment += string.Format("<description>{0}</description>", this.
CreateKMLDescription());

kmlFragment += string.Format("<Point><coordinates>{0},{1})
</coordinates></Point>", this.X, this.Y);
kmlFragment += string.Format("</Placemark>");

return kmlFragment;
}
```

6. This is the time for creating a KML file from the list of `City` objects. Append the following code to the `click` event handler of `btnCreateKMLFile`:

```
//create kml
StringBuilder sb = new StringBuilder();
//append the kml prologue
sb.Append(@"<?xml version='1.0' encoding='UTF-8'?><kml xmlns=
'http://www.opengis.net/kml/2.2'><Document>");

foreach (City ct in cities)
{
    sb.Append(ct.WriteKMLFragment());
}

//append the epilog of the kml file
sb.Append(@"</Document></kml>");
fs = new FileStream(@"c:\test.kml", FileMode.Create);
StreamWriter sw = new StreamWriter(fs);

try
{
    sw.Write(sb.ToString());
}
catch (Exception ex)
{
    MessageBox.Show(ex.Message);
}
finally
{
    sw.Close();
    fs.Close();
}
```

7. Run your application. A KML file should be created. You can open this file using Google Earth or ArcGIS Explorer. Figure 4-14 shows the file in Google Earth.

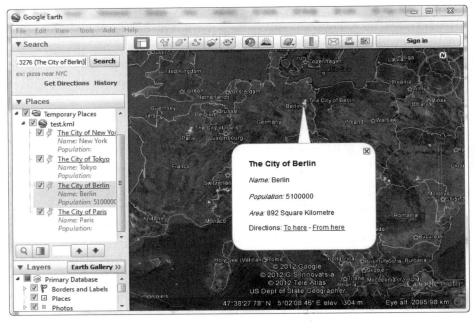

FIGURE 4-14

How It Works

You have seen how to create a simple KML file out of a list of objects. In addition, you used the String Builder class to hold the contents of a text file. You could use a String object instead of StringBuilder, but you have to know that String objects are *immutable*. This means once a String object is assigned a value (initialized) its value cannot be changed. As a matter of fact, when you reassign a string variable, behind the scenes the .NET Framework creates a new String object and assigns that object to that variable.

The String class is the perfect choice for representing basic character data, but when you build a text file it is better to use the StringBuilder class. The StringBuilder class (in the System.Text namespace) is the perfect choice when you make heavy use of text data. What makes this perfect is the capability to directly modify the internal character data. When you are using one of the members of the StringBuilder class, you don't obtain a copy of the contents of it in a modified format.

In addition to using FileStream, .NET includes functionality for reading and writing simple text and binary files using the File class. This functionality enables you to read and write a file with a single line of code. Here is an example:

```
string[] linesOfData = {
    "New York, 16500000, 1210, -74.0999, 40.7500",
    "Tokyo, 23650000, 2187, 139.8092, 35.6830",
```

```
    "Berlin, 5100000, 892, 13.3276, 52.5163" };

    //writing all lines in one shot
    File.WriteAllLines(@"c:\test.txt",linesOfData);

    //reading the text file line by line
    string[] contents = File.ReadAllLines(@"c:\test.txt");
```

These methods of accessing files (and other methods provided by the `File` class) are efficient for small amounts of data. In the case of writing a file, behind the scenes the .NET Framework reads all the data into memory and then flushes it to the specified file. A similar process happens when you try to read the file using these methods. The entire content is loaded into memory at once and put into a variable. It is recommended that when you deal with files and other unmanaged resources like databases you read one piece of data at a time and process the read data bit by bit.

You created a KML file in the preceding Try It Out. You can also create a KMZ file, which is a zipped version of a KML file. Unfortunately, there is no straightforward and easy approach to create `.zip` files using .NET 4.0. Fortunately, one of the new changes in .NET 4.5 is the vast improvement in the `System.IO.Compression` namespace. Using the types in that namespace in a very simple manner, you can perform zip and unzip actions (archiving and unarchiving). But as long as you are using Visual Studio 2010 and .NET 4.0 you cannot make use of them without installing .NET 4.5. So you have to resort to third-party components. Several free and commercial components can be used for performing packaging related tasks. One of the simplest is the free DotNetZip library. You can download it from `http://dotnetzip.codeplex.com/`. DotNetZip is managed code written completely in C# and can be used in any type of .NET application. The last Try It Out in this chapter shows how to create a KMZ file.

PACKAGING IN .NET 3.0 AND ABOVE

.NET 3.0 introduced the `System.IO.Packaging` namespace (in the `WindowsBase` `.dll` assembly), which can be used to create zip archives. The `ZipPackage` class in this namespace has the required members to perform zip-related actions. But because the `ZipPackage` class is not straightforward to work with, most developers resort to other solutions. This is changed in .NET 4.5, but this book uses Visual Studio 2010 throughout, so NET 4.5 features are not covered.

TRY IT OUT   Creating a KMZ File (KMZ.zip)

1. Open the KML project you created in the preceding Try It Out. Go to `http://dotnetzip .codeplex.com` and download the `DotNetZip` library. Unpack the library to a convenient location on your machine (such as `C:\ZipLibrary`).

2. To use a library, you have to add a reference to the assembly contained in the `DotNetZip` library. In Solution Explorer, right-click on the References folder and choose Add Reference. The Add

Reference window appears. Select the Browse tab and go to the extraction folder (where you extracted the .zip file). Find the zip-v1.9 folder as shown in Figure 4-15 and double-click it. You will see two other folders: Double-click the Release folder, which contains the assembly. Select the `Ionic.Zip.dll` file and then click the OK button to add the assembly to your project.

3. Notice that a reference (`Ionic.Zip`) is added at the top of your references in the Solution Explorer window. Add a button to the MainWindow of your application. As always, change its name and content to something meaningful (such as **btnKMZ** and **Convert KML to KMZ**, respectively).

FIGURE 4-15

4. Add the following code to create a `.zip` archive from the KML file in the `click` event handler of the newly added button.

```
private void btnKMZ_Click(object sender, RoutedEventArgs e)
{
    Ionic.Zip.ZipFile zf = new Ionic.Zip.ZipFile();
    try
    {
        //you created the kml file in the preceding step
        //you can create the kmz file in a single step as well
        zf.AddFile(@"C:\test.kml");
        zf.Save(@"C:\test.kmz");
    }
    catch (Exception ex)
    {
        MessageBox.Show(ex.Message, ex.Source);
    }
    finally
    {
        //cleanup code
        zf.Dispose();
    }
}
```

5. Run your code by pressing F5 or the Start Debugging button in Visual Studio. Click the newly added button. A KMZ file is created that can be viewed in most Earth viewer applications such as Google Earth, ArcGIS Explorer, and NASA's World Wind.

How It Works

In this Try It Out, you saw the process of adding an external assembly file. You also saw how easy and intuitive it is to work with the `DotNetZip` library. You write just three lines of code (exception handling and declaration code excluded) to create a `.zip` file. The most important line of code in those three lines is the `Dispose()` method. You have to call this method on every object to release memory that is occupied by the unmanaged resources within your code. The proper location for calling this method is the `finally` block. Note that many types provide a `Close()` method (such as the `FileStream` class) to perform the same action. So keep in mind that in spite of the fact that .NET provides automatic garbage collection, you always have to provide cleanup code for unmanaged resources.

> **NOTE** Codeplex (http://www.codeplex.com) is Microsoft's website dedicated to free and open source projects. You can create new innovative projects to share with the world, collaborate with others on existing projects, and download open source software from this site. Spend some time on this site and you will find some useful pieces of open source software.

SUMMARY

This chapter is the second and last chapter on pure .NET programming. In this chapter, you have completed the big picture of object-oriented programming in C# by exploring object-oriented principles and techniques. You reviewed the types in .NET and saw how reference types differ from value types. Also you examined debugging in Visual Studio and the use of structured exception handling in .NET. Then you delved into the `System.IO` namespace and accessing files using the types inside that namespace. Finally, through creating a KMZ file (and making use of an external tiny component), you were ready to make use of external components that have revolutionized the GIS world since its beginning. I mean ArcObjects. The remaining chapters of this book focus on ArcObjects. In Chapter 5, you see what ArcObjects is and how you can use ArcObjects types in .NET.

EXERCISES

1. Method overloading and method overriding are part of which object-oriented principle?

2. Is the `string` type a reference type or value type? What is the result of an assignment operator on it?

3. Which part of the exception handling block is optional? Which part is suitable for cleanup code?

4. It is recommended not to use the `ArrayList` class in all .NET code since .NET 2.0. What is wrong with the `ArrayList` class?

You will find the answers to these exercises in this book's appendix.

▶ WHAT YOU LEARNED IN THIS CHAPTER

TOPIC	KEY CONCEPTS
Main object-oriented principles	Abstraction, encapsulation, polymorphism, and inheritance
Method overriding	In general, method overriding allows a child class to override a specific implementation of a method that is already provided by its parent (super) class.
Differences between reference types and value types	Differences between reference types and value types lie in three important cases: in assignment operations, in comparison operations, and when passing parameters between methods. Also they are managed in two different places in memory by CLR.
.NET types	Classes, enumerations, structures, interfaces, and delegates compose what is called .NET types.
Namespace and assembly	All .NET types are logically organized in namespaces and all of them reside physically in assemblies (such as .dll files). There is a many-to-many relationship between namespaces and assemblies.
Casting objects in C#	You can cast objects in C# using an explicit casting operator or as keyword.

PART III
ArcObjects Programming

5

Understanding ArcObjects Object Model Diagrams

WHAT YOU WILL LEARN IN THIS CHAPTER:

➤ Interface-based programming

➤ Types of classes in ArcObjects

➤ Different kinds of relationships in ArcObjects

➤ Navigating a relationship

➤ Working with tools such as Object Browser and ILSpy

WROX.COM CODE DOWNLOADS FOR THIS CHAPTER

The wrox.com code downloads for this chapter are found at www.wrox.com/remtitle
.cgi?isbn=1118442547 on the Download Code tab. The code is in the Chapter05 folder
and individually named according to the names throughout the chapter.

ArcObjects is a set of reusable components developed using Microsoft's Component Object
Model (COM) specification. This specification is one of the rare successful standards for interface-based programming. Put simply, in interface-based programming, you don't use objects
directly; rather, you access the members of classes through their implemented interfaces. So
in ArcObjects development, you have to know the details of working with interfaces. In this
chapter, you first scratch the surface of interface-based programming in the .NET Framework.
Then you delve into the topic of interpreting ArcObjects object model diagrams, which you
often use as a source of planning for development.

WHAT IS ARCOBJECTS?

ArcObjects is a library of COM components that build up the foundation of the ArcGIS platform. ArcObjects is written mostly in C++ programming language. All the ArcGIS for Desktop applications are based on ArcObjects. In other words, when you are working with ArcMap or ArcCatalog, behind the scenes you are making use of ArcObjects.

A *component* is a discrete piece of software that does some specific, predefined task. Microsoft COM is a formal standard that everyone can use to create components, ensuring that they are compatible and reusable. Put simply, COM enables you to write a component once and then use it everywhere. Then you can correct or enhance the component's functionality simply by updating and replacing the component. This means that COM is not a programming language, a library of code, or a compiler. Rather, because COM is a binary specification, it enables you to build components that can communicate with each other regardless of the programming language or tool you choose to build them.

Since ArcGIS is completely built on top of ArcObjects, you can make use of COM services and capabilities to fully customize and extend the ArcGIS platform — meaning that extending the ArcObjects data model can be done easily and with virtually all COM-compatible programming languages. In platforms other than ArcGIS, extending the software platform could be done only using proprietary programming languages — or even worse, only the original GIS software vendor had the complete customization capabilities.

COM enables components to be reused at a binary level. In other words, developers do not require access to the source code of ArcObjects in order to extend the ArcGIS platform. For this reason, an ArcObjects programmer can make use of any type inside the ArcObjects system without knowing the inner details of the type. The developer only needs to know what the type is able to do. Because ArcObjects is based on the COM standard, you can easily work with it in conjunction with other COM objects and applications.

As previously mentioned, the ArcGIS platform was built using ArcObjects types (such as classes, interfaces, and enumerations). In the world of ArcObjects, classes use interfaces to organize properties and methods. Put simply, classes inside ArcObjects use only COM interfaces to expose their public members and communicate with each other. When working with an ArcObjects COM class, you never work with the properties and methods of the class; rather, you always access its properties and methods via one of its implemented interfaces. As an example, when you instantiate an object, you can only use one interface. However, after instantiation, you can query for any other interface that is implemented by that object. This process is sometimes called a *Query Interface* (QI). Classes in ArcObjects often have many interfaces. Since working with interfaces is a fundamental skill in ArcObjects programming, the next section briefly provides a foundation for interface-based programming.

INTERFACE-BASED PROGRAMMING IN BRIEF

When working with ArcObjects, you almost always use the interfaces it provides. In other words, you don't author or implement an interface in most cases. But in this section, you briefly see what authoring and implementing an interface looks like.

You define an interface with the `Interface` keyword in C#. Because an interface is nothing more than a named set of abstract members, there is no need to provide implementation for them. The following code defines an interface with one method and one property. By convention, COM and .NET interfaces are prefixed with a capital letter "I." When you create your own custom interfaces, it is considered a best practice to do the same.

```
interface I2DShape
{
    double CalculateArea();
    int NumberOfVertices { get;}
}
```

Interfaces are useless until they are implemented by a class. Here, `I2DShape` is an interface that expresses the behavior of "being a 2D shape." When a class chooses to extend its functionality by implementing interfaces, it does so using an interface name after a colon operator, as shown in the following code.

```
public class Square : I2DShape
{
    private double side;
    public Square(double side)
    {
        this.side = side;
    }
    double I2DShape.CalculateArea()
    {
        return side * side;
    }
    int I2DShape.NumberOfVertices
    {
        get
        {
            return 4;
        }
    }
}
```

Suppose that for some reason the authors of `I2DShape` decide to extend the interface. Directly changing the interface members (the number of members, names of members, and so on) results in breaking the existing code of the `Square` class (and all classes that implement the `I2DShape` interface). Here is the reason: Implementing an interface is an all-or-nothing task. The implementing type (in this case, the `Square` class) is not able to selectively choose which members it will implement. For this reason, instead of changing the functionality of an existing interface, the authors have to publish a new interface such as `I2DShape2`.

```
interface I2DShape2
{
    double CalculatePerimeter();
}
```

At this point, using a comma-delimited list you can indicate which interfaces should be implemented by the `Square` class.

```
public class Square : I2DShape, I2DShape2
    {
        private double side;
        public Square(double side)
        {
            this.side = side;
        }

        double I2DShape.CalculateArea()
        {
            return side * side;
        }

        int I2DShape.NumberOfVertices
        {
            get
            {
                return 4;
            }

        }

        double I2DShape2.CalculatePerimeter()
        {
            return 4 * this.side;
        }
    }
```

As you can see, a class can implement multiple interfaces. Using this approach, you ensure that existing code (existing clients) never breaks — and this is one of the benefits of interface-based programming.

When you want to use objects of the Square class, notice that you cannot access the members directly; rather, you have to use one of the implemented interfaces. As you can see in Figure 5-1, although the Square class has some members, it is not possible to access members of the Square class via the mySQ variable.

FIGURE 5-1

The following code snippet demonstrates using the I2DShape interface for a Square object.

```
//only members of I2DShape are available
        I2DShape mySQ = new Square(2.0);
        double area = mySQ.CalculateArea();
        int numOfVertices = mySQ.NumberOfVertices;

        //to access perimeter you have to cast (Query) the interface
        I2DShape2 mySQ2 = mySQ as I2DShape2;
        double perimeter = mySQ2.CalculatePerimeter();
        //mySQ and mySQ2 are the same object
        //with two different ways of exposing members
```

To work with a class through its interfaces, you need to declare a variable that points to an interface supported by that class. Declaring an interface variable does not give you access to any particular object; it simply defines how you will eventually communicate with the object once it is referenced.

The next step, therefore, is to initialize the variable to point to an actual object. Some objects can be created by using the new keyword, while others can only be returned from another object (for example, a FeatureClass can create a Feature, as you see later in this chapter). Once you point your variable to a specific object, you can use any methods or properties that exist on that particular interface.

If you need to access members on a different interface, you need to declare another variable that points to the required interface. In this case, there is no need for using the new keyword because the object existed beforehand and all that is needed is to cast or query the interface.

The previous code snippet uses the as keyword to cast the variable to the I2DShape2 interface type. In real-world applications, it is always a good idea to check whether the underlying object implemented an interface before casting. You do this using the is keyword. Here is an example:

```
//using the is keyword
if (mySQ is I2DShape2)
{
    //following lines of code are the same
    I2DShape2 mySQ3 = (I2DShape2)mySQ;
    mySQ3 = mySQ as I2DShape2;
}
```

As you notice, interfaces help a class evolve over time because new interfaces can be added to the class to provide additional functionalities. However, once an interface is created, it can never be updated to provide additional functionality or remove existing functionality. The actual implementation of existing members of an interface can be enhanced but additional members cannot be added to an existing interface. If the class needs to be reprogrammed to provide additional functionalities, new interfaces must be created. This way, the class evolves without breaking the existing client code. When a new interface is published, the class stays the same, but the client can interact with the class through the newest interface.

Figure 5-2 illustrates the two interfaces the Square class implements. The I2DShape interface provides NumberOfVertices as a read-only property (left-hand barbell) and the CalculateArea() method. The I2DShape2 interface provides only the CalculatePerimeter() method. These symbols are heavily used in ArcObjects programming. If you are familiar with Unified Modeling Language (UML), you have noticed the similarity between these symbols and the symbols of the UML Class diagram. Esri customized the UML Class diagram to create the ArcObjects object model diagrams. The ArcObjects object model diagrams are sets of diagrams in which almost all ArcObjects types and their relationships are illustrated.

One of the primary tasks in programming ArcObjects is to find relevant types, properties, and methods for the task at hand. Among the best starting points for finding relevant types in the world of ArcObjects are object model diagrams. Therefore, understanding object model diagrams is as important as writing C# code. The next section provides a comprehensive explanation of understanding ArcObjects object model diagrams.

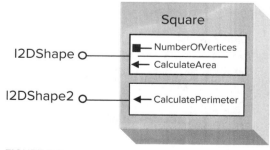

FIGURE 5-2

> **NOTE** All COM components must (at the very least) implement the standard `IUnknown` interface, and thus all COM interfaces are derived from `IUnknown`. The `IUnknown` interface consists of three methods. `AddRef()` implements a reference counting mechanism and `Release()` controls the lifetime of interfaces. The third method is `QueryInterface()`, which allows a caller to retrieve references to the different interfaces implemented by the object. The effect of `QueryInterface()` is similar to a cast operator in VB.NET and C#. In the COM specification, the `IUnknown` interface is the ultimate parent of all the interfaces. Thus, casting (the `QueryInterface()` method) is available to all interfaces and objects in ArcObjects.

UNDERSTANDING OBJECT MODEL DIAGRAMS

ArcObjects Help for .NET (which is installed with the ArcObjects SDK for Microsoft .NET) includes several object model diagrams that describe how the ArcObjects libraries are put together. In addition to the object model diagrams, there is a vast amount of sample code, best practices, and descriptive help for all aspects of ArcObjects programming. Before you can use the ArcObjects Developer help system efficiently, you have to be familiar with using ArcGIS because if you don't know what tool or command to use to select features based on a spatial criterion, you are unlikely to find the required types in the Developer help system. On the other hand, if you have experience using ArcGIS for Desktop, you will easily recognize that a map that has a feature layer has a feature class behind it, which can be queried. Also consider that the same concept can have different names, depending on whether you use ArcGIS as a user or as a developer (in the same way that users call a container of files a *folder* and developers call the same thing a *directory*). So your knowledge of ArcGIS is an important tool for ArcObjects development.

> **NOTE** The installed version of Developer help is a static version of the help system for ArcGIS development. You can find the most current documentation and help for any topic about ArcGIS development in the ArcGIS Resource Center. You can find any development-related topic somewhere in the following address: `resources.arcgis.com`. Specifically, ArcObjects help for .NET can be found at `http://resources.arcgis.com/en/help/arcobjects-net/conceptualhelp/`.

Object model diagrams are an important part of ArcGIS Developer Help. Object model diagrams can help you find not only classes and interfaces, but also the relationships between them and useful details about them. These diagrams are invaluable tools that help you plan how to write your code. Object model diagrams indicate how to work with certain types (so you know if objects can be created from a specific type or they must be obtained from a live object), and how each type is related to others (a table is composed of several rows, for example).

In fact, a few thousands interfaces and classes compose ArcObjects. Just like the .NET platform, ArcObjects is logically divided into several namespaces. In ArcGIS Developer Help, for the sake of simplicity each namespace is provided as a distinct object model diagram. These diagrams are accessible through static help (installed on your machine when you install the ArcObjects SDK for Microsoft .NET) as well as through the online ArcGIS Resource Center.

Types of Classes in ArcObjects

Figure 5-3 shows the user interface of ArcMap. Let's see what types (such as classes, interfaces, and structures) in ArcObjects can be found in this figure. In this figure, the currently running ArcMap application is an `Application` object. `Application` objects can open only one `*.mxd` file. If the file was previously saved, the name of the `*.mxd` file is displayed in the title bar; otherwise, a temporary document is created and *Untitled* is displayed. In Figure 5-3, the `Application` object opens the `TestDoc.mxd` file. `*.mxd` files in ArcObjects are called MxDocument. `MxDocument` objects can be composed of multiple (at least one) Data Frames. In ArcObjects, Data Frames are called Maps. Any Map (or Data Frame) can be composed of various types of Layers. Three Feature Layers (Layers) can be found in Figure 5-3.

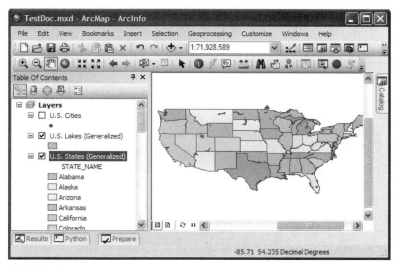

FIGURE 5-3

Figure 5-4 shows a simplified object model diagram of Figure 5-3. As in mathematics and algebra, there are standard notations and symbols in all object model diagrams.

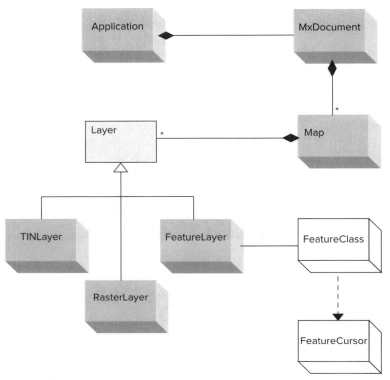

FIGURE 5-4

The following list describes the three classes in ArcObjects.

➤ **Abstract Classes:** As the name suggests, abstract classes cannot be instantiated. In other words, you cannot create an instance of an abstract class. They are used for modeling specialization or parent-child relationships to group a set of shared properties and methods for their subclasses. Therefore, you always find that abstract classes have multiple subclasses. In Figure 5-4, Layer is an abstract class which has FeatureLayer, TINLayer, and RasterLayer as its subtypes (or child classes or subclasses). All child classes inherit all the interfaces of their own super class (parent or base class). In ArcObjects object model diagrams, abstract classes are always presented using a 2D shaded rectangle.

➤ **Classes:** This kind of class represents ordinary classes with one limitation. You can use their instances but their instances must be created from other classes. For this reason, they are sometimes called *instantiable classes*. Instances of these classes are often created by the object that will contain them. In Figure 5-4, FeatureCursor (which in turn is used to create Feature instances) can only be created by Feature class. The purpose of creating instances of some classes using instances of other classes is consistency. In other words, when you create instances of (instantiable) classes using other classes, the newly created instances will be automatically put into the right context. For example, if you create a Feature instance using an instance of a specific FeatureClass class (say the Sea FeatureClass), you will be sure that the newly created `Feature` will reside in that specific `FeatureClass` (in other words, you create a `Sea` `Feature`). This makes more sense than creating a new `Feature` and then adding it to a specific `FeatureClass`. ArcObjects Classes are shown by a 3D rectangle without shading.

➤   **CoClasses:** CoClasses are concrete classes — they are the only kinds of classes which can be instantiated directly using the `new` keyword. `FeatureLayer`, `Map`, and `Application` are examples of CoClasses in Figure 5-4. As mentioned previously, an instance of a CoClass can be created directly. Sometimes you access the instances of CoClasses that exist as live objects or as properties of other objects. For example, since `MxDocument` (which represents an ArcMap `*.mxd` file) is a CoClass, you can create brand new instances, but usually you refer to an existing `MxDocument` using the `Document` property of the `Application` CoClass. (`Application.Document` represents a live `MxDocument` instance.) CoClasses are represented as 3D shaded rectangles in object model diagrams.

> **NOTE** As mentioned in this section, there are three types of classes in ArcObjects. To avoid confusion from this point forward, in this book, all the references to these ArcObject classes will be capitalized: Abstract Class, Class, and CoClass. The word "class" when lowercase refers to any type of class (that is, any Class, Abstract Class, or CoClass). Also remember that "types" refers to simple data types such as `double` as well as complex data types such as interfaces and classes.

Relationships between Classes

There are also relationships between various kinds of classes. In general, there are four kinds of relationships, as described in the following list.

➤   **Type inheritance (inheritance):** This is a relationship between parent and child classes. Often a parent class is an Abstract Class. By default, all the interfaces of a parent class are inherited to child classes. In Figure 5-4, the relationship between `Layer` (as a parent class) and `FeatureLayer`, `RasterLayer`, and `TINLayer` (as child classes) is an example of this kind of relationship. As shown in Figure 5-4, type inheritance relationships are represented by a solid line with an open triangle pointing to the parent class.

➤   **Composition:** This is a relationship between the container and contained classes. Sometimes the container and contained classes are called *whole* and *part* classes, respectively. The lifetime of part classes is controlled by the lifetime of the whole class. As an example of composition, a `Map` CoClass is composed by several `Layer` classes. If a `Map` instance is destroyed (for example, if a user removes the Data Frame), all `Layer` instances inside that `Map` will be destroyed. In Figure 5-4, the composition relationship is represented by a solid line with a filled diamond attached to the whole class.

➤ **Instantiation:** At least one of the participants of this relationship is a Class. Usually there is a member in one of the interfaces of the origin Class which creates an instance of the destination Class. In Figure 5-4, the relationship between FeatureClass and FeatureCursor is a type of instantiation and FeatureClass has a method (you see that in Chapter 7) to create a FeatureCursor instance. This relationship is displayed by a dashed line with a filled triangle pointing to the target Class.

➤ **Association:** Relationships other than inheritance, instantiation, and composition are called *associations*. In contrast to composition, in this relationship there is no control on lifetimes of each participant. In other words, if one participant is destroyed, the other participant could live independently. In Figure 5-4, there is an association relationship between FeatureClass and FeatureLayer. The association is shown using a solid line between participants. If more than two participants are involved in an association relationship, a diamond is placed at the intersection of all participants. For example, as a user of ArcMap, in order to perform the Select By Attribute operation on a table, you utilize the Select By Attribute window, then build a query, and finally execute the built query. As a result, some records of the table might be selected. To perform the same task in code, one instance of the Table Class and one instance of the QueryFilter CoClass should be used to create an instance of a SelectionSet Class (see Figure 5-5). Simply speaking, the SelectionSet instance contains selected records.

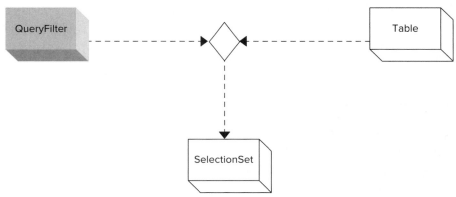

FIGURE 5-5

Association and composition relationships should indicate multiplicity or cardinality. Multiplicity or cardinality refers to the number of objects that can participate in a relationship. It should be displayed on both ends of the association and composition. In Figure 5-6, one or more Field Instances are associated with exactly one instance of the Fields CoClass. In addition, exactly one instance of the Fields CoClass is associated with one instance of the Table Class. Note that if nothing is shown as multiplicity, you can always consider it as 1. So Figure 5-6 shows exactly the same multiplicity or cardinality as Figure 5-7.

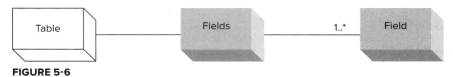

FIGURE 5-6

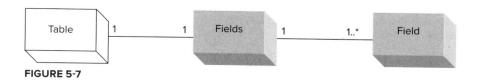

FIGURE 5-7

> **NOTE** *Relationships between interfaces are discussed in the "Interface Inheritance" section later in this chapter. The list in this section describes the relationship between classes only.*

Members of Interfaces

Classes in ArcObjects expose their members through interfaces. All the interfaces of a class are listed on object model diagrams. But all the members of only some of the more common interfaces are displayed on the diagrams. A complete list of the members of each interface can be found in the ArcGIS Developer Help. As you already know, properties, methods, and events comprise members of an interface.

Properties on the object model diagrams are generally illustrated using a barbell symbol. Since properties can be read-only, write-only, or read-write, different symbols are used to denote these characteristics. Figure 5-8 shows various kinds of properties.

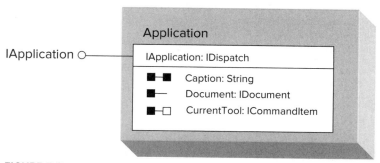

FIGURE 5-8

As shown in Figure 5-8, IApplication is one of the interfaces of the Application CoClass. All the interfaces on object model diagrams are shown using a lollipop symbol. Data types of all properties are specified after the name of each property. For example, Caption is of type String and Document is of type IDocument. If the data type of a property is interface, then it points to an object that implements that interface. In this example, the Document property is of type IDocument. The IDocument interface is implemented by the MxDocument CoClass. So the Document property is a live instance of the MxDocument CoClass. As a result, the relationship between Application and MxDocument CoClasses is made using the Document property of the IApplication interface. This is an important point in understanding object model diagrams. To summarize, if two classes have an association with each other, you can always find a member of one participant that references an implemented interface of the other participant.

The left box of the barbell denotes the capability to get the property, whereas the right box shows the capability to set the property. So in Figure 5-8, Caption is a read-write property and Document is a read-only property.

In addition, a filled box denotes Value types while a hollow box denotes Reference types. As you can see in Figure 5-8, the Caption property is a Value type whereas the CurrentTool is a Reference type property — meaning that if you assign a String variable as the Caption of IApplication, modification of the value of the String variable has no effect on the Caption of ArcMap. On the other hand, any change in the referenced CurrentTool of Application will be reflected to the CurrentTool property. This concept is covered in more detail in Chapter 4.

Methods are symbolized on the diagrams with a solid arrow. In addition to the name of the method, any required arguments from the method, return values from the method, or both will be specified as part of the diagram listing.

In Figure 5-9, RefreshWindow doesn't require any parameter. SaveDocument needs an input parameter, which is denoted by the In keyword of type String. As you can see, the object model diagram provides little help to find out what a method does and what it expects. The third method returns the IExtension interface, which is a reference to a live object that implements the interface.

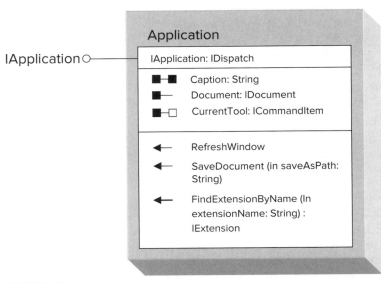

FIGURE 5-9

Events are illustrated like methods. They often reside on interfaces that contain the Events keyword. In addition, they usually have no return value. In Figure 5-10, IFindPanelEvents is an interface that is implemented by FindWindowUI.

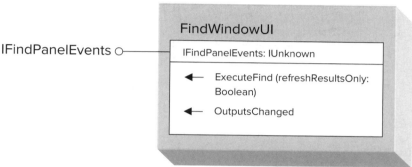

FIGURE 5-10

Interface Inheritance

To this point in this chapter, you have learned that one of the possible relationships between classes is *inheritance*. Through inheritance, all the interfaces of the parent class are inherited by its child classes. Also you have seen that ArcObjects is a huge set of COM components. Interfaces in COM define the public functionality of components that other components can use. In other words, interaction between components in COM is performed using interfaces.

In the COM specification, IUnknown is the ultimate parent interface of all interfaces. In other words, all the components in a COM system must directly or indirectly implement it. As mentioned previously in this chapter, the capability to switch or cast between various interfaces of a class is achieved through this interface (more specifically, through the QueryInterface() method of IUnknown).

Often in an ArcObjects object model diagram, you see the IUnknown interface after the name of many interfaces. This notation is used to express interface inheritance. For example, in Figure 5-10, the IFindPanelEvents inherits from the IUnknown interface; in Figure 5-9, the IApplication interface is inherited from the IDispatch interface. In interface inheritance, all members of a parent interface are inherited to the child interfaces. (The IDispatch interface is implemented by a class if there is a need to access that class from a scripting environment [such as JavaScript]).

To summarize, IUnknown must be defined for any component to make it a COM component. The IDispatch interface, which derives from the IUnknown interface, is implemented primarily for the benefit of scripting languages. Whenever you program in high-level programming languages such as C# or VB.NET, these interface inheritance relationships don't have any tangible effect on the way you code. The majority of ArcObjects interfaces are inherited directly from IUnknown or IDispatch. The remaining interfaces have a direct parent other than the two famous COM interfaces. As illustrated in Figure 5-12, FeatureClass inherits from ObjectClass. In addition to this ordinary type inheritance, the IFeatureClass interface inherits from the IObjectClass interface. By this interface inheritance, you get all the members of IObjectClass on IFeatureClass directly and without needing to cast an interface.

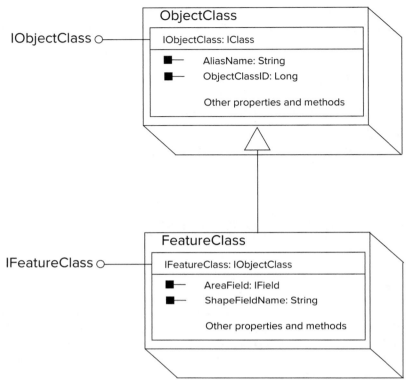

FIGURE 5-11

You can check interface inheritance using the autocomplete feature of Visual Studio, as shown in Figure 5-12.

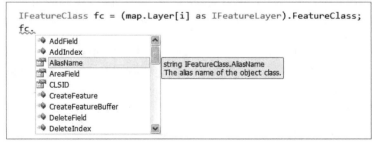

FIGURE 5-12

Wormhole

In addition to providing ArcObjects namespaces, to make the lives of ArcObjects developers a little bit simpler, object model diagrams are logically organized into various diagrams. When a class in one diagram (namespace) is related to a class in another diagram, an ellipsoid is used to create what is called a *wormhole*. The wormhole specifies the related class and the diagram on which it appears. In the example shown in Figure 5-13, the wormhole shows the composition between Map CoClass in a Carto diagram and MxDocument in an ArcMapUI diagram.

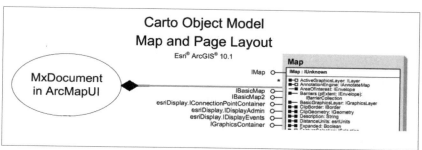

FIGURE 5-13

This relationship is also presented in the ArcMapUI as well, as shown in Figure 5-15.

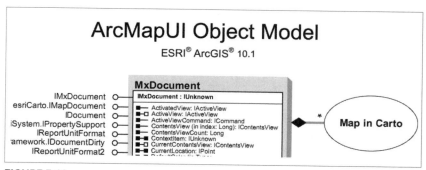

FIGURE 5-14

Additional Tips for Using Object Model Diagrams

Object model diagrams are invaluable tools for ArcObjects developers. They represent all the interfaces of all types inside ArcObjects. They also express the relationships between types. But they have some limitations.

They don't provide all the members for all the interfaces of a class. They only provide a complete list of members of a few common interfaces for each class. Another limitation is that not all the relationships are represented on the diagrams. In addition, they provide little help on parameters and the return values of methods. In other words, they don't provide descriptive tips and help for each member. Object model diagrams are valuable tools for planning how to write code, but other tools are needed for efficient ArcObjects programming.

In order to get brief tips as well as descriptive help for all members of all interfaces, Visual Studio's Object Browser window and ArcGIS Developer Help can be used.

To try Object Browser, open in Visual Studio the first add-in project you developed in Chapter 2 (Simplest add-in). From the View menu, select Object Browser to open the Object Browser window. The left panel in Object Browser lists all the available assemblies. If you expand the ESRI.ArcGIS .Carto assembly from the left panel, as shown in Figure 5-15, you will see all types (enumerations, classes, and interfaces) inside this assembly. Scroll down to `IFeatureLayer` to see its members. Alternatively, you can type the name of any type in the textbox above the Object Browser window to search for it. Click on one of its members to see a brief tip for that member.

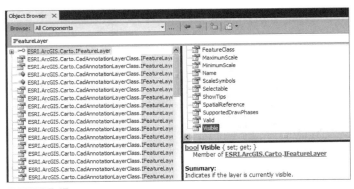

FIGURE 5-15

In addition to Object Browser, ArcGIS Developer Help provides all necessary information for successful ArcObjects development. The ArcGIS Developer Help is installed locally as part of ArcObjects SDK for .NET. In fact, ArcObjects object model diagrams are a part of ArcGIS Developer Help. All the object model diagrams are available in Adobe Portable Document Format (.pdf) and can be accessed using the following address on your machine: `<ArcGIS installation folder>\DeveloperKit10.10\Diagrams`.

As previously mentioned, the most current topics on development of ArcObjects as well as ArcGIS Developer Help can be accessed through the ArcGIS Resource Center (`http://resources.arcgis .com/en/help/arcobjects-net/conceptualhelp/`).

The final tip that is good to know is that the Object Browser does not show the explicit relationships between types as the object model diagrams do. With all your knowledge of object model diagrams, you still need to address two questions: What is your entry point into the ArcObjects system and how can you navigate between the types? The next sections walk you through the steps needed for addressing these questions.

Where to Start with ArcObjects

When developing ArcObjects, whether using Desktop Add-Ins or Extending ArcObjects project templates, you always have a preset and public variable that is the entry point of your code in the ArcObjects world. The public variable is always, regardless of the kind of desktop application, of type IApplication interface.

In the case of Desktop Add-Ins, the name of this public variable is Application. Based on the type of project template, it can point to different applications. For example, if you select the ArcMap Add-in project template, you can easily discover that the Application variable is of type IApplication interface of ArcMap's Application CoClass (the Application CoClass in the ArcMap object model diagram); if you select the ArcCatalog add-in project template, the Application variable is of type IApplication of ArcCatalog's Application CoClass. To discover this fact, you can simply open the Config.Designer.cs (for C#) in the Solution Explorer window inside Visual Studio and scroll down to the declaration section of ArcMap Class, as shown in Figure 5-16.

```csharp
internal static class ArcMap
{
  private static IApplication s_app = null;
  private static IDocumentEvents_Event s_docEvent;

  public static IApplication Application
  {
    get
    {
      if (s_app == null)
        s_app = Internal.AddInStartupObject.GetHook<IMxApplication>() as IApplication;

      return s_app;
    }
  }
}
```

FIGURE 5-16

As you see in Figure 5-16, the ArcMap class is defined with the keyword static, which means this class can be used without using a live instance of this class (remember the System.Math class in Chapter 3 in the "Operations on Variables" section). Also, you can see that the Application property is of type IApplication and all the ArcGIS for Desktop applications implement this interface, but with a little exploration it is discovered that the add-in hooks into the execution of an object that exactly implements IMxApplication interface. (Is it ArcMap?)

In addition to the `Application` property, the `IApplication` interface provides the `Document` property. Because you usually need to interact with the contents of an application (such as layers inside a map or features in a feature class inside ArcMap), you usually use this property directly. Alternatively, you can access the contents of an application using `Application`'s static `Document` property.

The only difference between these approaches is that the `Application.Document` property always, regardless of the kind of application (such as ArcMap, ArcCatalog, or ArcScene), points to the `IDocument` interface. However, the `Document` property of a specific kind of application (such as ArcMap, ArcCatalog, or ArcScene) points to the most common interface of that application.

You can discover similar patterns in other types of templates for Desktop Add-Ins. Table 5-1 summarizes the entry points for different ArcGIS for Desktop applications and the type of `Document` property of them.

TABLE 5-1: Entry Points

TEMPLATE OF ADD-IN	ADD-IN ENTRY POINT	TYPE OF DOCUMENT PROPERTY (TYPE OF ARCXXX.DOCUMENT)
ArcMap	`ArcMap.Application`	`IMxDocument`
ArcCatalog	`ArcCatalog.Application`	`IDocument`
ArcScene	`ArcScene.Application`	`ISxDocument`
ArcGlobe	`ArcGlobe.Application`	`IGMxDocument`

In the case of Extending ArcObjects project templates, the public and preset variable is called `m_application`, which, as in the case of Desktop Add-Ins, is of type `IApplication` interface. Because Extending ArcObjects project templates have no definition for static classes for different kinds of ArcGIS Desktop applications (such as ArcMap class and ArcCatalog class), the main entry point of your code is the `m_application` variable. As you do with Desktop Add-Ins, usually you rely on your knowledge of ArcObjects development to explore, manipulate, and process the contents of various ArcGIS for Desktop applications. So you use the `Document` property of this variable (`m_application.Document`).

In summary, you start coding by using the `Application` or `m_application` preset and public variables in Desktop Add-Ins and Extending ArcObjects project templates, respectively. With those two variables, you begin your journey of ArcObjects development.

How to Find an Associated Member

ArcGIS Developer Help is often used as the main resource for discovering the types and relationships between various types. As a part of Developer Help, object model diagrams display all interfaces of all classes and explicitly illustrate the majority of relationships between classes. But in order to explore all interfaces of all classes and all members of any interface, you have to resort to other parts of Developer Help and tools, such as Object Browser in Visual Studio. That could be an easy but time-consuming task.

In order to explore the relationships between types, you have to make use of object model diagrams. In all the relationships except type inheritance, there is always at least one member (property, method, or event) in one participant that enables the relationship between two types. Suppose that TypeA and TypeB have a relationship other than inheritance and the enabling member belongs to TypeA. If the member that enables the relationship is a property, that property points to one of the implemented interfaces of TypeB. If the member that enables the relationship is a method, then the method returns one of the implemented interfaces of TypeB or the method expects one of the implemented interfaces of TypeB as an input parameter. Figure 5-17 illustrates this.

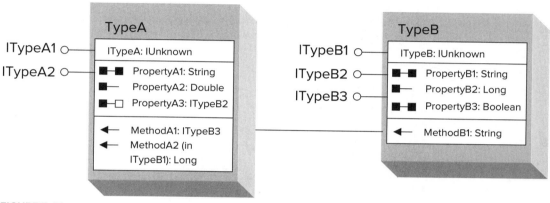

FIGURE 5-17

But now three important questions come to mind: How can you find a member that enables the relationship between two specific types? Is there a logical way to find that member? Can you explore that member programmatically?

At first finding this member seems to be hard. But as you work with ArcObjects, you will discover your own way of finding it. You simply need the experience of working with ArcGIS as a user with curiosity, patience, and willingness to invest enough elbow grease, as well as using available tools such as ArcGIS Developer Help. The next Try It Out walks you through using ArcGIS Developer Help and Visual Studio's Object Browser to find the member(s) that makes the relationship between the MxDocument and Map Classes. Remember that you can search for specific topics in the ArcGIS Developer Help (in fact, ArcGIS Developer Help works as a search engine that provides all the related topics of a subject matter) and find how to write the necessary code for the task at hand. But this approach should be used when you have sufficient experience working with ArcObjects. For this reason, throughout this book you only use the ArcGIS Developer Help as a source for exploring object model diagrams as well as finding types and members of types. But feel free to play around and learn with this resource.

> **NOTE** As you know, in inheritance relationships, all the interfaces of a parent class are inherited by the child class, which is why there are no members in child classes which enable the inheritance relationship.

TRY IT OUT   **Exploring the Relationship between MxDocument and Map CoClasses**

1. Your experience and knowledge of ArcMap tells you that the enabling member of the relationship between the MxDocument and Map CoClasses should be in one of the interfaces of the MxDocument CoClass. As previously mentioned, MxDocument (*.mxd file) can contain multiple Maps (Data Frames). Any specific Map will not belong to more than one MxDocument. So an MxDocument should have at least one member that points to its Maps.

2. Open the local ArcGIS Developer Help or browse to the online ArcGIS Resource Center. Search for "MxDocument." From the results, select MxDocument Class to see helpful information about this type. At the top of the page you can see the assembly containing this type. In addition, you can find a link to the object model diagram file in which you can find this type. MxDocument is documented in the ArcMapUI object model diagram and is contained in the ESRI.ArcGIS .ArcMapUI assembly.

3. Perform the same search for "Map class" to see its description, interfaces, and assembly information. This type resides in the ESRI.ArcGIS.Carto.dll assembly and you can see its object model in CartoObjectModel.pdf.

4. Open CartoObjectModel.pdf. You can find it locally in <ArcGIS installation folder>\DeveloperKit10.1\Diagrams or in the Online Resource Center. Search for MxDocument class in CartoObjectModel.pdf. With the help of object model diagrams, you find out that the type of relationship between those two classes is *composition*: Several maps compose a single MxDocument. So it is also logically correct that there should be a member in the MxDocument CoClass that has a reference to one of the implemented interfaces of the Map CoClass. Figure 5-18 displays a simplified view of the relationship.

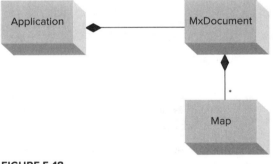

FIGURE 5-18

5. At this point, you have to explore members of the MxDocument type. You can use ArcGIS Developer Help as well as Visual Studio's Object Browser to find a member or members that point to the implemented interfaces of the Map CoClass. Since it is easier to explore the members in Visual Studio Object Browser, open the FirstAddin project (you developed it in Chapter 2), and from the View menu select Object Browser. In the previous steps, you found that the MxDocument type resides in the ESRI.ArcGIS.ArcMapUI assembly. So look for MxDocument inside that namespace.

6. The MxDocument CoClass implements more than 20 interfaces. In the right panel, you can see the list of members. If you select a specific interface from the left panel, all the members of that interface will be shown in the right panel. If the class is selected, all the members on all interfaces will be shown. Select the class to see all the members. By right-clicking in the right panel, you can control the way members are displayed. Right-click somewhere in the right panel and select the Group By Member Type item from the context menu (see Figure 5-19).

7. There are more than 200 members in the MxDocument CoClass and you have to find a member with one of the implemented interfaces of the Map CoClass. Unfortunately, there is no way to search members inside Object Browser by providing criteria. You have to explore all the members one by one. To make matters even worse, you have to scroll down to each member to see its details, such as data type, return type (in the case of methods),

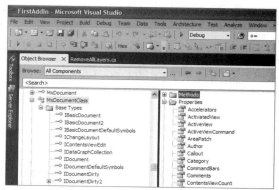

FIGURE 5-19

and so on. But you can discover from the ArcMapUI object model diagram that IMxDocument is the main interface of the MxDocument type. So you can limit your search to the members of the IMxDocument interface. So in the left panel click on the IMxDocument interface.

9. You can find a member named FocusMap of type IMap interface, which seems to have some sort of relationship with the Map Class. If you check the Map CoClass in the Carto object model diagram, you will see that the Map CoClass implements the IMap interface. So the FocusMap property of the MxDocument CoClass is the member that enables the relationship between the MxDocument and Map Classes.

How It Works

In this Try It Out, you learned how to find a member that enables a relationship. You have used ArcGIS Developer Help and Visual Studio's Object Browser to find a specific type, list of implemented interfaces, and details of members of a specific interface. Often you deal with the main interfaces of classes in ArcObjects. Fortunately in most cases, all members of the main interfaces are shown on the object model diagram. So in order to find a member that enables a relationship, you can limit your search to a small set of members displayed on object model diagrams and then, if you can't find any related member, you can explore other interfaces.

The Visual Studio Object Browser uses a concept of reflection to discover the details of any type. More specifically, metadata of assemblies can be queried to find out the details, such as the containing namespaces, types (classes, interfaces, structures, and enumerations), and the details of each type. In .NET, types inside the System.Reflection namespace provide services to examine the types and get all the necessary information for using each type. In addition, types inside the System.Reflection namespace enable you to obtain that information programmatically. In fact, Visual Studio's Object Browser uses the types inside the System.Reflection namespace to list all information about types. *Reflection* is an advanced topic in .NET programming, and it is outside the scope of this book. But if you are familiar with reflection, you can create a simple application that automatically finds members that enable the relationship between types.

.NET Reflector (`http://www.reflector.net`) and ILSpy (`http://wiki.sharpdevelop.net/ILSpy.ashx`) are two famous tools which use reflection to provide access to a type's metadata. These two tools provide all the information (and many more features) provided by Visual Studio's Object Browser, but in a friendlier fashion. Also custom add-ins can be developed for both tools to add custom functionality. One interesting add-in (Assembly Visualizer), developed by Denis Markelov, provides a friendly visual representation of each member. You can download this add-in from `http://www.denismarkelov.com/p/assembly-visualizer.html`. This add-in is available for both ILSpy and Reflector. You can see ILSpy in Figure 5-20.

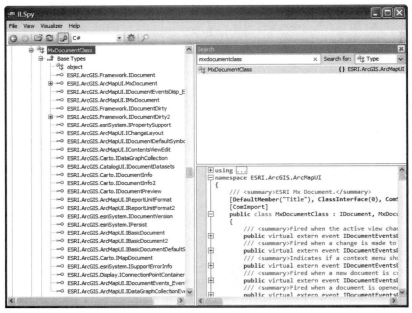

FIGURE 5-20

As you can see, ILSpy shows the data type of each property and the signature of each method for each type. Download ILSpy from `http://wiki.sharpdevelop.net/ILSpy.ashx`. In order to use the Assembly Visualizer add-in, first download the add-in (which is a `.dll` file) and just copy the downloaded add-in file beside the executable file (`ILSpy.exe`) of the ILSpy software. The add-in adds some context menu items to ILSpy. You can search for any type by selecting the Search item from the View menu. The following Try It Out uses ILSpy with the plug-in downloaded to discover the member in the `MxDocument` class that enables the relationship between the `MxDocument` and `Map` Classes.

TRY IT OUT   **Using ILSpy to Explore the Relationship between the MxDocument and Map Classes**

1. Run ILSpy by double-clicking on the `ILSpy.exe` file.

2. Add two assemblies that contain the `MxDocument` and `Map` Classes. From the File menu, select the Open item. Navigate to `<ArcGIS installation folder>\DeveloperKit10.1\DotNet` and select `ESRI.ArcGIS.ArcMapUI.dll` and `ESRI.ArcGIS.Carto.dll`, then click the Open button.

3. Click the Search button on the main toolbar or press F3. Enter the `MxDocumentClass` into the search box. You will notice that as you type, results are filtered accordingly. Double-click on the first result (see Figure 5-21).

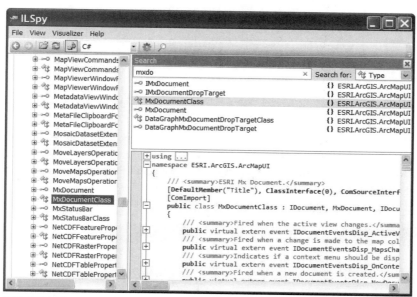

FIGURE 5-21

4. Right-click on the MxDocumentClass in the Catalog list on the left-hand side and select Browse Ancestry from the context menu. A new window pops up, which shows all the members of `MxDocument` and its parent. As shown in Figure 5-22, in the box above the window enter `Map` to filter out the members using the entered string.

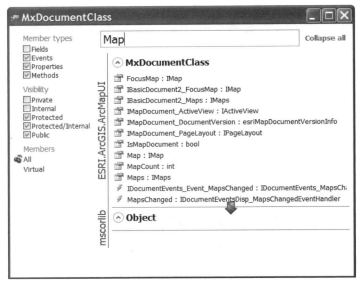

FIGURE 5-22

5. As you can see, the FocusMap property is of type IMap. For ensuring that the Map class also implements the IMap interface, you can search for MapClass in ILSpy, as shown in Figure 5-23. So
enter MapClass in the Search textbox of ILSpy. As you can see, there are two MapClass items in
the search results. Double-click the MapClass that resides in the ESRI.ArcGIS.Carto namespace.
Then expand its Base Types node to see its interfaces.

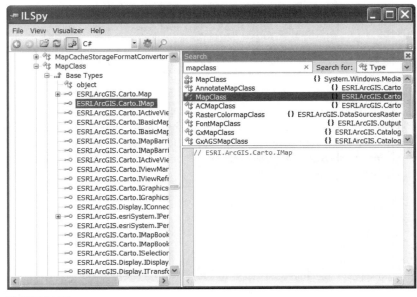

FIGURE 5-23

How It Works

Tools such as ILSpy provide friendlier ways to explore types and the relationships between types. ILSpy is faster than Visual Studio's Object Browser and also consumes less computer memory. It provides a signature for methods and the data type of properties in a more efficient manner. Searching for types is easier in ILSpy than in Visual Studio's Object Browser. There are also several free and useful add-ins for ILSpy.

Developing ArcObjects using any technology involves finding relevant types in ArcObjects and making use of those types to perform the task at hand. Although Microsoft is the creator of COM and .NET, they are two distinct technologies. Therefore there are many tips and tricks to working with COM-based ArcObjects in .NET.

As an important point of using ArcObjects in .NET, all classes of ArcObjects have the same name as in the object model diagrams, with "Class" appended. For example, the MxDocument class is converted to MxDocumentClass in .NET and SelectionSet is converted to SelectionSetClass. This is why you searched for MxDocumentClass in the preceding Try It Out.

SUMMARY

In this chapter, you learned the nuts and bolts of ArcObjects types using ArcGIS Developer Help. As special part of ArcGIS Developer Help, object model diagrams illustrate the interfaces that are implemented by various classes inside the ArcObjects, members of main interfaces of each class, and the relationships between classes. This chapter also covered the special visual symbols and notations used in object model diagrams. Now you understand the most important details of object model diagrams, but a few advanced details will be covered later in this book where appropriate. Finally in this chapter, you saw how working with tools such as Visual Studio's Object Browser and ILSpy can simplify the process of ArcObjects development.

EXERCISES

1. What are the types of Classes in ArcObjects?

2. What is a type inheritance relationship?

3. What is interface inheritance?

4. What is the main entry point to ArcObjects development in code?

You will find the answers to these exercises in this book's appendix.

▶ **WHAT YOU LEARNED IN THIS CHAPTER**

TOPIC	KEY CONCEPTS
Interface	Interfaces are a named set of abstract (not implemented) properties, methods, and events. Interfaces are mainly used for implementing an evolving software system. One of the main standards for interface-based software development is Microsoft COM. Microsoft COM is the basis for ArcObjects. ArcObjects types are accessed using their interfaces.
Members of an interface	The properties, methods, and events of an interface are the members of that interface. In addition, if one interface is inherited by another interface, the members of the parent interface are also members of the child interface.
Exploring relationships between types	In order to explore the relationships between types, you have to make use of object model diagrams. In all relationships, there are always one or more members (property, method, or event) in one participant that enable the relationship between two types.

Accessing Maps and Layers

➤ Exploring object model diagrams for accessing maps and layers

➤ Working with enums

➤ General characteristics of layers

➤ A first look at the FeatureLayer and RasterLayer CoClasses

➤ Adding a *.lyr file to a map

➤ Showing and tweaking the Add Data dialogbox

➤ Saving *.lyr and *.mxd files

WROX.COM CODE DOWNLOADS FOR THIS CHAPTER

The wrox.com code downloads for this chapter are found at www.wrox.com/remtitle .cgi?isbn=0123456789 on the Download Code tab. The code is in the Chapter06 folder and individually named according to the names throughout the chapter.

In Chapter 5, you learned the necessary skills for interpreting object model diagrams and finding related types in the ArcObjects system. In this chapter, you use those skills to study how to access Data Frames and the layers inside them in the ArcMap application. You will also learn how to work with *.mxd and *.lyr files.

INTRODUCTION TO MAPS AND LAYERS IN ARCOBJECTS

A map document (MxDocument instance) is composed of maps (Map instances) and layers (Layer instances). Maps are containers of layers, and layers provide a flexible way for representing geospatial data. Layers don't contain geospatial data; instead, they point to where geospatial data are stored. Layers are rendered in a specific order displayed in the map's table of contents. When a geospatial data item (such as a shapefile, a feature class of a geodatabase, or a satellite image) is added to a map, a temporary `Layer` object is created in memory. Based on the added geospatial data, the `Layer` object can be of various types, such as `FeatureLayer` and `RasterLayer`.

The `MxDocument` instance can stay temporarily in memory or be saved as an `*.mxd` file. Specifications for the contents of an `MxDocument` (maps and layers) comprise the most important information inside an `MxDocument` instance. Information such as the number of maps, the active map, and the number of layers inside each map can be extracted from the properties of a live `MxDocument` instance. Also, actions such as adding a layer to the active Data Frame can be done by a live instance of an `MxDocument` CoClass. All in all, the `MxDocument` CoClass is the central point in accessing maps and layers.

Same as an `MxDocument` instance, `Layer` instances also can be saved as `*.lyr` files. Similar to in-memory `Layer` instances, the `*.lyr` files just point to geospatial data and contain the necessary information that specifies how to render geospatial data.

Figure 6-1 provides a simplified diagram for accessing maps and layers. In this figure, the most commonly used interfaces of each type are presented. Feel free to explore other interfaces on your own.

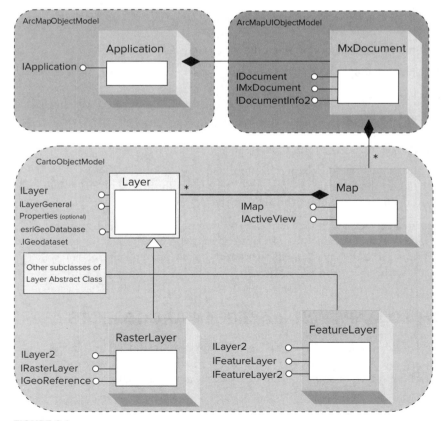

FIGURE 6-1

> **NOTE** As discussed in Chapter 5, there is virtually no difference between the entry point to the ArcObjects system using Desktop Add-Ins and the Extending ArcObjects project templates in Visual Studio. Most examples throughout this book are based on the Desktop Add-Ins template. In special cases when using one template is easier, the easier template will be discussed first and then differences with the other template will be explained.

The `Document` property of the `IApplication` object points to the `IDocument` interface. So to get to the `IMxDocument` interface all that is required is to cast from `IDocument` to `IMxDocument`. If you use the Desktop Add-Ins project template, the code for performing this task would be similar to the following code snippet:

```
IDocument doc = ArcMap.Application.Document;
//casting interface to get to IMxDocument
IMxDocument mxdoc = doc as IMxDocument;
```

`IMxDocument` has a property that enables the composition relationship with the `Map` CoClass. (Chapter 5 discusses this property.) The type of this property is `IMap` and it points to the active Data Frame in the Table Of Contents window.

```
IMap map = mxdoc.FocusMap;
```

If there is one map inside `MxDocument`, the `FocusMap` property points to that map. Sometimes an `MxDocument` contains more than one map. The `Maps` property must be used in order to access all maps inside an `MxDocument` instance. As the name suggests, this property behaves like a collection and provides members for iterating through each map.

```
IMaps maps = mxdoc.Maps;
for (int i = 0; i< maps.Count; i++)
{
    IMap map = maps.get_Item(i);
}
```

To access the active Data Frame (`FocusMap`) in this case, use the `IActiveView` interface of the `Map` CoClass. The `IActiveView` interface controls all rendering operations in the main window of ArcMap. This interface provides the `IsActive()` method, which returns a `bool` value indicating whether a `Map` object has focus (the Data Frame is activated) or not.

```
IMaps maps = mxdoc.Maps;
for (int i = 0; i< maps.Count; i++)
{
    IMap map = maps.get_Item(i);
    IActiveView activeView = map as IActiveView;

    if (activeView.IsActive() == true)
    {
        //do something with focus map
    } else
    {
        //do something with other maps
    }
}
```

> **NOTE** *Like the COM specification, the .NET platform has some predefined interfaces such as* `ICloneable`, `IEnumerable`, *and* `IComparer`. *Any class that implements these interfaces gets useful capabilities similar to those that internal .NET types have. For example, any collection-like class that implements* `IEnumerable` *or* `IEnumerator` *can provide the capability to iterate through its members using a* `foreach` *construct. The* `IEnumerator` *interface is implemented for all arrays of simple types as well as most collection types (generic and non-generic) in .NET. But unfortunately, neither the* `IEnumerable` *nor* `IEnumerator` *interfaces are implemented for collections inside ArcObjects. For this reason, the following code results in a compiler error.*

```
foreach (IMap map in maps)
{
//do something with map
}
```

As is true for an `MxDocument` instance that provides a collection for its comprising maps, each `Map` instance has members such as `Layer` and `Layer` properties to access its containing layers. The following Try It Out illustrates how to use those members.

TRY IT OUT   **Accessing Layers of Maps (LayersOfMaps.zip)**

1. Run Visual Studio and start a new project. Ensure that you have selected .NET Framework 3.5 as the target platform. In the New Project window, expand the Visual C# ⇨ ArcGIS node and select ArcMap Add-in from the Desktop Add-Ins templates. Provide **LayersOfMaps** as the name of the add-in and solution, and click the OK button.

2. The ArcGIS Add-Ins Wizard window is shown. Enter your information (see Figure 6-2) and click the Next button.

FIGURE 6-2

3. Select Button as the type of add-in and provide the necessary information as shown in Figure 6-3. Click the Finish button.

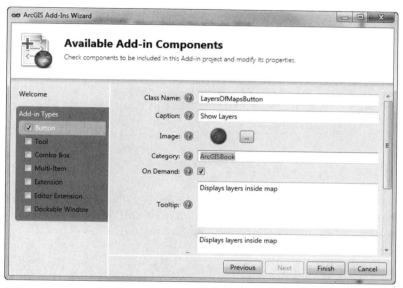

FIGURE 6-3

4. Adding necessary references is the first task to do. So from the Solution Explorer window inside Visual Studio, right-click on the References folder and select the Add ArcGIS Reference item. Add the ESRI.ArcGIS.Carto reference from the Desktop ArcMap folder to the project (This reference is needed to access Map and Layer objects in ArcMap).

5. In Solution Explorer, double-click the Button class (LayersOfMapsButton.cs) and add the following using directives at the top of the code:

```
using ESRI.ArcGIS.ArcMapUI;
using ESRI.ArcGIS.Carto;
using ESRI.ArcGIS.Framework;
```

6. Right-click on the project (LayersOfMaps) in Solution Explorer, and from the Add menu choose the Windows Form item as shown in Figure 6-4. In the Add New Item window, change the name of the form from Form1.cs to **Message.cs** and click the Add button.

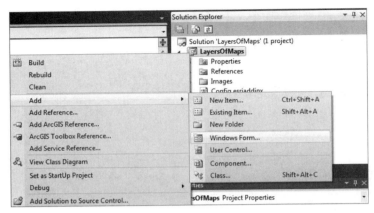

FIGURE 6-4

7. Add a Label control to the newly added form by double-clicking the Label item on the Toolbox window. If the Toolbox window is hidden, you can turn it on using the View menu. Select the label and change its name to **lbl**, AutoSize to False, and Size to 280;280 (width=280 and height=280) in the Properties window in Visual Studio.

8. Because you want to access the Label control (lbl) from outside the Windows Form (actually from outside the `Message.cs` class), you have to change its `Modifiers` property to Public or Internal. So change that property to Public as shown in Figure 6-5.

9. Double-click the Button class (`LayersOfMapsButton.cs`), then add the necessary code inside the click event handler to iterate through all `Layer` objects, and list the name of each `Layer` object in the Label control of the Message form. The following code uses both the `LayerCount` and `Layers` properties to iterate through all layers inside a map:

FIGURE 6-5

```
protected override void OnClick()
{
    string data = "";

    IDocument doc = ArcMap.Application.Document;
    IMxDocument mxDoc = doc as IMxDocument;

    IMap map = mxDoc.FocusMap;
    //using layerCount property
    data += "Using LayerCount Property \n";

    ILayer layer;
    for (int i = 0; i < map.LayerCount; i++)
    {
        layer = map.Layer[i];
```

```
        data += " >> " +layer.Name + "\n";
    }
    //Terminating layer object
    layer = null;
    data += string.Format("{0} Map contains {1} Layers\n", map.Name,
    map.LayerCount);
    data += "--------------------------------------\n";
    data += "Using Layers Property \n";
    IEnumLayer enumLayer = map.Layers;
    layer = enumLayer.Next();
    int j = 0;
    while (layer != null)
    {
        j++;
        data += " >> " + layer.Name + "\n";
        layer = enumLayer.Next();
    }
    data += string.Format("{0} Map contains {1} Layers", map.Name, j);

    Message msgForm = new Message();
    msgForm.lbl.Text = data;
    msgForm.ShowDialog();

}
```

10. Right-click on the project in Solution Explorer. Select Properties as shown in Figure 6-6 or press Alt+Enter when the project is selected in Solution Explorer to display a new tab in Visual Studio.

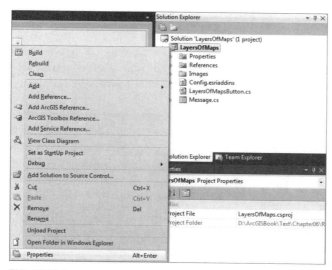

FIGURE 6-6

11. The newly opened tab is called Project Designer and contains settings for the project. Go to the Debug page shown in Figure 6-7.

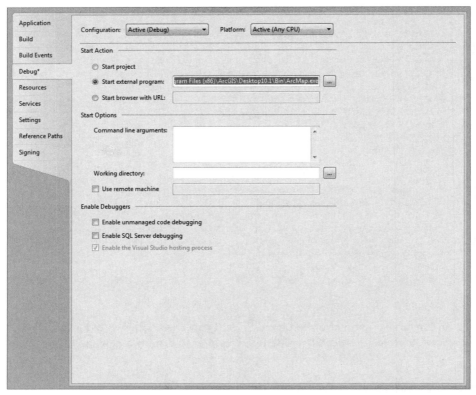

FIGURE 6-7

12. As you can see, ArcMap is set as the external program. This means that when you press F5 (or Start Debugging your project), Visual Studio runs ArcMap and listens to its events to debug your code. Because ArcGIS can be installed in different locations on various computers, whenever you get a Visual Studio solution for an ArcGIS project from other developers you have to check that ArcMap is set as the external program.

13. Press F5 to test your code. A few seconds later, ArcMap comes up. In both the Desktop Add-Ins and Extending ArcObjects project templates, you have to use the Customize window to test the functionality of your project. In ArcMap, select Customize Mode from the Customize menu. Remember that you set ArcGISBook as the category of your add-in button. So in the Commands tab, find the ArcGISBook Category as shown in Figure 6-8.

FIGURE 6-8

14. Select the Show Layers button from the Commands list and drag and drop it onto one of the existing toolbars. Notice that while dragging the button, the mouse cursor has a small "x" indicating that the current location of the cursor is not a valid place to drop the button. As you put the mouse cursor over somewhere that can be used as the command container (such as any toolbar or menu), the small "x" changes to a small "+" indicating that you can drop the button to add it. Also, as you learned in Chapter 2, you can use the Add-In Manager in ArcMap for this task.

15. Add some layers to your map and test the functionality of the button. Figure 6-9 displays a map containing some layers from the `TemplateData.gdb` file geodatabase that ships with ArcGIS.

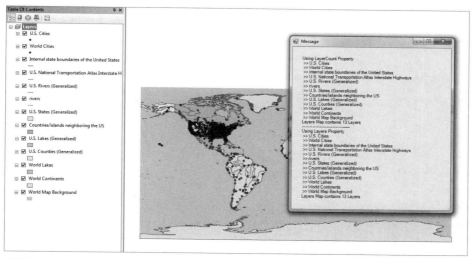

FIGURE 6-9

How It Works

You used two properties of the Map class to iterate through the layers it contains. The Layers property of the Map class is of type `IEnumLayer`. Generally speaking, `Enums` in ArcObjects are similar to `Reader` objects in .NET. If you look at the code for reading a text file using a `StreamReader` object, you will find many similarities in how you write code.

```
string oneLineOfData = sr.ReadLine();
while (oneLineOfData != null)
{
    //code to process a line of data goes here
    oneLineOfData = sr.ReadLine();
}
```

You always use the following pattern in working with `Enums`.

```
//Initializing the Enum object
IEnumLayer enumLayer = map.Layers;
//Use the next method for getting the first item in the enum
```

```
    layer = enumLayer.Next();

    //Using a while loop to iterate through all containing members
    while (layer != null)
    {
        //work with the members
        //use the Next() method to point to the next member
        layer = enumLayer.Next();
    }
```

At this point, it seems that both methods of working with layers inside a map are equal. But this is not the case when there is at least a group layer (GroupLayer CoClass) in the Data Frame. As you may know, a group layer is a special kind of Layer subclass that can contain other layers (even other group layers) and it is primarily used for organizing related layers. Compare Figure 6-9 with Figure 6-10 to see the difference between the results of the two methods to access layers inside a map when there are multiple group layers.

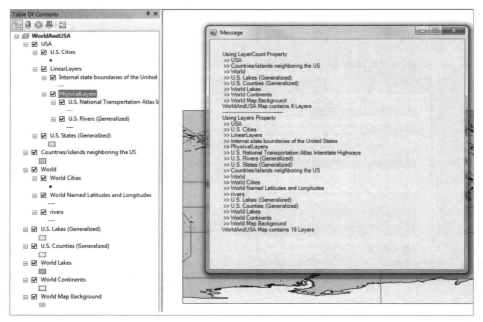

FIGURE 6-10

As you can see, by using the first method (the LayerCount property) you can only access the first level layers. With the second method (by using the Layers property), you can access all layers. So it is always more efficient and safe to use the Layers property and IEnumLayer object to iterate through all layers.

NOTE *If you want to use the Extending ArcObjects project template for the preceding Try It Out, you have to select the Class Library (ArcMap) item after selecting the Extending ArcObjects template. Then use the ArcGIS Project Wizard to add the required ArcGIS references.*

Visual Studio adds a new class file, but interestingly you don't need the created class file. Right-click on the project, and then select Add New Item from the Add submenu. Next, select the Base Command component from the list of available components when Extending ArcObjects has been chosen. Finally, choose the Desktop ArcMap Command as the type of command to be created. That is it!

An Enum object in ArcObjects contains a group of similar items much like a generic collection stores similar type objects in .NET. But the former has many subtle differences with all collections. Since an Enum object just provides Next() and Reset() methods (and no properties), there is only one way to access items inside an Enum object. But working with Enum objects is more efficient than working with arrays or collections in terms of memory consumption.

When an Enum is initialized, a pointer (which is controlled by the Enum object) is pointing above the first item in the Enum. As items are brought out of the Enum using the Next() method, the pointer points to the successive position in the Enum. Later in this book, you will see that all Enum objects have basically the same methods for working with contained items. There are several Enum interfaces inside ArcObjects, each named after the type of object it contains. For example, IEnumLayer contains ILayer objects and IEnumElement contains IElement objects. As the name suggests, the Reset() method brings back the pointer above the first item in the Enum.

GENERAL PROPERTIES OF ALL LAYERS

The ILayer interface is defined as the ultimate parent class of all types of layers (Layer Abstract Class). As a result, all types of layers are inherited by the ILayer interface. In other words, all the members of the ILayer interface can be seen in the Property window (the last item when you right-click on a layer in the Table Of Contents window) of all Layer types. At this point, you just use the Name property of this interface. The ILayer interface has more interesting properties than Name. Figure 6-11 shows the properties of the ILayer interface.

```
ILayer : IUnknown

■—    AreaOfInterest: IEnvelope
■—■   Cached: Boolean
■—■   MaximumScale: Double
■—■   MinimumScale: Double
■—■   Name: String
■—■   ShowTips: Boolean
—□    SpatialReference: ISpatialReference
■—    SupportedDrawPhases: Long
■—    TipText (in x: Double, in y: Double, in
            Tolerance: Double): String
■—    Valid: Boolean
■—■   Visible: Boolean
```

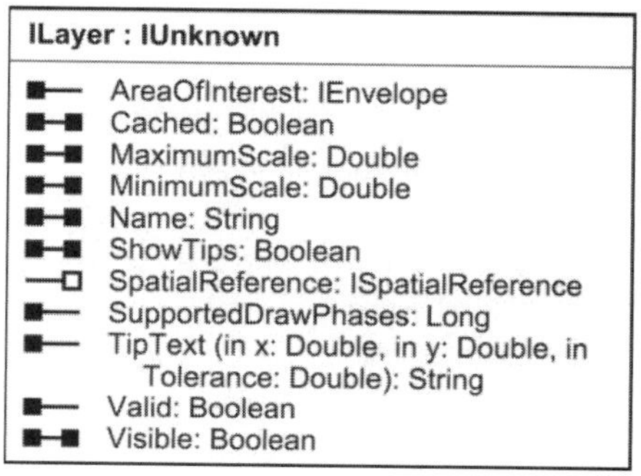

FIGURE 6-11

As you can see, the first property (AreaOfInterest) defines the minimum bounding rectangle of the Layer instance. This property is of type IEnvelope, which is defined in the Geometry library. All geometry objects have an associated envelope that is defined by the XMin, XMax, YMin, and YMax properties of the object. In fact, when you zoom into the specific layer or feature in ArcMap, you are looking at the minimum bounding rectangle of that object. In other words, ArcMap sets the minimum bounding box of the object as the extent of the main window of ArcMap.

As mentioned previously in this chapter, the IActiveView interface that is implemented by the Map CoClass controls all rendering operations in the main window of ArcMap. So if a code snippet makes any change in the representation of geospatial data (in the main window of ArcMap), you have to invoke the Refresh() method of the IActiveView interface. The following code can be used to zoom into the selected layer in the Table Of Contents:

```
IMxDocument mxdoc = ArcMap.Application.Document as IMxDocument;
    //the following two lines of code are the same
    IActiveView activeView = mxdoc.ActiveView;
    //IActiveView activeView = mxdoc.FocusMap as IActiveView;

    //get the selected layer in TOC
    ILayer layer = mxdoc.SelectedLayer;

    //check if there is a selected layer or not
    if (layer != null)
    {
        activeView.Extent = layer.AreaOfInterest;
        //invoking Refresh method
        //results in redrawing the whole view
        activeView.Refresh();
    }
```

Note that the selected layer in the Table Of Contents might not be in the active Data Frame.

In addition to Name and AreaOfInterest, you can use the MinimumScale, MaximumScale, ShowTips, and Visible properties to control the display of all types of layers. The following code snippet finds the layer with the name of U.S. Cities and changes some of its display properties and then makes all other layers invisible.

```
IMxDocument mxdoc = ArcMap.Application.Document as IMxDocument;
IMap map = mxdoc.FocusMap;

for (int i = 0; i < map.LayerCount; i++)
{
    if (map.Layer[i].Name.ToLower() == "u.s. cities")
    {
        ILayer usCities = map.Layer[i];
        usCities.Name = "Cities of the U.S";
        usCities.ShowTips = true;
        usCities.Visible = true;
        usCities.MaximumScale = 2500000;
    }
    else
    {
        map.Layer[i].Visible = false;
    }
        }
IActiveView activeView = map as IActiveView;
activeView.Refresh();
mxdoc.UpdateContents();
```

The preceding code snippet changes the Table Of Contents window of ArcMap by modifying the visibility of layers. So you have to call the UpdateContents() method of the IMxDocument interface. The Table Of Contents window of ArcMap contains multiple tabs or contents views. The first contents view in the Table Of Contents window is the Display contents view. It lists layers based on their drawing order. You can access a specific contents view by using the `get_ContentsView()` method of the `IMxDocument` interface. So as an alternative approach for refreshing the Display contents view, you can use the following line of code:

```
mxdoc.get_ContentsView(0).Refresh(null);
```

In this case, you have to provide an index to get to the specific tab in the Table of Contents window of ArcMap. As mentioned previously in this chapter, the Display tab is always the first tab. Note that using this approach just refreshes the specific tab in the Table of Contents window.

As previously mentioned, all types of layers implement the `ILayer` interface; as a result, all members of this interface are available to them. If you explore the Carto object model, you can see that the `Layer` Abstract Class has a few optional interfaces. Put simply, optional interfaces are the interfaces that can be optionally implemented by subclasses such as `ILayerGeneralProperties`. As you can see in Figure 6-12, optional interfaces are identified by the word "Optional" in object model diagrams.

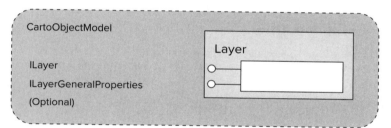

FIGURE 6-12

Any subclass that implements the optional interface lists it on an object model diagram. This way, you can easily check the implementation of any optional interface by a specific class in ArcObjects.

`ILayerGeneralProperties` is a simple but useful interface that provides three properties for most types of layers. Among the three properties, `LayerDescription` offers a lovely placeholder for describing anything related to the layer. This property is more useful for saved layer files (`*.lyr`) than for temporary in-memory `Layer` objects. The following code snippet uses this property to set the opening time for the U.S. Cities layer:

```
IMxDocument mxdoc = ArcMap.Application.Document as IMxDocument;
IMap map = mxdoc.FocusMap;
for (int i = 0; i < map.LayerCount; i++)
{
    if (map.Layer[i].Name.ToLower() == "u.s. cities")
    {
        ILayer usCities = map.Layer[i];
        ILayerGeneralProperties usGProperties = usCities as
        ILayerGeneralProperties;
        usGProperties.LayerDescription = "This layer is opened on:" +
        DateTime.Now.ToLongTimeString();
    }
}
```

Another interface which can be found on the `Layer` Abstract Class is `IGeoDataset`. This interface is defined in the Geodatabase library and can be found in the Geodatabase object model diagram. This is why its name is followed by esriGeoDatabase, as shown in Figure 6-13.

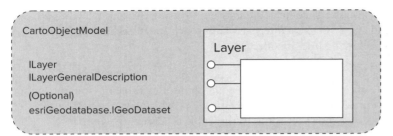

FIGURE 6-13

Using this interface, you can access the spatial reference of all layers. Consider the following code, which writes some information regarding the spatial reference in the layer description field of the U.S. Cities layer.

```
for (int i = 0; i < map.LayerCount; i++)
{
    if (map.Layer[i].Name.ToLower() == "u.s. cities")
    {
        ILayer usCities = map.Layer[i];
        ILayerGeneralProperties usGProperties = usCities as
        ILayerGeneralProperties;

        IGeoDataset usGDSet = usCities as IGeoDataset;
        usGProperties.LayerDescription += " SRS of this layer is " +
        usGDSet.SpatialReference.Name;
        usGProperties.LayerDescription += "\r\n" +" Well known ID of
        this SRS is " + usGDSet.SpatialReference.FactoryCode;
}
```

> **NOTE** Since the IGeoDataset interface is defined in the esriGeodatabase
> library, you have to add that library to your project references. In addi-
> tion, to avoid typing the fully qualified name of this interface (ESRI.ArcGIS.
> Geodatabase.IGeoDataset), you can take advantage of the using directive
> (using ESRI.ArcGIS.Geodatabase).

Also you can use the IGeoDataset interface to zoom into a specific layer using its Extent property, as shown in the following snippet. As you may guess, there are several methods to do the same task in ArcObjects.

```
activeView.Extent = usGDSet.Extent;
```

So far you have seen how easy it is to use the ILayer, IGeneralProperties, and IGeoDataset interfaces. Also you have learned about optional interfaces as an additional tip on reading object model diagrams. In general, ILayer is a standard interface to work with all layer types. However, the ILayer interface is superseded by the ILayer2 interface. This means if you want your ArcObjects code to work with future versions of ArcGIS, you have to consider working with the ILayer2 interface instead of ILayer. In addition to all the members of the ILayer interface, the ILayer2 defines a property (ScaleRangeReadOnly) that indicates whether or not the scale range properties are read-only. Besides, the `AreaOfInterest` property of the `ILayer2` interface is a two-headed barbell, which means it is a read and write property.

In contrast to `ILayer`, `ILayer2` is not defined on the `Layer` Abstract Class. Quite the contrary, it is implemented directly by most `Layer` types, such as `RasterLayer` and `FeatureLayer` CoClasses. An interesting fact about the `ILayer2` interface is that it is not implemented for all layer types. For example, if you deal with `KMLLayer` (in the GlobeCore library) and `WCSLayer` (in the Carto library) you can see that the `ILayer2` interface is not implemented for these two layer types.

WORKING WITH FEATURELAYERS

`FeatureLayers` are one of the most common types of layers in ArcGIS. A `FeatureLayer` points to vector data of the same geometry type (point, polyline, polygon, and so forth) in a single spatial reference system and with a common set of attributes. A `FeatureLayer` is based on a vector-based dataset that is called a `FeatureClass`. Examples of `FeatureClasses` are `Shapefiles` and Feature Classes in a Geodatabase. Figure 6-14 illustrates the detailed inheritance hierarchy for a `FeatureLayer` CoClass. As you might expect, all the interfaces of all parent classes in this hierarchy are implemented by the `FeatureLayer` CoClass; as a result, all the interfaces are available for use.

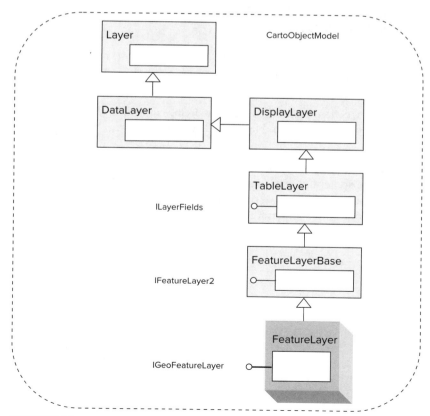

FIGURE 6-14

In previous versions of ArcObjects, the IFeatureLayer was the main interface for working with general aspects of FeatureLayer instances. In the current version of ArcObjects, the IFeatureLayer interface is superseded by IFeatureLayer2. As you might expect, IFeatureLayer2 provides all members of the IFeatureLayer interface as well as a method and a read-only property — ShapeType. The ShapeType property is of type esriGeometryType enumeration. This enumeration is defined in the Geometry library of ArcObjects and contains 20 distinct types of geometry that can be used to construct a geometry object.

As the name implies, the ILayerFields interface that is defined by the TableLayer Abstract Class provides an easy way to access fields of table-based layers. This interface provides the FieldCount property, which indicates the number of fields or columns inside the attribute table of a FeatureLayer. In addition to FieldCount, it provides Field and FieldInfo properties to access the columns at a specified index. The Field class is defined in the Geodatabase library. As a result, if there is a need to use the Field object (for example, using the Field property of the ILayerFields interface) the Geodatabase reference must be added to the project.

The IGeoFeatureLayer interface provides access to rendering properties for FeatureLayers. If you look at the IGeoFeatureLayer interface in a Carto object model diagram or examine it with ILSpy or Reflector, you will notice that this interface inherits from IFeatureLayer. In the following Try It Out, you inspect the general properties of FeatureLayers.

TRY IT OUT **Inspecting General Properties of FeatureLayers (FeatureLayerInspector.zip)**

1. Open the LayersOfMaps add-in solution that you created in a previous Try It Out. In the Solution Explorer window of Visual Studio, right-click on the project and choose New Item from the Add menu.

2. Expand the Visual C# Items ⇨ ArcGIS node in the Add New Item window, click Desktop Add-Ins, and choose the add-in component item. Name the component **FeatureLayerInspector**, and then click the Add button.

3. In the ArcGIS Add-Ins Wizard, choose Button as the type of add-in if it was not chosen already for you and change its caption to something meaningful like **General Properties of FeatureLayers**. As a convention for this book, set the Category of the add-in as **ArcGISBook**. Provide an image for your button and change its tooltip to some useful text. Finally, click the Finish button.

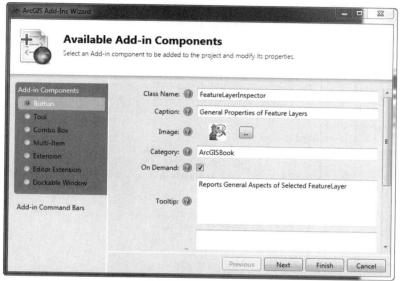

FIGURE 6-15

4. Visual Studio adds the necessary lines of code for the newly added component to the projects. As always in ArcObjects programming, the first step is to add necessary references and using directives. Because you want to use the classes in the Carto namespace, you have to add this ArcGIS reference to your project. Fortunately, you added this reference in the previous Try It Out. Because you want to take advantage of the ShapeType property of IFeatureLayer2 and the Field property of ILayerFields, in addition to the Carto namespace you have to add references for the Geometry and Geodatabase libraries, respectively. So right-click on the References folder in Solution Explorer and select the Add ArcGIS Reference item.

5. In the Add ArcGIS Reference window, expand the Desktop ArcMap tree, and select the ESRI .ArcGIS.Geometry item. Then click Add. Do the same for the ESRI.ArcGIS.Geodatabase item. Click Finish.

6. Add the following lines of code on top of the class file of your newly added add-in button (FeatureLayerInspector.cs) to make your life a little bit easier.

```
using ESRI.ArcGIS.ArcMapUI;
using ESRI.ArcGIS.Carto;
using ESRI.ArcGIS.Geodatabase;
using ESRI.ArcGIS.Geometry;
```

7. You want to report the general properties of the selected FeatureLayer in the Table Of Contents window. In addition, you want to make use of the labeling feature of ArcMap in its simplest form using IGeoFeatureLayer. So add the following code in the OnClick() method of the newly added button in the FeatureLayerInspector.cs file:

```
string data = "";
IMxDocument mxdoc = ArcMap.Application.Document as IMxDocument;
ILayer selectedLayer = mxdoc.SelectedLayer;

if (selectedLayer != null)
```

```
        {
            if (selectedLayer is IFeatureLayer2)
            {
                //using IFeatureLayer2 interface
                IFeatureLayer2 selectedFL = selectedLayer as IFeatureLayer2;
                data += "Data Source Type: " + selectedFL.DataSourceType + "\n";
                data += "Shape Type: " + selectedFL.ShapeType + "\n";
                data += "Is Selectable? " + selectedFL.Selectable + "\n";
                data += "Primary Display Field: " + selectedFL.DisplayField + "\n";

                //using ILayerFields interface
                ILayerFields selectedLayerFields = selectedFL as ILayerFields;
                data += "field count: " + selectedLayerFields.FieldCount + "\n";
                data += "Third Field Name: " + selectedLayerFields.Field[2].Name;

                //using IGeoFeatureLayer interface
                IGeoFeatureLayer selectedGFL = selectedFL as IGeoFeatureLayer;
                //toggle labeling for selected layer
                if (selectedGFL.DisplayAnnotation == true)
                {
                    selectedGFL.DisplayAnnotation = false;
                }
                else
                {
                    selectedGFL.DisplayAnnotation = true;
                }

                //since you modify rendering of the map by toggling labeling
                //you have to refresh the main window of ArcMap
                mxdoc.ActiveView.Refresh();

                Message msgForm = new Message();
                msgForm.lbl.Text = data;
                msgForm.ShowDialog();
            }

        }
```

8. Run your code and then use the Customize window in ArcMap to add your new button to somewhere pertinent and test the button's functionality. Select a layer in the Table Of Contents window and click the button to see some properties of the layer.

How It Works

You used the `SelectedLayer` property of the `IMxDocument` interface to get to the single selected layer in the Table Of Contents window. Because it is possible that the selected item in the Table Of Contents window is not of type `layer`, you have to check the `SelectedLayer` property against the null value.

To see whether or not the `SelectedLayer` is of type `IFeatureLayer2`, you used the `is` operator. In other words, to check the implementation of the `IFeatureLayer2` interface by the `SelectedLayer` object (is it an instance of the `FeatureLayer` CoClass or not?) you employed the `is` operator.

The interesting part of the code is the labeling part. As you see in the code, you didn't specify a field for labeling. In this case, the primary display field is used to make labels. The primary display field is the first string field that contains the literal name in its name (such as `StateName`, `CountyName`, and `name`). If no string field contains the literal name, the first string field is specified as the primary display field.

The `FeatureClass` property of `IFeatureLayer2` or the obsolete `IFeatureLayer` interfaces are the gate to access geospatial data represented by a `FeatureLayer`. You see this property in action in the next chapters.

WORKING WITH RASTERLAYERS

The other most common type of layer in ArcGIS is `RasterLayer`. All `RasterLayers` are represented as a two or more dimensional matrix of pixels of a `RasterDataset`. Each pixel in a `RasterLayer` contains a value that represents an average (or near average) value of a phenomenon covered by that pixel-like pollution, temperature, and reflection. Raster geospatial data comes from all kinds of photogrammetry and remote sensing resources as well as scanned paper documents like paper maps. Like `FeatureLayer`, `RasterLayer` has a long inheritance hierarchy (see Figure 6-16).

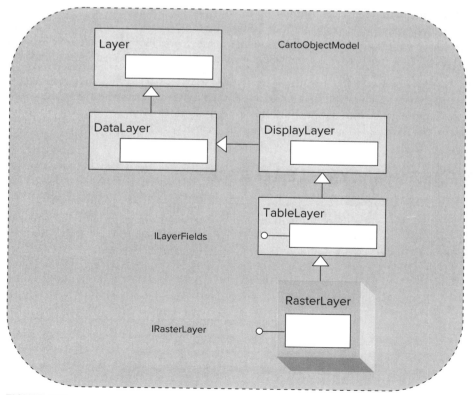

FIGURE 6-16

You can access general aspects of a `RasterLayer` using the `IRasterLayer` interface. The following code snippet performs a simple assessment for `RasterLayers` in the same way that the `FeatureLayerInspector` class does inspection for `FeatureLayers`.

```
string data = "";
IMxDocument mxdoc = ArcMap.Application.Document as IMxDocument;
ILayer selectedLayer = mxdoc.SelectedLayer;

if (selectedLayer != null)
{
    if (selectedLayer is IRasterLayer)
    {
        IRasterLayer selectedRL = selectedLayer as IRasterLayer;
        data += "Number of Bands: " + selectedRL.BandCount + "\n";
        data += "Number of Columns: " + selectedRL.ColumnCount + "\n";
        data += "Number of Rows: " + selectedRL.RowCount + "\n";
        data += "File Path: " + selectedRL.FilePath + "\n";
        data += "Is Pyramid Created? " + selectedRL.PyramidPresent;

        Message msgForm = new Message();
        msgForm.lbl.Text = data;
        msgForm.ShowDialog();
    }
}
```

To make use of this code, add another add-in button to your project and insert the preceding code into the newly added button's `OnClick()` method. To test the functionality of the code you can add an existing raster file to your map or download a satellite image from the web. The Earth Resources Observation and Science Center (EROS) of the USGS provides free satellite imagery for all around the world (`http://glovis.usgs.gov/`).

Same as the `FeatureClass` property of `IFeatureLayer`, the `Raster` property of `IRasterLayer` is the central gate to explore geospatial data behind this kind of layer. In other words, you get to the pixels that comprise the `RasterDataset` using the `Raster` property of the `IRasterLayer` interface.

ADDING AN EXISTING *.LYR FILE TO A MAP

As mentioned previously in this chapter, `Layer` instances can be saved as `*.lyr` files. Before discovering how to save layers of a map, you will explore the necessary steps for adding an existing `*.lyr` file to a map. The classes for adding existing `*.lyr` files are defined in the Catalog library of ArcObjects. Figure 6-17 illustrates a simplified object model diagram for this task.

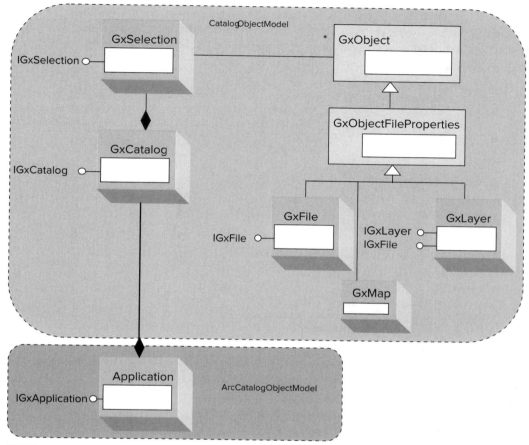

FIGURE 6-17

> **NOTE** *Everything related to ArcMap in ArcObjects contains the literal* Mx, *such as* IMxDocument *or* IMxdContents. *In turn, everything related to ArcCatalog has* Gx *in its name, such as* IGxCatalog *and* GxObject. Sx *and* GMx *play the same role for ArcScene and ArcGlobe, respectively. Regarding the explained theme, Figure 6-17 is part of the ArcCatalog and Catalog object model diagrams.*

For the time being, you need to concentrate on the right half of Figure 6-17. Items in the Catalog tree of ArcCatalog (which is available in ArcMap as well as ArcScene and ArcGlobe) represent multiple items such as files, disk connections, datasets, and so on. All the mentioned items are programmatically accessible by distinct and concrete subclasses of the GxObject Abstract Class such as GxFile and GxLayer.

For adding an existing *.lyr file to a map, an instance of IGxLayer must be used. The IGxLayer is defined by the GxLayer CoClass, so in order to instantiate it, use the following line of code:

```
            IGxLayer gxLayer = new GxLayerClass();
```

In addition to the `IGxLayer`, the `GxLayer` CoClass implements the `IGxFile` interface. The `IGxFile` interface has a `Path` property that can be used to specify the physical path of any `*.lyr` file. The following code explains all the steps for adding an existing `*.lyr` file to an active Data Frame:

```
            //creating a new IGxLayer instance
            IGxLayer gxLayer = new GxLayerClass();
            //cast the interface to IGxFile to
            //be able to use the Path property
            IGxFile gxFile = gxLayer as IGxFile;
            gxFile.Path = @"C:\cities.lyr";

            //make use of the Layer property of the IGxLayer instance
            ILayer layer = gxLayer.Layer as ILayer;

            if (layer != null)
            {//Add the layer to FocusMap

                //first method using IMxDocument
                IMxDocument mxdoc = ArcMap.Application.Document as IMxDocument;
                mxdoc.AddLayer(layer);

                //second method using IMap
                //IMap map = mxdoc.FocusMap;
                //map.AddLayer(layer);

                //update main window and TOC
                mxdoc.ActiveView.Refresh();
                mxdoc.UpdateContents();
            }
```

> **NOTE** In order to run the preceding code, the `ESRI.ArcGIS.Catalog` and `ESRI.ArcGIS.SystemUI` references and corresponding using directives must be added to the project.

As a related topic, it is also an easy task to open an existing `*.mxd` file using the `OpenDocument()` method of the `Application` property of the `ArcMap` static class.

```
            IMxDocument mxdoc = ArcMap.Application.Document as IMxDocument;
            string mapPath = @"C:\usa.mxd";
            ArcMap.Application.OpenDocument(mapPath);
```

ADDING *.LYR FILES USING GXDIALOG

Users of ArcGIS for Desktop applications often utilize the Add Data button as the first step to make use of geospatial and tabular datasets. Behind the scenes, the Add Data button initializes an `AddDataDialog` CoClass object and calls its `Show()` method. Figure 6-18 displays the small hierarchy of the `AddDataDialog` CoClass.

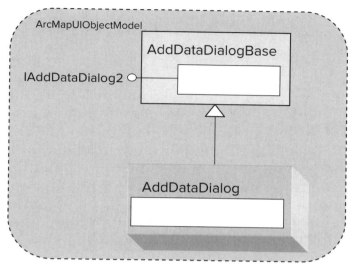

FIGURE 6-18

The following code shows the result of pressing the Add Data button:

```
IAddDataDialog2 addDataDialog = new AddDataDialogClass();
IMxDocument mxdoc = ArcMap.Application.Document as IMxDocument;
addDataDialog.Document = mxdoc;
addDataDialog.Map = mxdoc.FocusMap;

addDataDialog.Show(ArcMap.Application.hWnd, true);
```

All the properties of IAddDataDialog have to be set before calling the Show() method; otherwise, ArcGIS for Desktop applications will throw an exception.

Another important tip about the preceding code is the use of the hWnd property of the Application static property. Simply put, hWnd is an integer number that represents the window handle of an application in which the add-in is going to be executed. Think of it as a unique identifier of the executing application (for example, ArcMap). Sometimes your code needs to know this number to make the Windows kernel aware of the target application. You see this property several times in ArcObjects programming, especially when you want to open a window from within an ArcGIS for Desktop application.

> **NOTE** The IAddDataDialog interface and AddDataDialog CoClass are defined inside the ArcMapUI library. So make sure that you add the ESRI.ArcGIS .ArcMapUI reference to the project and its corresponding using directives in the code.

With the preceding code, users can select and add all supported data types to ArcGIS for Desktop applications. As always, developers need flexibility (for example, to permit users just to select one type of geospatial resource). In order to achieve that objective, developers should consult the Catalog and CatalogUI object model diagrams to find the required classes. Figure 6-19 illustrates a simplified view of the required classes.

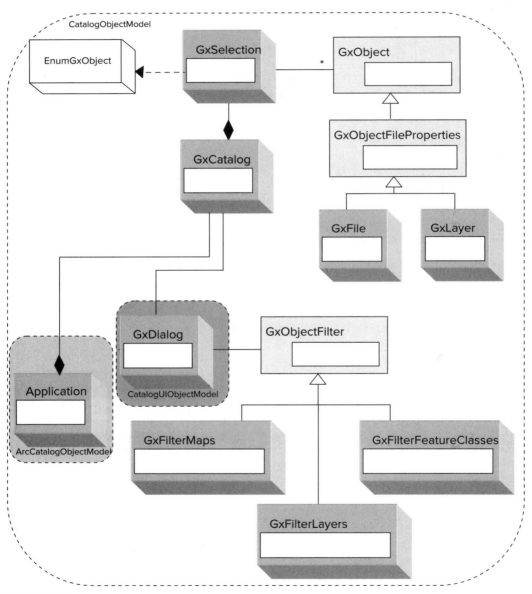

FIGURE 6-19

A central class in the diagram shown in Figure 6-19 is the GxDialog CoClass, which represents a dialog box for adding all kinds of geospatial resources. This class may have a filter object of type GxObjectFilter. The GxObjectFilter Abstract Class has as many concrete subclasses as the number of geospatial data types and datasets that ArcGIS can work with (and even more). For example, GxFilterMaps is for showing only those files with an .mxd extension and GxFilterTextFiles is for filtering out all files except *.txt files.

The GxDialog CoClass is associated with the GxCatalog CoClass by its InternalCatalog property. The GxCatalog CoClass represents the actual tree of geospatial data and resources. Among all the capabilities of the GxCatalog class, because this CoClass implements IGxObject and IGxObjectContainer interfaces it can contain other GxCatalog instances. It also can be contained by other GxCatalog instances. A file geodatabase which contains some feature classes, a folder full of shapefiles, and a toolbox with a set of geoprocessing tools are all GxCatalog instances.

Through the GxSelection CoClass, selected GxObjects of a GxCatalog instance can be accessed. As you have seen before, GxFile and GxLayer are two subclasses of the GxObject Abstract Class.

The GxSelection CoClass instantiates EnumGxObject to iterate through all selected GxObjects in a GxCatalog.

That is it! At first it seems quite complicated but it isn't. In the following Try It Out, you build a button for showing a native ArcGIS Desktop window that restricts users to selecting and adding only *.lyr files.

TRY IT OUT   **Adding *.lyr Files Using GxDialog CoClass (UsingAddDataDialog.zip)**

1. Open the LayersOfMap solution. Add a new add-in component by choosing the add-in component item in the Add New Item window. Name this component ShowAddDialog.

2. In the Add-Ins Wizard, select Button as the type of add-in if it was not chosen already for you. Change its caption to Show Add Dialog and its category to ArcGISBook. It is a good idea to provide an image for your add-in. Click the Finish button.

3. Required classes for the task at hand are inside the Catalog and CatalogUI libraries, so you need to add ESRI.ArcGIS.CatalogUI and ESRI.ArcGIS.Catalog references to your project by right-clicking the project in Solution Explorer and choosing Add ArcGIS Reference. Then as always when adding references, you need to add the necessary using directives. So add the following lines of code to the newly added class of your add-in button:

```
using ESRI.ArcGIS.ArcMapUI;
using ESRI.ArcGIS.CatalogUI;
using ESRI.ArcGIS.Carto;
using ESRI.ArcGIS.Catalog;
```

4. You need to create an instance of GxDialog to access its IGxDialog interface. Because GxDialog is a CoClass, you can use the new operator to create an instance of it. Also you can change its capability to select single or multiple items at once using the AllowMultiSelect property. So add the following code in the OnClick() method of the ShowAddDialog class:

```
IGxDialog gxd = new GxDialogClass();
gxd.AllowMultiSelect = true;
gxd.ButtonCaption = "Add Layer";
gxd.Title = "Add Layer Window";
gxd.RememberLocation = true;
```

5. The next step is to create an appropriate `GxObjectFilter` subclass and associate it with the `GxDialog` instance. Because you want to allow users to see only `*.lyr` files, you must make an instance of the `GxFilterLayersClass` CoClass.

```
IGxObjectFilter gxObjFilter = new GxFilterLayersClass();
gxd.ObjectFilter = gxObjFilter;
```

6. At this point, the `GxDialog` instance is ready to be displayed for users. Use the `DoModalOpen()` method of the `IGxDialog` interface to show the form as a modal window. This method needs two parameters. The first one is the handle of the parent application, and the second one is an output parameter of type `IEnumGxObject`. Remember that you need to use the `out` keyword for output parameters.

```
IEnumGxObject gxEnumObj;
gxd.DoModalOpen(ArcMap.Application.hWnd, out gxEnumObj);
```

The rest of the code is for working with the enum object (`IEnumGxObject` instance) and adding layers to the map one by one. The following code is the complete `OnClick()` method of the add-in button:

```
protected override void OnClick()
        {
            IMxDocument mxdoc = ArcMap.Application.Document as IMxDocument;

            //Setting some properties for GxDialog instance
            IGxDialog gxd = new GxDialogClass();
            gxd.AllowMultiSelect = true;
            gxd.ButtonCaption = "Add Layer";
            gxd.Title = "Add Layer Window";
            gxd.RememberLocation = true;

            //creating filter for GxDialog instance
            IGxObjectFilter gxObjFilter = new GxFilterLayersClass();
            gxd.ObjectFilter = gxObjFilter;

            //Adding each selected layer to map
            IEnumGxObject gxEnumObj;
            gxd.DoModalOpen(ArcMap.Application.hWnd, out gxEnumObj);

            IGxObject gxObj = gxEnumObj.Next();
            while (gxObj != null)
            {
                IGxLayer gxlayer = gxObj as IGxLayer;
                mxdoc.AddLayer(gxlayer.Layer);
                gxObj = gxEnumObj.Next();
            }
            //refreshing the main window and TOC
            mxdoc.ActiveView.Refresh();
            mxdoc.UpdateContents();
        }
```

7. Run the code in Visual Studio. Test the functionality of this button in ArcMap to add some `*.lyr` files to the active Data Frame. Remember, in order to make use of the button, you need to use the Customize window and place the button on some toolbar or menu.

How It Works

Using this code, you can take advantage of the native ArcGIS window and also require users to select the specific file type. With simple modification, you can use the preceding code to add different geospatial resources. For example, the following line of code requires the user to add `FeatureClass` datasets such as shapefiles and feature classes inside geodatabases:

```
IGxObjectFilter gxObjFilter = new GxFilterFeatureClasses();
         gxd.ObjectFilter = gxObjFilter;
```

In this Try It Out, you used the `out` keyword to create a new instance of the `IEnumGxObject` interface. This keyword and its use are explained in Chapter 4. You might want to quickly review Chapter 4, just to make sure you understand this.

SAVING *.LYR AND *.MXD FILES

As discussed in Chapter 5, the `Application` in the add-ins template and `m_application` in the Extending ArcObjects template act as the central points where access is gained to other types in the ArcObjects system. Both entry gates point to the `IApplication` interface. This interface represents all the ArcGIS for Desktop applications. The `IApplication` interface has several self-explanatory methods for working with `*.mxd` files. Table 6-1 summarizes most of them.

TABLE 6-1: Methods of the IApplication Interface

NAME OF METHOD	PURPOSE
NewDocument()	Closes the current document and creates a new one. Has the same effect as pressing the New Map File button. Two optional parameters can be supplied for this method. The first optional input parameter is used for showing the New Document Dialog to allow users to select a template. The second input parameter is used when the first parameter is set to true and is for specifying the path of a template file that will be the base for the new document.
OpenDocument()	As the name suggests, it opens a saved `*.mxd` file when the path of the `*.mxd` file is supplied. Otherwise, the Open dialog is displayed (same effect as pressing the Open button).
Save()	Saves the changes of an opened `*.mxd` file. Calling this method without specifying an input path parameter displays the Save As window.

continues

TABLE 6-1 *(continued)*

NAME OF METHOD	PURPOSE
SaveAsDocument()	Saves the current open *.mxd file as a different *.mxd file and opens the newly created *.mxd file. This method has two optional input parameters. The first parameter specifies the path of the new *.mxd file. Invoking this method without specifying the first input path parameter displays the Save As window.
	Setting the second parameter as true saves the open map document (in-memory or *.mxd) to an *.mxd file but doesn't open a newly created *.mxd file.

It is a good idea to have some simple metadata in the *.mxd file before saving it. As shown in the following code, by using the IDocumentInfo2 interface it is possible to provide information such as Name, Author, Description, and other fields that can be found in the Map Document Property window of all ArcGIS for Desktop applications.

```
IMxDocument mxdoc = ArcMap.Application.Document as IMxDocument;
IDocumentInfo2 docInfo = mxdoc as IDocumentInfo2;
docInfo.Author = "pouria amirian";
docInfo.Comments += "Last Saved in " + DateTime.Now.ToLongTimeString()
+ "\r\n";
docInfo.Subject = "Persian Gulf in Middle East";
docInfo.RelativePaths = true;

ArcMap.Application.SaveAsDocument(@"c:\PersianGulf.mxd");
```

Figure 6-20 illustrates the results of this code snippet.

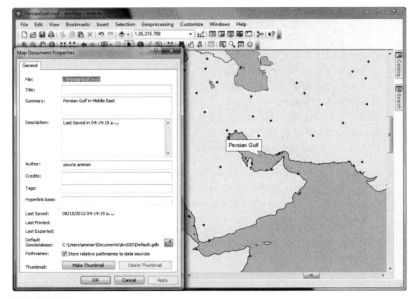

FIGURE 6-20

For saving `*.lyr` files, you resort to the `LayerFile` CoClass that can be found in the Carto object model diagram (See Figure 6-21).

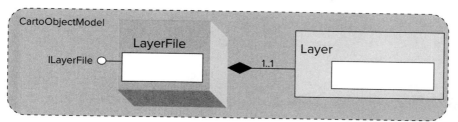

CartoObjectModel

LayerFile

ILayerFile

Layer

1..1

FIGURE 6-21

The `LayerFile` CoClass has the members required for read and write operations on in-memory and physical (saved on disc) `Layer` instances. The primary interface of the `LayerFile` CoClass is `ILayerFile`, illustrated in Figure 6-22.

The `Layer` property of the `ILayerFile` interface is a read-only property. In order to create a `*.lyr` file, a call to the `New()` method has to be made. `ReplaceContent()` then must be invoked to set the `Layer` instance as the content of the `*.lyr` file. The following code snippet iterates through all `Layer` instances inside the active Data Frame and saves only the `FeatureLayer` instances:

```
ILayerFile : IUnknown

    Filename: String
    IsLayerFile (in sFile: String): Boolean
    IsPresent (in sFile: String): Boolean
    IsReadOnly (in sFile: String): Boolean
    Layer: ILayer
    Thumbnail: IPicture

    Close
    New (in sFile: String)
    Open (in sFile: String)
    ReplaceContents (in pLayer: ILayer)
    Save
    SaveAs (in sFile: String)
```

FIGURE 6-22

```csharp
IMxDocument mxdoc = ArcMap.Application.Document as IMxDocument;
IMap map = mxdoc.FocusMap;
IEnumLayer enumLayer = map.Layers;
ILayerFile layerFile = new LayerFileClass();

ILayer layer = enumLayer.Next();
while (layer != null)
{
    if (layer is IFeatureLayer)
    {
        try
        {
            string layerPath = @"D:\" + layer.Name;
            if (!layer.Name.Contains(".lyr"))
            {
                layerPath += ".lyr";
            }
            layerFile.New(layerPath);
            layerFile.ReplaceContents(layer);
            layerFile.Save();
        }
        catch (Exception ex)
```

```
                    {
                         MessageBox.Show(ex.Message, ex.Source);
                    }
               }
          }
          layer = enumLayer.Next();
     }
```

Also, it is possible to use the `IGxFile` and `IGxLayer` interfaces to save `*.lyr` files; you can try this on your own if you are interested.

> **WARNING** The name of the `*.lyr` files must not contain certain alphanumeric characters such as \, |, or ". To be safe, you can check the names of layers against the mentioned characters.

SUMMARY

In this chapter, you learned how to access maps and layers using various classes in ArcObjects. You used your knowledge of reading object model diagrams to navigate through thousands of types to perform simple tasks.

Performing simple tasks and playing with classes is most effective for learning a new topic like ArcObjects. As you have seen often, many ArcObjects types are involved in performing simple tasks.

This chapter described the process of working with `Enum` instances. You will see more about `Enums` in upcoming chapters. In addition, this chapter illustrated some ways to read and modify the properties of all kinds of layers. The `FeatureLayer` and `RasterLayer` classes are explained briefly as another topic of this chapter. Saving and adding `*.lyr` files was the final topic of this chapter.

This chapter focused on only one type of component that can be added to ArcGIS for Desktop applications: the Button add-in (or Desktop ArcMap Command, as it is called in the Extending ArcObjects template in Visual Studio). You will see other types of components that can be added to ArcGIS for Desktop applications later in this book.

Working with maps and layers is the most basic task in ArcObjects programming. By reading this chapter, you have cleared the first hurdle in learning ArcObjects. Well done, but there are many other hurdles on your way to becoming a true ArcObjects programmer. The rest of this book will help put you on the track to success.

EXERCISES

1. Why can't the `foreach` construct be used in ArcObjects programming?

2. What is the difference between using the `LayerCount` property and using the `Layers` property to access layers inside a map?

3. What is the main interface for working with a layer that is created after adding a polygon shapefile to a map?

4. What interface should be used to provide simple metadata for `*.mxd` and `*.lyr` files?

5. How can you access the active Data Frame when there is more than one Data Frame inside the Table Of Contents window?

You will find the answers to these exercises in this book's appendix.

▶ **WHAT YOU LEARNED IN THIS CHAPTER**

TOPIC	KEY CONCEPTS
Optional interface	Optional interfaces are the interfaces that are optionally implemented by subclasses of a parent class, such as the `ILayerGeneralProperties` interface of the `Layer` Abstract Class.
Pattern for working with Enums	First step: Initialize the Enum. Second step: Use the `Next()` method of the Enum to point to the first item inside it. Third step: Use a `while` block to access all items inside the Enum. See the following code: ```\n//Initializing the Enum object\nIEnumLayer enumLayer = map.Layers;\n//Use the next method for getting the first item\nin the enum\nlayer = enumLayer.Next();\n\n//Using a while loop to iterate through all\ncontaining members\nwhile (layer != null)\n{\n //work with the members\n //use the Next() method to point to the next\nmember\n layer = enumLayer.Next();\n}\n```
Zoom to selected layer in the Table Of Contents window	```\nIMxDocument mxdoc = ArcMap.Application.Document\nas IMxDocument;\n\nIActiveView activeView = mxdoc.ActiveView;\n\nILayer layer = mxdoc.SelectedLayer;\n if (layer != null)\n {\nactiveView.Extent = layer.AreaOfInterest;\n//alternative method\n//IGeoDataset GDSet = layer as IGeoDataset;\n//activeView.Extent = GDSet.Extent;\n\nactiveView.Refresh();\n }\n```

7

Working with Tables and FeatureClasses

WHAT YOU WILL LEARN IN THIS CHAPTER:

➤   Exploring object model diagrams for data access and creation

➤   Adding and deleting existing fields

➤   Adding FeatureClasses, tables, and rasters to a map

➤   Creating new tables

➤   Filling tables with rows

➤   Using the family of Name objects

WROX.COM CODE DOWNLOADS FOR THIS CHAPTER

The wrox.com code downloads for this chapter can be found at www.wrox.com/remtitle .cgi?isbn=1118442548 on the Download Code tab. The code is in the Chapter07 folder and is individually named according to the names throughout the chapter.

The first part of this chapter discusses how to access tables and FeatureClasses inside a map. You learn how to create new fields and delete existing fields. In the second part of the chapter, you explore the classes for adding various datasets (such as FeatureClasses in file geodatabases or ArcSDE geodatabases, tables, and rasters) to a map. At the end of this chapter, you look at the topic of creating tables and records.

ACCESSING TABLES AND FEATURECLASSES

Vector-based geospatial data are one of the most widely used types of geospatial data (if not the most). Geospatial data have two elements: geometry and attribute. Different vector-based geospatial data store these two elements in various ways. There are quite a lot of formats and models for storage of vector-based geospatial data. Some of them store both elements in the same place (as in the case of spatial DBMS), and some of them use two (and more) different file structures for storing geometry and attributes of vector geospatial data (as in the case of a georelational model).

As an ArcGIS programmer, you often access geospatial data through a geodatabase model. Put simply, developers don't care about the format and model of storage of geospatial data. As you will see shortly, you access all geospatial data in the same way and independent of storage format and model. In fact, this is one of the promises of ArcObjects as an object-oriented system. (Polymorphism is explained in detail in Chapter 4).

The attribute table of vector geospatial data and tabular data that can be used in the ArcGIS platform plays an important role in all aspects of working with geospatial data, such as geoprocessing and visualization, just to name two. Additionally, geodatabase models provide ways to extend the capabilities of tables. Using the attribute domain to provide integrity and to take advantage of relationship classes to build traditional relationships of relational models are just two ways to make more efficient tables.

Figure 7-1 illustrates some classes for working with vector geospatial data and tabular data.

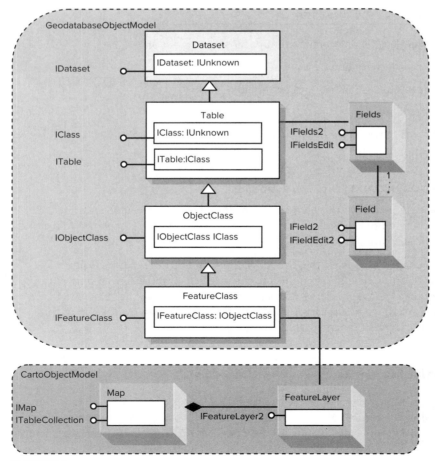

FIGURE 7-1

The core class of the geodatabase object model is the Dataset Abstract Class. It is a generic class with generic interfaces. A FeatureClass, a RasterClass, a FeatureDataset, a RelationshipClass, and a Table are concrete examples of a Dataset.

Let's see how you can access actual data behind a FeatureLayer inside a map. A FeatureClass behind a FeatureLayer can be accessed using the FeatureClass property of the IFeatureLayer2 interface (or the IFeatureLayer interface).

```
IFeatureLayer2 featureLayer = layer as IFeatureLayer2;
IFeatureClass fc = featureLayer.FeatureClass;
```

As shown in Figure 7-1, a FeatureClass is a type of Table. In fact, you can think of a FeatureClass as a Table that has a special capability to store the geometry of records or rows.

A Table inside a Map can be accessed using the ITableCollection interface of the Map CoClass. A Table instance contains a set of columns that are programmatically accessible through the Fields property. This property is of type Fields CoClass. The Fields CoClass has two major interfaces: IFields2 and IFieldsEdit. As you may guess, these two interfaces have the same set of properties; however, in the IFields2 interface all properties are read-only, while in the IFieldsEdit interface all properties are write-only.

```
IFields2 fields = table.Fields;
```

A Fields instance has a one-to-many relationship with the Field CoClass. The relationship between the Fields and Field CoClasses is similar to the relationship between the Map and Layer classes. In other words, the Fields CoClass has FieldCount and Field properties (which are like the LayerCount and Layer properties) to iterate through all fields.

```
for (int i = 0; i < fields.FieldCount; i++)
{
    IField2 field = fields.Field[i];
    //code for work with each field instance
}
```

The Field CoClass represents a single column in the table that has Name and Type among its useful properties. As with the Fields CoClass, the Field CoClass has two major interfaces. In this case, both interfaces have almost the same members but IField2 provides read-only properties whereas IFieldEdit2 offers the same properties as write-only. In the next Try It Out, you create a simple schema reporter add-in. In brief, a *schema* in geodatabase terminology is the structure or design of a geodatabase or geodatabase object, such as a table, or a feature class. The resulting add-in can report some properties on all columns of a selected table or FeatureLayer inside the Table Of Contents window of ArcMap.

TRY IT OUT Simple Schema Reporter (SchemaReporter.zip)

1. Create a new project in Visual Studio. For the last time in this book, be sure that you selected .NET Framework 3.5 as the target platform. Click on the Desktop Add-Ins template and select the ArcMap Add-in. Name your add-in something meaningful like SimpleSchemaReporter and click the OK button.

2. As always, provide your information and click Next in the ArcGIS Add-Ins Wizard. Select Button as the type of add-in and set other fields, as shown in Figure 7-2.

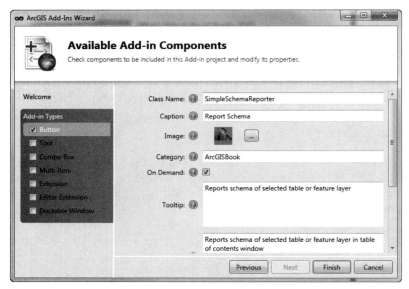

FIGURE 7-2

3. Add the ESRI.ArcGIS.Carto and ESRI.ArcGIS.Geodatabase references to your project. Then write the following, using directives at the top of the SimpleSchemaReporter.cs code window:

```
using ESRI.ArcGIS.ArcMapUI;
using ESRI.ArcGIS.Carto;
using ESRI.ArcGIS.Geodatabase;
```

4. You want to report just some properties of columns of the selected table or FeatureLayer inside the Table Of Contents window. For this reason, you are going to create a lightweight class for storing properties of Field instances. Later you take advantage of the generics feature of .NET and populate a List of these lightweight objects.

So right-click on the project and from the Add submenu, select the Class item. As shown in Figure 7-3, name the class **fldClass** and click Add.

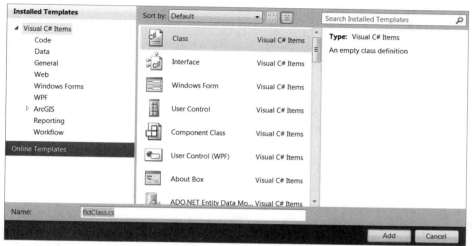

FIGURE 7-3

5. `fldClass.cs` is an information package class for storing data such as `Name`, `Alias`, `Length`, and `FieldType` for `Field` objects. It has a handful of properties just to provide a group of related information for a specific `Field`. The contents of your `fldClass.cs` file should be similar to the following code listing. Note that because you use the `esriFieldType` enumeration as the type of `FieldType` property, you have to add a reference to a geodatabase library (and write the corresponding `using` directives), which you have done in previous steps for the other class.

```csharp
using System;
using System.Collections.Generic;
using System.Linq;
using System.Text;
using ESRI.ArcGIS.Geodatabase;

namespace SimpleSchemaReporter

{
    class fldClass
    {
        public int No
        { get; set; }

        public string AliasName
        { get; set; }

        public string Name
        { get; set; }

        public esriFieldType FieldType
        { get; set; }
```

```
        public int Length
        { get; set; }

        public bool IsRequired
        { get; set; }

        public bool IsNullable
        { get; set; }



        public fldClass(int No)
        { this.No = No; }
    }
}
```

6. Add a new Windows Form to your project by right-clicking the project in the Visual Studio Solution Explorer window and selecting Windows Form from the Add submenu. Name it **frmGrid**, then click the Add button. This form is used to show the schema of all fields inside a grid.

7. Modify the `ShowInTaskBar` property of the form to `False`. Change the size of frmGrid to **726; 266**. Add a DataGridView control to the form. You can find the DataGridView control in the Data or All Windows Forms categories of the Toolbox window. Change the properties of the added DataGridView as indicated in Table 7-1.

TABLE 7-1: Properties of DataGridView

PROPERTY	VALUE
Name	dgv
ReadOnly	True
Modifiers	Public
Size	686;194

8. At this point, your form and information package class are ready. Go back to the main add-in class (`SimpleSchemaReporter.cs`) and write the following lines of code in the `OnClick()` method to cast the selected item in the Table Of Contents window to `ITable` if the selected item is of type `IFeatureLayer2` or `ITable`:

```
        protected override void OnClick()
        {
            IMxDocument mxDoc = ArcMap.Application.Document as IMxDocument;

            if (mxDoc.SelectedItem is IFeatureLayer2 || mxDoc.SelectedItem is ITable)
            {
                ITable selectedTbl = mxDoc.SelectedItem as ITable;
                reportSchema(selectedTbl);
            }
        }
```

A `FeatureClass` is a type of `Table`, so a single generic method will suffice to report the schema of the selected item. Name the method `ReportSchema`.

9. Finally, here is the `ReportSchema()` method, which requires an `ITable` instance as its input parameter:

```
void ReportSchema(ITable table)
{
    //Build a generic list of fldClass instances
    List<fldClass> fldClassList = new List<fldClass>();

    IFields2 fields = table.Fields as IFields2;
    for (int i = 0; i < fields.FieldCount; i++)
    {
        IField2 field = fields.Field[i] as IField2;
        fldClass fldClassInstance = new fldClass(i + 1);
        //code working with each field
        fldClassInstance.AliasName = field.AliasName;
        fldClassInstance.Name = field.Name;

        fldClassInstance.IsNullable = field.IsNullable;
        fldClassInstance.IsRequired = field.Required;

        fldClassInstance.FieldType = field.Type;
        fldClassInstance.Length = field.Length;
        //populating list
        fldClassList.Add(fldClassInstance);
    }
    //for being able to use the Name of Table or FeatureClass
    IDataset dsTable = table as IDataset;

    frmGrid gridForm = new frmGrid();
    //databinding
    gridForm.dgv.DataSource = fldClassList;
    gridForm.Text = "Simple Schema of: " + dsTable.Name;
    gridForm.ShowDialog();
}
```

10. Run the code by pressing F5 and test the functionality of the add-in. Note that you need to use the Customize window in order to add your add-in button to the user interface of ArcMap. Figure 7-4 is the result of clicking the add-in button when U.S. Cities is selected in the Table Of Contents window.

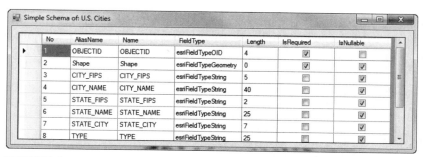

No	AliasName	Name	FieldType	Length	IsRequired	IsNullable
1	OBJECTID	OBJECTID	esriFieldTypeOID	4	☑	☐
2	Shape	Shape	esriFieldTypeGeometry	0	☑	☑
3	CITY_FIPS	CITY_FIPS	esriFieldTypeString	5	☐	☑
4	CITY_NAME	CITY_NAME	esriFieldTypeString	40	☐	☑
5	STATE_FIPS	STATE_FIPS	esriFieldTypeString	2	☐	☑
6	STATE_NAME	STATE_NAME	esriFieldTypeString	25	☐	☑
7	STATE_CITY	STATE_CITY	esriFieldTypeString	7	☐	☑
8	TYPE	TYPE	esriFieldTypeString	25	☐	☑

Simple Schema of: U.S. Cities

FIGURE 7-4

How It Works

In this example, you used a single method to populate a generic `List` of lightweight objects. Each of these lightweight objects conveys information about `Field` instances. In addition to generics, you have employed the data binding services of .NET.

The .NET Framework encapsulates much of the complexity of synchronizing controls (such as the DataGridView control) to a data source (such as a `List`) through a process called data binding. When you create a binding between a control and some data (for example, via the setting control's `DataSource` property), you are binding a *binding target* to a *binding source*. Behind the scenes, a *binding object* handles the interaction between the binding source and the binding target. In this example, you need to have one-way or read-only data binding. So with just one line of code, you display all the members of a `List` inside a DataGridView control.

Adding and Deleting Fields

In order to delete an existing field, a live `Field` instance must be supplied for the `DeleteField()` method of the `IClass` interface of the `Table` Class. Since the `IObjectClass` interface inherits from the `IClass` interface and the `IFeatureClass` inherits from the `IObjectClass`, all members of the `IClass` and the `IObjectClass` are available on the `IFeatureClass` interface. As a result, the `DeleteField()` method can be directly accessed using the `ITable` and `IFeatureClass` interfaces. For referencing an existing `Field` instance, you must use the `IFields` interface of the `Fields` CoClass.

The `IFields2` interface has two useful methods for finding the index of a specific `Field` instance: `FindField()` and `FindFieldByAliasName()`. The following code snippet uses the `FindField()` method of the `IFields2` interface to find the `Name` field of the first layer inside the active Data Frame:

```
ILayer layer = map.Layer[0];
//suppose that the first layer is FeatureLayer
IFeatureClass featureClass = (layer as IFeatureLayer2).FeatureClass;
//find Name field
IFields2 fields = featureClass.Fields as IFields2;
IField2 nameField =null;
int fieldIndex = fields.FindField("Name");
//the index of field is zero-based
if (fieldIndex >= 0)
{
    nameField = fields.Field[fieldIndex] as IField2;
}
```

The process for finding a specific field is the same for `Table` instances, with one exception: the way in which you get to the table itself. The following code snippet uses the second method to find a specific field of the first table in the List By Source contents view (the second view in the Table Of Contents window in ArcMap):

```
//accessing the first table inside
// the source contents view of TOC
ITable table = (map as ITableCollection).Table[0];
IFields2 fields = table.Fields as IFields2;
//find a field with Alias= City Name
IField2 cityNameField =null;
```

```
        int fieldIndex = fields.FindFieldByAliasName("City Name");
        //the index of field is zero-based
        if (fieldIndex >= 0)
        {
            cityNameField = fields.Field[fieldIndex] as IField2;
        }
```

An existing field can be easily deleted using the `DeleteField()` method.

```
Try
{
    if (cityNameField != null)
    {
        table.DeleteField(cityNameField);
        //or featureClass.DeleteField(NameField);
    }
}
catch (Exception ex)
{
    //work with ex object and perform appropriate actions
    System.Windows.Forms.MessageBox.Show(ex.Message,ex.Source);
}
```

It is always good programming practice to check for the existence of a `Field` instance before trying to delete it. In addition, using a `try` block ensures that the preceding code will cause the ArcGIS for Desktop application to behave unexpectedly.

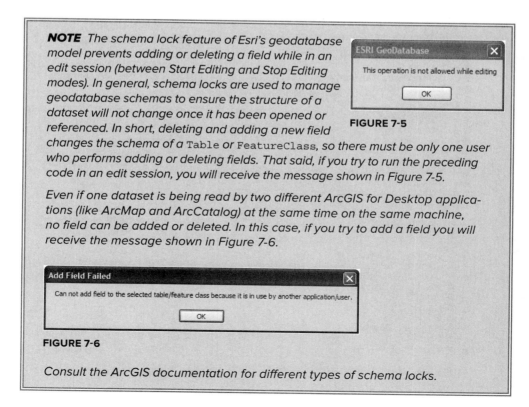

NOTE *The schema lock feature of Esri's geodatabase model prevents adding or deleting a field while in an edit session (between Start Editing and Stop Editing modes). In general, schema locks are used to manage geodatabase schemas to ensure the structure of a dataset will not change once it has been opened or referenced. In short, deleting and adding a new field changes the schema of a* Table *or* FeatureClass, *so there must be only one user who performs adding or deleting fields. That said, if you try to run the preceding code in an edit session, you will receive the message shown in Figure 7-5.*

FIGURE 7-5

Even if one dataset is being read by two different ArcGIS for Desktop applications (like ArcMap and ArcCatalog) at the same time on the same machine, no field can be added or deleted. In this case, if you try to add a field you will receive the message shown in Figure 7-6.

FIGURE 7-6

Consult the ArcGIS documentation for different types of schema locks.

For adding a new field to an existing `Table` or `FeatureClass`, you need to create a brand new field or reference an existing field, and then use the `AddField()` method of the `ITable` or `IFeatureClass` interfaces.

```
IMxDocument mxdoc = ArcMap.Application.Document as IMxDocument;
ILayer layer = mxdoc.FocusMap.Layer[0];
IFeatureClass featureClass = (layer as IFeatureLayer2).FeatureClass;
IFields2 fields = featureClass.Fields as IFields2;

IFieldEdit2 newField = new FieldClass();
string fieldName = "NewField";
newField.Name_2 = fieldName;
newField.Type_2 = esriFieldType.esriFieldTypeString;
newField.DefaultValue_2 = "no content";

if (fields.FindField(fieldName) < 0)
{
    try
    {
        featureClass.AddField(newField);
    }
    catch (Exception ex)
    {
        System.Windows.Forms.MessageBox.Show(ex.Message, ex.Source);
    }
}
```

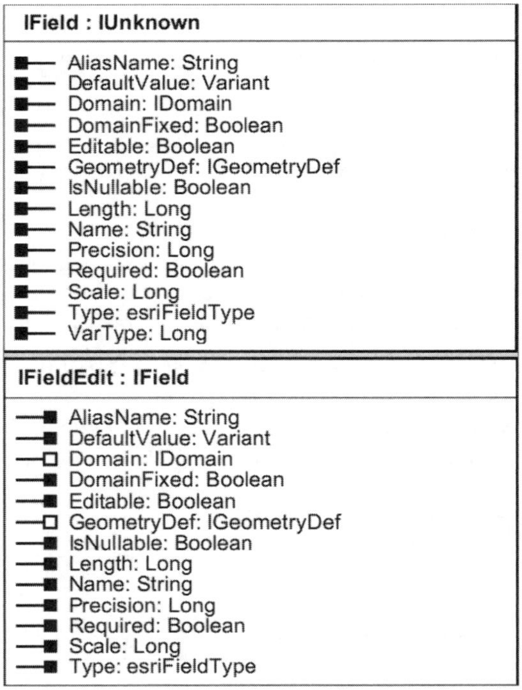

IField : IUnknown

- AliasName: String
- DefaultValue: Variant
- Domain: IDomain
- DomainFixed: Boolean
- Editable: Boolean
- GeometryDef: IGeometryDef
- IsNullable: Boolean
- Length: Long
- Name: String
- Precision: Long
- Required: Boolean
- Scale: Long
- Type: esriFieldType
- VarType: Long

IFieldEdit : IField

- AliasName: String
- DefaultValue: Variant
- Domain: IDomain
- DomainFixed: Boolean
- Editable: Boolean
- GeometryDef: IGeometryDef
- IsNullable: Boolean
- Length: Long
- Name: String
- Precision: Long
- Required: Boolean
- Scale: Long
- Type: esriFieldType

FIGURE 7-7

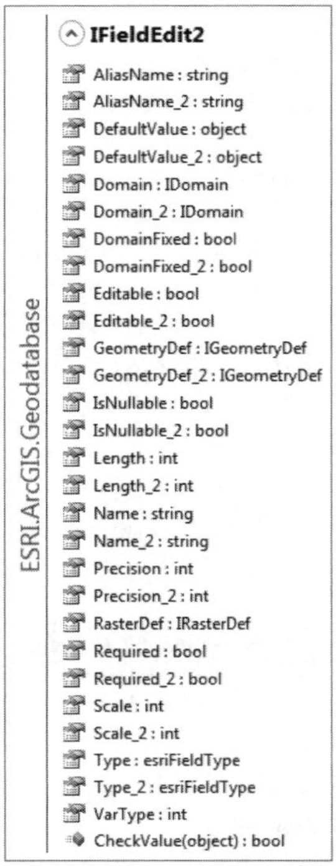

IFieldEdit2

ESRI.ArcGIS.Geodatabase

- AliasName : string
- AliasName_2 : string
- DefaultValue : object
- DefaultValue_2 : object
- Domain : IDomain
- Domain_2 : IDomain
- DomainFixed : bool
- DomainFixed_2 : bool
- Editable : bool
- Editable_2 : bool
- GeometryDef : IGeometryDef
- GeometryDef_2 : IGeometryDef
- IsNullable : bool
- IsNullable_2 : bool
- Length : int
- Length_2 : int
- Name : string
- Name_2 : string
- Precision : int
- Precision_2 : int
- RasterDef : IRasterDef
- Required : bool
- Required_2 : bool
- Scale : int
- Scale_2 : int
- Type : esriFieldType
- Type_2 : esriFieldType
- VarType : int
- CheckValue(object) : bool

FIGURE 7-8

The IFieldEdit2 interface inherits from the IField2 interface, so it has all the read-only properties of its parent. In addition, the IFieldEdit2 has a write-only version of all the properties of the IField2 interface. In contrast to what can be seen in the geodatabase object model diagram, write-only members of this interface have a literal _2 at the end of their names, such as Name_2 and Type_2. Figure 7-7 displays the IField and IFieldEdit interfaces on the geodatabase object model diagram.

The actual names of members of IFieldEdit2 and IField2 interfaces are shown in Figure 7-8.

Adding Existing FeatureClasses, Tables, and Rasters to a Map

In order to add existing FeatureClasses or tables to a map, a live instance of the appropriate IWorkspaceFactory interface is needed. The IWorkspaceFactory interface is implemented by the WorkspaceFactory Class. As shown in Figure 7-9, there are several subclasses of the WorkspaceFactory Class.

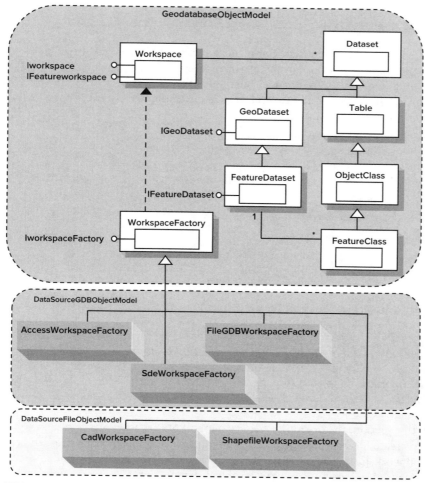

FIGURE 7-9

As the names of the subclasses imply, they are used to instantiate a corresponding `Workspace` object in order to access the datasets inside it. For example, a `ShapefileWorkspaceFactory` can create a `Workspace` object representing a folder containing shapefiles, a `FileGDBWorkspaceFactory` creates a `Workspace` instance representing a file geodatabase, and an `SdeWorkspaceFactory` can create a `Workspace` object, which indicates an instance of a local or remote ArcSDE spatial DBMS service.

Put simply, a workspace is a container of datasets and it comes in many flavors. More precisely, a workspace is a container of geospatial and non-geospatial datasets. Using a workspace, existing datasets can be accessed and new geospatial and non-geospatial data can be created. In order to instantiate a workspace, you need to first create a `WorkspaceFactory` instance. The following code creates a `FileGDBWorkspaceFactory` instance.

```
IWorkspaceFactory wsf = new FileGDBWorkspaceFactoryClass();
```

An instance of a workspace is created using the `OpenFromFile()` method of the `IWorkspaceFactory` interface.

```
string gdbFileAddress=@"D:/DataFolder/fileGDB.gdb";
IWorkspace ws = wsf.OpenFromFile(gdbFileAddress, ArcMap.Application.hWnd);
```

A workspace is associated with several datasets. So the next step for adding vector-based data to a map is to cast the `IWorkspace` interface to the `IFeatureWorkspace`. Then you can use the `OpenFeatureClass()` and `OpenFeatureDataset()` methods of the `IFeatureWorkspace` interface in order to access all the FeatureClasses and FeatureDatasets inside the workspace. The following code provides access to the cities FeatureClass.

```
IFeatureWorkspace fws = ws as IFeatureWorkspace;
IFeatureClass fc = fws.OpenFeatureClass("cities");
```

The rest of the code for adding a `FeatureClass` to a map is to create a `FeatureLayer` instance and add it to the map.

```
IFeatureLayer fl = new FeatureLayerClass();
fl.Name = "Cities of the US";
fl.FeatureClass = fc;
IMxDocument mxdoc = ArcMap.Application.Document as IMxDocument;
mxdoc.AddLayer(fl);

mxdoc.ActiveView.Refresh();
mxdoc.UpdateContents();
```

> **NOTE** *In order to run the preceding code, you must add references to* `ESRI` `.ArcGIS.DataSourcesGDB`, `ESRI.ArcGIS.Display`, `ESRI.ArcGIS.Geodatabase`, *and* `ESRI.ArcGIS.Carto` *to your ArcObjects project.*

As shown in earlier in this section, the `OpenFromFile()` method of the `IWorkspaceFactory` interface can be used to create file-based workspaces like shapefiles and file geodatabases. In order to create a DBMS-based workspace, you must use the `Open()` method of the `IWorkspaceFactory` interface. The `Open()` method solicits a `PropertySet` object. Simply put, a `PropertySet` is a bag of key and value pairs. The `PropertySet` CoClass resides in the System library of ArcObjects.

The required setting for opening a connection to an ArcSDE geodatabase (a *connection string* in DBMS terminology) can be stored in a single instance of the `PropertySet` CoClass. The following code illustrates the use of the `PropertySet` CoClass to connect to a remote data server called gisServer.

```
IWorkspaceFactory wsf = new SdeWorkspaceFactoryClass();

    IPropertySet pSet = new PropertySetClass();
    pSet.SetProperty("Server", "gisServer");//name of server
    pSet.SetProperty("Instance", "5151");//port
    pSet.SetProperty("Database", "MunicipalityGDB");//name of Database
    pSet.SetProperty("User", "sde");//name of user connecting to DB
    pSet.SetProperty("Password", "@Keep#Moving_Forward");//password
    pSet.SetProperty("Version", "sde.Default");//version to be connected

    IWorkspace ws = wsf.Open(pSet, ArcMap.Application.hWnd);
    IFeatureWorkspace fws = ws as IFeatureWorkspace;
```

> **NOTE** *Seasoned programmers know that hard coding usernames and passwords is a bad idea. Traditional approaches, such as getting these two sensitive pieces of information from users using a login window, are better.*
>
> *In order to connect to an ArcSDE geodatabase, in addition to a username and password, you need to provide the name or IP address of the server, the name of the database, and either ArcSDE service information (such as port) or a direct connection string (such as* `sde:sqlserver:serverName`*, in the case of Microsoft SQL Server DBMS). For different approaches and various parameters connecting to an ArcSDE geodatabase, consult the online ArcGIS Resource Center website* (`http://resources.arcgis.com/en/home/`)*.*

You can access datasets inside a workspace using the `Subsets` property of the `IFeatureDataset` interface. This is of type `IEnumDataset`, and as you may guess, the `Next()` method of this interface returns an `IDataset` instance. The following code snippet adds all FeatureClasses residing in the USA `FeatureDataset` of a `FileGDB`.

```
IWorkspaceFactory wsf = new FileGDBWorkspaceFactoryClass();
IFeatureWorkspace fws = wsf.OpenFromFile(fileGDBAddress,
ArcMap.Application.hWnd) as IFeatureWorkspace;

IFeatureDataset fds = fws.OpenFeatureDataset("USA");
IEnumDataset enumDS = fds.Subsets;
IDataset ds = enumDS.Next();

while (ds != null)
{
    if (ds is IFeatureClass)
    {
    IFeatureClass fc = ds as IFeatureClass;
        IFeatureLayer fl = new FeatureLayerClass();
        fl.Name = ds.Name;
        fl.FeatureClass = fc;
        mxdoc.AddLayer(fl);
        ds = enumDS.Next();
```

```
                    }
              }
              mxdoc.ActiveView.Refresh();
              mxdoc.UpdateContents();
        }
```

In order to get access to all `FeatureDatasets` in a geodatabase, you must use the `Datasets` property of the `IWorkspace` interface. When you are programming in .NET, Java, or C++, you need to consider situations in which the members of interfaces cannot be accessed in code. One of these situations is the `Datasets` property of `IWorkspace`. In VB 6.0, you can access this property by its name. In .NET and C++, you get to the same result using the `get_Datasets()` method, and in Java, use the `getDatasets()` method.

The next Try It Out uses the topics you have learned up to now in this chapter to create an add-in button for adding all `FeatureClasses` inside all `FeatureDatasets` of a selected file geodatabase.

TRY IT OUT   Adding All FeatureClasses inside All FeatureDatasets of a File Geodatabase (AddingAllFeatureClasses.zip)

1. Open the SimpleSchemaReporter solution by double-clicking its solution file (`SimpleSchema Reporter.sln`).

2. Add references for `Geodatabase`, `DataSourcesGDB`, `Catalog`, `CatalogUI`, and `Display` using the Add ArcGIS Reference window.

3. You need to add a new add-in component. To do that, right-click on your project in the Solution Explorer window and select New Item from the Add submenu. Then select the Desktop Add-Ins item under the ArcGIS template. Name your add-in component **AddAllFeatureClasses.cs** and click the Add button.

4. In the ArcGIS Add-Ins Wizard, select Button as the type of add-In, set its properties as shown in Figure 7-10, and click Finish.

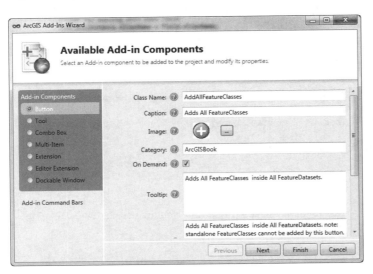

FIGURE 7-10

5. You are going to add a command container add-in (toolbar) to your project. The steps for adding a command container for versions 10 and 10.1 of ArcGIS are slightly different.

➤ For ArcGIS 10.1, right-click on your project in the Solution Explorer window and select New Item from the Add submenu. Then select the Desktop Add-Ins item under the ArcGIS template. Then select the Add-in Command Container item and name it **myToolbar.cs**. Select Toolbar as the type of Command Bar and add the ReferenceIDs of all add-in buttons in your project by clicking inside the Items grid. Finally click the Finish button (see Figure 7-11).

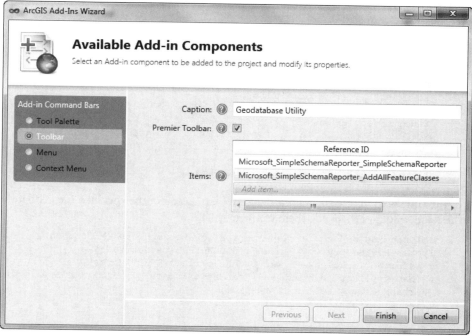

FIGURE 7-11

➤ For ArcGIS 10, right-click on your project in the Solution Explorer window and select New Item from the Add submenu. Then select the Desktop Add-Ins item under the ArcGIS template. Then select Add-in Component and name it **myToolbar.cs**.

Without specifying anything in the first page of the ArcGIS Add-Ins Wizard, go to the second page by clicking on Add-in Command Bars. Select Toolbar, configure its settings as shown in Figure 7-11, and click the Finish button.

6. If you run your code by pressing F5, you won't need to resort to the Customize window for adding your newly created button to the user interface of ArcMap. Both buttons are now on a toolbar. If you are in Run mode, press the Stop Debugging button and go to the code window of your newly added button class (AddAllFeatureClasses.cs). Add the following using directives at the top of the code file:

```
using ESRI.ArcGIS.Carto;
using ESRI.ArcGIS.DataSourcesGDB;
using ESRI.ArcGIS.Geodatabase;
using ESRI.ArcGIS.ArcMapUI;
using ESRI.ArcGIS.Catalog;
using ESRI.ArcGIS.CatalogUI;
```

7. You want to let users specify a file geodatabase. The best tool for this purpose is
   GxDialogClass(). So add the following lines of code to the OnClick() method of your
   AddAllFeatureClasses button:

```
IGxDialog gxd = new GxDialogClass();
gxd.AllowMultiSelect = false;
gxd.ButtonCaption = "Add FileGDB";
gxd.Title = "Add All FeatureClasses inside FileGDB";
gxd.RememberLocation = true;

IGxObjectFilter gxObjFilter = new GxFilterFileGeodatabasesClass();
gxd.ObjectFilter = gxObjFilter;

IEnumGxObject gxEnumObj;
gxd.DoModalOpen(ArcMap.Application.hWnd, out gxEnumObj);
IGxObject gxObj = gxEnumObj.Next();
//getting the address of fileGDB
string fileGDBAddress = gxObj.FullName;
```

8. The rest of the code is to iterate through all FeatureDatasets in the specified file geodatabase
   and add the FeatureClasses inside them to the map.

```
IMxDocument mxdoc = ArcMap.Application.Document as IMxDocument;
IWorkspaceFactory wsf = new FileGDBWorkspaceFactoryClass();
IFeatureWorkspace fws = wsf.OpenFromFile(fileGDBAddress,
ArcMap.Application.hWnd) as IFeatureWorkspace;
IWorkspace ws = fws as IWorkspace;
//get all FeatureDatasets inside fileGDB
IEnumDataset enumDS =
ws.get_Datasets(esriDatasetType.esriDTFeatureDataset);
try
{
    //first FeatureDataset
    IDataset featureDataSet = enumDS.Next();
    while (featureDataSet != null)
    {
        //get all FeatureClasses inside a FeatureDataset
        IEnumDataset featureClassesInFDS = featureDataSet.Subsets;
        IDataset singleFeatureClassAsDataset =
        featureClassesInFDS.Next();

        while (singleFeatureClassAsDataset != null)
        {
```

```
            if (singleFeatureClassAsDataset is IFeatureClass)
            {
                IFeatureClass singleFeatureClass =
                singleFeatureClassAsDataset as IFeatureClass;
                IFeatureLayer featureLayer = new FeatureLayerClass();
                featureLayer.Name = singleFeatureClassAsDataset.Name;
                featureLayer.FeatureClass = singleFeatureClass;
                mxdoc.AddLayer(featureLayer);
            }
            singleFeatureClassAsDataset = featureClassesInFDS.Next();
        }
        featureDataSet = enumDS.Next();
    }
    mxdoc.ActiveView.Refresh();
    mxdoc.UpdateContents();
}
catch (Exception ex)
{
    System.Windows.Forms.MessageBox.Show(ex.Message, ex.Source);
}
```

Press F5 to run the code and test the functionality of this button.

How It Works

This Try It Out used the get_Datasets() method of the IWorkspace interface and the Subset property of the IDataset interface to iterate through all FeatureClasses inside all FeatureDatasets of a file geodatabase. Note that since you use the esriDatasetType.esriDTFeatureDataset as input to the get_Datasets() method, stand-alone FeatureClasses of a file geodatabase cannot be added to the map.

In addition, you used a toolbar to contain the button you created in Step 4. When you added the toolbar to the project, behind the scenes, the XML configuration file of the add-in (Config.esriaddinx) was modified to include a toolbar with the setting introduced in the ArcGIS Add-In Wizard window, as shown in the following code:

```
<Toolbar id="Microsoft_SimpleSchemaReporter_Geodatabase_Utility"
caption="Geodatabase Utility" showInitially="true" >
        <Items>
          <Item refID="Microsoft_SimpleSchemaReporter_SimpleSchemaReporter" />
          <Button refID="Microsoft_SimpleSchemaReporter_AddAllFeatureClasses"
           separator="true" />
        </Items>
      </Toolbar>
```

The configuration file of the add-in is utilized to include the static aspects of all types of add-ins in a project — including captions, ToolTips, Help information, images, and initial layout details.

Adding a table to a map is similar to adding a FeatureClass to a map. `Table` instances don't have an associated `Layer` object; you have to directly add them to the map using the `ITableCollection` interface of the `Map` CoClass. The following code adds the first table in a file geodatabase to the Table of Contents window:

```
string fileGDBAddress =@"D:/DataFolder/fileGDB.gdb";
IMxDocument mxdoc = ArcMap.Application.Document as IMxDocument;
IWorkspaceFactory wsf = new FileGDBWorkspaceFactoryClass();
IWorkspace ws = wsf.OpenFromFile(fileGDBAddress,
ArcMap.Application.hWnd);
IEnumDataset enumDS = ws.get_Datasets(esriDatasetType.esriDTTable);
IDataset ds = enumDS.Next();
ITable table = ds as ITable;
IMap map = mxdoc.FocusMap;
ITableCollection tableColl = map as ITableCollection;
tableColl.AddTable(table);
mxdoc.UpdateContents();
```

In order to add raster data to the map, you should use some other related types in ArcObjects. Figure 7-12 illustrates the classes and relationship between them, which are relevant when adding a RasterDataset to a map.

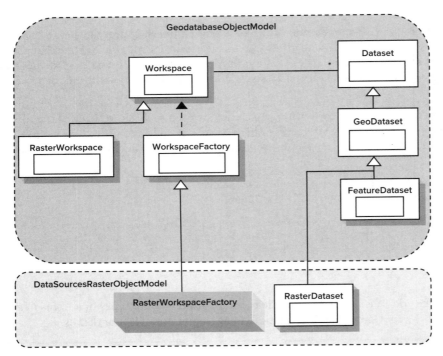

FIGURE 7-12

The process to get to an existing RasterDataset is a bit different in comparison with previous approaches to get to the existing FeatureClasses or tables. The following code demonstrates adding a satellite image with the name geoeye-1-endeavour.tif, which is located in D:\DataFolder. As you can see, the OpenRasterDataset() method of the IRasterWorkspace is used to create a RasterDataset. Note that you use the CreateFromDataset() method of IRasterLayer to reference the RasterDataset.

```
string parentDirectory = @"D:/DataFolder/";
IMxDocument mxdoc = ArcMap.Application.Document as IMxDocument;
IWorkspaceFactory wsf = new RasterWorkspaceFactoryClass();
IWorkspace ws = wsf.OpenFromFile(parentDirectory,
ArcMap.Application.hWnd);
IRasterWorkspace rasterWS = ws as IRasterWorkspace;
IRasterDataset rasterDataset =
rasterWS.OpenRasterDataset(@"geoeye-1-endeavour.tif");
IRasterLayer rasterLayer = new RasterLayerClass();
rasterLayer.CreateFromDataset(rasterDataset);
mxdoc.AddLayer(rasterLayer);
mxdoc.ActiveView.Refresh();
mxdoc.UpdateContents();
```

Deleting an Existing FeatureDataset, FeatureClass, Table, or Raster

To this point in this chapter, you have learned how to access existing FeatureClasses, rasters, tables, and FeatureDatasets. In addition to accessing these items, you might need to remove them as well. Fortunately, it is easy to delete any kind of class that implements the IDataset interface using its Delete() method. The following code demonstrates how to delete the first table in a file geodatabase:

```
string fileGDBAddress =@"D:/DataFolder/fileGDB.gdb";
IWorkspaceFactory wsf = new FileGDBWorkspaceFactoryClass();
IWorkspace ws = wsf.OpenFromFile(fileGDBAddress,
ArcMap.Application.hWnd);
IFeatureWorkspace fws = ws as IFeatureWorkspace;
IEnumDataset enumDS = ws.get_Datasets(esriDatasetType.esriDTTable);
IDataset ds = enumDS.Next();
if (ds.CanDelete() == true)
{
    ds.Delete();
}
```

Creating Tables and Rows

The IFeatureWorkspace interface of the Workspace Class plays a major role in creating geodatabase objects such as tables, FeatureClasses, and RelationshipClasses. A FeatureClass is a special kind of table, and features inside a FeatureClass are special kinds of rows of a table. This can be seen in Figure 7-13, which provides a simplified view of a Geodatabase object model diagram (see the specialization-inheritance between FeatureClass and Table as well as between Feature and Row).

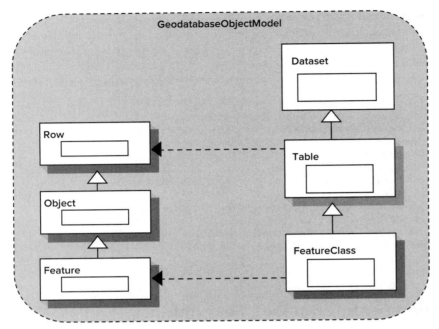

FIGURE 7-13

> **NOTE** *This section only discusses creating and populating tables. Chapter 8 covers the geometry of features and Chapter 13 explains the creation other types of geodatabase objects such as FeatureClasses and FeatureDatasets.*

Follow these steps in order to create and populate a table instance:

1. Create a `Fields` instance.
2. Create necessary `Field` objects and add them to the `Fields` instance.
3. Use the `IFeatureWorkspace` interface to create a `Table`.
4. Use the created `Table` to make an empty `Row` instance.
5. Set values for each column of the created `Row` instance.

Among all the types needed to create and populate a table, `Field` and `Fields` are CoClasses. After creating an instance of the `Fields` CoClass, the `FieldCount` property must be set. This is important because this collection object must know how many `Field` objects will be inside the collection. Because you create a brand new instance, you definitely want write access to the members of the `Fields` objects. For this reason, you must use the `IFieldsEdit` interface. A literal `_2` also must be added to names of members on this interface in .NET. In summary, the number of `Fields` must be known beforehand.

```
IFieldsEdit fields = new FieldsClass();
fields.FieldCount_2 = 3;
```

`Name` is the only mandatory property of a `Field` object. But it is common practice to specify the data type of each `Field` in addition to its name to create the bare bones of a `Field` object. If the data type of a `Field` wasn't specified, ArcObjects considers it a Long Integer (C# long) data type.

Note that each table must have one field of type `esriFieldTypeOID`. This field is an identity field and is basically a record number. The values stored by the OID field are integers that uniquely identify each record (starting from one and incrementing from top to bottom). These values are managed internally by ArcObjects and do not need to be explicitly set by the user or code. The following code snippet creates a string field and assigns it as the second field in a collection of `Field` instances:

```
IFieldEdit2 field1 = new FieldClass() as IFieldEdit2;
field1.Name_2 = "OID";
field1.Type_2 = esriFieldType.esriFieldTypeOID;
fields.Field_2[0] = field1;

IFieldEdit2 field2 = new FieldClass() as IFieldEdit2;
field2.Name_2 = "StateName";
field2.Type_2 = esriFieldType.esriFieldTypeString;
fields.Field_2[1] = field2;

IFieldEdit2 field3 = new FieldClass() as IFieldEdit2;
Field3.Name_2 = "StatePopulation";
Field3.Type_2 = esriFieldType.esriFieldTypeString;
fields.Field_2[2] = field3;
```

> **NOTE** In the preceding code, you added the OID field manually. You can also automatically provide required fields and then add the necessary fields manually. The `RequiredFields` property of an instance of the `IObjectClassDescription` interface returns a `Fields` instance that contains the mandatory `Field` instances, such as an OID field.

In the third step, you must use the `CreateTable()` method of the `IFeatureWorkspace` interface to create a table. This method solicits the name of `Table` and `Fields` objects as mandatory inputs. It is always a good idea to check for the existence of a table with the same name in the same location before creating it, as shown in the following code:

```
IWorkspaceFactory wsf = new FileGDBWorkspaceFactoryClass();
IWorkspace ws = wsf.OpenFromFile(fileGDBAddress,
ArcCatalog.Application.hWnd);
IWorkspace2 ws2 = ws as IWorkspace2;
if (!ws2.get_NameExists(esriDatasetType.esriDTTable, tableName))
{
    IFeatureWorkspace fws = ws as IFeatureWorkspace;
    ITable table = fws.CreateTable(tableName, fields, null,
    null, "");
}
```

> **NOTE** It is a good idea to validate the `Fields` instance before creating a table. For this task, you can take advantage of the `Validate()` method of an instance of the `FieldChecker` CoClass. This method creates a validated version of the input `Fields` object.

At this point, you can use a live instance of `Table` to create a record. Using a `Table` to create a `Row` instance ensures that the created `Row` has the necessary and appropriate placeholders for storing values for all columns in the table.

```
IRow row = table.CreateRow();
```

The `IRow` interface inherits from the `IRowBuffer` interface. The `IRowBuffer` interface has a `Value` property which must be utilized to fill each placeholder of a row. Finally, to save a row, the `Store()` method must be called.

```
row.Value[1] = "Texas";
row.Value[2] = 20000000;
row.Store();
```

There is no need to assign values for an OID field; that is why the index for the `Value` property in the preceding code starts from 1.

It's time to have some fun with the topics you have learned. In the next Try It Out, you create an ArcCatalog add-in that converts a Comma Separated Values (CSV) text file to a table in a file geodatabase. The first line in the text file indicates field names. The user of the add-in just needs to select the source text file and target file geodatabase. Behind the scenes, the add-in reads the first line of the text file to extract the field names and then infer the data type of each field based on the second line inside the text file. The rest of the code of the add-in creates a table with the same name as the input text file and populates it.

<hr>

TRY IT OUT   Converting a CSV Text File to a Table (CSV2Table.zip)

1. Create a new project in Visual Studio. Select ArcCatalog Add-in as the template (in the New Project window, expand the Visual C# ➪ ArcGIS node and select ArcCatalog Add-In from the Desktop Add-Ins templates) and name your solution **CSV2Table**. Then click OK.

2. In the Add-Ins Wizard, provide your information and click the Next button. On the next page, select Button as the type of add-in and change its setting, as shown in Figure 7-14.

FIGURE 7-14

3. Add `Catalog`, `DataSourcesFile`, `DataSourcesGDB`, and `Geodatabase` references to your project and the following lines of code to the top section of the `csvConvertor.cs` file's code window:

```
using ESRI.ArcGIS.Catalog;
using ESRI.ArcGIS.CatalogUI;
using ESRI.ArcGIS.DataSourcesGDB;
using ESRI.ArcGIS.Geodatabase;
```

4. You must determine the types of `Field` objects based on the data. For simplifying this task, it is a good idea to create an enumeration that contains three members for numeric, textual, and date data types. You can add the code of this enumeration anywhere in the class file (`csvConvertor .cs`) of your button as long as it is not inside other methods. Name the enumeration `FieldDataType` and add it as the first item in the class definition. Your class file should be similar to the following code:

```
public class csvConvertor : ESRI.ArcGIS.Desktop.AddIns.Button
    {
        public enum FieldDataType
        {
            numeric,
            text,
            date
        }
        public csvConvertor(){}
```

```
          protected override void OnClick(){}

          protected override void OnUpdate()
          { Enabled = ArcCatalog.Application != null;}
      }
```

5. In order to determine the data type of each field, you need to evaluate the data items (CSVs) of the second line in a text file. The following method evaluates its input and returns a member of FieldDataType enumeration indicating its input data type. Add the following method in the class definition of your button (csvConvertor.cs):

```
private FieldDataType DetermineTheFieldType(string item)
      {
          double num;
          DateTime date;
          if (double.TryParse(item, out num))
          {
              return FieldDataType.numeric;
          }
          else if (DateTime.TryParse(item, out date))
          {
              return FieldDataType.date;
          }
          //otherwise it is string
          return FieldDataType.text;
      }
```

6. As the beginning of this section states, the first step to create a table is to create a Fields instance. This instance must contain one OID field and other Field objects. The names of other Field objects should be extracted from the first line of the text file. In addition, the data type of Field objects must be inferred from the first line of data in the text file, which is the second line of the text file. So you need to write a method with two inputs representing the field names and data items of the first line of data for creating a table. In addition, this method uses the DetermineTheFieldType() method and returns an IFieldsEdit instance. Add the following method to your add-in (csvConvertor.cs):

```
private IFieldsEdit CreateTableSchema(string[] dataItemsOfFirstLine, string[]
fieldNames)
      {
          IFieldsEdit fields = new FieldsClass();
          fields.FieldCount_2 = fieldNames.Length + 1;
          //creating OID field
          IFieldEdit OIDField = new FieldClass() as IFieldEdit2;
          OIDField.Name_2 = "ObjectIDentifier";
          OIDField.Type_2 = esriFieldType.esriFieldTypeOID;
          fields.Field_2[0] = OIDField;

          for (int i = 0; i < fieldNames.Length; i++)
          {
              IFieldEdit2 newField = new FieldClass() as IFieldEdit2;
              FieldDataType FDT = DetermineTheFieldType(dataItemsOfFirstLine[i]);
```

```
newField.Name_2 = fieldNames[i].Trim();

switch (FDT)
{
    case FieldDataType.numeric:
        newField.Type_2 = esriFieldType.esriFieldTypeDouble;
        break;
    case FieldDataType.date:
        newField.Type_2 = esriFieldType.esriFieldTypeDate;
        break;
    default:
        newField.Type_2 = esriFieldType.esriFieldTypeString;
        break;
}

fields.Field_2[i + 1] = newField;
}
return fields;
}
```

7. Time to create a table, which is a simple task. All you need are the name, a `Fields` object, and the path to the file geodatabase in which the created table will be saved. Add the following method to create the table:

```
private ITable CreateTable(string tableName, IFieldsEdit fields, string
fileGDBAddress)
{

    IWorkspaceFactory wsf = new FileGDBWorkspaceFactoryClass();
    IWorkspace ws = wsf.OpenFromFile(fileGDBAddress,
    ArcCatalog.Application.hWnd);

    IFeatureWorkspace fws = ws as IFeatureWorkspace;
    IWorkspace2 ws2 = ws as IWorkspace2;
    if (!ws2.get_NameExists(esriDatasetType.esriDTTable, tableName))
    {
        ITable table = fws.CreateTable(tableName, fields, null, null, "");
        return table;
    }
    return null;
}
```

8. In order to make the process of interacting with your button more user friendly, it is good to use the GxDialog and show it to users to allow them to select the source text file and target file geodatabase. Add the following lines of code in the `OnClick()` method to do this:

```
//using gxdiaolog to get the text file
IGxDialog gxd = new GxDialogClass();
gxd.AllowMultiSelect = false;
gxd.ButtonCaption = "Select txt file";
gxd.Title = "Select a text file to be converted to a Table inside a
File GDB";
gxd.RememberLocation = true;
```

```
IGxObjectFilter gxTxtFilter = new GxFilterTextFilesClass();
gxd.ObjectFilter = gxTxtFilter;

IEnumGxObject gxEnumObj;
gxd.DoModalOpen(ArcCatalog.Application.hWnd, out gxEnumObj);

IGxObject gxObj = gxEnumObj.Next();
//user clicks on cancel button
if (gxObj == null)
{ return; }

//getting the address of text file
string fileAddress = gxObj.FullName;
//set the name of table as the name of text file
string tableName = gxObj.BaseName;
//again displaying gxDialog to select file GDB
gxd.ButtonCaption = "Select FileGDB";
gxd.Title = "Select target file Geodatabase ";
IGxObjectFilter gxGDBFilter = new GxFilterFileGeodatabasesClass();
gxd.ObjectFilter = gxGDBFilter;
gxd.DoModalOpen(ArcCatalog.Application.hWnd, out gxEnumObj);
gxObj = gxEnumObj.Next();
if (gxObj == null)
{ return; }
//getting the address of fileGDB
string fileGDBAddress = gxObj.FullName;
```

9. You need to read the first and second lines of the text file and call the `CreateTableSchema()` method in order to create a `Fields` instance. So add the following code to the `OnClick()` method:

```
FileStream fs = new FileStream(fileAddress, FileMode.Open);
StreamReader sr = new StreamReader(fs);
//read the first line (field names)
string lineOfTxtFile = sr.ReadLine();
//extracting fieldNames
string[] splitter = { "," };
string[] fieldNames = lineOfTxtFile.Split(splitter,
StringSplitOptions.RemoveEmptyEntries);
//read the second line of text file (first line of data)
lineOfTxtFile = sr.ReadLine();
//create fields based on the data type of first record
string[] dataItems = lineOfTxtFile.Split(splitter,
StringSplitOptions.RemoveEmptyEntries);
//Create collection of Fields to be used to build a Table
IFieldsEdit fields = CreateTableSchema(dataItems, fieldNames);
```

10. Next, use the `CreateTable()` method in the `OnClick()` method.

```
//create Table instance
ITable table = CreateTable(tableName, fields, fileGDBAddress);
//table exists
if (table == null)
{ return; }
```

11. Up to this point, you have read the first and second lines of the text file. You also have a table. Now you need to create rows and populate them and do the same for the other lines of the text file. Add the following code at the end of the `OnClick()` method:

```
//create each row as reader reads the text file
while (lineOfTxtFile != null)
{
    IRow row = table.CreateRow();
    //Important tip: any table must have one OID Field
    //the first field is OID
    for (int i = 0; i < table.Fields.FieldCount - 1; i++)
    {
        if (table.Fields.Field[i + 1].Type == esriFieldType.esriFieldTypeDouble)
        {
            row.Value[i + 1] = double.Parse(dataItems[i]);
        }
        else if (table.Fields.Field[i].Type == esriFieldType.esriFieldTypeDate)
        {
            row.Value[i + 1] = DateTime.Parse(dataItems[i]);
        }
        else
        {
            row.Value[i + 1] = dataItems[i].Trim();
        }
    }
    //saving a row in table
    row.Store();

    lineOfTxtFile = sr.ReadLine();
    if (lineOfTxtFile != null)
    {
        dataItems = lineOfTxtFile.Split(spliter,
                            StringSplitOptions.RemoveEmptyEntries);
    }
}
```

12. Run your code, use the Customize menu, and select the Customize mode to add your button to the user interface of the ArcCatalog. Test the button and enjoy it. You can use the CSV file created in Chapter 4 to test this add-in.

How It Works

This Try It Out uses the famous separation of concerns principle (in its simplest form) to write reusable and maintainable code. You focused on a specific concern in each method that you created. As an example, if you want to enhance the current version of this button to separate numeric values into integral and fractional, all you need to do is to modify a single method: `DetermineTheFieldType()`.

In addition to the classes that you have explored, the other family of objects can be used for data access and creation: the Name family.

A Name object represents a very light version of a geodatabase object (such as Table, FeatureClass, and FeatureDataset). The ultimate parent interface of all Name objects (IName interface) has an Open() method, which can be used to instantiate the actual geodatabase object. Figure 7-15 illustrates the simplified hierarchy of the Name family.

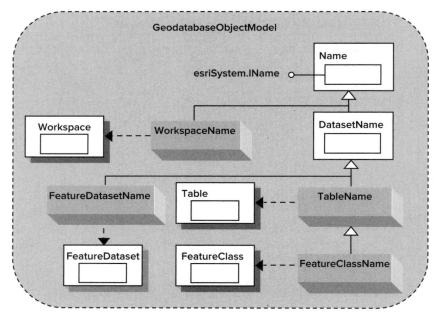

FIGURE 7-15

The following code uses the Open() method to create an IWorkspace instance:

```
IWorkspaceFactory wsf = new FileGDBWorkspaceFactoryClass();
//IWorkspace ws =wsf.OpenFromFile();
 IWorkspaceName wsn = wsf.Create(parentDir, gdbName, null,
 ArcCatalog.Application.hWnd);

IName name = wsn as IName;
//create the actual IWorkspace object
IWorkspace ws = name.Open() as IWorkspace;
```

Alternatively, you can make use of the Name family to create and access other geodatabase objects inside a workspace.

SUMMARY

From a user perspective, the geodatabase is a native format of data in the ArcGIS platform. The ArcGIS platform has various flavors, such as personal, file, and enterprise. And the ArcGIS platform manages geospatial and non-geospatial data inside various kinds of geodatabases using a relational database model.

From a developer's perspective, a geodatabase is a fully object-oriented model and system for accessing and creating various kinds of geospatial and non-geospatial data. The geodatabase model makes it possible to access geospatial and non-geospatial data which are stored in relational, georelational, and other database models using the same set of classes. The geodatabase model allows you to work with all supported formats of the ArcGIS platform based on Esri's documentations (see http://resources.arcgis.com/en/help/arcobjects-net/component help/index.html#//002500000n8v000000).

This chapter discusses some important topics about data access and creation. Use the knowledge you have gained in this chapter to get to the specific field inside a table or FeatureClass. In addition, you can create a record of a table and set its values. The next chapter discusses creating geospatial records (Feature instances).

EXERCISES

1. Which class can be used for creating a FeatureDataset inside a personal geodatabase?

2. What is the result of the following code?

```
string data=""
foreach (IField field in fields)
{
    data += field.Name +",";
}
```

3. Which attribute in the XML configuration file of an add-In indicates that a toolbar must be shown the first time ArcGIS for Desktop applications run?

You will find the answers to these exercises in this book's appendix.

▶ WHAT YOU LEARNED IN THIS CHAPTER

TOPIC	KEY CONCEPTS
Accessing fields of a FeatureLayer	A FeatureClass associated with a FeatureLayer can be accessed using the `FeatureClass` property of the `IFeatureLayer2` interface. Using the `Fields` property of the `IFeatureClass` interface, you can get a `Fields` object, which is a collection of `Field` objects composing the underlying FeatureClass.
Deleting a geodatabase object	Any class that implements the `IDataset` interface can call its `Delete()` method to delete itself. Fortunately, `IDataset` is the parent to lots of types in the geodatabase model.
Schema lock	Schema locks are used to manage geodatabase schemas (such as fields and their properties of FeatureClasses and tables) to ensure the structure of a dataset will not change once it has been opened or referenced.

8

Subsets of Records

WHAT YOU WILL LEARN IN THIS CHAPTER:

➤ Exploring object model diagrams for subsets of records

➤ Creating cursors

➤ Working with SelectionSets

➤ Performing select by attribute

➤ Performing select by location

➤ Calculating simple statistics for numerical fields

WROX.COM CODE DOWNLOADS FOR THIS CHAPTER

The wrox.com code downloads for this chapter can be found at `www.wrox.com/remtitle .cgi?isbn=1118442547` on the Download Code tab. The code is in the Chapter08 folder and is individually named according to the names throughout the chapter.

Users of ArcGIS for Desktop applications make use of subsets of features and rows in various ways. Usually they need to select and highlight features and rows in a map. Sometimes they create a subset of features to be displayed in a map. Developers have more options to work with subsets of features or rows. For example, you can work with subsets of features without highlighting them on a map.

In this chapter, you look at subsets of features and rows; how to work with existing selections; how to select subsets of features without highlighting them; and how to restrict a FeatureLayer to display just a subset of features. You also explore how you can calculate simple statistics out of a numeric field of a FeatureClass associated with a FeatureLayer.

USING OBJECT MODEL DIAGRAMS FOR SELECTING FEATURES AND ROWS

Selecting features in FeatureClasses and rows in tables is indispensable to a typical GIS workflow. Users of ArcMap applications can select features in FeatureClasses or rows in tables using the Select By Attributes window. By specifying a layer and a condition based on fields of a FeatureClass associated with the specified layer, you select features and highlight them on the map. A very similar task can be done for table objects in the List By Source contents view of the Table Of Contents window in ArcMap.

In addition to selecting features or rows by providing an attribute condition, features can be selected by their geometry and the topological relationship they have in relation with other features in and out of the parent FeatureClass. This is the basic idea of the Select By Location window of the ArcMap application, which is another way of selecting features. Figure 8-1 illustrates the object model diagram for selecting features and rows (records).

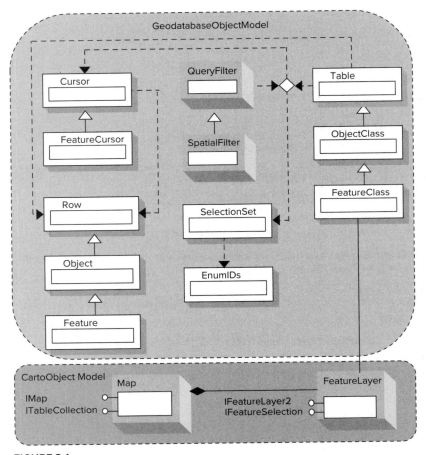

FIGURE 8-1

As described in Chapter 5 and shown here in Figure 8-1, a diamond placed at the intersection of a `Table` Class and `QueryFilter` CoClass means a `Table` instance in conjunction with a `QueryFilter` instance can create `Cursor` and `SelectionSet` objects. Since `FeatureClass` is a type of table, a `FeatureClass` can also create `FeatureCursor` and `SelectionSet` objects with the help of a `QueryFilter` instance or its spatial subclass, `SpatialFilter`.

In fact, central types in the Select By Attributes window of the ArcMap user interface are `FeatureClass` (or `Table`) and `QueryFilter` classes. As you may guess, `SpatialFilter` and `FeatureClass` compose essential types of logic behind the Select By Location window.

As you have seen in Chapter 7, a `Table` can create a brand new `Row` object. As shown in Figure 8-1, a `Cursor` can create `Rows` as well. But keep in mind that not all types of `Cursors` can create `Rows`. In this chapter I only discuss cursors that are created using the `Search()` method of a dataset (such as `Table` and `FeatureClass` instances) or a group of selected records (such as `SelectionSet` instances). These cursors (which are called *search cursors*) cannot create new records or modify or delete existing ones. Think of them as read-only cursors. Chapter 13 explains *update* and *insert* cursors.

> **NOTE** All the examples and code snippets in this chapter assume that you have some FeatureLayers of the USA FeatureDataset in ArcMap. In addition, to test the functionality of code snippets in this chapter, you can create an ArcMap Button Add-in, add the code snippet to the `OnClick()` method of the add-in, and run the code. When ArcMap pops up, after adding the button to the user interface of ArcMap, select some features or rows and select the layer or table in the Table Of Contents window, and finally click on the button. Make sure you add Geometry, Geodatabase, and Carto references to your project.

WORKING WITH EXISTING SELECTIONS

Usually, users of the ArcMap application select features using three different approaches: the Select By Attribute window, the Select By Location window, and selecting features interactively using the Select Feature By Graphics (such as Rectangle) tool. In all three approaches, the result selection will be highlighted on the map and accessible using the `IFeatureSelection` interface of the `FeatureLayer` CoClass.

Rows in tables can be selected using the Select By Attribute window or by clicking on them when the table is open. In this case, selected rows are highlighted in the Table window and can be accessed using the `Table` Class's `ITableSelection` interface.

Both `IFeatureSelection` and `ITableSelection` have a `SelectionSet` property which is of type `ISelectionSet`.

Selected records can be referenced by `SelectionSet` as well as by cursor. The `SelectionSet` instance has a very handy property that indicates the count of selected records: the `Count` property.

A FeatureLayer is associated with one SelectionSet instance, which represents selected features. The SelectionSet property of the IFeatureSelection interface that is implemented by the FeatureLayer class enables this relationship. SelectionSet will be empty if there is no selected feature in the FeatureLayer. The following code reports the count of selected features in the selected FeatureLayer in the status bar of ArcMap:

```
IMxDocument mxdoc = ArcMap.Application.Document as IMxDocument;
IStatusBar statusBar = ArcMap.Application.StatusBar;

if (mxdoc.SelectedItem is IFeatureLayer2)
{
    ILayer layer = mxdoc.SelectedLayer;
    IFeatureLayer2 featureLayer = layer as IFeatureLayer2;
    IFeatureSelection featureSelection = featureLayer as IFeatureSelection;
    ISelectionSet2 selectionSet = featureSelection.SelectionSet as ISelectionSet2 ;
    statusBar.Message[0] = string.Format("Number of selected Features in {0}: {1}",
    layer.Name, selectionSet.Count);

}

The same property on ITableSelection can be utilized to access
a SelectionSet of a Table.
else if (mxdoc.SelectedItem is ITable)
{
    ITable table = mxdoc.SelectedItem as ITable;
    IDataset dataset = table as IDataset;

    ITableSelection tableSelection = table as ITableSelection;
    ISelectionSet2 selectionSet = tableSelection.SelectionSet as ISelectionSet2;
    statusBar.Message[0] = string.Format("Number of selected Rows in {0}: {1}",
    dataset.Name, selectionSet.Count);
}
```

In addition to the Count property, the ISelectionSet2 interface provides an IDs property that references an IEnumIDs object. This object contains an object identifier of all selected records. The following code shows the object identifier of all selected rows or features in the status bar of ArcMap:

```
IMxDocument mxdoc = ArcMap.Application.Document as IMxDocument;
IStatusBar statusBar = ArcMap.Application.StatusBar;
ISelectionSet2 selectionSet = null;
if (mxdoc.SelectedItem is IFeatureLayer2)
{
    ILayer layer = mxdoc.SelectedLayer;
    IFeatureSelection featureSelection = layer as IFeatureSelection;
    selectionSet = featureSelection.SelectionSet as ISelectionSet2;
}
else if (mxdoc.SelectedItem is ITable)
{
    ITable table = mxdoc.SelectedItem as ITable;
    ITableSelection tableSelection = table as ITableSelection;
    selectionSet = tableSelection.SelectionSet as ISelectionSet2;
}
string message = "";
```

```
if (selectionSet != null)
{
    IEnumIDs enumIDs = selectionSet.IDs;
    int id = enumIDs.Next();
    while (id > 0)
    {
        message += id + ".";
        id = enumIDs.Next();
    }
}
statusBar.Message[0] = string.Format("IDs of selected Records: {0}",message);
```

In order to pull out records inside a `SelectionSet`, a `Cursor` object must be utilized. `Cursor` objects are common in Database Management System (DBMS) programming.

Generally speaking, `Cursors` are objects that manage the traversal of successive records. It is common to use a `Cursor` object to process records returned by the DBMS as a result of running a query.

In ArcObjects, cursors have the same duty: to access individual records in a `SelectionSet`, `FeatureClass`, `Table`, and any object representing a group of records. There are three different types of cursors with the same interface. Each type of cursor is used for a different purpose and is defined by the method used to create it.

Search cursors are used to return a subset of records for some type of read-only purpose, such as calculating a statistic value or getting a count of records. In this chapter, you only explore the search cursors that can be created using the `Search()` method. Other types of cursors (update and insert cursors) are discussed in later chapters.

`Cursor` objects have a `Fields` property that allows you to access the same `Field` objects that are in the parent table or FeatureClass from which the cursor was created. These `Field` objects are in the same order in the cursor as they are in the parent table, and once you access the `Fields` collection, you can reference a specific field by using its index position.

As shown in Figure 8-1, in order to create a `Cursor` object you must have a table or FeatureClass and a QueryFilter. What is not shown on this diagram is the capability of the `SelectionSet` class to create a `Cursor` object (of course, in conjunction with a `QueryFilter` object).

The `ISelectionSet2` interface has one method for creating a cursor: `Search()`. The `Search()` method creates a cursor that is able to iterate through all selected records referenced by the `SelectionSet` instance. In addition, using a `QueryFilter` instance, a subset of selected features or rows can be pulled out from the SelectionSet. Consider the following code:

```
IMxDocument mxdoc = ArcMap.Application.Document as IMxDocument;
IStatusBar statusBar = ArcMap.Application.StatusBar;
ISelectionSet2 selectionSet = null;
if (mxdoc.SelectedItem is IFeatureLayer2)
{
    string message = null;
    ILayer layer = mxdoc.SelectedLayer;
    if (layer.Name == "U.S. States (Generalized)")
    {
        IFeatureLayer2 featureLayer = layer as IFeatureLayer2;
```

```
                IFeatureSelection featureSelection =
                featureLayer as IFeatureSelection;
                selectionSet = featureSelection.SelectionSet as ISelectionSet2;
                ICursor Cursor = null;
                //all features in a SelectionSet
                selectionSet.Search(null, true, out Cursor);
                IFeatureCursor featureCursor = Cursor as IFeatureCursor;

                //finding the index of the STATE_NAME field
                //the following two methods have the same result
                //first method
                //int fieldIndex = featureLayer.FeatureClass.FindField("STATE_NAME");
                //second method
                int fieldIndex = featureCursor.Fields.FindField("STATE_NAME");

                IFeature feature = featureCursor.NextFeature();
                while (feature != null)
                {
                    message += feature.Value[fieldIndex] + ",";
                    feature = featureCursor.NextFeature();
                }
                statusBar.Message[0] ="Selected States:"+ message;
            }
        }
```

In order to pull out all the records inside a SelectionSet, a null value is provided as the QueryFilter.

> **NOTE** *The second input for the* `Search()` *method is a Boolean value that specifies whether memory occupied by the referenced record will be recycled. In other words, if set as* `true` *(in this case, the* `Cursor` *object is called the recycling cursor), each record referenced by the cursor will occupy the same memory location as the other successive records and as a result will optimize the read-only access. The reference to the fetched record will be lost when the recycling cursor points to the next record (as a result of calling to the* `NextRow()` *or* `NextFeature()` *methods). For this reason, records that are returned by a recycling cursor must not be updated.*
>
> *In summary, for read-only cursors (search cursors), setting this input parameter as* `true` *results in better performance. Later this chapter explains when you shouldn't use recycling for search cursors. For update and insert cursors, this parameter should be set as* `false`*. Chapter 13 furthur describes this topic.*

QueryFilter and its subclass SpatialFilter are CoClasses and can be created with the new keyword. A QueryFilter object has a WhereClause property, which is simply an expression that defines an attribute query.

```
    IQueryFilter2 queryFilter = new QueryFilterClass();
    queryFilter.WhereClause="STATE_NAME='California'";
```

Actually, the WhereClause property is a condition part of a Structured Query Language (SQL) statement. If you look at the Select By Attributes window, you will notice that ArcGIS provides the first part of the SQL statement and the second part (condition) should be provided by a QueryFilter object. Near the bottom of Figure 8-2, you can see SELECT * FROM states WHERE.

This statement is SQL, so you have to adhere to the rules of SQL, such as enclosing text literals in quotations. In addition, you can take advantage of SQL in the condition part of the query. Consider the following example: If you want to select California, Colorado, Georgia, Maryland, Nevada, and New York states you should provide the condition in the Select By Attributes window, as shown in Figure 8-3.

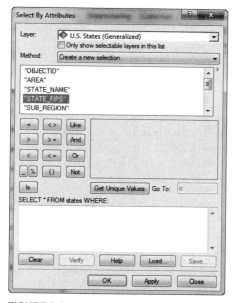

FIGURE 8-2

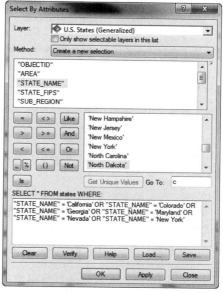

FIGURE 8-3

Instead, you can make use of the `in` operator to select all the mentioned states, as shown in Figure 8-4.

SELECTING ROWS AND FEATURES

In order to select rows or features based on attribute queries, you need to create a new instance of `QueryFilter` and use the `ITableSelection` or `IFeatureSelection` interfaces. The following code snippet first finds the U.S. Cities layer and then highlights all the cities that have the Texas value in their `STATE_NAME` column:

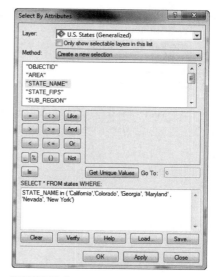

FIGURE 8-4

```
IMxDocument mxdoc = ArcMap.Application.Document as IMxDocument;
IMap map = mxdoc.FocusMap;
for (int i = 0; i < map.LayerCount; i++)
{
    if (map.Layer[i].Name == "U.S. Cities")
    {
        IFeatureLayer2 featureLayer = map.Layer[i] as IFeatureLayer2;
        IFeatureSelection featureSelection = featureLayer as IFeatureSelection;

        IQueryFilter qF = new QueryFilterClass();
        qF.WhereClause = "STATE_NAME = 'Texas'";

        featureSelection.SelectFeatures(qF,
        esriSelectionResultEnum.esriSelectionResultNew, false);
        mxdoc.ActiveView.Refresh();
    }
}
```

The second parameter of the `SelectFeatures()` method specifies how the result of the selection is created in relation to the current selection. As users of ArcGIS for Desktop, you can see various alternatives in the Method ComboBox, which has four members for creating a new selection, adding to the current selection, removing from the current selection, and selecting from the current selection.

As a developer, you access the same methods through the `esriSelectionResultEnum` enumeration, which has five members. The additional member (`esriSelectionResultXOR`) performs an exclusive OR operation with the existing selection.

For selecting features based on their location, you have to resort to the `SpatialFilter` CoClass. `SpatialFilter` has a `Geometry` property, which is a basis for spatial search. It is of type `IGeometry`, which is a parent interface of all types in the geometry library. That means that you can use geometry of all feature types for this property.

The `SpatialRel` property specifies the type of spatial relationship to be used in selecting features. `SpatialRel` is of type `esriSpatialRelEnum` and contains members for various spatial relationships. The following Try It Out uses the visible extent of a map as geometry and selects all the features of all visible layers inside that.

TRY IT OUT   **Selecting Visible Features of Visible Layers (VisibleFeatures.zip)**

1. Create a new ArcMap Add-in project. Name the solution **SelectionAddIn**. In the Add-Ins Wizard, provide the necessary information as shown in Figure 8-5 and then click Finish.

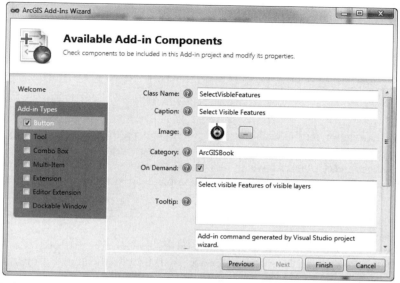

FIGURE 8-5

2. Add ESRI.ArcGIS.Carto, ESRI.ArcGIS.Geodatabase, and ESRI.ArcGIS.Geometry references to your project and type the following using directives at the top of the SelectVisibleFeatures .cs code window:

```
using ESRI.ArcGIS.Carto;
using ESRI.ArcGIS.Geodatabase;
using ESRI.ArcGIS.ArcMapUI;
```

3. Add the following code to the OnClick() method of the button:

```
IMxDocument mxdoc = ArcMap.Application.Document as IMxDocument;
IMap map = mxdoc.FocusMap;
IEnumLayer enumLayer = map.Layers;
ILayer layer = enumLayer.Next();

ISpatialFilter spatialFilter = new SpatialFilter();
spatialFilter.Geometry = (map as IActiveView).Extent;
spatialFilter.SpatialRel = esriSpatialRelEnum.esriSpatialRelContains;

while (layer != null)
{
    if (layer is IFeatureLayer2)
    {
        if (layer.Visible)
        {
            IFeatureLayer2 featureLayer = layer as IFeatureLayer2;
            IFeatureSelection featureSelection = featureLayer as IFeatureSelection;
```

```
            featureSelection.SelectFeatures(spatialFilter,
                esriSelectionResultEnum.esriSelectionResultNew, false);
        }
    }
    layer = enumLayer.Next();
}
mxdoc.ActiveView.Refresh();
```

How It Works

As mentioned in Chapter 6, you can get or set the visible extent of a map using the `Extent` property of the `IActiveView` interface. This property is of type `IEnvelope`, which is the minimum bounding rectangle of a geometry type. All geometry objects have an associated `Envelope` (this is applicable even for point features). In this Try It Out, you select features that are completely contained by the visible area of the map.

Most of the time, the geometry or shape of a feature is used as the `Geometry` property of a `SpatialFilter` instance. The geometry of a feature can be accessed through the `Shape` property of the `IFeature` interface. The following code snippet first selects Colorado and uses its geometry to select rivers that intersect its shape:

```
IMxDocument mxdoc = ArcMap.Application.Document as IMxDocument;
IMap map = mxdoc.FocusMap;
IGeometry geometry = null;
IFeatureSelection featureSelection = null;
for (int i = 0; i < map.LayerCount; i++)
{
    ILayer layer = map.Layer[i];
    if (map.Layer[i].Name == "U.S. Rivers (Generalized)")
    {
        IFeatureLayer2 featureLayer = map.Layer[i] as IFeatureLayer2;
        featureSelection = featureLayer as IFeatureSelection;
    }
    else if (layer.Name == "U.S. States (Generalized)")
    {
        //selects Colorado state and gets the shape of it
        IFeatureLayer2 featureLayer = map.Layer[i] as IFeatureLayer2;
        IFeatureSelection statesSelection = featureLayer as IFeatureSelection;

        IQueryFilter2 queryFilter = new QueryFilterClass();
        queryFilter.WhereClause = "STATE_NAME='Colorado'";

        statesSelection.SelectFeatures(queryFilter,
        esriSelectionResultEnum.esriSelectionResultNew, true);
        ICursor cursor = null;
        statesSelection.SelectionSet.Search(null, true, out cursor);
        IFeatureCursor featureCursor = cursor as IFeatureCursor;
        //get the geometry needed for SpatialFilter
        IFeature colorado = featureCursor.NextFeature();
```

```
            geometry = colorado.Shape;

        }

    }

    ISpatialFilter spatialFilter = new SpatialFilter();
    spatialFilter.Geometry = geometry;
    spatialFilter.SpatialRel = esriSpatialRelEnum.esriSpatialRelIntersects;

    featureSelection.SelectFeatures(spatialFilter,
    esriSelectionResultEnum.esriSelectionResultNew, false);
    mxdoc.ActiveView.Refresh();
```

For clearing selected records the `Clear()` method of `IFeatureSelection` or `ITableSelection` interfaces should be called. Using the `ClearSelection()` method of `IMap` interface, all selected Features as well as selected rows inside a map will be cleared.

```
            IMxDocument mxdoc = ArcMap.Application.Document as IMxDocument;
            mxdoc.FocusMap.ClearSelection();
            mxdoc.ActiveView.Refresh();
```

Accessing a Subset of Records

As an ArcGIS developer, you can access a subset of records without highlighting them in a map. As shown in Figure 8-1, in conjunction with a `QueryFilter` object (or its spatial subclass) the `IFeatureClass` and `ITable` interfaces are able to directly create a `FeatureCursor` and `Cursor`, respectively. In this case, there is no need to create a `Cursor` object using the `SelectionSet` Class. The following code reports the number of cities inside Texas without highlighting them on the map.

```
    IMxDocument mxdoc = ArcMap.Application.Document as IMxDocument;
    for (int i = 0; i < mxdoc.FocusMap.LayerCount; i++)
    {
        ILayer layer = mxdoc.FocusMap.Layer[i];
        if (layer.Name == "U.S. Cities")
        {
            IFeatureLayer2 featureLayer = layer as IFeatureLayer2;
            IFeatureClass featureClass = featureLayer.FeatureClass;

            IQueryFilter qF = new QueryFilterClass();
            qF.WhereClause = "STATE_NAME = 'Texas'";
            IFeatureCursor featureCursor = featureClass.Search(qF, true);
            IFeature feature = featureCursor.NextFeature();
            int count = 0;
            while (feature != null)
            {
                count++;
                feature = featureCursor.NextFeature();
            }
            ArcMap.Application.StatusBar.Message[0] = count + " cities are inside
            Texas state";
        }
    }
```

In most cases, attribute and spatial queries must be combined to get the most out of queries. In the next Try It Out, you use a new type of ArcObjects component: a dockable window. Creating a dockable window in an add-in template is a little tricky, so you first create a dockable window component using the Extending ArcObjects template, and then learn about a little difference which should be considered when using add-in templates.

TRY IT OUT   **Dockable Window for Selection (DockableSelection.zip)**

Before you start, take a look at what exactly a dockable window is. A dockable window is a window inside ArcGIS for Desktop applications which contains other Windows controls and can be used for various purposes. A common example of a dockable window is the Table Of Contents window in ArcMap, which provides different tabs (Contents view) for accessing various properties of added data. For example, it contains a TreeView control to display geospatial data in tree structure.

As the name suggests, a dockable window can be moved and docked (that is, attached at various places) within the application, or it can float. Usually a separate button in the user interface is responsible for showing or hiding it.

1. Start a new project in Visual Studio and name it **DockableSelection**. Choose the Extending ArcObjects template, select Class Library (ArcMap) as shown in Figure 8-6, and click OK.

FIGURE 8-6

2. In the ArcGIS Project Wizard, add ArcMapUI, Carto, Geodatabase, and Geometry references to your project, as shown in Figure 8-7, and click the Finish button.

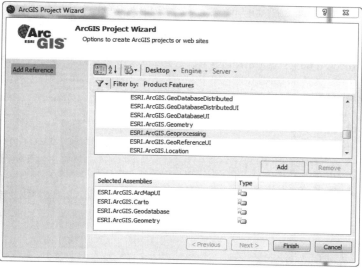

FIGURE 8-7

After a few seconds, the Wizard will create a default class file for you. You don't need this class, so you can delete it permanently. Right-click on your project and from the Add submenu, select New Item. In the Extending ArcObjects template, select the Dockable Window (Desktop) item and name it `selectionDockable.cs`, as shown in Figure 8-8, then click the Add button.

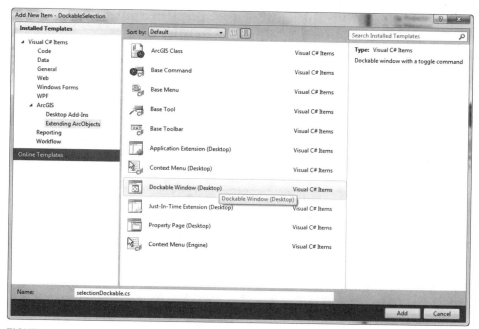

FIGURE 8-8

3. Select the Desktop ArcMap item in the newly opened window, as shown in Figure 8-9, and click OK.

4. Visual Studio adds an empty UserControl and a command button to the project. The UserControl is used for adding necessary Windows controls and the functionality behind them. The button is used for displaying the dockable window in the user interface of ArcMap. Open the code for the button (`selectionDockableCommand.cs`), and modify the public `selectionDockableWindow` method to match Figure 8-10. That is all the modification in the button's code. Leave all the remaining code as is.

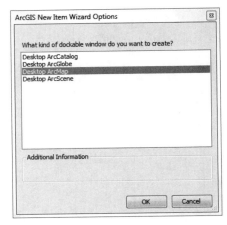

FIGURE 8-9

```
COM Registration Function(s)

public selectionDockableCommand()
{
    //
    // TODO: Define values for the public properties
    //
    base.m_category = "ArcGISBook";
    base.m_caption = "Show/Hide Selection Dockable window";
    base.m_message = "Show/Hide Selection Dockable window in the user interface of ArcMap";
    base.m_toolTip = "Show/Hide Selection Dockable window";
    base.m_name = "ArcGISBook_selectionDockableCommand";
```

FIGURE 8-10

5. In Solution Explorer, double-click on the `selectionDockable.cs` file to open its designer. At the moment, it just contains a single label (LabelPlaceHolder) control. Clear its text property and change its size to 250;570.

6. Add three Button controls, one ListBox control, and a Label control to the LabelPlaceHolder and name them **btnPopulateList, btnSelect, btnClear, lstStates,** and **lblReport.** Change their properties as listed in Table 8-1.

TABLE 8-1: Properties of Controls

CONTROL	PROPERTY	VALUE
btnPopulateList	Text	Populate List of States
lstStates	Size	210;200
btnSelect	Text	Select Cities in the Selected State

btnClear	Text	Clear Selection
lblReport	AutoSize	False
lblReport	Size	210;100

Position the controls as shown in Figure 8-11.

7. Double-click on btnPopulateList to go to the code window of the dockable window. At the top of the code window, type the following using directives:

```
using ESRI.ArcGIS.Geodatabase;
using ESRI.ArcGIS.ArcMapUI;
using ESRI.ArcGIS.Carto;
using ESRI.ArcGIS.Geometry;
```

8. Above the event handler of btnPopulate list, add the declaration of three variables.

```
string selectedState = null;
        IFeatureLayer2 citiesFL = null;
        IFeatureLayer2 statesLayer = null;
```

9. Add the names of all states from the U.S. States FeatureLayer to a Listbox control. To perform this task, you need to create a FeatureCursor for the mentioned layer and iterate through all features, as shown in the following code:

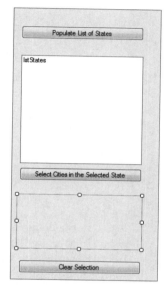

FIGURE 8-11

```
private void btnPopulateList_Click(object sender, EventArgs e)
        {
            lstStates.Items.Clear();
            IMxDocument mxdoc = m_application.Document as IMxDocument;
            IMap map = mxdoc.FocusMap;

            IEnumLayer enumLayer = map.Layers;
            ILayer layer = enumLayer.Next();

            while (layer != null)
            {
                if (layer is IFeatureLayer2 && layer.Name == "U.S. States
                (Generalized)")
                {
                    statesLayer = layer as IFeatureLayer2;
                }
                layer = enumLayer.Next();
            }

            if (statesLayer == null)
            { return; }

            IFeatureCursor statesFCursor = statesLayer.FeatureClass.Search(null,
            true);
            int state_nameIndex = statesFCursor.Fields.FindField("STATE_NAME");
```

```
        IFeature state = statesFCursor.NextFeature();

        if (state_nameIndex < 0)
        { return; }

        while (state != null)
        {
            lstStates.Items.Add(state.Value[state_nameIndex]);
            state = statesFCursor.NextFeature();
        }
    }
```

10. Press Shift+F7 or select View Designer in Solution Explorer to go to the designer window. This time, double-click lstStates to create skeleton code for the SelectedIndexChanged event handler. In this event handler, you want to figure out which state the user has selected.

```
        private void lstStates_SelectedIndexChanged(object sender, EventArgs e)
        {
            if (lstStates.SelectedIndex >= 0)
            {
                selectedState = lstStates.SelectedItem.ToString();
            }
        }
```

11. Again in the designer window, double-click on btnSelect to create stub code for handling the click event. In this handler, you want to perform a selection based on the geometry of the selected state. In other words, you want to select all cities contained by a selected state. As a result, you need to first find the state feature that was selected by the user and use its shape as the geometry of a SpatialFilter object. Also you want to zoom to selected cities and calculate a summation of their population. The following code illustrates the click event handler of btnSelect.

```
private void btnSelect_Click(object sender, EventArgs e)
    {
        IMxDocument mxdoc = m_application.Document as IMxDocument;

        IFeatureClass stateFC = statesLayer.FeatureClass;
        IQueryFilter2 qF = new QueryFilterClass();
        qF.WhereClause = string.Format("STATE_NAME='{0}'", selectedState);
        IFeatureCursor stateFCursor = stateFC.Search(qF, true);
        //just one state is selected
        IFeature selectedStateFeature = stateFCursor.NextFeature();
        IGeometry5 shapeOfSelectedState = selectedStateFeature.Shape as
        IGeometry5;

        IMap map = mxdoc.FocusMap;
        IEnumLayer enumLayer = map.Layers;
        ILayer layer = enumLayer.Next();

        while (layer != null)
        {
            if (layer.Name == "U.S. Cities" && layer is IFeatureLayer2)
            {
                citiesFL = layer as IFeatureLayer2;
            }
            layer = enumLayer.Next();
```

```
        }

        ISpatialFilter sF = new SpatialFilterClass();
        sF.Geometry = shapeOfSelectedState;
        sF.SpatialRel = esriSpatialRelEnum.esriSpatialRelContains;

        IFeatureSelection citiesFeatureSelection = citiesFL as
        IFeatureSelection;
        citiesFeatureSelection.SelectFeatures(sF,
        esriSelectionResultEnum.esriSelectionResultNew, false);

        ICursor citiesCursor = null;
        citiesFeatureSelection.SelectionSet.Search(null, true, out
        citiesCursor);
        int pop1990Index = citiesCursor.Fields.FindField("POP1990");
        long totalPopulation = 0;
        IRow city = citiesCursor.NextRow();
        while (city != null)
        {

            totalPopulation += long.Parse(city.Value[pop1990Index].ToString());

            city = citiesCursor.NextRow();
        }

        //zoom to selected features
        mxdoc.ActiveView.Extent = shapeOfSelectedState.Envelope;
        //IFeatureClass citiesFC = citiesFL.FeatureClass;
        mxdoc.ActiveView.Refresh();

        lblReport.Text = String.Format("Number of Selected Cities: {0} \n",
         citiesFeatureSelection.SelectionSet.Count);
        lblReport.Text += String.Format("Total Population: {0}",
        totalPopulation);

    }
```

12. When a user clicks the btnClear button, the selected features and selected states in the ListBox should be cleared and the extent of the map should be restored to the envelope of all states. Double-click the btnClear button in Designer view and add the following code:

```
    private void btnClear_Click(object sender, EventArgs e)
    {
        selectedState = "";
        lstStates.ClearSelected();
        lblReport.Text = "";
        //todo: clear selected features in specified layer
        (citiesFL as IFeatureSelection).Clear();

        IMxDocument mxdoc = m_application.Document as IMxDocument;
        if (statesLayer != null)
        {
            mxdoc.ActiveView.Extent = (statesLayer as ILayer).AreaOfInterest;
        }
        mxdoc.ActiveView.Refresh();
    }
```

13. Just one remaining point: The caption of the dockable window is defined in the region called `IDockableWindowDef Members`. This region can be found just above the code that you write in this Try It Out. (See Figure 8-12.)

```
public partial class selectionDockable : UserControl, IDockableWindowDef
{
    private IApplication m_application;

    COM Registration Function(s)

    public selectionDockable()...

    IDockableWindowDef Members

    string selectedState = null;
    IFeatureLayer2 citiesFL = null;
    IFeatureLayer2 statesLayer = null;

    private void btnPopulateList_Click(object sender, EventArgs e)
    {
        lstStates.Items.Clear();
        IMxDocument mxdoc = m_application.Document as IMxDocument;
        IMap map = mxdoc.FocusMap;
```

FIGURE 8-12

Expand this region, and in the `IDockableWindowDef.Caption` replace the default string (`my C# Dockable Window`) with `Selection Dockable window`.

14. Run your project. After a few seconds, ArcMap will appear. You have to use the Customize window for adding the button to the user interface of ArcMap. So in the Commands tab, select the ArcGISBook category and you will see a button with a clever rabbit icon. Drag and drop it somewhere appropriate in the user interface (such as any toolbar or menu). Add the USA FeatureDataset of `TemplateData.gdb` and test the functionality of the dockable window. You can change the button's icon using basic tools provided by Visual Studio.

How It Works

The dockable window is a flexible component which can contain many controls in order to perform useful tasks. In this Try It Out, you combined attribute and spatial subsets of features to select cities in a selected state. Usually, a button should provide functionality for displaying a dockable window in the user interface.

When you create a dockable window using the Extending ArcObjects template, a button will be created automatically. But this is not the case when using the Desktop Add-Ins template. That is why you use the Extending ArcObjects project template. But with little effort, you can achieve the same result with the Desktop Add-ins template.

Simple Statistics of Features

Sometimes you need to calculate simple statistics such as summation, standard deviation, and average for a numerical field in a table or a FeatureClass. It is possible to iterate through all records and calculate these statistics, but there are two classes in the ArcObjects library that can simplify this task. These two classes and their relationships are shown in Figure 8-13. The `DataStatistics` class can be used to retrieve simple statistics of a single field. As shown in Figure 8-13, in order to calculate statistics of a specific field, an instance of the `Cursor` object is needed. After setting the `Field` and `Cursor` properties, the statistics of the specified field can be accessed through the `Statistics` property.

The `Statistics` property is of type `IStatisticsResults`, which is implemented by the `BaseStatistics` CoClass.

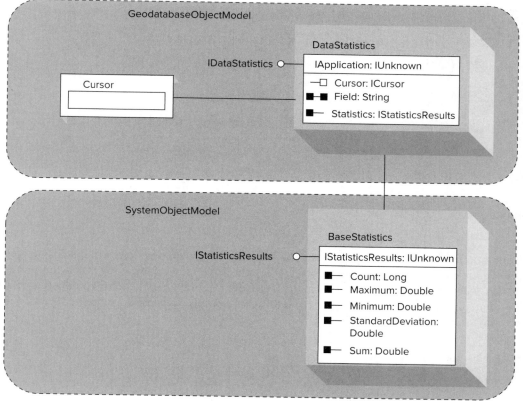

FIGURE 8-13

In the next Try It Out, you create a dockable window add-in that calculates statistics for numerical fields.

TRY IT OUT Dockable Window for Statistics (DockableWindowStatistics.zip)

1. Create a new project in Visual Studio. Click on the Desktop Add-Ins template and select the ArcMap Add-in. Name your add-in **DockableWindowStatistics** and click the OK button.

2. As always, provide your information and Click Next in the ArcGIS Add-Ins Wizard. Select Dockable Windows as the type of the add-In, set other fields as shown in Figure 8-14, and click Finish. Note that you don't specify a category for the dockable window component.

FIGURE 8-14

3. In Solution Explorer, double-click on the DockableWinStatistics component to open its designer. At the moment, it is an empty UserControl. Using the Toolbox window, add two buttons, one ListBox, one ComboBox, and a Label to the UserControl, and name them **btnPopulateLayerList**, **btnCalculate**, **lstLayers**, **cboNumFields**, and **lblReport**, respectively. Change their properties as listed in Table 8-2.

TABLE 8-2: Properties of Controls

CONTROL	PROPERTY	VALUE
btnPopulateLayerList	Text	List of Layers
btnCalculate	Text	Calculate Statistics
lblReport	BorderStyle	FixedSingle
lblReport	AutoSize	False

Position the controls as shown in Figure 8-15.

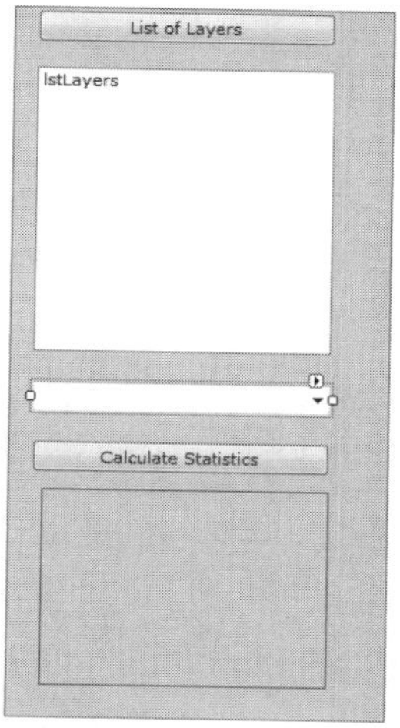

4. Add Carto and Geodatabase references to your project. Double-click on btnPopulateLayerList to go to the code window of the dockable window. At the top of the code window, type the following using directives:

```
using ESRI.ArcGIS.ArcMapUI;
using ESRI.ArcGIS.Carto;
using ESRI.ArcGIS.Geodatabase;
using ESRI.ArcGIS.esriSystem;
```

5. Above the event handler of btnPopulateLayerList, add the declaration of one variable to be shared between some blocks of code.

```
IMxDocument mxdoc = ArcMap.Application.Document as IMxDocument;
```

6. Click on the btnPopulateLayerList results to add the names of all FeatureLayer objects inside the Table Of Contents window to the ListBox. The event handler should be similar to the following code:

```
private void btnPopulateLayerList_Click(object sender, EventArgs e)
{
    lstLayers.Items.Clear();
    cboNumFields.Tag = null;

    IMap map = mxdoc.FocusMap;
    IEnumLayer enumLayer = map.Layers;
    ILayer layer = enumLayer.Next();

    while (layer != null)
    {
        if (layer is IFeatureLayer2)
        {
            lstLayers.Items.Add(layer.Name);
        }
        layer = enumLayer.Next();
    }
}
```

FIGURE 8-15

7. Suppose a user clicks the btnPopulateLayerList and a list of all existing layers is displayed for him or her. The next step is to provide logic to determine which item (which represents the name of a layer) of ListBox (lstLayers) the user selects. Then you need to add the names of all numerical fields of the FeatureClasses associated with the selected FeatureLayer and add them to the ComboBox. Press Shift+F7 to go to the designer window of Visual Studio and double-click on lstLayers to create the stub code for its SelectedIndexChanged event handler. Following is the complete code for this event handler:

```
private void lstLayers_SelectedIndexChanged(object sender, EventArgs e)
{
    cboNumFields.Items.Clear();
    string selectedLayerName = null;
    if (lstLayers.SelectedIndex >= 0)
    {
        selectedLayerName = lstLayers.SelectedItem.ToString();
    }

    if (selectedLayerName == null)
```

```
    { return; }

    //getting all the numerical fields
    IMap map = mxdoc.FocusMap;
    IEnumLayer enumLayer = map.Layers;
    ILayer layer = enumLayer.Next();
    IFeatureLayer2 featureLayer = null;

    while (layer != null)
    {
        if (layer.Name == selectedLayerName)
        {
            featureLayer = layer as IFeatureLayer2;
        }
        layer = enumLayer.Next();
    }

    IFeatureClass FC = featureLayer.FeatureClass;
    for (int i = 0; i < FC.Fields.FieldCount; i++)
    {
        IField field = FC.Fields.Field[i];
        if (field.Type == esriFieldType.esriFieldTypeDouble || field.Type ==
          esriFieldType.esriFieldTypeInteger || field.Type ==
          esriFieldType.esriFieldTypeSingle || field.Type ==
          esriFieldType.esriFieldTypeSmallInteger)
        {
            cboNumFields.Items.Add(field.Name);
        }
        //to be able to reach to the parent FeatureLayer
        cboNumFields.Tag = (featureLayer as ILayer).Name;
    }
}
```

Note that you use the `Tag` property of the ComboBox in order to remember the parent FeatureLayer.

8. At this point, you have the names of all numerical fields so users can select one of them from the ComboBox. All that is needed is to calculate the statistics using the `DataStatistics` CoClass. The following code illustrates the steps necessary to perform this task. Go to the designer window of Visual Studio and double-click btnCalculate to create the event handler for click event, then insert the code inside it.

```
private void btnCalculate_Click(object sender, EventArgs e)
{
    string selectedFieldName = null;
    if (cboNumFields.SelectedIndex >= 0)
    {
        selectedFieldName = cboNumFields.SelectedItem.ToString();
    }

    if (selectedFieldName == null)
    { return; }

    if (cboNumFields.Tag == null)
    {
```

```
            lblReport.Text = "";
            return;
        }

        string featureLayerName = cboNumFields.Tag.ToString();

        IMap map = mxdoc.FocusMap;
        IEnumLayer enumLayer = map.Layers;
        ILayer layer = enumLayer.Next();
        IFeatureLayer2 featureLayer = null;

        while (layer != null)
        {
            if (layer.Name == featureLayerName)
            {
                featureLayer = layer as IFeatureLayer2;
            }
            layer = enumLayer.Next();
        }

        if (featureLayer == null)
        { return; }

        IFeatureClass FC = featureLayer.FeatureClass;
        IFeatureCursor featureCursor = FC.Search(null, true);


        IDataStatistics dataStatistics = new DataStatisticsClass();
        dataStatistics.Field = selectedFieldName;
        dataStatistics.Cursor = featureCursor as ICursor;

        IStatisticsResults sR = dataStatistics.Statistics;

        lblReport.Text = string.Format("Count: {0}\n", sR.Count);
        lblReport.Text += string.Format("Min: {0:#.00}\n", sR.Minimum);
        lblReport.Text += string.Format("Max: {0:#.00}\n", sR.Maximum);
        lblReport.Text += string.Format("Sum: {0:#.00}\n", sR.Sum);
        lblReport.Text += string.Format("Average: {0:#.00}\n", sR.Mean);
        lblReport.Text += string.Format("Standard Deviation: {0:#.00}\n",
        sR.StandardDeviation);
    }
```

9. The dockable window is ready, but you need a button to show it on ArcMap's user interface. Right-click on your project and select New Item from the Add submenu. Choose Add-in Component and name it **showDockableWinStatistics**, then click the Add button.

10. The ArcGIS Add-Ins Wizard appears. Provide settings for the new button as displayed in Figure 8-16 and click Finish.

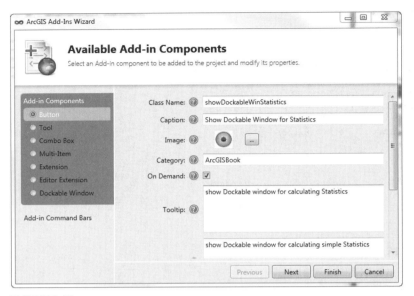

FIGURE 8-16

11. Double-click `showDockableWinStatistics.cs` in the Solution Explorer window and add the following `using` directives at the top of the newly added button's code window:

```
using ESRI.ArcGIS.esriSystem;
using ESRI.ArcGIS.Framework;
```

12. Add the following lines of code for getting a reference to the dockable window and providing it to the `OnClick()` method of the newly created button:

```
UID dockableWinUID = new UIDClass();
dockableWinUID.Value = ThisAddIn.IDs.DockableWinStatistics;

IDockableWindow statsticsDockableWin =
ArcMap.DockableWindowManager.GetDockableWindow(dockableWinUID);
statsticsDockableWin.Show(true);
```

13. That is it! Run your project and test it. Add the button to ArcMap's user interface using the Customize window. You can find the button in the ArcGISBook commands category.

How It Works

The `UID` CoClass is usually used for referencing the Globally Unique Identifier (GUID) of interfaces and CoClasses in ArcObjects. For example, you can get to the built-in tools and commands using their UIDs. You explore this topic in Chapter 13. In this Try It Out, you get at the dockable window add-in using the `UID` CoClass. Then you use the `IDockableWindow` interface to show the referenced dockable window. As you have noticed, the logic for showing the dockable window was quite easy but you have to provide a button for this logic. This is the main difference between developing a dockable window using add-ins and Extending ArcObjects templates.

Some Important Points about Using Cursors

Cursors play a major role in working with geospatial data, so understanding their behavior as described in this section is quite important.

Recycling

As previously stated, recycling is a characteristic of cursors that determines whether rows (or features) retrieved by a cursor occupy the same location in memory.

In general, recycling should be enabled for referencing one feature only, although it might seem that you should enable recycling for any kind of read access. Also, in certain situations when using search cursors you have to disable recycling. As a rule of thumb for read access, whenever you need to reference more than one row (or feature) you have to disable recycling, otherwise you might get unexpected behavior. In other words, when you want to work directly with the rows (or feature) retrieved by the cursor, enabling recycling will always result in retrieving a reference to just one row (or feature), which is the last retrieved row (or feature). The following code creates a recycling search cursor and retrieves three features from the first FeatureLayer in the active Data Frame. Since the cursor is recycling, all the retrieved features point to the feature3 object (the last feature retrieved by the cursor).

```
void testRecycling()
    {
        IMxDocument mxdoc = ArcMap.Document as IMxDocument;
        IMap map = mxdoc.FocusMap;
        IEnumLayer enumLayer = map.Layers;
        ILayer layer = enumLayer.Next();
        IFeatureLayer2 fLayer = null;
        while (layer != null)
        {
            if ( layer is IFeatureLayer2)
            {
                fLayer = layer as IFeatureLayer2;
                break;
            }
            layer = enumLayer.Next();
        }
        if (fLayer == null)
        { return; }

        IFeatureClass fClass = fLayer.FeatureClass;
        bool recyclingEnabled = true;
        IFeatureCursor featureCursor = fClass.Search(null, recyclingEnabled);
        IFeature feature1 = null;
        IFeature feature2 = null;
        IFeature feature3 = null;

        feature1 = featureCursor.NextFeature();
        feature2 = featureCursor.NextFeature();
        feature3 = featureCursor.NextFeature();
        ESRI.ArcGIS.Framework.MessageDialogClass msgBox =
            new ESRI.ArcGIS.Framework.MessageDialogClass();
```

```
string message = "OID of Feature1 :" + feature1.OID + "\n";
message += "OID of Feature2 :" + feature2.OID + "\n";
message += "OID of Feature3 :" + feature3.OID + "\n";
msgBox.DoModal("Recycling is " + recyclingEnabled, message, "OK",
    "", ArcMap.Application.hWnd);
}
```

The result of running the preceding code is shown in Figure 8-17.

If you change the `recyclingEnabled` variable to `false` the result of the preceding code is shown in Figure 8-18.

So if you don't need more than one row (or feature) to be referenced at once, it is possible to use both recycling and non-recycling cursors, but in this case recycling cursors provide a more efficient approach. If you need to reference more than one feature at once and keep the distinct references in memory you need non-recycling cursors. In this case, using recycling cursors might result in inaccurate results. The next chapter provides an example of the non-recycling search cursors.

FIGURE 8-17

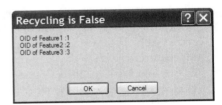

FIGURE 8-18

> **NOTE** *In order to run the preceding code, you need to add ESRI.ArcGIS.Carto and ESRI.ArcGIS.Geodatabase references to your project.*

Memory Management

Some objects require explicit execution of code to release resources such as open files, database connections, operating system handles, and other unmanaged objects. In .NET terminology, this is called *disposal*. The .NET Framework defines a special interface (`IDisposable`) for types requiring a cleanup method. In the .NET realm, disposal is in charge of cleaning up the handles for open files, database connections, and other unmanaged objects.

The managed memory occupied by unused objects must also be reclaimed at some point; this function is known as *garbage collection* and is performed by the Common Language Runtime (CLR). Garbage collection occurs behind the scenes, without any programmer intervention and in a nondeterministic way. (*Nondeterministic* means that it is not known when exactly the garbage collector will reclaim the memory.) You can think of it like this: When no reference to an object exists, that object (memory allocated by that object) is marked as garbage. The actual garbage collection process is performed sporadically during execution of your .NET code.

It is possible to call the `Collect()` method of the `System.GC` class to request garbage collection manually. But because of the way the garbage collector works in the .NET Framework, explicitly requesting garbage collection doesn't mean that the memory will be reclaimed as soon as you request garbage collection. Also, manually initiating garbage collection is not recommended for most situations, since it can lead to inefficiencies.

Disposal differs from garbage collection in that disposal is usually explicitly initiated while garbage collection is totally automatic. In other words, the developer takes care of such things as releasing file handles, database connections, and operating system resources while the CLR takes care of releasing memory.

When you are working with pure .NET code (which is called *managed code*) you almost never care about how the .NET Framework manages the memory. The `IDisposable` interface has a single method: `Dispose()`. The `Dispose()` method is in charge of releasing a type's unmanaged resources such as file handles and database connections. Interestingly, some types in the .NET Framework have a `Close()` method for the same purpose. In Chapter 4, you worked with the `FileStream`, `StreamReader`, and `StreamWriter` types to access files. All these types implement `IDisposable`. In addition to the `Dispose()` method they provide the `Close()` method for the same purpose.

> **NOTE** *If you are interested in a more in-depth description of memory management in the .NET Framework, good reference books include* Professional C# 2012 and .NET 4.5 *by Christian Nagel, Bill Evjen, Jay Glynn, Karli Watson, and Morgan Skinner and* C# 5.0 in a Nutshell: The Definitive Reference *by Joseph Albahari and Ben Albahari.*

There are also some types in ArcObjects that need explicit disposal, in particular cursors (and FeatureCursors). As a rule of thumb, when performing any operation with a cursor, you must release the resources it occupies. If you don't release the resources, unexpected behaviors can occur. Consider the following code, which creates 256 FeatureCursors without disposing them:

```
IMxDocument mxdoc = ArcMap.Document as IMxDocument;
IMap map = mxdoc.FocusMap;
IEnumLayer enumLayer = map.Layers;
ILayer layer = enumLayer.Next();
IFeatureLayer2 fLayer = null;
while (layer != null)
{
    if (layer is IFeatureLayer2)
    {
        fLayer = layer as IFeatureLayer2;
        break;
    }
    layer = enumLayer.Next();
}
if (fLayer == null)
{ return; }

IFeatureClass featureClass = fLayer.FeatureClass;
int iterator = 255;
try
{
    for (int i = 0; i < iterator; i++)
    {
        //creating a new featureCursor
        IFeatureCursor featureCursor = featureClass.Search(null, true);
        //using featureCursor
```

```
        }
    }
    catch (Exception ex)
    {
        new ESRI.ArcGIS.Framework.MessageDialogClass().DoModal(ex.Source,
            ex.Message, "", "", ArcMap.Application.hWnd);
    }
```

If you test this code for a feature class in a personal geodatabase you will get the error shown in Figure 8-19. The reason for this error is that by design, a maximum of 255 open connections are possible for a personal geodatabase (Microsoft Jet engine). In other words, any attempt to open more than 255 connections results in an error for this type of data source.

FIGURE 8-19

To overcome this issue you must dispose of any open cursors when there is no need for them using the `Marshal` class's `ReleaseComObject()` method. You can find the `Marshal` class in the `System.Runtime.InteropServices` namespace. If you replace the `for` block in the preceding code with the following `for` block you will not get an error when connecting to a personal geodatabase:

```
for (int i = 0; i < iterator; i++)
{
    //creating a new featureCursor
    IFeatureCursor featureCursor = featureClass.Search(null, true);
    //using featureCursor then dispose it
    System.Runtime.InteropServices.Marshal.ReleaseComObject(featureCursor);
}
```

DISPLAYING SUBSETS OF GEOSPATIAL DATA

To this point in this chapter, you have learned how to use attribute queries as well as spatial queries to select and make a subset of features. Sometimes you need to use an attribute query to just display subsets of features. In order to perform this task, users of ArcGIS for Desktop applications can use the Definition Query tab of the Layer Properties window. Developers have the same capability through the `IFeatureLayerDefinition2` interface, which is implemented by the `FeatureLayer` CoClass. This interface has a `DefinitionExpression` property that should be used for defining the query expression (same as the `WhereClause` property of a `QueryFilter`). The following code snippet displays states which have populations that exceed six million:

```
IMxDocument mxdoc = ArcMap.Application.Document as IMxDocument;
IMap map = mxdoc.FocusMap;
for (int i = 0; i < map.LayerCount; i++)
{
    ILayer layer = map.Layer[i];
    if (layer.Name == "U.S. States (Generalized)")
    {
        IFeatureLayerDefinition2 flDefinition =
        layer as IFeatureLayerDefinition2;
```

```
                    flDefinition.DefinitionExpression =
                    "POP2000 > 6000000";
                    mxdoc.ActiveView.Refresh();
            }
       }
```

In order to display all the features, you can simply provide an empty string for the `DefinitionExpression` property.

SUMMARY

Making a subset of geospatial data is one of the most common tasks in ArcObjects programming. `SelectionSet`, `Cursor`, `SpatialFilter`, and `QueryFilter` are central classes for performing this task. Criteria for selection are defined using the `QueryFilter` or `SpatialFilter` classes. References to selected features or rows are managed by the `SelectionSet` and `Cursor` classes. As you have seen, the search cursor is used for high performance read-only access to records. In addition, this chapter has shown how a `Cursor` object can be used for calculating simple statistics for a numerical field. You see more about cursors in the remaining chapters of this book.

EXERCISES

1. What is a search cursor?

2. In order to calculate simple statistics using the `DataStatistics` CoClass, what properties of `IDataStatistics` should be set?

3. Which class is used for referencing the unique identifier of interfaces and CoClasses in ArcObjects?

4. Write the code to perform switch selection for the cities FeatureLayer. (You can use the `ISelectionSet` interface for this task.)

You will find the answers to these exercises in this book's appendix.

► WHAT YOU LEARNED IN THIS CHAPTER

TOPIC	KEY CONCEPTS
Recycling	If the recycling parameter (which is one of the `Search()` method's input parameters) is set as true, each record referenced by the cursor will occupy the same memory address as the other successive records and as a result optimize the read-only access. In this case, a cursor is called the recycling cursor. The reference to the retrieved record will be lost when the recycling cursor points to the next record. For this reason, records which were returned by the recycling cursor must not be updated.
Cursor	An object which is in charge of accessing individual records in a SelectionSet, FeatureClass, Table, and any object representing a group of records. There are three different types of cursors with three different functionalities. All the different kinds of cursors implement the same interface. In other words, they have the same methods.
Selecting and highlighting features on map	The IFeatureSelection interface must be used in conjunction with a QueryFilter or a SpatialFilter object.
Iterating through subsets of features	IFeatureClass interface should be used in conjunction with a QueryFilter or a SpatialFilter object to create a cursor.
Displaying subsets of geospatial data	IFeatureLayerDefinition2 interface should be used with providing a criterion for Features to be displayed.
Disposing of cursors	As a rule of thumb, when performing any operation with a cursor, you must release the resources it occupies. If you don't release the resources, unexpected behaviors might occur. You can dispose of any open cursor when there is no need for it using the `Marshal` class's `ReleaseComObject()` method. You can find the `Marshal` class in the `System.Runtime.InteropServices` namespace.

Constructing and Using the Geometry of Features

WHAT YOU WILL LEARN IN THIS CHAPTER:

- ➤ Exploring object model diagrams for geometry
- ➤ Relationships between segments, paths, rings, polylines, and polygons
- ➤ Displaying geometries without persisting them
- ➤ Creating and drawing different types of geometries
- ➤ Creating interior and exterior rings for polygons
- ➤ Performing common geoprocessing operations
- ➤ Calculating distance between geometries
- ➤ Examining the spatial relationships between geometries
- ➤ Finding length, area, and centroid of geometries

WROX.COM CODE DOWNLOADS FOR THIS CHAPTER

The wrox.com code downloads for this chapter can be found at www.wrox.com/remtitle .cgi?isbn=1118442547 on the Download Code tab. The code is in the Chapter09 folder and is individually named according to the names throughout the chapter.

One of the first steps in making any GIS database is modeling the natural or man-made phenomena of interest. This means that real-world objects need to be simplified to be represented in GIS. For vector representation of real-world objects, ArcObjects provides the Geometry library.

This chapter looks at the Geometry library. This is the library provided by ArcObjects to facilitate constructing geometries. In addition to geometry construction, this library has numerous interfaces for geoprocessing operations such as buffer, overlay, and union, just to name a few.

OBJECT MODEL DIAGRAM FOR THE GEOMETRY OF FEATURES AND GRAPHICS

The Geometry library contains classes to construct and use points, polylines, polygons, and multipatches. In addition to representing real-world objects, classes in the Geometry library can be used to construct graphic elements. This chapter focuses on constructing and using geometry classes for features. Chapter 10 covers displaying and using various rendering options and different kinds of symbols available in ArcGIS, and Chapter 11 uses the materials described in this chapter to construct and add various kinds of graphic elements. To be able to focus on geometry topics, you will make use of quick drawing techniques in ArcGIS rather than persisting them as features.

Before exploring the Geometry library's object model diagram, it is a good idea to know the common terminology. The most basic constructor of all geometries is a point, which includes at least a single pair of X and Y coordinates. Any geometry can be directly and indirectly created from a set of point instances.

In addition to X and Y coordinates, points can have optional properties. M, Z, and ID are properties that can be used for different purposes. For example, the M attribute can be used for linear referencing, and the Z attribute is usually used for storing height values for points. The ID property of points is an integer value that can be used for establishing relationships with other entities in a database (as a foreign key).

When points (or vertices) of any geometry have the mentioned optional properties, ArcObjects will be aware of them using attribute awareness interfaces such as IZAware, IMAware, and IPointIDAware.

A *multipoint feature* is a single feature that stores the coordinates of several points in a specific order. A feature class with several locations for a single supermarket chain is an example of a multipoint feature.

A segment that consists of two points is the basis for polyline and polygon features. The Segment Abstract Class consists of two ordered points and a function to connect those two points. Since several functions can be defined to be used as the connecting curve, there are four concrete subclasses for the Segment Abstract Class in the Geometry library. Figure 9-1 shows all available segment types in ArcObjects.

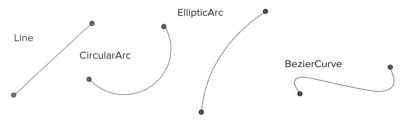

FIGURE 9-1

Several segments can compose complex geometry classes, such as Path, Ring, Polyline, and Polygon. A collection of several connected or disconnected paths can be used to generate a polyline, as shown in Figure 9-2.

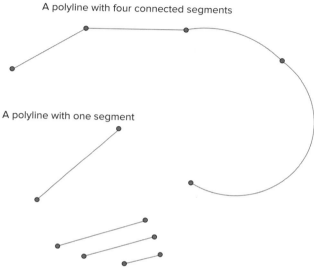

A polyline with four connected segments

A polyline with one segment

A polyline with three disconnected segments

FIGURE 9-2

As Figure 9-3 illustrates, a closed sequence of connected segments constructs a ring and a collection of one or more rings generates a polygon. (When a polygon has more than one ring it is called a multipart polygon.)

As mentioned in previous chapters, all geometries have an *envelope* (even points). The envelope of any geometry instance defines the minimum bounding rectangle or extent of that geometry. The IGeometry interface, defined by the Geometry Abstract Class, has the Envelope property, which can be used to get (but not set) the envelope of any geometry.

Figure 9-4 shows the simplified object model diagram of geometry.

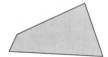

A polygon with one ring

A polygon with four rings

FIGURE 9-3

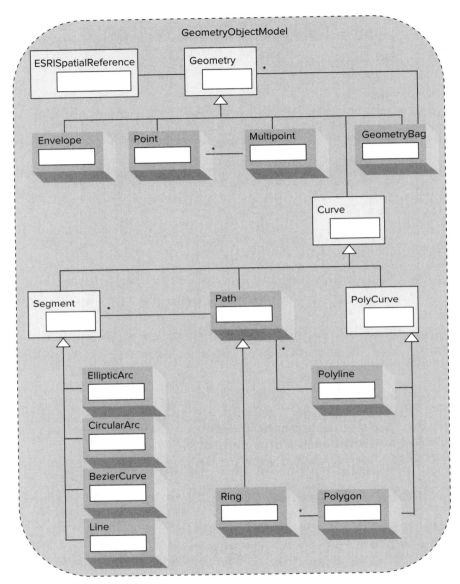

FIGURE 9-4

DISPLAYING GEOMETRIES ON THE SCREEN

In order to focus on drawing geometries, in this chapter you make use of the `IScreenDisplay` interface. This interface, which represents a normal application window, can be obtained from an `IActiveView` instance. It provides a temporary drawing surface.

The following code demonstrates how to get a reference to an `IScreenDisplay` object:

```
IMxDocument mxdoc = ArcMap.Application.Document as IMxDocument;
IActiveView activeView = mxdoc.ActiveView;
IScreenDisplay screenDisp = activeView.ScreenDisplay;
```

After getting a reference to an object of type `IScreenDisplay`, you can use one of several methods for drawing geometries. All the drawing methods must be invoked between the `StartDrawing()` and `FinishDrawing()` methods. The following code illustrates how `IScreenDisplay` can be used to draw two points:

```
//any call to draw methods must be between the
//StartDrawing() and FinishDrawing() methods
screenDisp.StartDrawing(screenDisp.hDC, screenCache);
screenDisp.DrawPoint(point1);
screenDisp.DrawPoint(point2);
screenDisp.FinishDrawing();
```

As mentioned, `IScreenDisplay` just provides a temporary drawing surface. In other words, the drawn geometry will disappear when the application window is refreshed.

The `StartDrawing()` method expects two input parameters. The first one is an integer value that indicates the target device context where drawing will occur. This target device can be a display, printer, or bitmaps.

The second input, which is a short value (`int16` .NET data type), specifies the cache for drawing. ArcGIS for Desktop applications usually use different caches for drawing layers, selections, graphics, and annotations to provide a more responsive user interface.

In most cases `ScreenDisplay.hDC` is provided for the first input and `esriNoScreenCache` should be specified as the second input. Consult the ArcObjects API Reference for .NET if you need more details about this method.

Creating and Drawing Points

A point is a zero-dimensional object that is represented by a single pair of X and Y coordinates. Because it is a CoClass, it can be generated by using the `new` keyword. The coordinates of a point can be set using the `PutCoord()` method or by setting X and Y properties directly. In addition, the `IConstructPoint2` interface provides various methods for generating points from other geometries and measurements, such as distance and angles. In the next Try It Out, you create a Button add-in to draw some points in the display window of ArcMap. You continue to use this approach in several later Try It Outs to create other kinds of geometries.

TRY IT OUT   Creating and Drawing Points (DrawingPoints.zip)

1. Create a new ArcMap Add-in project. Name the solution GeometrySolution. In the Add-Ins Wizard, provide the necessary information as shown in Figure 9-5 and click Finish.

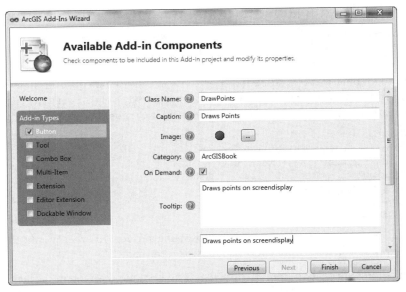

FIGURE 9-5

2. Add ESRI.ArcGIS.Display, ESRI.ArcGIS.Carto, and ESRI.ArcGIS.Geometry references to your project and type the following using directives at the top of the code window of your button's class (DrawPoints.cs):

```
using ESRI.ArcGIS.Carto;
using ESRI.ArcGIS.Display;
using ESRI.ArcGIS.Geometry;
using ESRI.ArcGIS.ArcMapUI;
```

3. Add the following code to the button's OnClick() method:

```
IPoint p1 = new PointClass();
p1.X = 10; p1.Y = 10;

IPoint p2 = new PointClass();
p2.X = 20; p2.Y = 20;

IPoint p3 = new PointClass();
p3.PutCoords(35, 15);

IPoint p4 = new PointClass();
p4.X = 40; p4.Y = 17;

IPoint p5 = new PointClass();
p5.X = 50; p5.Y = 19;

IPoint p6 = new PointClass();
p6.X = 60; p6.Y = 18;

IMxDocument mxdoc = ArcMap.Application.Document as IMxDocument;
```

```
IActiveView activeView = mxdoc.ActiveView;

IScreenDisplay screenDisp = activeView.ScreenDisplay;
short screenCache = Convert.ToInt16(esriScreenCache.esriNoScreenCache);

screenDisp.StartDrawing(screenDisp.hDC, screenCache);
IRgbColor color = new RgbColorClass();
color.Red = 0; color.Blue = 255; color.Green = 0;

ISimpleMarkerSymbol simpleMarkerSymbol = new SimpleMarkerSymbolClass();
//any call to draw methods must be between the
//StartDrawing() and FinishDrawing() methods
simpleMarkerSymbol.Color = color;
screenDisp.SetSymbol(simpleMarkerSymbol as ISymbol);
screenDisp.DrawPoint(p1);
screenDisp.DrawPoint(p2);
screenDisp.DrawPoint(p3);
screenDisp.DrawPoint(p4);
screenDisp.DrawPoint(p5);
screenDisp.DrawPoint(p6);
screenDisp.FinishDrawing();
```

4. Next you need to add a toolbar to your add-in and put the button on the toolbar. The procedure for adding a toolbar is slightly different in ArcGIS 10 and 10.1. Please refer to the "Adding All FeatureClasses inside All FeatureDatasets of a File Geodatabase" Try It Out in Chapter 7 for more details. Name the toolbar GeometryToolbar and add the reference to the button as shown in Figure 9-6.

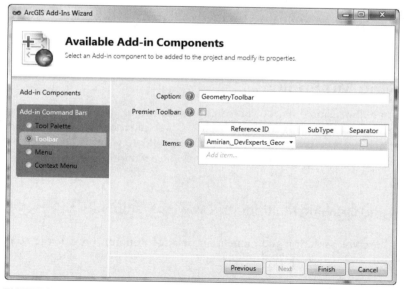

FIGURE 9-6

5. Run your code by pressing F5. After a few seconds, ArcMap will appear. Click the Draw Points button (the only button on the Geometry toolbar). If you used the specified values for the coordinates of all points, you will see Figure 9-6. If you don't, use the Go To XY command on ArcMap's Tools toolbar and provide 35 and 15 as X and Y and then click the Draw Points button.

How It Works

You have to provide a symbol for `IScreenDisplay` to be able to draw geometries. Symbols and colors are covered in Chapter 10. But for the purpose of drawing geometries, you use the simplest possible types of symbol classes. In this Try It Out, you used `SimpleMarkerSymbol` to draw point geometries. If you run ArcMap, using the GeometryToolbar add-in you can draw six points. If you don't see the points, first use the Go To XY command (on the ArcMap Tools toolbar) to navigate to somewhere near the coordinates of points (such as 20,20) and then press the button to see the points. You should see something similar to Figure 9-7.

FIGURE 9-7

> **NOTE** Most subclasses of the `Geometry` *Abstract Class implement the* `IPointCollection` *interface. This interface can be used to get, set, update, and query the points in a* `Geometry` *subclass object. This interface provides an easy approach to construct most types of geometries without a need to aggregate. In other words, there is no need to aggregate segments to a path and paths to a polyline to create a polyline. Because* `Polyline` *implements the* `IPointCollection` *interface, any number of points can be directly used to create a polyline.*

Creating and Drawing Multipoints

A multipoint feature is a one-dimensional object that can be used to store an ordered collection of points. Multipoints can be constructed using methods of the `IConstructMultipoint` interface as well as by directly using the `IPointCollection` interface. In the following Try It Out, you first create a CircularArc using three points and then divide it to produce a multipoint geometry based on a specified distance.

TRY IT OUT **Creating and Drawing Multipoints (DrawingMultipoints.zip)**

1. Add a new add-in button to your solution and name it DrawingMultipoint. Provide the necessary settings as shown in Figure 9-8. Click the Finish button.

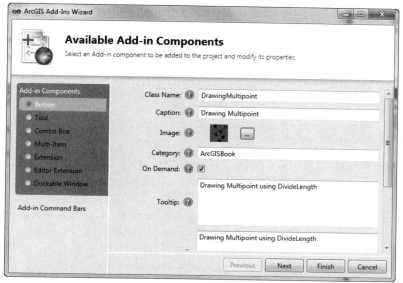

FIGURE 9-8

2. Type the following using directives at the top of the DrawingMultipoint.cs file's code window:

```
using ESRI.ArcGIS.Carto;
using ESRI.ArcGIS.Display;
using ESRI.ArcGIS.Geometry;
using ESRI.ArcGIS.ArcMapUI;
```

3. Add the following code to the button's OnClick() method:

```
            IPoint centerPoint = new PointClass();
            centerPoint.PutCoords(0, 0);

            IPoint fromPoint = new PointClass();
            fromPoint.PutCoords(100, 0);

            IPoint toPoint = new PointClass();
            toPoint.PutCoords(0, 200);

            ICircularArc circularArcConstruction = new CircularArcClass();
            circularArcConstruction.PutCoords(centerPoint, fromPoint, toPoint,
     esriArcOrientation.esriArcClockwise);

            IMultipoint multipoint = new MultipointClass();
            IConstructMultipoint multipointConst = multipoint as
     IConstructMultipoint;
            //divide the circularArc in equal-length parts
            multipointConst.ConstructDivideLength(circularArcConstruction as ICurve,
     50);

            IMxDocument mxdoc = ArcMap.Application.Document as IMxDocument;
            IActiveView activeView = mxdoc.ActiveView;
```

```
IScreenDisplay screenDisp = activeView.ScreenDisplay;
short screenCache = Convert.ToInt16(esriScreenCache.esriNoScreenCache);
screenDisp.StartDrawing(screenDisp.hDC, screenCache);

IRgbColor color = new RgbColorClass();
color.Red = 100; color.Blue = 255; color.Green = 0;

ISimpleMarkerSymbol simpleMarkerSymbol = new SimpleMarkerSymbolClass();
simpleMarkerSymbol.Color = color;
screenDisp.SetSymbol(simpleMarkerSymbol as ISymbol);
screenDisp.DrawMultipoint(multipoint);

screenDisp.FinishDrawing();
```

4. If you look at the add-in's XML configuration file (`Config.esriaddinx`), you will notice that the toolbar is defined as an XML element (`<Toolbar>`) with `id`, `caption`, and `showInitially` attributes. Each item on the toolbar is a child element of the `Items` element (between `<Items>` and `</items>`). The following is the fragment of the `Config.esriaddinx` file that represents the toolbar:

```
<Toolbar id="Amirian,_DevExperts_GeometrySolution_GeometryToolbar"
caption="GeometryToolbar" showInitially="false">
        <Items>
          <Item refID="Amirian,_DevExperts_GeometrySolution_DrawPoints" />
        </Items>
      </Toolbar>
```

Note that the `refID` attribute of the `Item` element is exactly the same as the `id` attribute of the `Button` element, which is declared earlier in the configuration file. Based on the setting of your add-in solution, it might be different from what is presented here.

```
<Button id="Amirian,_DevExperts_GeometrySolution_DrawPoints" class="DrawPoints"
 message="Draws points on screendisplay" caption="Draws Points"
tip="Draws points on screendisplay" category="ArcGISBook"
image="Images\DrawPoints.png" />
```

If you take a look at the `id` attribute of the button, you will notice that its value contains the content of the `Company` element, the name of the solution, and the content of the `Name` element.

The company and the name of the solution are defined in the `Name` and `Company` elements in the configuration file and are set by you when you create a new add-in solution.

```
<Name>GeometrySolution</Name>
<AddInID>{2b720261-b563-4f8e-bf0e-624976b82175}</AddInID>
<Description>Working with Geometries</Description>
<Version>1.0</Version>
<Image>Images\GeometrySolution.png</Image>
<Author>Pouria Amirian</Author>
<Company>Amirian, DevExperts</Company>
```

This is the expressive power of XML, which makes it both machine-readable and human-readable.

5. Next you add this button on the existing toolbar. Modify the `Toolbar` XML element to contain a new item with the `refID` value of the newly added button.

```
<Toolbar id="Amirian,_DevExperts_GeometrySolution_GeometryToolbar"
caption="GeometryToolbar" showInitially="false">
  <Items>
    <Item refID="Amirian,_DevExperts_GeometrySolution_DrawPoints" />
    <Item refID="Amirian,_DevExperts_GeometrySolution_DrawingMultipoint" />
  </Items>
</Toolbar>
```

6. Run the ArcMap and you should see the Geometry toolbar with two buttons. The `showInitially` attribute of the `Toolbar` element specifies whether the toolbar is shown the first time the add-in is installed. Use the Go To XY command to pan to somewhere around 0,0 and press the button. Figure 9-9 shows what you see.

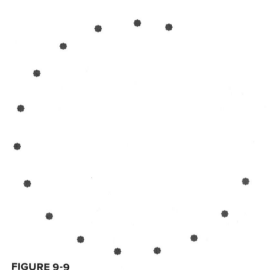

FIGURE 9-9

7. If you want to add a separator between two buttons on the toolbar, all you need to do is add a `separator="true"` attribute to the second `Item` element of the `Items` element. The following is the full toolbar element and its children:

```
<Toolbar id="Amirian,_DevExperts_GeometrySolution_GeometryToolbar"
caption="GeometryToolbar" showInitially="false">
      <Items>
        <Item refID="Amirian,_DevExperts_GeometrySolution_DrawPoints" />
        <Item refID="Amirian,_DevExperts_GeometrySolution_DrawingMultipoint"
  separator="true" />
      </Items>
    </Toolbar>
```

How It Works

In this Try It Out, you used a method of the `IConstructMultipoint` interface to create a multipoint geometry. In addition, you modified the XML configuration file to add the newly created button to the existing toolbar. In fact, command bars such as toolbars and menus are nothing but XML elements.

As a result, you can easily configure the items contained in a menu and a toolbar. Also note that static information about add-in buttons such as caption, ToolTip, category, and image are stored in the configuration file. As you progress through this book, you learn new topics about this extensible mechanism of configuration. XML has been used for more than a decade for configuring most applications, but it's only recently been used to configure for most GIS software.

NOTE *Consider the following XML fragment:*

```
<Geometry id="43">
    <SRS name="WGS84" />
    <Shape>Polygon </Shape>
    <points>
        <point>70, 70</point>
        <point>110, 70</point>
        <point>110, 20</point>
        <point>70, 20</point>
    </points>
    </Geometry>
```

In XML terminology, a markup construct (called a tag*) begins with* < *and ends with* >*. There are three types of tags:*

➤   *start tag:* `<Shape>`

➤   *end tag:* `</Shape>`

➤   *empty element tag:* `<SRS />`

An XML element begins with a start tag and ends with the corresponding end tag. An XML element also can be composed of a single tag (an empty element tag). The characters between the start and end tags of an element are called the element's content. *For example, the content of the* `Shape` *element in this example is* `Polygon`*.*

A name=value pair *in a start tag or in the empty element tag is called an* attribute. *For example, the* `Geometry` *element in this example has an attribute with the name of* `id` *and with a value of* `43`*.*

Creating and Drawing Polylines

As mentioned previously in this chapter, a polyline is an ordered collection of one or more connected or disconnected (disjoint) paths. The easiest (and also most limited) approach to create a polyline is to use the `IPointCollection` interface. The following code creates six points and adds them to an `IPointCollection` instance:

```
Point p1 = new PointClass();
p1.X = 10; p1.Y = 10;

IPoint p2 = new PointClass();
```

```
      p2.X = 20; p2.Y = 20;

      IPoint p3 = new PointClass();
      p3.X = 35; p3.Y = 15;

      IPoint p4 = new PointClass();
      p4.X = 40; p4.Y = 17;

      IPoint p5 = new PointClass();
      p5.X = 50; p5.Y = 19;

      IPoint p6 = new PointClass();
      p6.X = 60; p6.Y = 18;

      IPolyline polyline = new PolylineClass();
      IPointCollection5 pointColl = polyline as IPointCollection5;
      pointColl.AddPoint(p1);
      pointColl.AddPoint(p2);
      pointColl.AddPoint(p3);
      pointColl.AddPoint(p4);
      pointColl.AddPoint(p5);
      pointColl.AddPoint(p6);

      IMxDocument mxdoc = ArcMap.Application.Document as IMxDocument;
      IActiveView activeView = mxdoc.ActiveView;
      IScreenDisplay screenDisp = activeView.ScreenDisplay;
      short screenCache = Convert.ToInt16(esriScreenCache.esriNoScreenCache);
      screenDisp.StartDrawing(screenDisp.hDC, screenCache);

      IRgbColor color = new RgbColorClass();
      color.Red = 255; color.Blue = 128; color.Green = 120;

      ISimpleLineSymbol simpleLineSymbol = new SimpleLineSymbolClass();
      simpleLineSymbol.Color = color;
      simpleLineSymbol.Width = 2;

      screenDisp.SetSymbol(simpleLineSymbol as ISymbol);
      screenDisp.DrawPolyline(polyline);

      screenDisp.FinishDrawing();
```

You have to provide a LineSymbol instance to IScreenDisplay to enable it to draw polylines. The order of adding points to IPointCollection defines the indexes of each point in the collection; the indexes of points are important especially for retrieving and editing a geometry object. Add another add-in button to the GeometrySolution and add the above code to the OnClick() method of the button. Then modify the configuration file to put the button on the toolbar. When you run the code, you will see what is shown in Figure 9-10. You can find the code of this add-in button in the DrawingPolylineUsingPointColl.zip file in this book's download files on Wrox.com.

FIGURE 9-10

In addition to `IPointCollection`, two other interfaces (`IGeometryCollection` and `ISegmentCollection`) can be used to create and manipulate polylines with higher flexibility. The `IGeometryCollection` interface provides some useful methods to access, manipulate, insert, and remove the geometry parts of a polyline. For a polyline, the geometry parts are paths. At a little lower level, `ISegmentCollection` can be used to access each composing segment of a polyline.

In the next Try It Out, you create and draw a polyline using the `ISegmentCollection` interface. You create three different segments and add them to an instance of `ISegmentCollection` and finally draw them.

TRY IT OUT Creating and Drawing Polylines (DrawingPolylines.zip)

1. Add a new add-in button to your solution and name it DrawingPolylines. Provide the necessary settings as shown in Figure 9-11. Make sure that you provide DrawingPolylines as the class name for the button and then click Finish.

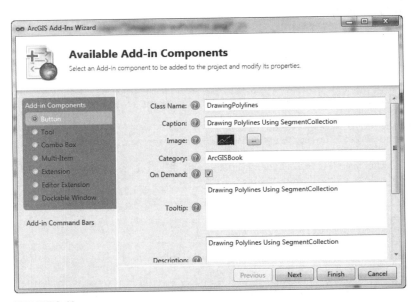

FIGURE 9-11

2. Type the following `using` directives at the top of the `DrawingPolylines.cs` file's code window:

```
using ESRI.ArcGIS.Carto;
using ESRI.ArcGIS.Display;
using ESRI.ArcGIS.Geometry;
using ESRI.ArcGIS.ArcMapUI;
```

3. Add the following code to the button's `OnClick()` method:

```
//create a Line Segment
Point p1 = new PointClass();
p1.X = 10; p1.Y = 10;

IPoint p2 = new PointClass();
p2.X = 20; p2.Y = 20;

ILine lineSegment = new LineClass();
lineSegment.FromPoint = p1;
lineSegment.ToPoint = p2;

//create a CircularArc Segment
IPoint p3 = new PointClass();
p3.X = 35; p3.Y = 15;

IPoint p4 = new PointClass();
p4.X = 40; p4.Y = 17;

ICircularArc circularSegment = new CircularArcClass();
circularSegment.PutCoords(p3, p2, p4,
esriArcOrientation.esriArcClockwise);

//create a BezierCurve Segment
IPoint p5 = new PointClass();
p5.X = 50; p5.Y = 19;

IPoint p6 = new PointClass();
p6.X = 60; p6.Y = 18;

IPoint p7 = new PointClass();
p7.X = 70; p7.Y = 29;

IPoint p8 = new PointClass();
p8.X = 80; p8.Y = 38;

IBezierCurve bezierSegment = new BezierCurveClass();
IPoint[] controlPoints = { p5, p6, p7, p8 };
IBezierCurveGEN bezierSegmenGen = bezierSegment as IBezierCurveGEN;
bezierSegmenGen.PutCoords(ref controlPoints);

//create a Polyline out of Segments
ISegmentCollection path = new PathClass();
path.AddSegment(lineSegment as ISegment);
path.AddSegment(circularSegment as ISegment);
path.AddSegment(bezierSegment as ISegment);

IGeometryCollection polyline = new PolylineClass();
polyline.AddGeometry(path as IGeometry);

//draw the Polyline
IMxDocument mxdoc = ArcMap.Application.Document as IMxDocument;
IActiveView activeView = mxdoc.ActiveView;
IScreenDisplay screenDisp = activeView.ScreenDisplay;
```

```
short screenCache = Convert.ToInt16(esriScreenCache.esriNoScreenCache);
screenDisp.StartDrawing(screenDisp.hDC, screenCache);

IRgbColor color = new RgbColorClass();
color.Red = 255; color.Blue = 28; color.Green = 20;

ISimpleLineSymbol simpleLineSymbol = new SimpleLineSymbolClass();
simpleLineSymbol.Color = color;
simpleLineSymbol.Width = 2;

screenDisp.SetSymbol(simpleLineSymbol as ISymbol);
screenDisp.DrawPolyline(polyline as IGeometry);

screenDisp.FinishDrawing();
```

4. Modify the configuration file to put the button on the toolbar. Your `Toolbar` element in the configuration file should be similar to the following XML fragment:

```
<Toolbar id="Amirian,_DevExperts_GeometrySolution_GeometryToolbar"
caption="GeometryToolbar" showInitially="false">
        <Items>
            <Item refID="Amirian,_DevExperts_GeometrySolution_DrawPoints" />
            <Item refID="Amirian,_DevExperts_GeometrySolution_DrawingMultipoint"
separator="true" />
            <Item refID="Amirian,_DevExperts_GeometrySolution_DrawingPolylines"
separator="true" />
        </Items>
    </Toolbar>
```

5. Run the ArcMap and test the functionality of the newly developed button. Use the Go To XY command to pan to somewhere around 20,20 and click the button. You will see what is shown in Figure 9-12.

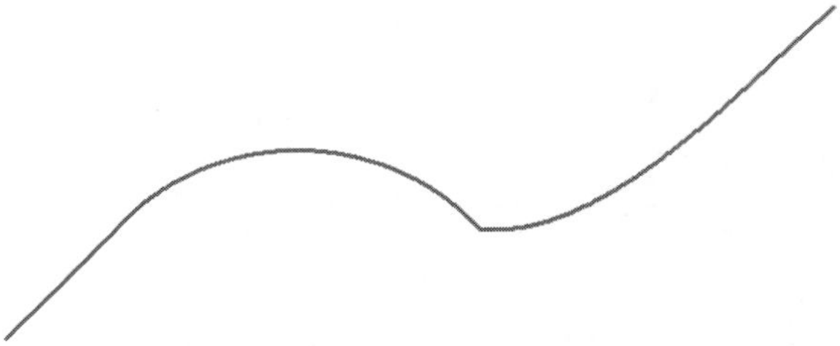

FIGURE 9-12

How It Works

Most complex geometry objects such as paths, rings, polylines, and polygons can be created by aggregating segments. As you have seen in this Try It Out, subclasses of the `Segment` Abstract Class (except the `Line` CoClass) provide numerous constructor methods. Consult the online ArcGIS Resource Center to find out more about them.

Creating and Drawing Polygons

As shown in Figure 9-4, a polygon is an ordered collection of rings. A ring can be inside another ring and create what is generally called a hole. Holes define the interior boundary of a polygon and are oriented counterclockwise in ArcObjects. In contrast, rings that define the exterior boundary of a polygon are oriented clockwise. In other words, when working with rings composing the polygon, traveling from the first point to the last point of any interior ring, the polygon is always on the left side. On the other hand, traveling from the first point to the last point of the exterior ring of a polygon, the polygon is always on the right side. Because of this, it is an easy task to create a polygon using the IPointCollection interface. The following code creates and draws a polygon with two rings (an external and an internal):

```
//exterior Ring
IPoint p1 = new PointClass();
p1.X = 70; p1.Y = 70;

IPoint p2 = new PointClass();
p2.X = 110; p2.Y = 70;

IPoint p3 = new PointClass();
p3.X = 110; p3.Y = 20;

IPoint p4 = new PointClass();
p4.X = 70; p4.Y = 20;

IPointCollection exRing = new RingClass();
exRing.AddPoint(p1);
exRing.AddPoint(p2);
exRing.AddPoint(p3);
exRing.AddPoint(p4);

//interior Ring
IPoint p5 = new PointClass();
p5.X = 100; p5.Y = 55;

IPoint p6 = new PointClass();
p6.X = 80; p6.Y = 55;

IPoint p7 = new PointClass();
p7.X = 80; p7.Y = 40;

IPoint p8 = new PointClass();
p8.X = 100; p8.Y = 40;

IPointCollection inRing = new RingClass();
inRing.AddPoint(p5);
inRing.AddPoint(p6);
inRing.AddPoint(p7);
inRing.AddPoint(p8);

IGeometryCollection polygon = new PolygonClass();
polygon.AddGeometry(exRing as IGeometry);
polygon.AddGeometry(inRing as IGeometry);

IMxDocument mxdoc = ArcMap.Application.Document as IMxDocument;
IActiveView activeView = mxdoc.ActiveView;
IScreenDisplay screenDisp = activeView.ScreenDisplay;
short screenCache = Convert.ToInt16(esriScreenCache.esriNoScreenCache);
screenDisp.StartDrawing(screenDisp.hDC, screenCache);

IRgbColor color = new RgbColorClass();
color.Red = 255; color.Blue = 28; color.Green = 20;
```

```
ISimpleFillSymbol simpleFillSymbol = new SimpleFillSymbolClass();
simpleFillSymbol.Color = color;

screenDisp.SetSymbol(simpleFillSymbol as ISymbol);
screenDisp.DrawPolygon(polygon as IGeometry);

screenDisp.FinishDrawing();
```

FIGURE 9-13

The result of running this code is shown in Figure 9-13. The code for this example is located in the `DrawingPolygonInExRing.zip` file on the book's download tab on Wrox.com.

Similar to polylines, polygons can be created with higher flexibility using interfaces such as `ISegmentCollection` and `IGeometryCollection`. In the following example, four segments create two rings of a polygon. The `Close()` method of the `IRing` interface creates a line segment between the first and last points of the ring.

```
Point p1 = new PointClass();
p1.X = 10; p1.Y = 10;

IPoint p2 = new PointClass();
p2.X = 20; p2.Y = 20;

ILine lineSegment1 = new LineClass();
lineSegment1.FromPoint = p1;
lineSegment1.ToPoint = p2;

IPoint p3 = new PointClass();
p3.X = 35; p3.Y = 15;

IPoint p4 = new PointClass();
p4.X = 40; p4.Y = 17;

ICircularArc circularSegment = new CircularArcClass();
circularSegment.PutCoords(p3, p2, p4,
esriArcOrientation.esriArcClockwise);


ISegmentCollection ringSegColl1 = new RingClass();
ringSegColl1.AddSegment(lineSegment1 as ISegment);
ringSegColl1.AddSegment(circularSegment as ISegment);

IRing ring1 = ringSegColl1 as IRing;
ring1.Close();

IPoint p5 = new PointClass();
p5.X = 50; p5.Y = 19;

IPoint p6 = new PointClass();
p6.X = 60; p6.Y = 18;

IPoint p7 = new PointClass();
```

```
p7.X = 70; p7.Y = 29;

ILine lineSegment2 = new LineClass();
lineSegment2.FromPoint = p5;
lineSegment2.ToPoint = p6;

ILine lineSegment3 = new LineClass();
lineSegment3.FromPoint = p6;
lineSegment3.ToPoint = p7;

ISegmentCollection ringSegColl2 = new RingClass();
ringSegColl2.AddSegment(lineSegment2 as ISegment);
ringSegColl2.AddSegment(lineSegment3 as ISegment);

IRing ring2 = ringSegColl2 as IRing;
ring2.Close();

IGeometryCollection polygon = new PolygonClass();
polygon.AddGeometry(ring1 as IGeometry);
polygon.AddGeometry(ring2 as IGeometry);

IMxDocument mxdoc = ArcMap.Application.Document as IMxDocument;
IActiveView activeView = mxdoc.ActiveView;
IScreenDisplay screenDisp = activeView.ScreenDisplay;
short screenCache = Convert.ToInt16(esriScreenCache.esriNoScreenCache);
screenDisp.StartDrawing(screenDisp.hDC, screenCache);

IRgbColor color = new RgbColorClass();
color.Red = 255; color.Blue = 28; color.Green = 20;

ISimpleFillSymbol simpleFillSymbol = new SimpleFillSymbolClass();
simpleFillSymbol.Color = color;
screenDisp.SetSymbol(simpleFillSymbol as ISymbol);
screenDisp.DrawPolygon(polygon as IGeometry);
screenDisp.FinishDrawing();
```

Add another add-in button to GeometrySolution and insert the preceding code in the OnClick() method of the button. Then place the button on the toolbar by modifying the configuration file and finally test the button. The button should create the output shown in Figure 9-14. You can find the source code of this example in the DrawingPolygonSegmentColl.zip file on the book's download tab on Wrox.com.

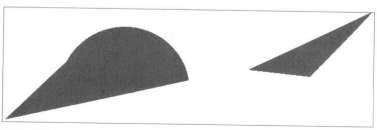

FIGURE 9-14

CREATING A NEW FEATURE AND EDITING AN EXISTING FEATURE'S GEOMETRY

Chapter 7 explains how to create and store a new row. In order to insert a new row into a table, first a new row object must be created using the `CreateRow()` method of the `ITable` interface, then values for each `Field` have to be assigned using `IFieldEdit`. Finally, using the `Store()` method of `IRow`, the `Row` object is persisted in the table.

The `CreateFeature()` method of the `IFeatureClass` interface can be used to create a new feature. The newly created feature will have a unique ID and null value or default values for other fields.

```
IFeature newState = StatesFeatureLayer.FeatureClass.CreateFeature();
```

After assigning values to all necessary fields, calling the `Store()` method will persist the feature in the geodatabase.

```
newState.Store();
```

If a FeatureClass is a versioned FeatureClass, any call to `CreateFeature()` should be within an edit session. An edit session can be started and stopped with a call to the `IWorkspaceEdit.StartEditing()` and `IWorkspaceEdit.StopEditing()` methods, respectively. In addition, if a FeatureClass participates in topologies or geometric networks, a call to `CreateFeature()` must be surrounded by an edit session.

> **NOTE** There are two primary approaches to creating features in a geodatabase:
>
> ➤ Use `IFeatureClass.CreateFeature()` and then `IFeature.Store()`
>
> ➤ Use `IFeatureClass.CreateFeatureBuffer()` and then `InsertCursor.InsertFeature()`
>
> For bulk insertion of features or rows in a geodatabase, the second approach provides higher performance for simple tables and FeatureClasses. But for FeatureClasses and tables that implement the custom behavior (such as participating in topologies, geometric networks, and class extensions), there is no difference between these two methods. Chapter 13 provides more explanation of these methods as well as other geospatial data management related topics.

In the following Try It Out, you create a new city in the cities FeatureClass of the USA FeatureDataSet.

TRY IT OUT Creating a New Feature (CreatingANewFeature.zip)

1. Add a new add-in button to your solution and name it CreatingANewCity. Provide the necessary setting as shown in Figure 9-15. Click Finish.

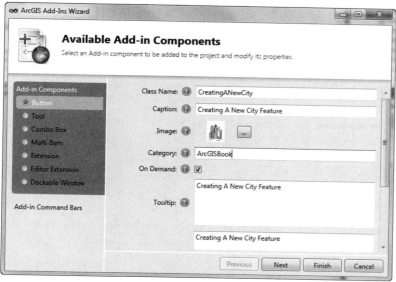

FIGURE 9-15

2. Add a reference to ESRI.ArcGIS.Geodatabase and then insert the following using directives at the top of the CreatingANewCity.cs file code window:

```
using ESRI.ArcGIS.Carto;
using ESRI.ArcGIS.Display;
using ESRI.ArcGIS.Geometry;
using ESRI.ArcGIS.ArcMapUI;
using ESRI.ArcGIS.Geodatabase;
using ESRI.ArcGIS.Framework;
```

3. Add the following code to the button's OnClick() method:

```
//finding cities layer
IMxDocument mxdoc = ArcMap.Application.Document as IMxDocument;
IMap map = mxdoc.FocusMap;
IEnumLayer enumLayer = map.Layers;

ILayer layer = enumLayer.Next();
IFeatureLayer2 cityFLayer = null;

while (layer != null)
{
    if (layer.Name == "U.S. Cities" && layer is IFeatureLayer2)
    {
        cityFLayer = layer as IFeatureLayer2;
    }
    layer = enumLayer.Next();
}

if (cityFLayer == null)
{ return; }

try
```

```
        {
            IFeature newCity = cityFLayer.FeatureClass.CreateFeature();
            IPoint citypoint = new PointClass();
            citypoint.PutCoords(-118.802581987, 34.020762811);
            newCity.Shape = citypoint;
            IFeatureClass cityFClass = cityFLayer.FeatureClass;
            int nameFieldIndex = cityFClass.Fields.FindField("CITY_NAME");
            int stateFieldIndex = cityFClass.Fields.FindField("STATE_NAME");
            int popFieldIndex = cityFClass.Fields.FindField("POP1990");
            newCity.Value[nameFieldIndex] = "Malibu";
            newCity.Value[stateFieldIndex] = "California";
            newCity.Value[popFieldIndex] = 12000;

            newCity.Store();
        }
        catch (Exception ex)
        {
        new MessageDialogClass().DoModal(ex.Source, ex.Message, "", "",
                ArcMap.Application.hWnd);

        }
```

4. Next you add a menu to the add-in and put this button on the menu. Right-click your project in the Solution Explorer window, then select New Item from the New submenu. Select Desktop Add-in in Installed Templates and then choose the Add-in Component Container (or Add-in Component for ArcGIS 10) item. Name the new item GeometryMenu and click Add.

5. In the ArcGIS Add-Ins Wizard window, select Menu in the Add-in Command Bars section, set its caption, and add a ReferenceID as shown in Figure 9-16.

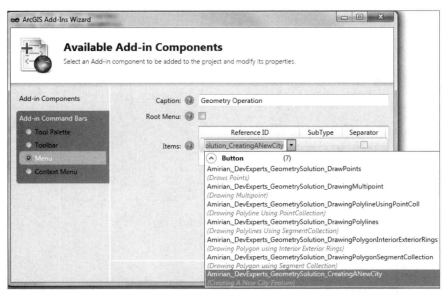

FIGURE 9-16

6. If you take a look at the configuration file you will observe have been some new elements added, which reflect that the existence of a menu and an item on the menu.

```
<Menu id="Amirian,_DevExperts_GeometrySolution_Geometry_Operation"
caption="Geometry Operation" isRootMenu="false">
        <Items>
          <Item refID="Amirian,_DevExperts_GeometrySolution_CreatingANewCity" />
        </Items>
      </Menu>
```

Because you want to place this menu on the toolbar, you have to modify the configuration file as you have in previous Try It Outs in this chapter. In order to add a menu to a toolbar, you need to add an Item element inside the Items element and provide the value of the menu's id attribute as the value for the refID attribute of the newly added Item element.

```
<Toolbar id="Amirian,_DevExperts_GeometrySolution_GeometryToolbar"
caption="GeometryToolbar" showInitially="false">
        <Items>
          <Item refID="Amirian,_DevExperts_GeometrySolution_DrawPoints" />
          <Item refID="Amirian,_DevExperts_GeometrySolution_DrawingMultipoint"
 separator="true" />
          <Item
refID="Amirian,_DevExperts_GeometrySolution_DrawingPolylineUsingPointColl"
separator="true" />
          <Item refID="Amirian,_DevExperts_GeometrySolution_DrawingPolylines"
 separator="true" />
          <Item
refID="Amirian,_DevExperts_GeometrySolution_DrawingPolygonInteriorExteriorRings"
separator="true" />
          <Item
refID="Amirian,_DevExperts_GeometrySolution_DrawingPolygonSegmentCollection"
separator="true" />
          <Item
refID="Amirian,_DevExperts_GeometrySolution_Geometry_Operation"
 separator="true" />

        </Items>
      </Toolbar>
```

7. Run the code and add the cities FeatureClass (from the USA feature dataset within the TemplateData.gdb file that ships with ArcGIS for Desktop) to the ArcMap and test the functionality of the button. The button should insert the city Malibu in California (see Figure 9-17). It is a good idea to check the number of cities before and after clicking the button.

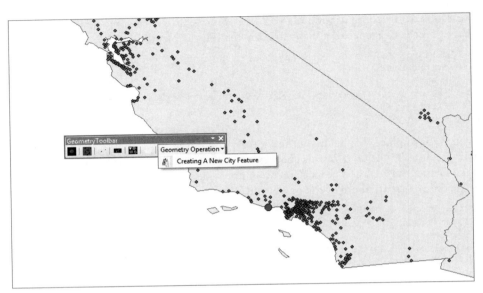

FIGURE 9-17

How It Works

In this Try It Out, you see how easy it is to insert a new feature into an existing FeatureClass. In fact, the procedure for adding a new feature is similar to adding a new row except that you must set the `Shape` property of a feature. You also used a menu as another type of Desktop Add-in. Both menus and toolbars are containers for other items (such as buttons and tools). This fact is reflected in the configuration file.

Same as creating a new feature, there are a few ways to update the geometry as well as the attribute properties of a feature.

> **NOTE** *Updating values of a row in a table is similar to this topic.*

For updating the geometry and attribute properties of a feature, an update cursor can be used. Update cursors are cursors that are initialized using the `Update()` method of a table or FeatureClass. Chapter 13 explains their use updating rows or features. In addition to update cursors, another type of cursor can be used to update properties of a feature: search cursors!

As you learned in Chapter 8, you create a search cursor using the `Search()` method of table or FeatureClass instances. Then you use the `Value` property to get the specific attributes of a feature. The `Value` property is a read-and-write property. As a result, you can use this property to set values for all fields, including the shape for features. Then you can call the `Store()` method of feature to persist the modification. The following code illustrates using a search cursor to update the geometry of Malibu (which you have added in the preceding Try It Out):

```
IMxDocument mxdoc = ArcMap.Application.Document as IMxDocument;
IMap map = mxdoc.FocusMap;
IEnumLayer enumLayer = map.Layers;

ILayer layer = enumLayer.Next();
IFeatureLayer2 cityFLayer = null;

while (layer != null)
{
    if (layer.Name == "U.S. Cities" && layer is IFeatureLayer2)
    {
        cityFLayer = layer as IFeatureLayer2;
    }
    layer = enumLayer.Next();
}
if (cityFLayer == null)
{ return; }
    IQueryFilter2 qF = new QueryFilterClass();
    qF.WhereClause = "CITY_NAME='Malibu'";


    IFeatureCursor featureCursor = cityFLayer.FeatureClass.Search(qF,
    false);
    IFeature city = featureCursor.NextFeature();
    if (city != null)
    {
        (city.Shape as IPoint).X += 1;
        (city.Shape as IPoint).Y += 2;
        city.Store();
    }
    mxdoc.ActiveView.Refresh();
```

WORKING WITH SPATIAL OPERATORS

There are several spatial operators for working with the geometry of features in ArcObjects. These operators can be used to perform common geoprocessing tasks such as buffer, merge, overlay, and union, as well as geographical measurements of features and examining the topological relationship among the geometry of different features. This section of this chapter explores the IRelationalOperator, IProximityOperator, and ITopologicalOperator interfaces.

Examining Spatial Relationships

In order to examine the spatial relationships between two geometries, the IRelationalOperator interface should be used. The IRelationalOperator has several methods for examining the relationship, which return a boolean value indicating whether or not the desired relationship exists among two geometries. In the following Try It Out, you use the Equals() method on IRelationalOperator to find duplicate features in the U.S. States FeatureLayer. Because the test data for the next Try It Out (the states feature class in the USA feature dataset) doesn't have any duplicates, it is a good idea to create some duplicate features in it. Open ArcMap and add the states feature class to your map. Click the Editor Toolbar command on the Standard toolbar, then from the Editor menu on the Editor toolbar click Start Editing. Use the Edit tool on the Editor toolbar (or any Select Features by Graphics tools on the Tools toolbar), select a feature, then copy (Ctl+C) and paste (Ctl+V) a feature. When you paste the feature, make sure that you select the correct layer (since you want to create duplicate features, select the U.S. States layer). Click Stop Editing on the Editor menu and save your edits.

TRY IT OUT　Finding Duplicate Features (FindingDuplicateFeatures.zip)

1. Add a new add-in button to your solution and name it FindDuplicateStates. Provide the necessary information and settings as shown in Figure 9-18. Click Finish.

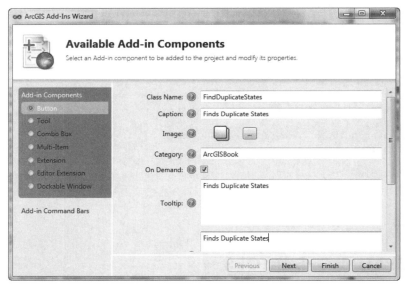

FIGURE 9-18

2. Insert the following using directives at the top of the FindDuplicateStates.cs file's code window:

```
using ESRI.ArcGIS.Carto;
using ESRI.ArcGIS.Display;
using ESRI.ArcGIS.Geometry;
using ESRI.ArcGIS.ArcMapUI;
using ESRI.ArcGIS.Geodatabase;
```

3. Add the following code to the button's OnClick().

```
IMxDocument mxdoc = ArcMap.Application.Document as IMxDocument;
IMap map = mxdoc.FocusMap;
IEnumLayer enumLayer = map.Layers;
ILayer layer = enumLayer.Next();
IFeatureLayer2 statesFLayer = null;

while (layer != null)
{
```

```
            if (layer.Name == "U.S. States (Generalized)"
                && layer is IFeatureLayer2)
            {
                statesFLayer = layer as IFeatureLayer2;
            }
            layer = enumLayer.Next();
        }

        if (statesFLayer == null)
        { return; }

        string message = null;

        IPolygon polygon1 = null;
        IPolygon polygon2 = null;

        IFeatureClass statesFC = statesFLayer.FeatureClass;
        IRelationalOperator2 relOperator;
        for (int i = 1; i < statesFC.FeatureCount(null); i++)
        {
            polygon1 = statesFC.GetFeature(i).Shape as IPolygon;
            for (int j = i + 1; j <= statesFC.FeatureCount(null); j++)
            {
                polygon2 = statesFC.GetFeature(j).Shape as IPolygon;
                relOperator = polygon1 as IRelationalOperator2;
                // if polygon1 == polygon2
                if (relOperator.Equals(polygon2) == true)
                {
                    message += string.Format("{0} and {1},", i, j);
                }
            }
        }

        if (message != null)
        {
            ArcMap.Application.StatusBar.Message[0] =
                "Duplicate Features: " + message;
        }
        else
        {
            ArcMap.Application.StatusBar.Message[0] =
                "There is no duplicate in U.S. States Layer";
        }
```

4. Next you modify the configuration file to place the newly created button on the menu. The menu is positioned on the toolbar, so there is no need to add the button to the toolbar. Add an `Item` element to the `Items` element inside the `Menu` element and use the `Item` element's `refID` value as the button's ID. The following XML fragment indicates two buttons are placed on the menu:

```
        <Menu id="Amirian,_DevExperts_GeometrySolution_Geometry_Operation"
caption="Geometry Operation" isRootMenu="false">
            <Items>
                <Item refID="Amirian,_DevExperts_GeometrySolution_CreatingANewCity" />
    <Item refID="Amirian,_DevExperts_GeometrySolution_FindDuplicateStates" />
            </Items>
        </Menu>
```

Note that in the configuration file the `Button` element is defined in the `Commands` element and the `Commands` element is defined as the direct child of the `ArcMap` element.

5. Run the solution and add the states FeatureClass to your map (from USA feature dataset inside TemplateData.gdb). If you copy and paste some features representing states (creating some duplications), this button can report the IDs of the duplicate features in the lower left corner of ArcMap's window in the status bar.

How It Works

In this example, you used the `IRelationalOperator` interface to find duplicate features. As you might know, finding duplicate data is a common task in quality control procedures.

> **NOTE** Note that the methods of `IRelationalOperator` are only applicable on points, multipoints, polylines, polygons, and envelopes. To use this interface for other types of geometry, such as lines, CircularArcs, paths, and rings, they first must be wrapped in an appropriate geometry. For example, rings must be wrapped into polygons, and lines must be wrapped into polylines.

Common Geoprocessing Operations

Geoprocessing operations such as buffer, overlay, and union are an indispensable part of almost any GIS workflow. Methods of the `ITopologicalOperator` interface are in charge of performing these common geoprocessing operations. These methods are limited to points, multipoints, polylines, and polygons. Most methods of `ITopologicalOperator` return geometry and require additional geometry as input. In the next Try It Out, you create a union of three states: California, Arizona, and Oregon.

TRY IT OUT Creating a Union of Some Features (UnionSomeFeatures.zip)

1. Add a new add-in button to your solution and name it UnionSomeFeatures. Provide necessary settings and then click the Finish button.

2. Insert the following `using` directives at the top of the code window of the `UnionSomeFeatures.cs` file:

```
using ESRI.ArcGIS.Carto;
using ESRI.ArcGIS.Display;
using ESRI.ArcGIS.Geometry;
using ESRI.ArcGIS.ArcMapUI;
using ESRI.ArcGIS.Geodatabase;
using System.Runtime.InteropServices;
```

3. You need a method for getting an individual state feature by its name. So add the following method in the `UnionSomeFeatures` class file:

```
private IFeature GetState(string stateName)
    {
        IMxDocument mxdoc = ArcMap.Application.Document as IMxDocument;
        IActiveView activeView = mxdoc.ActiveView;
        IMap map = activeView as IMap;
        IEnumLayer enumLayer = map.Layers;
        ILayer layer = enumLayer.Next();
        IFeatureLayer2 statesFLayer = null;

        while (layer != null)
        {
            if (layer.Name == "U.S. States (Generalized)"
                && layer is IFeatureLayer2)
            {
                statesFLayer = layer as IFeatureLayer2;
            }
            layer = enumLayer.Next();
        }

        if (statesFLayer == null)
        { return null; }

        IQueryFilter qF = new QueryFilterClass();
        qF.WhereClause = string.Format("STATE_NAME='{0}'", stateName);
        IFeatureCursor featureCursor = statesFLayer.FeatureClass.Search(qF, true);
        IFeature state = featureCursor.NextFeature();
        //releasing the cursor
        Marshal.ReleaseComObject(featureCursor);
        return state;
    }
```

4. Add the following code to the `OnClick()` method of the button to get the three states, and union them to create a new geometry.

```
IFeature california = GetState("California");
IFeature arizona = GetState("Arizona");
IFeature oregon = GetState("Oregon");

if (california == null || arizona == null || oregon == null)
{ return; }

ITopologicalOperator topoOperator =
    california.Shape as ITopologicalOperator;

IPolygon5 unionPolygon = topoOperator.Union(arizona.Shape) as IPolygon5;
IPolygon5 unionPolygon2 = (unionPolygon as ITopologicalOperator).
    Union(oregon.Shape) as IPolygon5;

IMxDocument mxdoc = ArcMap.Application.Document as IMxDocument;
IActiveView activeView = mxdoc.ActiveView;

IScreenDisplay screenDisp = activeView.ScreenDisplay;
short screenCache = Convert.ToInt16(esriScreenCache.esriNoScreenCache);
screenDisp.StartDrawing(screenDisp.hDC, screenCache);
```

```
IRgbColor color = new RgbColorClass();
color.Red = 214; color.Blue = 156; color.Green = 78;

ISimpleFillSymbol simpleFillSymbol = new SimpleFillSymbolClass();
simpleFillSymbol.Color = color;
screenDisp.SetSymbol(simpleFillSymbol as ISymbol);

screenDisp.DrawPolygon(unionPolygon2 as IGeometry);
screenDisp.FinishDrawing();
```

5. Modify the configuration file to place the button on the menu. Run your code and add the `states` FeatureClass and finally test the button. You will see Figure 9-19.

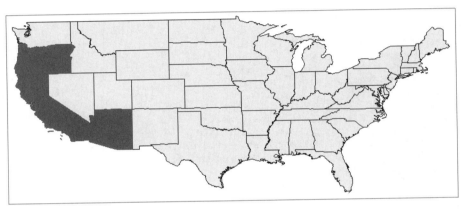

FIGURE 9-19

How It Works

In this Try It Out, you used the `ITopologicalOperator` interface to perform a union of three state features. As you can see, you can chain union polygons, but this is a very tedious and inefficient approach. In order to make a union for several geometries, you can make use of the `GeometryBag` CoClass and the `ConstructUnion()` method of the `ITopologicalOperator` interface. The following code demonstrates making a union of all features in the `states` FeatureClass.

```
IMxDocument mxdoc = ArcMap.Application.Document as IMxDocument;
IActiveView activeView = mxdoc.ActiveView;
IMap map = activeView as IMap;
IEnumLayer enumLayer = map.Layers;
ILayer layer = enumLayer.Next();
IFeatureLayer2 statesFLayer = null;

while (layer != null)
{
    if (layer.Name == "U.S. States (Generalized)"
    && layer is IFeatureLayer2)
    {
        statesFLayer = layer as IFeatureLayer2;
```

```
        }
        layer = enumLayer.Next();
}

if (statesFLayer == null)
{ return; }

IGeometry geometryBag = new GeometryBagClass();

// we have to use nonrecycling cursor in order to retain
//each individual Feature as a separate object in memory
IFeatureCursor featureCursor = statesFLayer.FeatureClass.Search(null, false);
IGeometryCollection geometryColl = geometryBag as IGeometryCollection;
IFeature aFeature = featureCursor.NextFeature();

while (aFeature != null)
{
    geometryColl.AddGeometry(aFeature.Shape);
    aFeature = featureCursor.NextFeature();
}
Marshal.ReleaseComObject(featureCursor);
ITopologicalOperator topoOperator = new PolygonClass();
topoOperator.ConstructUnion(geometryColl as IEnumGeometry);

IScreenDisplay screenDisp = activeView.ScreenDisplay;
short screenCache = Convert.ToInt16(esriScreenCache.esriNoScreenCache);
screenDisp.StartDrawing(screenDisp.hDC, screenCache);

IRgbColor color = new RgbColorClass();
color.Red = 214; color.Blue = 156; color.Green = 78;

ISimpleFillSymbol simpleFillSymbol = new SimpleFillSymbolClass();
simpleFillSymbol.Color = color;

screenDisp.SetSymbol(simpleFillSymbol as ISymbol);
screenDisp.DrawPolygon(topoOperator as IGeometry);
screenDisp.FinishDrawing();
```

As mentioned in the comments of the preceding code, you have to use a nonrecycling cursor to keep the reference to the individual feature in memory while iterating through features. This behavior is necessary, otherwise you'll lose the reference to the retrieved feature (the shape of the feature in this example) with each iteration. In other words, the result of preceding code, with recycling disabled, will be the last feature of the states feature class — that is, it unions with itself several times (up to the number of features in the states feature class).

Determining the Nearest Points and Distance

In order to find the distance between two geometries or locate the nearest point geometry in relation to other geometries, IProximityOperator can be used. Unlike IRelationalOperator and ITopologicalOperator, IProximityOperator is implemented by almost all geometry types. In the following Try It Out, you create a dockable window add-in to calculate distances between a specific city and all cities inside a specified state.

TRY IT OUT   **Nearest Cities (FindingNearestCities.zip)**

1. Add a new add-in component to your solution and name it NearestDockableWindow. Select Dockable Window as the type of add-in component, provide the necessary settings as shown in Figure 9-20, and then click the Finish button.

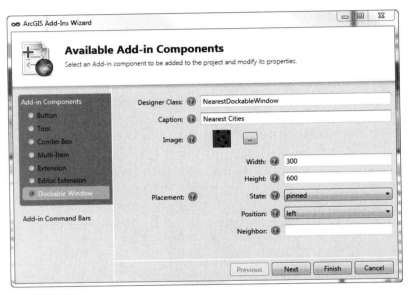

FIGURE 9-20

2. Add a class file to your solution and name it NearCity. Add Name and Distance properties to the class and a constructor that solicits Name as the input parameter. Instances of this NearCity class need to be sorted based on the Distance property. A standard way to do this is to implement the IComparable interface. The following code is the full code of the NearCity class.

```
public class NearCity : IComparable<NearCity>
    {
        public string Name
        { get; set; }

        public double Distance
        { get; set; }

        public NearCity(string Name)
        {
            this.Name = Name;
        }

        public int CompareTo(NearCity other)
        {
            if (this.Distance > other.Distance)
```

```
        {
            return 1;
        }
        else if (this.Distance < other.Distance)
        {
            return -1;
        }
        else
        {
            return 0;
        }
    }
}
```

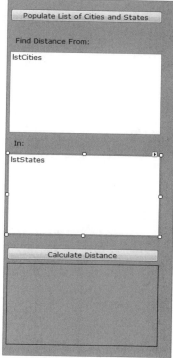

FIGURE 9-21

3. In the Solution Explorer window, double-click on the NearestDockable window to bring up the designer. Put two buttons, two list boxes, two labels, and a DataGridView on the dockable window and arrange them as shown in Figure 9-21.

4. Type the following using directives at the top of the NearestDockableWindow.cs file's code window:

```
using ESRI.ArcGIS.Carto;
using ESRI.ArcGIS.Display;
using ESRI.ArcGIS.Geometry;
using ESRI.ArcGIS.ArcMapUI;
using ESRI.ArcGIS.Geodatabase;
using System.Runtime.InteropServices;
```

5. Double-click on btnPopulateListOfCitiesStates (the button at the top of the dockable window) to create stub code for handling the Click event. Insert the following code inside the event handler:

```
lstCities.Items.Clear();
lstStates.Items.Clear();
lstCities.Sorted = true;
lstStates.Sorted = true;

IFeatureLayer2 statesFLayer = GetFeatureLayer("U.S. States (Generalized)");
IFeatureLayer2 citiesFLayer = GetFeatureLayer("U.S. Cities");

if (statesFLayer == null || citiesFLayer == null)
{ return; }

IFeatureCursor stateFeatureCursor = statesFLayer.Search(null, true);
IFeature state = stateFeatureCursor.NextFeature();
IFeatureClass stateFC = statesFLayer.FeatureClass;
int statenameFieldIndex = stateFC.Fields.FindField("STATE_NAME");
while (state != null)
{
    lstStates.Items.Add(state.Value[statenameFieldIndex]);
    state = stateFeatureCursor.NextFeature();
}
```

```
        Marshal.ReleaseComObject(stateFeatureCursor);

        IFeatureCursor cityFeatureCursor = citiesFLayer.Search(null, true);
        IFeature city = cityFeatureCursor.NextFeature();
        IFeatureClass cityFC = citiesFLayer.FeatureClass;
        int citynameFieldIndex = cityFC.Fields.FindField("CITY_NAME");
        while (city != null)
        {
            lstCities.Items.Add(city.Value[citynameFieldIndex]);
            city = cityFeatureCursor.NextFeature();
        }
        Marshal.ReleaseComObject(cityFeatureCursor);
```

6. Add a method to return a FeatureLayer based on the name of the layer.

```
public IFeatureLayer2 GetFeatureLayer(string layerName)
    {
        IMxDocument mxdoc = ArcMap.Application.Document as IMxDocument;
        IMap map = mxdoc.FocusMap;
        IEnumLayer enumLayer = map.Layers;
        ILayer layer = enumLayer.Next();
        while (layer != null)
        {
            if (layer.Name == layerName && layer is IFeatureLayer2)
            {
                return layer as IFeatureLayer2;
            }
            layer = enumLayer.Next();
        }
        return null;
    }
```

7. Go to the Designer window and double-click on btnCalculateDistance (the button with Calculate Distance text), then insert the following code inside the click event handler:

```
        List<NearCity> nearCities = new List<NearCity>();

        if (lstCities.SelectedIndex < 0 || lstStates.SelectedIndex < 0)
        { return; }

        string specifiedState = lstStates.SelectedItem.ToString();
        string specifiedCity = lstCities.SelectedItem.ToString();

        //select cities inside the specified state
        //select specified city and use its geometry as
        //ProximityOperator to calculate all distances

        IQueryFilter qF = new QueryFilterClass();
        qF.WhereClause = string.Format("CITY_NAME='{0}'", specifiedCity);
        IFeatureClass citiesFC = GetFeatureLayer("U.S. Cities").FeatureClass;
        IFeatureSelection citiesFSelection = GetFeatureLayer("U.S. Cities")
        as IFeatureSelection;

        IFeatureCursor featureCursor = citiesFC.Search(qF, true);
```

```
IFeature city = featureCursor.NextFeature();
citiesFSelection.SelectFeatures(qF,
    esriSelectionResultEnum.esriSelectionResultNew, true);

IProximityOperator proximityOp = city.Shape as IProximityOperator;

qF.WhereClause = string.Format("STATE_NAME='{0}'", specifiedState);
citiesFSelection.SelectFeatures(qF,
esriSelectionResultEnum.esriSelectionResultAdd, false);

featureCursor = citiesFC.Search(qF, true);
IFeature candidateCity = featureCursor.NextFeature();

int citynameFieldIndex = citiesFC.Fields.FindField("CITY_NAME");

while (candidateCity != null)
{
    NearCity aNearCity = new NearCity(
        candidateCity.Value[citynameFieldIndex].ToString());
    aNearCity.Distance = proximityOp.ReturnDistance(
        candidateCity.Shape as IGeometry4);
    nearCities.Add(aNearCity);
    candidateCity = featureCursor.NextFeature();
}

nearCities.Sort();
dgv.DataSource = nearCities;
IMxDocument mxdoc = ArcMap.Application.Document as IMxDocument;
mxdoc.ActiveView.Extent = city.Shape.Envelope;
mxdoc.ActiveView.Refresh();
```

8. Same as all add-in dockable window components, you need an additional button to display or activate it in ArcMap. So add a new add-in component button to your solution and name it NearestToggle. Add the following using directives in the code file of the newly added button:

```
using ESRI.ArcGIS.esriSystem;
using ESRI.ArcGIS.Framework;
```

9. Add the following code to the button's OnClick() method to display or activate the dockable window:

```
UID dockableWinUID = new UIDClass();
dockableWinUID.Value = ThisAddIn.IDs.NearestDockableWindow;
IDockableWindow nearestDockableWin = ArcMap.DockableWindowManager.
GetDockableWindow(dockableWinUID);
nearestDockableWin.Show(true);
```

10. As the final step, modify the configuration file to place the NearestToggle button on the menu. Then run the add-in and add cities and states FeatureClasses to the ArcMap and test the functionality of the dockable window.

How It Works

In this Try It Out, you used one of the standard and generic interfaces of .NET to provide sort functionality. In order to implement this interface, all that is required is the definition of a single method called CompareTo(). This method indicates whether the position of the current instance in the sort order is before, after, or the same as a second object of the same type. When you call the Sort() method on the generic List<NearCity>, the CompareTo() method will sort the list.

You also saw how to use the IProximityOperator interface to calculate the distance between two geometries. Note that the ReturnDistance() method reports minimum distances in the dataset's units. As a result, in order to obtain distances in different units you have to multiply it by a constant or apply a different projection to the geometries.

LENGTH, AREA, CENTROID, AND ENVELOPE OF GEOMETRIES

In order to obtain the length of any one-dimensional geometry (such as paths and polylines) or the perimeter of any two-dimensional geometry (such as rings and polygons), the Length property of ICurve (or the most recent version, ICurve3) interface can be used. The ICurve interface is defined on the Curve Abstract Class and as a result is inherited by all subclasses.

The area and centroid of a two-dimensional geometry can be easily obtained using the IArea interface. The centroid of a geometry object is a point indicating the center of gravity of that geometry, which can be inside or outside of the geometry. Same as other things related to geometry, the area, length, and position of the centroid are in the units of the dataset.

The Envelope property is defined in the IGeometry interface, which is the primary interface of the ultimate parent class of all geometry classes (the Geometry Abstract Class). This property can be used to get the extent of a geometry. Note that Envelope is also a CoClass, meaning that there is no need to get a reference to an envelope from an existing geometry. For example, you can define a specific extent as a live instance of the Envelope CoClass for creating a spatial bookmark within a map document (.mxd) file.

The following code demonstrates the use of these interfaces to obtain common geometrical properties:

```
ICurve3 polygonICurve = polygon as ICurve3;
IArea polygonIArea = polygon as IArea;

double perimeter = polygonICurve.Length;
double area = polygonIArea.Area;
IPoint centroid = polygonIArea.Centroid;
//zooming to the polygon's envelope
IMxDocument mxdoc = ArcMap.Application.Document as IMxDocument;
IActiveView activeView = mxdoc.ActiveView;
activeView.Extent = polygon.Envelope;
//instantiating a new envelope
IEnvelope envelope = new EnvelopeClass();
envelope.XMin = -170; envelope.XMax = -66;
envelope.YMin = 20; envelope.YMax = 74;
activeView.Extent = envelope;
```

SUMMARY

The geometry of geospatial data is one of the distinguishing aspects of GIS from any other information system. In this chapter, you learned the basics of creating geometries. Working with the geometry of features and performing common geoprocessing operations was also covered in this chapter. In addition, you explored another type of desktop add-in. There wasn't anything related to spatial reference systems in this chapter. Those are covered in Chapter 13.

EXERCISES

1. Which attribute in a configuration file indicates if an add-in toolbar is automatically displayed the first time after the installation of the add-in?

2. Which interface provides the functionality to examine the spatial relationship between two geometries?

3. Why should a non-recycling cursor be used to create a union of all the features in a FeatureClass?

You will find the answers to these exercises in this book's appendix.

▶ **WHAT YOU LEARNED IN THIS CHAPTER**

TOPIC	KEY CONCEPTS
Displaying geometries on the screen	The `IScreenDisplay` interface provides a temporary drawing surface that can be easily used to draw geometries. This interface, which represents a normal application window, can be obtained from an `IActiveView` instance.
Adding items (such as buttons) to an existing toolbar	In order to add any add-in component to a toolbar (such as buttons and menus), you have to insert a new `Item` element as a child of the toolbar's `Items` element in the configuration file (`config.esriaddinx`). Then the value of the `refID` attribute of the `Item` element (as a child of the `Items` element) must be set to the `id` attribute of the add-in component.
Defining interior and exterior rings of a polygon	The interior rings, which define the interior boundary of a polygon, are oriented counterclockwise in ArcObjects. In contrast, rings that define the exterior boundary of polygons are oriented clockwise. In other words, when working with rings composing the polygon, traveling from the first point to the last point of any interior ring, the polygon is always on the left side. On the other hand, traveling from the first point to the last point of the exterior ring of a polygon, the polygon is always on the right side. Using this characteristic, it is an easy task to create a polygon using the `IPointCollection` interface. All that has to be done is to define two rings and then add points to those rings according to their orientations.
Creating a new feature	In order to create a new feature, the `CreateFeature()` method of the `IFeatureClass` interface can be used. The newly created feature will have a unique ID and null value or default values for other fields. Also it is possible to use an insert cursor to create a new feature. As an important tip, insert cursors provide higher performance for creating a large amount of features.
Updating a feature's geometry	To update the geometry as well as the attribute properties of a feature, an update cursor can be used. In addition to update cursors, search cursors can be used to update feature properties (geometry as well as attributes). Search cursors are created using the `Search()` method of a table or FeatureClass. Then the `Value` property has to be used to get the specific attribute of a feature. The `Value` property is a read-and-write property. As a result, this property can be used to set values (including the shape) for features for all fields. Then in order to persist the modifications, the `Store()` method of a feature must be called.

10

Rendering Geospatial Data and Using Hyperlinks and MapTips

WHAT YOU WILL LEARN IN THIS CHAPTER:

➤ Exploring object model diagrams for rendering, including colors, ColorRamps, and symbols

➤ Making use of various renderers for vector and raster data

➤ Using different classification methods

➤ Refreshing the ActiveView

➤ Examining simple and advanced MapTips

➤ Creating hyperlinks and dynamic hyperlinks

WROX.COM CODE DOWNLOADS FOR THIS CHAPTER

The wrox.com code downloads for this chapter can be found at www.wrox.com/remtitle .cgi?isbn=1118442547 on the Download Code tab. The code is in the Chapter10 folder and is individually named according to the names throughout the chapter.

Users of ArcGIS for Desktop applications set the symbology of layers using the Symbology and Display tabs of the Layer Properties window. There are several rendering options for each layer, such as Single Symbol, Unique Values, and Graduated Colors. Setting a symbology for a specific layer will change the appearance of its contents (for example, features in the case of FeatureLayer) as well as the legend of the layer in the application's Table Of Contents window.

Developers of ArcGIS for Desktop applications access the same functionality (and more) through a multitude of types inside several libraries in ArcObjects such as Display, Carto, and System. This chapter presents an overview of setting symbology for vector and raster layers and explores some widely needed types when working with Renderer classes. This chapter first discusses how to change the appearance of geospatial data and then deals with how to make features to go beyond display through hyperlinks and MapTips.

GEOSPATIAL DATA DISPLAY

The geospatial data display has a key role for data exploration and evaluation. Proper display of geospatial data leads to much easier understanding of real-world phenomena that are represented by geospatial data. Proper display of geospatial data even can result in stimulation of the visual reasoning of users and ultimately support the decision-making process. So it consists of cartography as well as art, digital technology, psychology, human-computer interaction, and many other disciplines. However, ArcObjects developers need only to focus on working with the proper types inside ArcObjects rather than the other tasks involved with proper data display. The following sections provide information about working with the necessary types for setting and defining symbology for geospatial data.

Color and ColorRamp Classes

An indispensable part of symbology is color. The Display library of ArcObjects includes a `Color` Abstract Class that has five creatable subclasses. Figure 10-1 shows how these five CoClasses can be used to define colors using different methods.

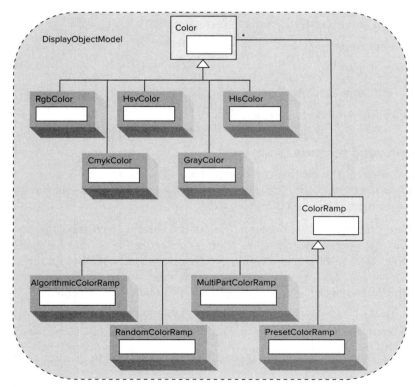

FIGURE 10-1

Each of the five CoClasses has a distinct interface to define the parameters needed to specify a color. For example, the HsvColor CoClass has an IHsvColor interface with three properties: Hue, Saturation, and Value. Table 10-1 provides all the needed properties of a color for a different interface.

TABLE 10-1: Various Color CoClasses

COLOR INTERFACE	PROPERTIES	RANGE (LONG)
IRgbColor	Red	0-255
	Green	0-255
	Blue	0-255
IHsvColor	Hue	0-360
	Saturation	0-100
	Value	0-100
IHlsColor	Hue	0-100
	Lightness	0-100
	Saturation	0-100
ICmykColor	Cyan	0-255
	Magenta	0-255
	Yellow	0-255
	Black	0-255
IGrayColor	Level	0-255

A color ramp is simply a collection of unique or sequential colors. ArcGIS for Desktop applications offer a set of predefined color ramps in the Symbology tab of the Layer Properties window. The same color ramp objects can be accessed using the Style Manager window, as shown in Figure 10-2.

Developers can create a ColorRamp instance using four concrete subclasses of the ColorRamp Abstract Class. The ColorRamp Abstract Class defines an interface called IColorRamp, which has Size, Color, Colors, and Name properties. All the interfaces of all subclasses of ColorRamp inherit from this interface. In other

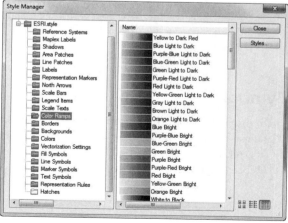

FIGURE 10-2

words, Size, Color, Colors, and Name properties are available to all the instances of ColorRamp subclasses.

In order to work with an instance of a ColorRamp subclass, after instantiation, the Size property (which indicates the number of colors to be created by the instance of ColorRamp) must be set. Then the CreateRamp() method has to be called to create a series of Color objects. The created Color objects can be accessed using the Colors property of the ColorRamp instance which is of type IEnumColors. Like any Enum, IEnumColors has a Next() method that points to the next item. The following code snippet creates a RandomColorRamp instance and gets the first Color object created by the RandomColorRamp:

```
IRandomColorRamp randomColorRamp = new RandomColorRampClass();
randomColorRamp.Size = 25;
bool ok = true;
randomColorRamp.CreateRamp(out ok);
IEnumColors enumColors = randomColorRamp.Colors;
IColor color = enumColors.Next();
```

The most commonly used ColorRamp subclass is the AlgorithmicColorRamp CoClass. An instance of this class must be defined using two Color objects and an algorithm to be used to fill the color space between those two colors. There are three possible algorithms for creating an AlgorithmicColorRamp instance.

Discussion about these algorithms is out of the scope of this book. The following code creates a color ramp, based on AlgorithmicColorRamp.

```
IAlgorithmicColorRamp algColorRamp = new AlgorithmicColorRampClass();
IRgbColor startColor = new RgbColorClass();
startColor.Red = 255; startColor.Green = 20; startColor.Blue = 232;

IRgbColor toColor = new RgbColorClass();
toColor.Red = 242; toColor.Green = 239; toColor.Blue = 136;

algColorRamp.FromColor = startColor;
algColorRamp.ToColor = toColor;
algColorRamp.Size = 25;
algColorRamp.Algorithm = esriColorRampAlgorithm.esriLabLChAlgorithm;
bool ok = true;
algColorRamp.CreateRamp(out ok);
```

Symbols

In order to display anything in ArcGIS for Desktop applications, some kind of Symbol object must be used. Lots of things (such as features, charts, pictures, texts, and north arrows) can be displayed in ArcGIS for Desktop applications, so a large number of classes define different kinds of symbol objects. Figure 10-3 presents a simple and brief view of the Symbol hierarchy.

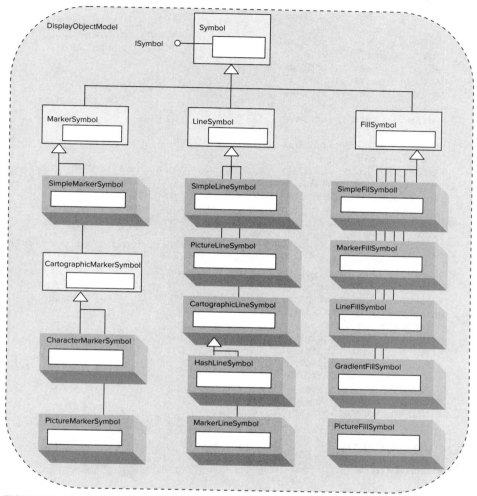

FIGURE 10-3

You used `SimpleMarkerSymbol`, `SimpleLineSymbol`, and `SimpleFillSymbol` in Chapter 9. Each `Symbol` subclass has members such as `Color`, `Style`, and `Size` through which an ArcObjects developer can tweak the appearance of the symbol. For example, the following code draws some points on the screen using an instance of `PictureMarkerSymbol`. Note that this code assumes that the specified address includes an image file.

```
IPoint p1 = new PointClass();
p1.X = 10; p1.Y = 10;
IPoint p2 = new PointClass();
p2.X = 20; p2.Y = 20;
IPoint p3 = new PointClass();
p3.PutCoords(35, 15);
IPoint p4 = new PointClass();
p4.X = 40; p4.Y = 17;
IPoint p5 = new PointClass();
p5.X = 50; p5.Y = 19;
IPoint p6 = new PointClass();
p6.X = 60; p6.Y = 18;
IMxDocument mxdoc = ArcMap.Application.Document as IMxDocument;
IActiveView activeView = mxdoc.ActiveView;
IScreenDisplay screenDisp = activeView.ScreenDisplay;
short screenCache = Convert.ToInt16(esriScreenCache.esriNoScreenCache);
screenDisp.StartDrawing(screenDisp.hDC, screenCache);
string picAddress = @"D:\GIS.bmp";
IPictureMarkerSymbol picMarkerSymbol = new PictureMarkerSymbolClass();
picMarkerSymbol.CreateMarkerSymbolFromFile
(esriIPictureType.esriIPictureBitmap, picAddress);
picMarkerSymbol.Size = 30;
screenDisp.SetSymbol(picMarkerSymbol as ISymbol);
screenDisp.DrawPoint(p1);
screenDisp.DrawPoint(p2);
screenDisp.DrawPoint(p3);
screenDisp.DrawPoint(p4);
screenDisp.DrawPoint(p5);
screenDisp.DrawPoint(p6);
screenDisp.FinishDrawing();
```

Figure 10-4 shows what you see when you run this code.

Renderers for Vector and Raster Geospatial Data

Each `Layer` object needs an appropriate type of renderer in order to be displayed by ArcGIS for Desktop applications.

FIGURE 10-4

For vector data, the `IGeoFeatureLayer` interface of the `FeatureLayer` CoClass has a `Renderer` property through which any renderer can be associated. As shown in Figure 10-5, there are several creatable subclasses of the `FeatureRenderer` Abstract Class. In this book, you explore `SimpleRenderer`, `UniqueValueRenderer`, `ClassBreaksRenderer`, and `ScaleDependentRenderer` for vector geospatial data.

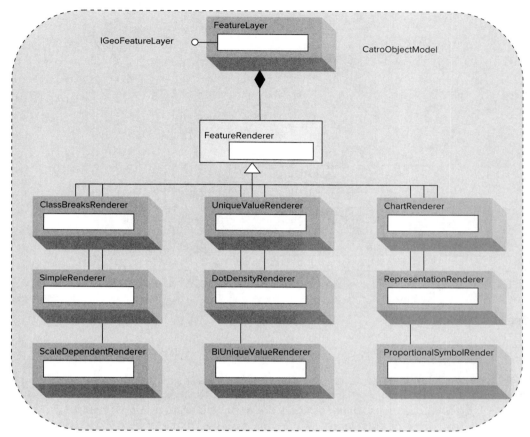

FIGURE 10-5

Raster data also has several `Renderer` CoClasses (see Figure 10-6). The `Renderer` object of a `RasterLayer` can be set or obtained through the `Renderer` property of the `IRasterLayer` interface. This book covers only the `RasterRGBRenderer` CoClass.

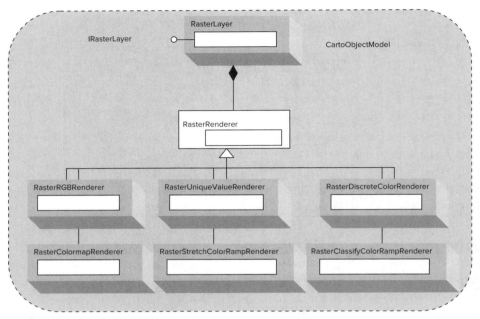

FIGURE 10-6

> **NOTE** *The default renderer for vector data is* `SimpleRenderer`. *In other words, when adding vector data (such as FeatureClasses or shapefiles) to ArcGIS for Desktop applications, all the features are displayed using a single symbol. In contrast to vector data, there is no default renderer for raster data. Based on the type of data in the Raster dataset, ArcObjects automatically uses the appropriate* `RasterRenderer` *to display it. For example, if a multispectral or hyperspectral satellite image is added to ArcMap, it uses* `RasterRGBRenderer` *to display a satellite image as an RGB composite and if a digital elevation model (DEM) is added to ArcMap, it uses* `RasterStretchColorRampRenderer` *to display DEM. Also some rasters have a predefined color map that ArcGIS for Desktop applications automatically use to display them.*

SimpleRenderer for Vector Data

This renderer is the default renderer that ArcGIS for Desktop applications use to display vector data. `SimpleRenderer` displays all features of a FeatureLayer using a single symbol. So in order to associate a `SimpleRenderer` with a FeatureLayer, all that is needed is to create an appropriate type of symbol and then assign it as the symbol used by SimpleRenderer. You see this in action in the next Try It Out.

TRY IT OUT Rendering Vector Data Using SimpleRenderer (SimpleRenderer.zip)

1. Create a new ArcMap Add-in project. Name the solution **GeospatialDataRenderer**. In the ArcGIS Add-Ins Wizard, provide the necessary information in the Welcome page and then click the Next button. Select Button as the type of add-in and provide the information shown in Figure 10-7, and then click Finish.

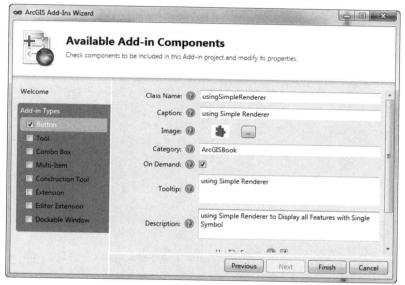

FIGURE 10-7

2. Add ESRI.ArcGIS.Display, ESRI.ArcGIS.Geometry, and ESRI.ArcGIS.Carto references to your project and type the following `using` directives at the top of the code window in the `usingSimpleRenderer.cs` file:

```
using ESRI.ArcGIS.Carto;
using ESRI.ArcGIS.Display;
using ESRI.ArcGIS.ArcMapUI;
```

3. Add the following code to the button's `OnClick()` method:

```
IRgbColor fillColor = new RgbColorClass();
fillColor.Red = 243; fillColor.Green = 188; fillColor.Blue = 245;

IRgbColor outlineColor = new RgbColorClass();
outlineColor.Red = 14; outlineColor.Green = 99; outlineColor.Blue = 24;

ISimpleLineSymbol outlineSymbol = new SimpleLineSymbolClass();
outlineSymbol.Color = outlineColor;
outlineSymbol.Width = 1.5;

ISimpleFillSymbol simpleFillSymbol = new SimpleFillSymbolClass();
```

```
        simpleFillSymbol.Style = esriSimpleFillStyle.esriSFSSolid;
        simpleFillSymbol.Color = fillColor;
        simpleFillSymbol.Outline = outlineSymbol;

        ISimpleRenderer simpleRenderer = new SimpleRendererClass();
        simpleRenderer.Label = "USA States in the same Color";
        simpleRenderer.Symbol = simpleFillSymbol as ISymbol;

        IMxDocument mxdoc = ArcMap.Application.Document as IMxDocument;
        IMap map = mxdoc.FocusMap;

        IEnumLayer layers = map.Layers;
        ILayer layer = layers.Next();
        IFeatureLayer2 statesFL = null;
        while (layer != null)
        {
            if (layer is IFeatureLayer2 && layer.Name == "U.S. States
            (Generalized)")
            {
                statesFL = layer as IFeatureLayer2;
            }
            layer = layers.Next();
        }
        if (statesFL == null)
        { return; }

        IGeoFeatureLayer geoFL = statesFL as IGeoFeatureLayer;
        geoFL.Renderer = simpleRenderer as IFeatureRenderer;
        mxdoc.ActiveView.Refresh();
        mxdoc.ActiveView.PartialRefresh(esriViewDrawPhase.esriViewGeography,
geoFL, mxdoc.ActiveView.Extent);
        mxdoc.UpdateContents();
```

4. Add a new command container (toolbar) to your project. Procedures for adding a command container for versions 10 and 10.1 of ArcGIS are slightly different.

➤ For ArcGIS 10.1 right-click on your project in the Solution Explorer window and select New Item from the Add submenu. Then select the Desktop Add-Ins item under the ArcGIS template. Then select Add-in Command Container item, and name it **RendererToolbar.cs**. Select Toolbar as the type of Command Bar and add the ReferenceID of the using SimpleRenderer button in your project by clicking inside the Items grid, and finally click the Finish button (see Figure 10-8).

➤ For ArcGIS 10, right-click on your project in the Solution Explorer window and select New Item from the Add submenu. Then select the Desktop Add-Ins item under the ArcGIS template. Then select Add-in Component and name it **RendererToolbar.cs**. Without specifying anything in the first page of the ArcGIS Add-Ins Wizard, go to the second page by clicking on Add-in Command Bars. Select Toolbar, configure its settings as shown in Figure 10-8, and click the Finish button.

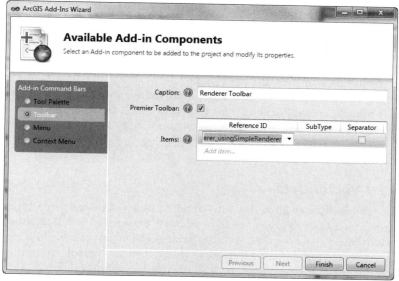

FIGURE 10-8

5. Run the code and add the states FeatureClass from the USA FeatureDataset, click on the newly created button, and you should see Figure 10-9.

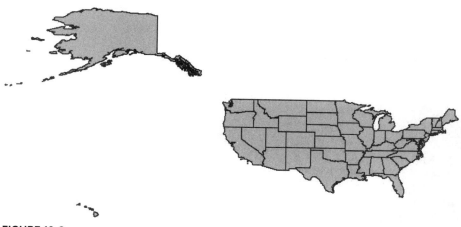

FIGURE 10-9

How It Works

In this Try It Out, you defined outline and fill symbols for a `SimpleRenderer` and used the `IGeoFeatureLayer` interface to associate the created `SimpleRenderer` with the FeatureLayer. In addition, in order to refresh the ActiveView, instead of calling the `Refresh()` method, you called the `PartialRefresh()` method. As its name implies, the `PartialRefresh()` method partially refreshes the display and as a result improves drawing performance. You learn more about this method later in this chapter. One of the inputs of the `PartialRefresh()` method is of type `IEnvelope`, defined in the `Geometry` assembly, which is why you added a reference to the `ESRI.ArcGIS.Geometry` assembly.

UniqueValueRenderer for Vector Data

As the name suggests, this renderer can assign a distinct symbol to each unique value (category) in attribute tables of vector data. The unique values can be of any type, such as text and number. In other words, a `UniqueValueRenderer` uses one or more fields in the attribute table of a FeatureClass in order to render each unique value (category) with a distinct symbol. Up to three fields can be specified for a `UniqueValueRenderer`, but usually just one field is used to create the categories. In the following Try It Out, you create an example of a `UniqueValueRenderer`.

TRY IT OUT   **Rendering Vector Data Using UniqueValueRenderer (UniqueValueRenderer.zip)**

1. Add a new add-in component to your project and name it **usingUniqueValueRenderer**. Select Button as the type of add-in, provide the information displayed in Figure 10-10, and click Finish.

FIGURE 10-10

2. You need to get all the unique values from a field in the attribute table of the counties FeatureClass. So add a reference to ESRI.ArcGIS.Geodatabase and then enter the following using directives at the top of the code window:

```
using ESRI.ArcGIS.ArcMapUI;
using ESRI.ArcGIS.Carto;
using ESRI.ArcGIS.Display;
using ESRI.ArcGIS.Geodatabase;
using ESRI.ArcGIS.Geometry;
using System.Runtime.InteropServices;
```

3. In order to use different colors for unique categories of attribute values, you need to create a color ramp. Insert the following method in your code in the usingUniqueValueRenderer.cs file:

```
private IEnumColors GetColorRamp(int size)
{
    IRandomColorRamp randomColorRamp = new RandomColorRampClass();
    randomColorRamp.Size = size;
    bool ok = true;
    randomColorRamp.CreateRamp(out ok);
    return randomColorRamp.Colors;
}
```

4. Add the following code to the button's OnClick() method:

```
IMxDocument mxdoc = ArcMap.Application.Document as IMxDocument;
IMap map = mxdoc.FocusMap;
IEnumLayer layers = map.Layers;
ILayer layer = layers.Next();
IFeatureLayer2 countiesFL = null;

while (layer != null)
{
    if (layer is IFeatureLayer2 && layer.Name == "U.S. Counties
    (Generalized)")
    {
        countiesFL = layer as IFeatureLayer2;
    }
    layer = layers.Next();
}
if (countiesFL == null)
{ return; }

IFeatureLayer2 FL = map.Layer[map.LayerCount - 1] as IFeatureLayer2;
IFeatureCursor fCursor = FL.FeatureClass.Search(null, true);

List<string> uniqueValues = new List<string>();
IFeature feature = fCursor.NextFeature();
int fieldIndex = FL.FeatureClass.Fields.FindField("STATE_NAME");

while (feature != null)
{
    if (uniqueValues.Contains(feature.Value[fieldIndex].ToString())
    == false)
    {
        uniqueValues.Add(feature.Value[fieldIndex].ToString());
```

```
            }
            feature = fCursor.NextFeature();
    }
    Marshal.ReleaseComObject(fCursor);
    IUniqueValueRenderer uVRenderer = new UniqueValueRendererClass();
    uVRenderer.FieldCount = 1;
    uVRenderer.Field[0] = "STATE_NAME";

    IEnumColors enumColors = GetColorRamp(uniqueValues.Count);
    for (int i = 0; i < uniqueValues.Count; i++)
    {
        ISimpleFillSymbol simpleFSymbol = new SimpleFillSymbolClass();
        simpleFSymbol.Color = enumColors.Next();
        uVRenderer.AddValue(uniqueValues[i], "States",
        simpleFSymbol as ISymbol);
    }

    IGeoFeatureLayer geoFL = FL as IGeoFeatureLayer;
    geoFL.Renderer = uVRenderer as IFeatureRenderer;
    mxdoc.ActiveView.PartialRefresh(esriViewDrawPhase.esriViewGeography,
geoFL, mxdoc.ActiveView.Extent);
    mxdoc.UpdateContents();
```

5. Modify the configuration file to place the button on the toolbar.

```
    <Toolbar id="Amirian,_devExperts_GeospatialDataRenderer_Renderer_Toolbar"
caption="Renderer Toolbar" showInitially="true">
        <Items>
            <Item refID="Amirian,_devExperts↲
_GeospatialDataRenderer_usingSimpleRenderer" />
            <Item refID="Amirian,_devExperts↲
_GeospatialDataRenderer_usingUniqueValueRenderer" />
        </Items>
    </Toolbar>
```

6. Run your code and add the counties FeatureClass of USA FeatureDataset then click the newly added button to the toolbar. Figure 10-11 shows what you should see.

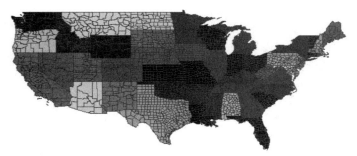

FIGURE 10-11

How It Works

In this example, you used a `RandomColorRamp` to create distinct `Color` objects for unique values. Since the `RandomColorRamp` creates random `Color` objects, each time you click the button, you get a different series of colors, and as a result, a different view of the same FeatureClass.

ClassBreaksRenderer for Vector Data

Up to this point in this chapter, you have used two types of `FeatureRenderers` to create single or multiple symbols for all features in a FeatureClass without any classification. In order to display various classes of features of a FeatureClass using classification of a numeric field, an `IClassBreaksRenderer` interface can be utilized.

In order to set the symbology of a FeatureLayer using an ArcGIS for Desktop application's user interface, you first set a numeric field and number of classes, and then tweak the method of classification. In other words, you can choose different classification methods, the number of classes, break values, and color ramps for the symbology of a FeatureLayer. In addition, in the Classification window you can see the histogram for data values, which consists of unique data values and their frequencies.

As an ArcObjects developer, you use the same procedure in reverse. First you need to get the histogram of a specific field of a FeatureClass. For this purpose, the `IHistogram` and `ITableHistogram` interfaces must be used (see Figure 10-12).

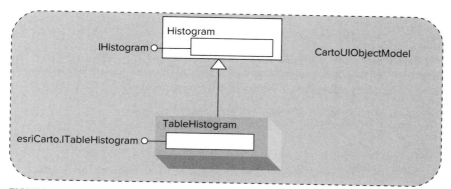

FIGURE 10-12

The following code shows that an `ITableHistogram` is set for the desired table and field. Then, using the `IHistogram` interface as shown, you can get the data values and their frequencies.

```
ITableHistogram tableHistogram = new TableHistogramClass();
tableHistogram.Table =countiesFeatureClass as ITable;
tableHistogram.Field = "POP2000";

IHistogram histogram = tableHistogram as IHistogram;
object dataValues, dataFrequencies;
histogram.GetHistogram(out dataValues, out dataFrequencies);
```

The next step is to create an appropriate classification instance and call its `Classify()` method to create appropriate break points based on the data and its method of classification. Figure 10-13 displays available classification CoClasses in ArcObjects.

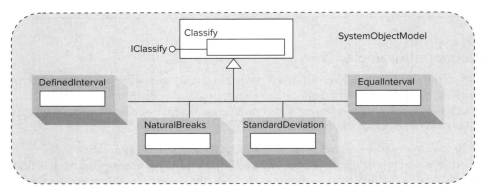

FIGURE 10-13

Before calling the `Classify()` method, the histogram data of the dataset must be set for the `Classify` object. In addition to histogram data, the number of classes must be known before performing classification. The following code shows how to obtain this information:

```
IClassify classify = new NaturalBreaksClass();
classify.SetHistogramData(dataValues, dataFrequencies);
int numOfClasses=5;
classify.Classify(ref numOfClasses);
```

The `Classify` object has a `ClassBreaks` property which is defined in the `IClassify` interface. The `ClassBreaks` property is an object containing actual break points. In order to use the data inside the `ClassBreaks` object, you have to cast it to an array of type `double`.

```
double[] classBreaks = new double[numOfClasses];
classBreaks = (double[])classify.ClassBreaks;
```

Then an instance of `ClassBreaksRenderer` has to be created and several properties have to be set.

```
IClassBreaksRenderer classBreaksRen = new ClassBreaksRendererClass();
classBreaksRen.Field = "POP2000";//name of the numeric field
classBreaksRen.BreakCount = numOfClasses;
classBreaksRen.MinimumBreak = classBreaks[0];
```

Then you have to create different symbols for different classes and add them to the renderer in a loop. In the following Try It Out, you use `ClassBreaksRenderer` in an add-in button.

TRY IT OUT | **Rendering Vector Data Using ClassBreaksRenderer (ClassBreaksRenderer.zip)**

1. Add a new add-in component to your project and name it **usingCBRenderer**. Select Button as the type of add-in, provide the information as shown in Figure 10-14, and click Finish.

FIGURE 10-14

2. Add a reference to the ESRI.ArcGIS.CartoUI and ESRI.ArcGIS.DisplayUI assemblies, and then enter the following using directives at the top of the usingCBRenderer.cs file's code window:

```
using ESRI.ArcGIS.ArcMapUI;
using ESRI.ArcGIS.Carto;
using ESRI.ArcGIS.Display;
using ESRI.ArcGIS.Geodatabase;
using ESRI.ArcGIS.DisplayUI;
using ESRI.ArcGIS.CartoUI;
using ESRI.ArcGIS.esriSystem;
```

3. In order to use different colors for different classes of values, you need to create a color ramp. In the previous Try It Out, you used the RandomColorRamp. This time you make use of the AlgorithmicColorRamp CoClass. So add the following code in the usingCBRenderer.cs file:

```
private IEnumColors GetColorRamp(int size)
{
    IAlgorithmicColorRamp algColorRamp = new AlgorithmicColorRampClass();
    IRgbColor startColor = new RgbColorClass();
    startColor.Red = 255; startColor.Green = 204; startColor.Blue = 204;

    IRgbColor toColor = new RgbColorClass();
    toColor.Red = 219; toColor.Green = 0; toColor.Blue = 0;

    algColorRamp.FromColor = startColor;
    algColorRamp.ToColor = toColor;
```

```
        algColorRamp.Size = size;
        algColorRamp.Algorithm = esriColorRampAlgorithm.esriHSVAlgorithm;
        bool ok = true;
        algColorRamp.CreateRamp(out ok);
        return algColorRamp.Colors;
    }
```

4. Add the following code to the button's `OnClick()` method:

```
            IMxDocument mxdoc = ArcMap.Application.Document as IMxDocument;
IMap map = mxdoc.FocusMap;
IEnumLayer layers = map.Layers;
ILayer layer = layers.Next();
IFeatureLayer2 countiesFL = null;
while (layer != null)
{
    if (layer is IFeatureLayer2 && layer.Name == "U.S. Counties
    (Generalized)")
    {
        countiesFL = layer as IFeatureLayer2;
    }
    layer = layers.Next();
}
if (countiesFL == null)
{ return; }

ITableHistogram tableHistogram = new TableHistogramClass();
tableHistogram.Table = countiesFL.FeatureClass as ITable;
tableHistogram.Field = "POP2000";

IHistogram histogram = tableHistogram as IHistogram;
object dataValues, dataFrequencies;
histogram.GetHistogram(out dataValues, out dataFrequencies);

IClassify classify = new QuantileClass();
classify.SetHistogramData(dataValues, dataFrequencies);

int numOfClasses = 5;
classify.Classify(ref numOfClasses);
double[] classBreaks = new double[numOfClasses];
classBreaks = (double[])classify.ClassBreaks;

IClassBreaksRenderer classBreaksRen = new ClassBreaksRendererClass();
classBreaksRen.Field = "POP2000";
classBreaksRen.BreakCount = numOfClasses;
classBreaksRen.MinimumBreak = classBreaks[0];


IEnumColors colors = GetColorRamp(numOfClasses);
IFillSymbol fillSymbol = null;
for (int i = 0; i < numOfClasses; i++)
{
    fillSymbol = new SimpleFillSymbolClass();
    fillSymbol.Color = colors.Next();
    classBreaksRen.Symbol[i] = fillSymbol as ISymbol;
```

```
            classBreaksRen.Break[i] = classBreaks[i + 1];
            classBreaksRen.Label[i] = string.Format("{0}___{1}", classBreaks[i],
            classBreaks[i + 1]);
        }

        IGeoFeatureLayer countiesGFL = countiesFL as IGeoFeatureLayer;
        countiesGFL.Renderer = classBreaksRen as IFeatureRenderer;
        mxdoc.ActiveView.PartialRefresh(esriViewDrawPhase.esriViewGeography,
countiesGFL, mxdoc.ActiveView.Extent);
        mxdoc.UpdateContents();
```

5. Modify the configuration file to place the button on the toolbar:

```
<Toolbar id="Amirian,_devExperts_GeospatialDataRenderer_Renderer_Toolbar"
caption="Renderer Toolbar" showInitially="true">
        <Items>
            <Item refID="Amirian,_devExperts
_GeospatialDataRenderer_usingSimpleRenderer" />
            <Item refID="Amirian,_devExperts
_GeospatialDataRenderer_usingUniqueValueRenderer" separator="true" />
            <Item refID="Amirian,_devExperts
_GeospatialDataRenderer_usingCBRenderer" separator="true" />
        </Items>
    </Toolbar>
```

6. Run your code and add the counties FeatureClass of the USA FeatureDataset. Test the functionality of your newly developed add-in button.

How It Works

Using `ClassBreaksRenderer` includes making use of several interfaces for extracting the histogram of data as well as classifying the data. As you can see, with just instantiating from different subclasses of the `Classify` Abstract Class, you can use different classification methods. So if you want to use the NaturalBreaks classification, all you need to do is to provide the `NaturalBreaksClass` as the instantiation class, as shown in the following line of code:

```
IClassify classify = new NaturalBreaksClass();
```

ScaleDependentRenderer for Vector Data

The `ScaleDependentRenderer` is available only to ArcObjects developers. Put simply, this type of `FeatureRenderer` is an ordered collection of other types of `FeatureRenderers`. Each `FeatureRenderer` in this collection has a corresponding scale for displaying the data of a FeatureLayer. In other words, using this renderer makes it possible to specify several FeatureRenderers for a single FeatureLayer. Geospatial data can be displayed in only a single scale at a time in ArcGIS, so only one `FeatureRenderer` in `ScaleDependentRenderer` is enabled at any time.

The `ScaleDependentRenderer` has a `Breaks` property for specifying scale ranges and the `AddRenderer()` method for adding `FeatureRenderers`. Remember: This `FeatureRenderer` is an ordered collection of other `FeatureRenderers` and the order in which the `FeatureRenderers` are added must match the order of scale breaks. The following code creates an instance of `ScaleDependentRenderer`, adds two `FeatureRenderers` to it, and specifies the scale ranges:

```
IScaleDependentRenderer sDR = new ScaleDependentRendererClass();
//Suppose that we have two live objects of type
//UniqueValueRenderer (uVR) and ClassBreaksRenderer (cBR)
    sDR.AddRenderer(cBR as IFeatureRenderer);

sDR.Break[0] = 10000000;
sDR.AddRenderer(uVR as IFeatureRenderer);
sDR.Break[1] = 40000000;
countiesGFL.Renderer = sDR as IFeatureRenderer;
```

This code uses the `ClassBreaksRenderer` for displaying features at scales greater than 1:10,000,000 (scale denominator <= 10,000,000). In the ranges of 1:10,000,000 and 1:40,000,000, a `UniqueValueRenderer` is used to render all the features (10,000,000 < scale denominator <= 40,000,000). At 1:40,000,000 scale and smaller, the layer will not be rendered at all! Note that break values indicate the absolute scale (or the scale denominator). Figures 10-15 and 10-16 show counties in 1:12,500,000 and 1:8,000,000 scales, which have been rendered using the preceding code. Source code for this `FeatureRenderer` is available in the `ScaleDependentRenderer.zip` file on this book's page on Wrox.com.

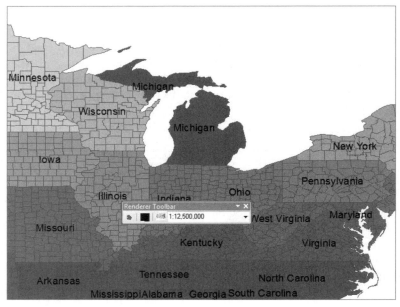

FIGURE 10-15

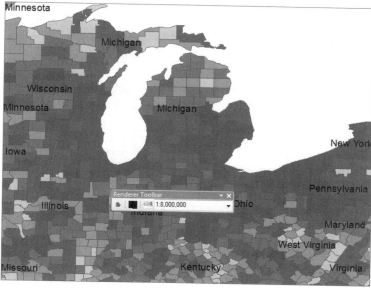

FIGURE 10-16

RasterRGBRenderer for Raster Data

The `RasterRGBRenderer` is used to display raster data as an RGB composite. This `RasterRenderer` is usually used to display multiband rasters, such as aerial and satellite images, as a composite of red, green, and blue colors. Figure 10-17 shows the main interface and properties for working with this renderer.

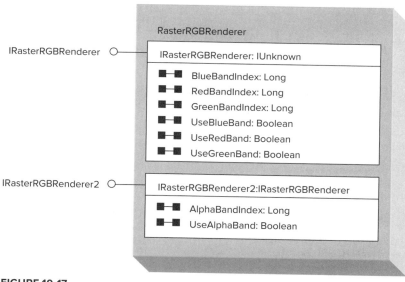

FIGURE 10-17

As you can see, indices of a raster's band are specified through the first three properties and their usage is determined using the rest of `IRasterRGBRenderer`'s properties. The `AlphaBandIndex` provides transparency for each pixel of the raster using the value of the specific band for that pixel. In the following Try It Out you learn how to use this type of renderer.

> **TRY IT OUT** **Rendering Raster Data Using RasterRGBRenderer (RasterRGBRenderer.zip)**

1. Open the GeospatialDataRenderer solution. Add a new add-in component to your project and name it **usingRasterRGBRenderer**. Select Button as the type of add-in, provide the information as presented in Figure 10-18, and click Finish.

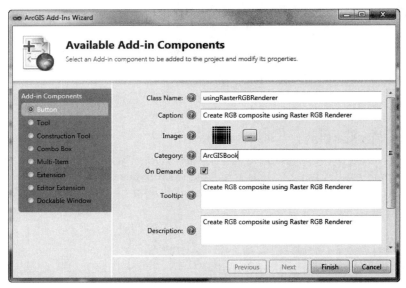

FIGURE 10-18

2. Add a reference to the ESRI.ArcGIS.DataSourcesRaster assembly, and then enter the following using directives at the top of the usingRasterRGBRenderer.cs file's code window:

```
using ESRI.ArcGIS.ArcMapUI;
using ESRI.ArcGIS.Carto;
using ESRI.ArcGIS.Geodatabase;
using ESRI.ArcGIS.DataSourcesRaster;
```

3. Add the following code to the button's `OnClick()` method:

```
IMxDocument mxdoc = ArcMap.Application.Document as IMxDocument;
IMap map = mxdoc.FocusMap;
IEnumLayer layers = map.Layers;
ILayer layer = layers.Next();
IRasterLayer rasterLayer = null;
while (layer != null)
```

```
        {
            if (layer is IRasterLayer)
            {
                rasterLayer = layer as IRasterLayer;
            }
            layer = layers.Next();
        }
        if (rasterLayer == null)
        { return; }

        IRaster raster = rasterLayer.Raster;
        IRasterBandCollection rasterBC = raster as IRasterBandCollection;
        if (rasterBC.Count < 3)
        { return; }

        IRasterRGBRenderer2 rgbRen = new RasterRGBRendererClass();
        IRasterRenderer rasRen = rgbRen as IRasterRenderer;
        //little playing with the raster display
        rgbRen.RedBandIndex = 1;
        rgbRen.GreenBandIndex = 2;
        rgbRen.BlueBandIndex = 0;
        //use channel 2 value as transparency value for each pixel
        rgbRen.UseAlphaBand = true;
        rgbRen.AlphaBandIndex = 2;
        rasterLayer.Renderer = rasRen;
        //update is needed
        rasRen.Update();
        mxdoc.UpdateContents();
        mxdoc.ActiveView.Refresh();
```

4. Modify the configuration file to put the button on the existing toolbar. Then run your code and add a raster dataset to your map. Test the functionality of your newly developed add-in button.

How It Works

You can tweak the way any multiband raster is displayed in ArcGIS for Desktop applications using the properties of the IRasterRGBRenderer2 interface. It's important to note that after any changes to the renderer associated with a RasterLayer, you have to update it by calling the Update() method. Also, as the name suggests, you can access information about the bands of a raster dataset through the IRasterBandCollection interface.

> **NOTE** As stated in Chapter 6, you can download free satellite images from the web. For example, the Earth Resources Observation and Science Center (EROS) of USGS provides satellite images of the world (http://glovis.usgs.gov/).

Refreshing the ActiveView

As mentioned in Chapter 6, the main application window is controlled by the IActiveView interface. Chapter 9 shows how the ScreenDisplay object, which is accessible through the IActiveView interface, performs drawing operations in ArcGIS for Desktop applications. Because

ArcMap is used as the target of most of the materials in this book, in this section's discussion of refreshing, the display is based on ArcMap.

ArcMap has two `IActiveView` objects: `Map` and `PageLayout`. Each object has its own `ScreenDisplay` object to perform drawing. The `ScreenDisplay` object uses different caches to draw different things. The cache is a bitmap (in memory or saved on disk) representing the main window of the application. Since reading and writing bitmaps is more efficient than reading and writing data from and to a database, using caches improves drawing performance.

The `Map` object in ArcMap has three caches for Layers, Selections, and Graphics and Annotations. The second cache (Selection) is for all features and graphics that are highlighted and accessible by `IActiveView`'s `Selection` property. If there is no selected feature or graphic in `Map` or `PageLayout`, the Selection cache is empty. The third cache is for Graphics and Annotations. ArcMap draws each of these caches within a separate `StartDrawing()` and `FinishDrawing()` block of the `ScreenDisplay` object.

It is possible to create a cache for any layer. The `ILayer` interface has a `cached` property which is of type `Boolean`. When this property is set to `true`, the Map creates another cache for the specified layer.

There are two methods for refreshing the main window of ArcGIS for Desktop applications. `IActiveView` provides `Refresh()` as well as `PartialRefresh()` methods to redraw the main display of the application. Both methods cause a cache invalidation process, which means all entries in the cache are deleted. But the `Refresh()` method invalidates all the caches and as a result redraws all the view phases, while `PartialRefresh()` redraws the specified view phase. Specified view phases are defined in the `esriViewDraw` enumeration.

The `PartialRefresh()` method solicits for three input parameters. The first input is of type `esriViewDraw` enumeration. The second and third parameters are optional. The second input is used to specify the data that is going to be invalidated, and the third input is for specifying the envelope to be invalidated.

In summary, using the `PartialRefresh()` method provides higher performance as well as a smoother user experience.

GOING BEYOND SIMPLE DISPLAY

MapTips go beyond simply labeling the features with text by providing interactive access to data via the map. When enabled, MapTips pop up as users of ArcGIS for Desktop applications hover the mouse pointer over a feature. MapTips provide a quick way to explore any feature without using the Identify tool or opening the attribute table, both of which give users all the feature's attributes. Prior to ArcGIS version 10.0, it was only possible to select one field as a source of MapTips. Fortunately, this behavior has been changed in versions 10.0 and 10.1. Whether simple or advanced, MapTips make working with geospatial data easier and more comfortable.

In addition to MapTips, hyperlinks provide an easy way to work with geospatial data's related information. In contrast to MapTips, hyperlinks can provide additional information about features and are not limited to values in a FeatureClass's attribute table. Hyperlinks must be defined before a user can utilize them.

Simple and Advanced MapTips

By default, a value inside the DisplayField is the only piece of data that can be displayed for each feature as a MapTip. The ShowTips property, which is defined on the ILayer interface, enables the display of MapTips. The following code demonstrates how to enable MapTips for a layer:

```
ILayer aLayer = mxdoc.SelectedLayer;
aLayer.ShowTips = true;
```

Prior to ArcGIS 10.0, this was the only way to create and manage MapTips. In ArcGIS 10.0 and 10.1, it is also possible to provide expressions in a scripting language to create flexible and advanced MapTips. ArcMap contains parsers for VBScript, JScript, and Python, and these parsers can be used to display MapTips as well as labels.

> **NOTE** In ArcGIS 10.0 there are VBScript and JScript parsers for labeling and MapTips. In addition to VBScript and JScript, Python parser is added in ArcGIS 10.1 for the same purpose.

The primary interface for displaying flexible MapTips is IDisplayExpressionProperties. The simplest way to use this interface is just to set its Expression property. The Expression property is a string which may contain string literals, the names of fields, and the functions of the specified parser. In the next Try It Out, you create this relatively new feature of ArcObjects.

TRY IT OUT Displaying Advanced MapTips (MapTips.zip)

1. Open the GeospatialDataRenderer solution, add a new add-in component to your project, and name it **advancedMapTips**. Select Button as the type of add-in, provide the information shown in Figure 10-19, and click Finish.

FIGURE 10-19

2. Type the following `using` directives at the top of the `advancedMapTips.cs` file's code window:

```
using ESRI.ArcGIS.ArcMapUI;
using ESRI.ArcGIS.Carto;
```

3. Add the following code to the button's `OnClick()` method:

```
IMxDocument mxdoc = ArcMap.Application.Document as IMxDocument;
IMap map = mxdoc.FocusMap;
IEnumLayer layers = map.Layers;
ILayer layer = layers.Next();
IFeatureLayer2 statesFL = null;
while (layer != null)
{
    if (layer is IFeatureLayer2 &&
        layer.Name == "U.S. States (Generalized)")
    {
        statesFL = layer as IFeatureLayer2;
    }
    layer = layers.Next();
}
if (statesFL == null)
{ return; }

IDisplayString displayString = statesFL as IDisplayString;
IDisplayExpressionProperties dEP = displayString.ExpressionProperties;
if ((statesFL as ILayer).ShowTips == false)
{
    (statesFL as ILayer).ShowTips = true;

    dEP.Expression = string.Format("\"State Name: \" +  [STATE_NAME]
        + vbNewline + \"State Abbreviation: \" + [STATE_ABBR]
        + vbNewline + \"Population :\" + [POP2000]");
    this.Checked = true;
}
else
{
    ILayer aLayer = mxdoc.SelectedLayer;
    aLayer.ShowTips = true;
    (statesFL as ILayer).ShowTips = false;
    this.Checked = false;
    dEP.Expression = "";
}
```

4. Modify the configuration file to put the button on the existing toolbar. Then run your code, add the states FeatureClass from the USA FeatureDataset, and test the functionality of your newly developed add-in button. You should see Figure 10-20 when you click the button.

How It Works

You set the `Expression` property of `IDisplayExpressionProperties` to display

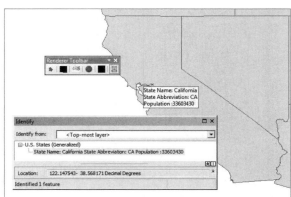

FIGURE 10-20

flexible MapTips. As you can see in Figure 10-20, the button is checked when MapTips are shown. In other words, by setting the add-in button's Checked property, you can create a toggle button.

It is also possible to use the built-in functions of scripting languages to create cool MapTips. Consider the following line of code:

```
dEP.Expression = string.Format("\"State Name: \" +  UCase([STATE_NAME]) + vbNewline
    + \"State Abbreviation: \" + [STATE_ABBR] + vbNewline + \"Population: \" +
    FormatNumber([POP2000],0)");
```

This code uses two built-in functions of VBScript, both of which are self-explanatory. The UCase() function converts a string to uppercase, and the FormatNumber() function returns a formatted number value for numeric expression. The output of the preceding line of code is shown in Figure 10-21.

FIGURE 10-21

Another important point in this example is that the same expression can be seen in the Identify window.

Hyperlinks

Hyperlinks are a basic and primitive facility of ArcGIS for communicating with the outside world. Hyperlinks make it possible to jump to a website or open a Microsoft Word document from inside ArcGIS for Desktop applications.

NOTE *As you will see shortly, you have to use different interfaces based on the type of resource you want to use. Hyperlinks come in two flavors. Hyperlinks defined based on a field are called* field-based hyperlinks, *and you have to use the* IHotlinkContainer *interface for them. If you want to use dynamic hyperlinks, you have to use the* IHyperlinkContainer. *Both interfaces are supported by the* FeatureLayer *CoClass and both support URLs as well as documents.*

For creating field-based hyperlinks through the user interface of ArcGIS for Desktop applications, the Display tab of the Layer Properties window must be used. To set a dynamic hyperlink for a feature, click on a feature with the Identify tool. Right-click the feature name in the Identify dialog box and choose Add Hyperlink from the context menu. Select the type of hyperlink (Document or URL) and specify the address of the document or Uniform Resource Locator (URL) of the website. It is possible to add multiple dynamic hyperlinks for the same feature.

The following code sets the field-based hyperlink for a FeatureLayer based on a field called HotLinkFieldName. This example assumes that there is a field in a FeatureClass's attribute table with values in the form of URLs.

```
string hotlinkField = "HotLinkFieldName";
IFeatureLayer2 featureL =
(ArcMap.Application.Document as IMxDocument).FocusMap.Layer[0] as
IFeatureLayer2;
IHotlinkContainer hLContainer = featureL as IHotlinkContainer;
hLContainer.HotlinkField = hotlinkField;
hLContainer.HotlinkType = esriHyperlinkType.esriHyperlinkTypeURL;
```

As previously mentioned, field-based hyperlinks are dependent on a resource. In addition, in ArcObjects it is possible to create dynamic hyperlinks that have no dependency on fields. This facility can be used to create more intelligent hyperlinks. You learn how to create dynamic hyperlinks in the following Try It Out.

TRY IT OUT **Creating Dynamic Hyperlinks (Hyperlinks.zip)**

1. Add a new add-in component to your project and name it **usingDynamicHyperlink**. Select Button as the type of add-in.

2. Type the following using directives at the top of the usingDynamicHyperlink.cs file's code window:

```
using ESRI.ArcGIS.Carto;
using ESRI.ArcGIS.Geodatabase;
using ESRI.ArcGIS.ArcMapUI;
using ESRI.ArcGIS.Geometry;
using System.Runtime.InteropServices;
```

3. Add the following code to the button's `OnClick()` method:

```csharp
IMxDocument mxdoc = ArcMap.Application.Document as IMxDocument;
IMap map = mxdoc.FocusMap;
IEnumLayer layers = map.Layers;
ILayer layer = layers.Next();
IFeatureLayer2 statesFL = null;
while (layer != null)
{
    if (layer is IFeatureLayer2 &&
        layer.Name == "U.S. States (Generalized)")
    {
        statesFL = layer as IFeatureLayer2;
    }
    layer = layers.Next();
}
if (statesFL == null)
{ return; }

IHyperlinkContainer statesHLC = statesFL as IHyperlinkContainer;
if (this.Checked == false)
{
    this.Checked = true;

    IFeatureCursor featureCursor = statesFL.FeatureClass.
        Search(null, true);

    IFeature feature = featureCursor.NextFeature();

    while (feature != null)
    {
        IHyperlink hyperlink = new HyperlinkClass();
        hyperlink.LinkType = esriHyperlinkType.esriHyperlinkTypeURL;
        IPoint centroid = (feature.Shape as IArea).Centroid;
        string link = string.Format(
            "http://www.openstreetmap.org/?lat={0}&lon={1}&zoom=9",
            centroid.Y, centroid.X);
        hyperlink.Link = link;
        hyperlink.FeatureId = feature.OID;
        statesHLC.AddHyperlink(hyperlink);
        feature = featureCursor.NextFeature();
    }
}
else
{
    this.Checked = false;
    int numberOfHL = statesHLC.HyperlinkCount;
    for (int i = 1; i <= numberOfHL; i++)
    {
        statesHLC.RemoveHyperlink(0);
    }
}
```

4. Modify the configuration file to put the button on the existing toolbar. Then run your code and add the states FeatureClass from the USA FeatureDataset. In order to test the functionality of the add-in button, click on the button, use the Hyperlink tool on ArcMap's Tools toolbar, and click one of the features.

How It Works

In this example, you iterate through all features in a FeatureClass and create a hyperlink based on the location of each feature's centroid, one by one. The hyperlinks are in the form of a shortlink URL of OpenStreetMap. Then you add all hyperlinks to the FeatureLayer using the `IHyperlinkContainer` interface.

Clicking the add-in button activates the Hyperlink tool on the Tools toolbar of ArcMap. This means dynamic hyperlinks are added to one of the layers in the map. Note that the container acts like a collection, which means adding or removing items to and from it will change the index of items inside it. This is why you have to call the `RemoveHyperlink()` method to remove the first item several times in order to remove all hyperlinks in `HyperlinkContainer`. You can also tweak the zoom level of hyperlinks (use the `zoom=9` key-value pair in the URL) based on the `MapScale` property of the `IMap` interface. (As an exercise, try to change the code slightly to create a more synchronized view between the map and OpenStreetMap.)

SUMMARY

One of the primary tasks of a GIS professional is to make maps. Properly displaying geospatial data is the first step in the process of map creation. ArcObjects contains a rich set of types for displaying geospatial data; fortunately or unfortunately, that means there are several ways to display geospatial data properly. In this chapter, you explored some of the most widely used methods for displaying geospatial data. Some features of ArcGIS for Desktop applications, such as MapTips and hyperlinks, provide an easier way to deal with geospatial data and bring additional information into GIS. Having mastered all the material covered in this chapter (colors, color ramps, symbols, and so forth), you are ready to work through the next chapter.

EXERCISES

1. What is the default renderer for raster data?

2. Which interface of the `FeatureLayer` CoClass is used for assigning a FeatureRenderer to a FeatureLayer?

3. Which interfaces are in charge of classification of a numeric field?

4. Which renderer type is not available in the ArcGIS for Desktop application user interface?

You will find the answers to these exercises in this book's appendix.

▶ WHAT YOU LEARNED IN THIS CHAPTER

TOPIC	KEY CONCEPTS
Refreshing ActiveView	There are two methods for refreshing the main window of ArcGIS for Desktop applications. `IActiveView` provides `Refresh()` as well as `PartialRefresh()` methods to redraw the main display of applications. Both methods cause a cache invalidation process, which means all entries in the cache are deleted. The `Refresh()` method invalidates all the caches, and as a result, redraws all the view phases. `PartialRefresh()` redraws the specified view phase. As a result, `PartialRefresh()` provides higher performance.
Using multiple fields in MapTips	In ArcGIS 10.0 and 10.1, it is possible to provide expressions in VBScript, JScript, and Python (in just ArcGIS 10.1) scripting languages to create flexible and advanced MapTips. These parsers can be used to display MapTips as well as labels. The primary interface for displaying flexible MapTips is `IDisplayExpressionProperties`. In addition to multiple fields, it is also possible to make use of built-in functions of the scripting language to create more flexible and helpful MapTips.
Creating dynamic hyperlinks	In ArcObjects, in addition to field-based hyperlinks, it is also possible to create dynamic hyperlinks that have no dependency on fields. This facility can be used to create more intelligent hyperlinks. Through dynamic hyperlinks, it is also possible to set multiple hyperlinks for a single feature. The primary interfaces for creating dynamic hyperlinks are `IHyperlink` and `IHyperlinkContainer`.

11

Labeling, Exporting ActiveView, and Working with Elements

WHAT YOU WILL LEARN IN THIS CHAPTER:

- ➤ Displaying flexible labels
- ➤ Labeling with the Maplex engine
- ➤ Exporting an ActiveView to different formats
- ➤ Including attribute data in PDF files
- ➤ Adding a graphic element
- ➤ Getting an item from the Style Manager window
- ➤ Adding north arrows and scale bars to a page layout
- ➤ Working with tools and the Tool Palette Add-in

WROX.COM CODE DOWNLOADS FOR THIS CHAPTER

The wrox.com code downloads for this chapter can be found at www.wrox.com/remtitle .cgi?isbn=1118442547 on the Download Code tab. The code is in the Chapter11 folder and is individually named according to the names throughout the chapter.

This chapter covers topics related to creating softcopy outputs out of geospatial data. Creating outputs can be seen as a final step of working with geospatial data. Often, the softcopy output of geospatial data is all that is needed as the first step of a decision-making process. In this regard, creating flexible, intuitive, and appropriate outputs is an important aspect of working with geospatial data.

This chapter presents an overview of making different kinds of labels using the standard as well as the Maplex labeling engine. Exporting an ActiveView is covered in detail next, and working with elements is the last topic. Along the way, you also learn about getting items from the Style Manager window and developing a Tools add-in. Placing tools on the Tool Palette is also covered in this chapter.

LABELING

Figure 11-1 shows the object model diagram for labeling. The map (Data Frame) uses a single labeling engine for all FeatureLayers. There are two possible labeling engines. The default labeling engine is called the *Standard Label Engine*. In addition to the standard (default) labeling engine, it is also possible to take advantage of a more flexible labeling engine — the Esri Maplex Label Engine.

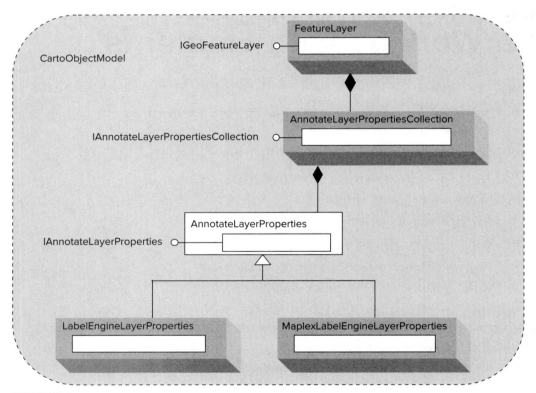

FIGURE 11-1

As mentioned in previous chapters, the IGeoFeatureLayer interface controls the display settings for FeatureLayer instances. One of these settings is *labeling*, which is controlled by a collection called AnnotateLayerPropertiesCollection. Using this collection, it is possible to assign more than one labeling setting for a given FeatureLayer.

The following line of code demonstrates the relationship between `IGeoFeatureLayer` and the collection.

```
IAnnotateLayerPropertiesCollection annotateLPC = geoFeatureLayer.
AnnotationProperties;
```

The actual labeling settings such as the expression of labels and the minimum and maximum scales for displaying one set of labels for a FeatureLayer are managed by the `IAnnotateLayerProperties` interface. This interface is defined by the `AnnotateLayerProperties` Abstract Class. There are two concrete subclasses for this Abstract Class (see Figure 11-1). The `LabelEngineLayerProperties` CoClass is the default and standard container for labeling settings. In other words, there is no need to have a special extension or to modify the settings in order to use this labeling engine.

Previous versions of ArcGIS included an extension called Maplex. Maplex provided a way to create more flexible and professional labels and have a lot more control on the labeling process. Starting with the release of ArcGIS 10.1, the functionality of Maplex is included in the core ArcGIS for Desktop software along with the Standard Label Engine. As a curious user of ArcGIS for Desktop applications, you can check this as shown in Figure 11-2 if you right-click on any Data Frame and select Properties in ArcGIS 10.1.

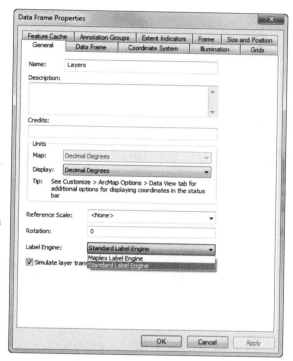

FIGURE 11-2

> **NOTE** Maplex labeling is available for ArcGIS 10.0 through a separate extension that you can purchase.

Labeling with the Default Labeling Engine

The following lines of code demonstrate how to create an instance of the default label engine class and set its properties:

```
IAnnotateLayerProperties annotateLP = new LabelEngineLayerPropertiesClass();
annotateLP.Class = "Between 5m and 20m";
annotateLP.AnnotationMaximumScale = 5000000;
annotateLP.AnnotationMinimumScale = 20000000;
```

In order to define the expression for labeling, you need to switch to another interface. Suppose that you want to create labels based on the Name field.

```
ILabelEngineLayerProperties2 labelELP = annotateLP as ILabelEngineLayerProperties2;
labelELP.Expression = string.Format("\"Name: \" + UCase([NAME])");
```

At this point, you need to add these settings to the collection that is associated with the FeatureLayer (`AnnotateLayerPropertiesCollection`) and then refresh the ActiveView.

```
annotateLPC.Clear();
geoFeatureLayer.DisplayAnnotation = true;
annotateLPC.Add(annotateLP);
ActiveView.Refresh();
```

In the following Try It Out, you create two classes of label settings and display them using the default label engine.

TRY IT OUT Labeling Using the Default Labeling Engine (DefaultLabelling.zip)

1. As always, create a new ArcMap Add-in project. Name the solution **CreatingOutputs**. In the Add-Ins Wizard, provide the necessary information in the Welcome page and then click the Next button. Select Button as the type of add-in, and provide the information as it is shown in Figure 11-3 and click Finish.

FIGURE 11-3

2. Add an `ESRI.ArcGIS.Carto` reference to your project and type the following `using` directives at the top of the **defaultLabelling.cs** file's code window:

```
using ESRI.ArcGIS.Carto;
using ESRI.ArcGIS.ArcMapUI;
```

3. Add the following code to the button's `OnClick()` method:

```
IMxDocument mxdoc = ArcMap.Application.Document as IMxDocument;
IMap map = mxdoc.FocusMap;

IEnumLayer layers = map.Layers;
ILayer layer = layers.Next();
IFeatureLayer2 statesFL = null;

while (layer != null)
{
    if (layer is IFeatureLayer2 && layer.Name == "U.S. States
    (Generalized)")
    {
        statesFL = layer as IFeatureLayer2;
    }
    layer = layers.Next();
}
if (statesFL == null)
{ return; }
IGeoFeatureLayer geoFeatureL = statesFL as IGeoFeatureLayer;
IAnnotateLayerPropertiesCollection annotateLPC = geoFeatureL.
AnnotationProperties;

annotateLPC.Clear();
geoFeatureL.DisplayAnnotation = true;

IAnnotateLayerProperties annotateLP = new
LabelEngineLayerPropertiesClass();
IAnnotateLayerProperties annotateLP2 = new
LabelEngineLayerPropertiesClass();

annotateLP.Class = "LowerScale";
annotateLP.AnnotationMaximumScale = 5000000;
annotateLP.AnnotationMinimumScale = 20000000;

annotateLP2.Class = "HigherScale";
annotateLP2.AnnotationMaximumScale = 1000000;
annotateLP2.AnnotationMinimumScale = 5000000;

ILabelEngineLayerProperties2 labelELP1 = annotateLP as
ILabelEngineLayerProperties2;
ILabelEngineLayerProperties2 labelELP2 = annotateLP2 as
ILabelEngineLayerProperties2;

labelELP1.Expression = string.Format("\"State Name: \" +
UCase([STATE_NAME]) + vbNewline + \"State Abbreviation: \" +
[STATE_ABBR] + vbNewline + \"Population: \" + FormatNumber([POP2000],0)");

labelELP2.Expression = "\"State Name: \" +  [STATE_NAME]";

annotateLPC.Add(annotateLP);
annotateLPC.Add(annotateLP2);

mxdoc.ActiveView.Refresh();
```

4. Add a new add-in command container (toolbar) and name it OutputToolbar. Select Toolbar as the type of Add-in Command Bars and add the reference to the newly created button. Run the code and add the states FeatureClass from the USA FeatureDataset. Click the button and change the display scale to 1:9,000,000; you should see what is shown in Figure 11-4.

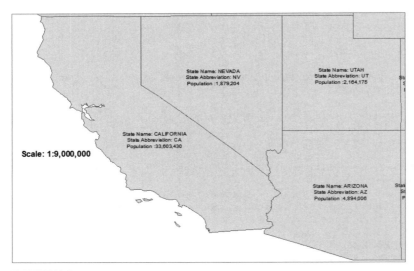

FIGURE 11-4

If you change the display scale to 1:5,000,000, the label engine will display both label classes, as shown in Figure 11-5.

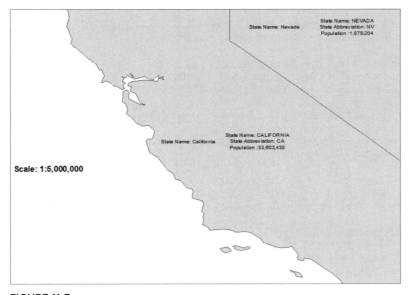

FIGURE 11-5

How It Works

In this example you set the minimum and maximum scales and the expression for two classes of labels. As you saw, these scales are inclusive. This is why both classes of labels were displayed at scale of 1:5,000,000. In addition to the scale of display, you can make use of conditions to determine the features to be labeled. For example, if you add the following line of code, you enforce the labeling engine to just create labels for those states with a population of more than four million.

```
annotateLP.WhereClause = "POP2000 > 4000000";
```

The result of this code is shown in Figure 11-6.

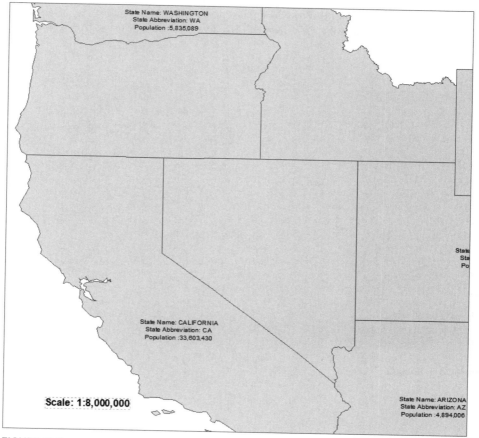

FIGURE 11-6

Labeling with the Maplex Labeling Engine

In order to use the Esri Maplex Label Engine, you need to change the `Map` object's `AnnotationEngine` property. In this case, the default labeling engine, which is of type `AnnotateMap`, should be changed to an instance of `MaplexAnnotateMap`. Consider the following code, which creates a new `MaplexAnnotateMap` instance and sets it as the `AnnotationEngine` of the `Map` object:

```
IAnnotateMap2 annMap = new MaplexAnnotateMapClass();
map.AnnotationEngine = annMap as IAnnotateMap;
```

In addition, you need to instantiate from an appropriate `AnnotateLabelProperties` subclass.

```
IAnnotateLayerProperties annotateLP = new MaplexLabelEngineLayerPropertiesClass();
```

In order to run this code, you need to add a reference to the `ESRI.ArcGIS.Display` and `ESRI.ArcGIS.Maplex` assemblies. Figure 11-7 displays the result of using the Maplex Label Engine.

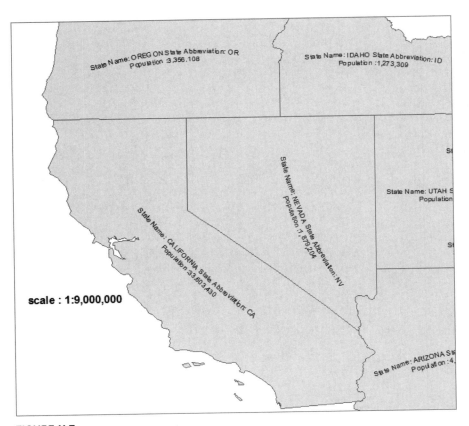

FIGURE 11-7

WARNING As shown in Figure 11-8, you may not find the `ESRI.ArcGIS.Maplex` assembly in the Add ArcGIS Reference window.

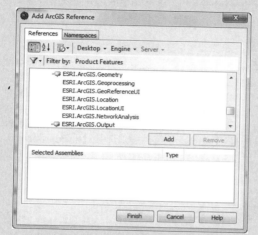

FIGURE 11-8

In this case, right-click the References folder in the Solution Explorer window and choose Add Reference. Then select the `Esri.ArcGIS.Maplex` assembly below the .NET tab, as shown in Figure 11-9.

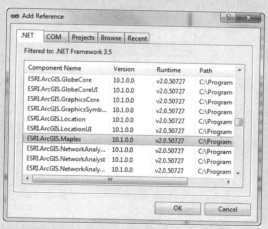

FIGURE 11-9

Note that if you change the labeling engine to Maplex, in order to use the default labeling engine you need to change it back to an instance of the `AnnotateMap` class. So as a best programming practice, make sure to include the following lines of code when working with the default labeling engine.

```
IAnnotateMap2 annMap = new AnnotateMapClass();
map.AnnotationEngine = annMap as IAnnotateMap;
```

In most cases, using the Maplex engine provides more natural labels (refer to Figure 11-7); as a result, users can communicate with the map in a more intuitive manner. For this reason, if you are going to print and disseminate a paper version of the map, consider using the Maplex Label Engine. You can find the whole source code for using the Maplex labeling button in the `MaplexLabeling.cs` file on this book's page on Wrox.com.

EXPORTING THE ACTIVEVIEW

Some situations make it necessary to export the ActiveView — for example, exporting ActiveView to `*.png` files to put them in a web page or Microsoft Word document. In these cases, you can take advantage of the types in the ArcObjects Output library to perform this task. There are ten supported formats for exporting maps: BMP, JPEG, PNG, TIFF, GIF, EMF, PostScript, Adobe Illustrator artwork, PDF, and SVG. Figure 11-10 shows most classes in the Output library.

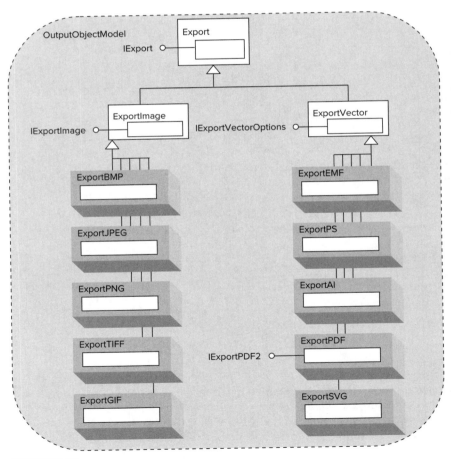

FIGURE 11-10

As Figure 11-10 illustrates, the ultimate parent class of all export classes is the Export Abstract Class, which defines the IExport interface. In most cases, all you need to export an ActiveView to a raster or vector file is the address of the output file and the target resolution. The following steps demonstrate the simplest approach to exporting ActiveView.

1. Create and instantiate the appropriate exporter object. Then set the address of the output file and its resolution using the properties of the IExport interface.

```
IMxDocument mxdoc = ArcMap.Application.Document as IMxDocument;
IActiveView activeView = mxdoc.ActiveView;
IExport exporter = new ExportPNGClass();
exporter.ExportFileName = @"c:\test.png";
exporter.Resolution = 96;
```

In order to change the output's format, you can easily change the instantiation phrase. The following code creates *.SVG output:

```
IExport exporter = new ExportSVGClass();
exporter.ExportFileName = @"c:\test.svg";
```

2. Define an envelope that specifies the pixel bounds of the output file. This rectangle must be set using the PixelBounds property of the exporter object. You can use the ExportFrame property of the ActiveView to create this envelope:

The ExportFrame property is of type tagRECT structure. For this reason, you cannot simply type the following line of code.

```
//the following line of code doesn't compile
exporter.PixelBounds = activeView.ExportFrame;
```

> **NOTE** The type of Envelope is a class while the type of tagRECT is a structure. There is a significant difference in the way that .NET manages classes and structures. Remember that when you speak about types in .NET, you mean precisely the members of the following set: enumerations, classes, structures, interfaces, and delegates. All these types can be categorized as either value types or reference types. Put simply, structures are value types and are created in the stack part of memory. In contrast, classes are reference types and reside in the managed heap in memory.

In addition to the subtle difference between classes and structures, there the tagRECT structure and the Envelope class have another important difference. As Figure 11-11, illustrates, the direction of the y axis in the Envelope coordinate system is the opposite of the y axis of the tagRECT coordinate system.

For this reason, if you need to define an Envelope instance that covers the whole ActiveView, you should use the following code pattern:

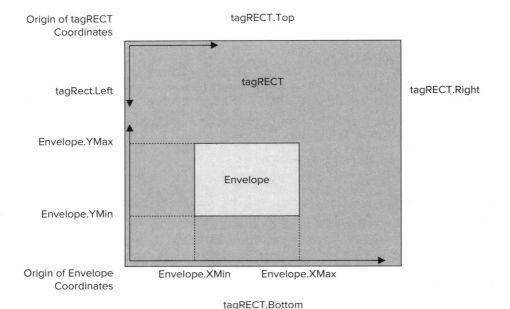

Origin of tagRECT
Coordinates

tagRECT.Top

tagRECT

tagRect.Left

tagRECT.Right

Envelope.YMax

Envelope

Envelope.YMin

Origin of Envelope
Coordinates

Envelope.XMin   Envelope.XMax

tagRECT.Bottom

FIGURE 11-11

```
IEnvelope pixelBBOX = new EnvelopeClass();
pixelBBOX.XMin = activeView.ExportFrame.left;
pixelBBOX.XMax = activeView.ExportFrame.right;

pixelBBOX.YMin = activeView.ExportFrame.top;
pixelBBOX.YMax = activeView.ExportFrame.bottom;

exporter.PixelBounds = pixelBBOX;
```

3. Allocate the required memory for the exporter object and then call the ActiveView's
Output() method to perform the export process. The required memory is allocated using
the exporter object's StartExporting() method.

The StartExporting() method returns an integer number representing the device context handle
that is managed by the Windows operating system. Then the ActiveView's Output() method can be
invoked.

```
int hdc = exporter.StartExporting();
//since a property cannot be passed as ref or out parameter
//you need another tagRECT variable
tagRECT exporterRectangle;
exporterRectangle = activeView.ExportFrame;
activeView.Output(hdc, (int)exporter.Resolution
```

```
, ref exporterRectangle, null, null);
//cleanup code to deallocate the memory
exporter.FinishExporting();
exporter.Cleanup();
```

The Output() method asks for three mandatory parameters. The first parameter specifies the handle of the output device and is an integer number that has its value assigned by the exporter object's StartExporting() method. The second parameter is an integer representing the DPI (dots per inch) resolution of the output file. The last parameter defines the export rectangle and is identical to the ActiveView's ExportFrame property. The rest of the code is for memory cleanup. The complete code for the simplest possible export of the ActiveView follows.

```
using ESRI.ArcGIS.Geometry;
using ESRI.ArcGIS.esriSystem;
using ESRI.ArcGIS.Output;
using ESRI.ArcGIS.Carto;

protected override void OnClick()
    {
        IMxDocument mxdoc = ArcMap.Application.Document as IMxDocument;
        IActiveView activeView = mxdoc.ActiveView;

        IExport exporter = new ExportPNGClass();
        exporter.ExportFileName = @"c:\test.png";
        exporter.Resolution = 96;

        IEnvelope pixelBBOX = new EnvelopeClass();
        pixelBBOX.XMin = activeView.ExportFrame.left;
        pixelBBOX.XMax = activeView.ExportFrame.right;
        pixelBBOX.YMin = activeView.ExportFrame.top;
        pixelBBOX.YMax = activeView.ExportFrame.bottom;

        exporter.PixelBounds = pixelBBOX;

        int hdc = exporter.StartExporting();
        tagRECT exporterRectangle = activeView.ExportFrame;
        activeView.Output(hdc, (int)exporter.Resolution, ref exporterRectangle,
            null, null);
        exporter.FinishExporting();
        exporter.Cleanup();
    }
```

In order to run this code, you need to add references to the ESRI.ArcGIS.Geometry and ESRI.ArcGIS.Output assemblies. The preceding source code can be found on this book's page on Wrox.com in the SimpleExportingActiveView.cs file.

NOTE *The preceding code used 96 as the output resolution (the exporter object's* `Resolution` *property). In reality, most Windows operating systems are shipped with the display resolution set to 96 DPI. If you need to export at higher resolutions (such as 300 DPI), all you need is to multiply the size of* `exporter` `Rectangle` *and* `PixelBounds` *of the exporter by the ratio of target resolution and screen resolution.*

In order to get the screen resolution, you must add a Reference to the `System` `.Windows.Forms` *assembly and use the following code:*

```
private int getScreenResolution()
{
    System.Windows.Forms.Form myForm = new System.Windows.
        Forms.Form();
    System.Drawing.Graphics myGraphic = myForm.
        CreateGraphics();
    return (int)myGraphic.DpiX;
}
```

Then you need to calculate the ratio to make the correct rectangle for output as well as for the envelope that covers all the pixels of the map.

```
int screenRes = getScreenResolution();
        int outputRes = 300;
        exporter.Resolution = outputRes;
        double ratio = (double)outputRes / screenRes;

        IEnvelope pixelBBOX = new EnvelopeClass();
        pixelBBOX.XMin = activeView.ExportFrame.left * ratio;
        pixelBBOX.XMax = activeView.ExportFrame.right * ratio;
        pixelBBOX.YMin = activeView.ExportFrame.top * ratio;
        pixelBBOX.YMax = activeView.ExportFrame.bottom * ratio;
        exporter.PixelBounds = pixelBBOX;

        tagRECT exporterRectangle;
        exporterRectangle.left = activeView.ExportFrame.left *
            (int)ratio;
        exporterRectangle.bottom = activeView.ExportFrame.
            bottom * (int)ratio;
        exporterRectangle.top = activeView.ExportFrame.top *
            (int)ratio;
        exporterRectangle.right = activeView.ExportFrame.
            right * (int)ratio;

        int hdc = exporter.StartExporting();
        activeView.Output(hdc, outputRes, ref
            exporterRectangle, null, null);
        exporter.FinishExporting();
        exporter.Cleanup();
```

You can find the code for high-resolution exporting of an ActiveView on this book's page on Wrox.com in the `HighResExportingActiveView.cs` *file.*

The ExportPDF CoClass (a subclass of the Export Abstract Class) provides some interesting facilities. In the following Try It Out, you export attributes and create standard output using the export process.

TRY IT OUT   Creating a PDF with Additional Content (PDFwithAdditionalContent.zip)

1. Add a new add-in component to the CreatingOutputs solution you created in the preceding Try It Out and name the component **PDFwithAdditionalContent**. Select Button as the type of add-in, set the configuration of the button as shown in Figure 11-12, then click Finish.

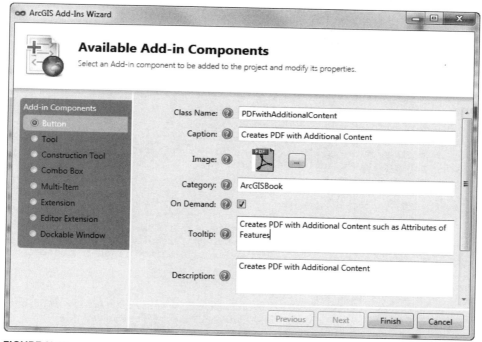

FIGURE 11-12

2. Add references to ESRI.ArcGIS.Display and System.Windows.Forms, then enter the following using directives at the top of the PDFwithAdditionalContent.cs file's code window.

```
using ESRI.ArcGIS.ArcMapUI;
using ESRI.ArcGIS.Geometry;
using ESRI.ArcGIS.esriSystem;
using ESRI.ArcGIS.Output;
using ESRI.ArcGIS.Carto;
```

3. In the code file of newly created button, add a method to get the resolution of the current screen.

```
private int getScreenResolution()
{
    System.Windows.Forms.Form myForm = new System.Windows.Forms.Form();
    System.Drawing.Graphics myGraphic = myForm.CreateGraphics();
    return (int)myGraphic.DpiX;
}
```

4. Add the following code to the button's `OnClick()` method:

```
IMxDocument mxdoc = ArcMap.Application.Document as
    IMxDocument;
IActiveView activeView = mxdoc.ActiveView;

IExport exporter = new ExportPDFClass();
exporter.ExportFileName = @"c:\MapWithContent.pdf";
int screenRes = getScreenResolution();
int outputRes = 300;
exporter.Resolution = outputRes;
double ratio = (double)outputRes / screenRes;

IEnvelope pixelBBOX = new EnvelopeClass();
pixelBBOX.XMin = activeView.ExportFrame.left * ratio;
pixelBBOX.XMax = activeView.ExportFrame.right * ratio;
pixelBBOX.YMin = activeView.ExportFrame.top * ratio;
pixelBBOX.YMax = activeView.ExportFrame.bottom * ratio;
exporter.PixelBounds = pixelBBOX;

tagRECT exporterRectangle;
exporterRectangle.left = activeView.ExportFrame.left * (int)ratio;
exporterRectangle.bottom = activeView.ExportFrame.bottom * (int)ratio;
exporterRectangle.top = activeView.ExportFrame.top * (int)ratio;
exporterRectangle.right = activeView.ExportFrame.right * (int)ratio;

IExportPDF2 ePDF = exporter as IExportPDF2;
ePDF.ExportMeasureInfo=true;
ePDF.ExportPDFLayersAndFeatureAttributes = esriExportPDFLayerOptions.
    esriExportPDFLayerOptionsLayersAndFeatureAttributes;

int hdc = exporter.StartExporting();
activeView.Output(hdc, outputRes, ref exporterRectangle, null, null);
exporter.FinishExporting();
exporter.Cleanup();
```

5. Place the newly created button on the Output toolbar by modifying the configuration file and run the code. In ArcMap, add the cities and states FeatureClasses to the map and press the PDFwithAdditionalContent button to export the map along with all the attributes of the two FeatureClasses.

6. Open the created file (`C:\MapWithContent.pdf`) with Adobe Reader software. From the Navigation panels in the View menu, select Model Tree. The Model Tree appears on the left side of the application and displays two expandable nodes for two layers. Using the Model Tree, it is possible to select a feature (by selecting the name of the feature), and its attributes will be displayed in the lower list, as shown in Figure 11-13.

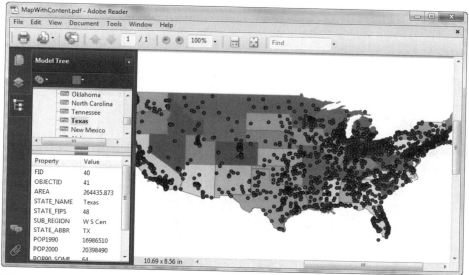

FIGURE 11-13

7. Using the Model Tree it is possible to select and zoom to a feature by its name. In order to select a feature interactively you can use the Object Data tool from the Analysis toolbar. Display the Analysis toolbar by selecting the Analysis item from the View menu's Toolbars submenu. Then select the Object Data tool (a tool with an icon similar to the Identify tool in ArcMap) and double click on a feature to make it selected on the map and show its attributes in the Model Tree at the same time, as shown in Figure 11-14.

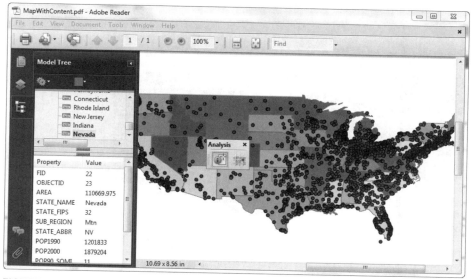

FIGURE 11-14

8. The PDF document contains the geographical coordinates from the map and is therefore aware of the mouse pointer's location. From the Analysis toolbar, select the Geospatial Location tool and the software will display the geospatial location of the mouse cursor (see Figure 11-15).

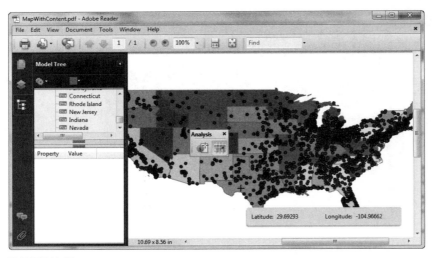

FIGURE 11-15

9. Because the Geospatial Location tool is selected in Adobe Reader, it is also possible to find a location based on its coordinates pair. Right-click somewhere in the PDF file when the Geospatial Location tool is selected and select Find A Location from the context menu. Enter values for latitude and longitude (for example, 32 and -99) and click the Find Next button to mark the entered coordinates in the PDF file, as shown in Figure 11-16.

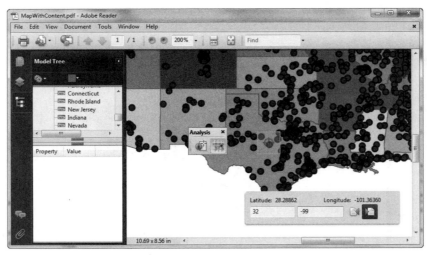

FIGURE 11-16

How It Works

You learn in this Try It Out that by means of setting two properties of an interface, you can embed attributes and measurement information in PDF output. Also, it is possible to control the visibility of layers in a PDF file using the Layers panel. Just select Layers from the Navigation panel's submenu in the View menu (see Figure 11-17). `ExportPDFClass` provides this capability by default.

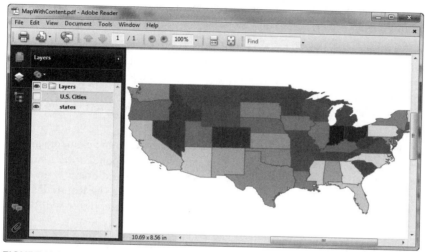

FIGURE 11-17

In addition to measurement information, visibility, and attribute data, it is possible to set user and master passwords using the `IExportPDFPasswordSecurity` interface, which is implemented by the `ExportPDF` CoClass. As you have witnessed, exporting an ActiveView as a PDF file can include advanced functionality that makes PDF a suitable softcopy format for simple exchanging of geospatial data.

Keep in mind, however, that exporting an ActiveView to a PDF file (including attribute data) can result in large files, which leads to performance problems when viewing the file in supported PDF readers. It is a good idea to limit exported attributes to one layer per map.

> **NOTE** *There are quite a lot of software applications capable of reading and editing the PDF file format. Usually the name of tools, panels, toolbars, and menus in various software applications are different. In the preceding Try It Out, all the instructions are based on the free Adobe Reader. Note that if you use software other than Adobe Reader, you might not have all the capabilities indicated in this Try It Out. If you run the code and open the created file but you don't find all the capabilities, download the free Adobe Reader and test the functionality of the newly created button.*

WORKING WITH ELEMENTS

Chapter 10 explains that in order to display anything in ArcGIS for Desktop applications, some kind of symbol object should be used, and there are many different kinds of symbols. This section's topic — elements — is similar to the topics discussed in Chapter 10.

Elements are things like north arrows, scale bars, markers, and text that can be added to a map (Data view) or page layout (Layout view). When working with elements, it is always necessary to work with symbols, colors, and geometries to define and set different properties.

Figure 11-18 illustrates the simplified object model diagram of working with elements. This diagram makes it obvious that a map and PageLayout can be composed of several elements. Each element has a geometry that is defined in the `IElement` interface. In fact, `IElement` defines the location of an element using the `Geometry` property. An important tip is that the geometry of an element can be defined using map or PageLayout units. For example, if the element must be added to the map, its geometry has to be defined using map units.

There are two categories of elements: *graphic elements* and *frame elements*. Graphic elements are the elements that are not related to a map's content, while frame elements are dependent on a map's content. For example, if you add a marker element (a graphic element instance) and north arrow (a frame element instance) to a page layout and then rotate the Data Frame (using the Rotate Data Frame command on the Data Frame Tools toolbar), you will see that just the north arrow will be rotated automatically to be synchronized with the map.

Both types of elements can be added using the `IGraphicsContainer` interface, which is implemented by both the `Map` and `PageLayout` classes. This interface has many methods to add, delete, and find elements. The following code demonstrates how to iterate through all elements in a page layout and report basic information about all the elements:

```
IMxDocument mxdoc = ArcMap.Application.Document as IMxDocument;
IGraphicsContainer graphicsContainer = mxdoc.PageLayout as IGraphicsContainer;
        graphicsContainer.Reset();

        IElement element = graphicsContainer.Next();
        string elementReport = null;
        while (element != null)
        {
            //use IElementProperties interface to get or set the Name of an
            //Element
            IElementProperties elementProp = element as IElementProperties;
            elementReport += string.Format("Name:{0} Type:{1} \n",
                elementProp.Name, elementProp.Type);
            element = graphicsContainer.Next();
        }
        MessageBox.Show(elementReport);
```

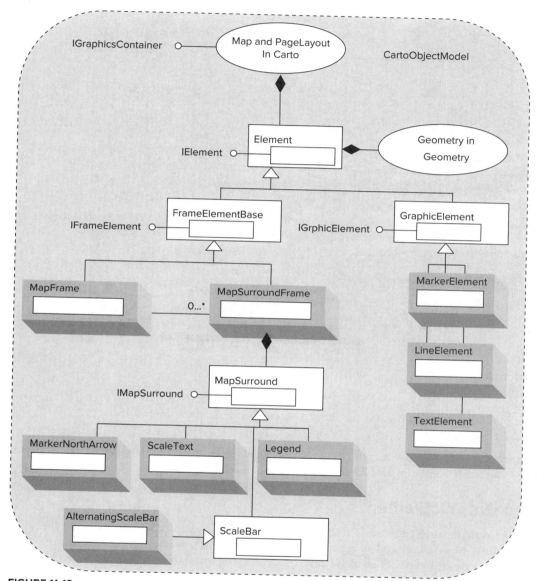

FIGURE 11-18

To test the preceding code, you can create a button add-in and paste the code into its `OnClick()` method. Add some elements such as north arrow, scale bar, and so on to the Layout view and press the button. (See Figure 11-19.)

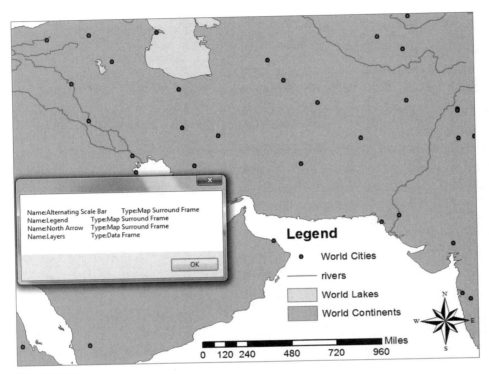

FIGURE 11-19

As the preceding code shows, it is possible to access the name of an element using `IElementProperties`.

Apart from this dependency to a map's content, FrameElements can be added only to PageLayout, while GraphicElements can be added to a PageLayout as well as a map.

Adding GraphicElements

In order to add a `GraphicElement` instance to a map or PageLayout, you need to create the appropriate `Symbol` object and assign it to the GraphicElement's `Symbol` property. Then the GraphicElement should be added to the map or PageLayout using the `IGraphicsContainer` interface.

```
IRgbColor color = new RgbColorClass();
color.Red = 255; color.Blue = 0; color.Green = 0;

IRgbColor outlineColor = new RgbColorClass();
outlineColor.Red = 0; outlineColor.Blue = 255; outlineColor.Green = 0;

ISimpleMarkerSymbol simpleMarkerSymbol = new SimpleMarkerSymbolClass();
simpleMarkerSymbol.Color = color;
simpleMarkerSymbol.Outline = true;
simpleMarkerSymbol.OutlineColor = outlineColor;
```

```
simpleMarkerSymbol.Size = 12;
simpleMarkerSymbol.Style = esriSimpleMarkerStyle.esriSMSDiamond;

//define the Element
IElement element = null;
IMarkerElement markerElement = new MarkerElementClass();
markerElement.Symbol = simpleMarkerSymbol;
element = (IElement)markerElement;
IPoint point = new PointClass();
//coordinates are in Map unit
point.X = 94; point.Y = -24;
element.Geometry = point;

IMxDocument mxdoc = ArcMap.Application.Document as IMxDocument;
IGraphicsContainer gContiner = mxdoc.FocusMap as IGraphicsContainer;
gContiner.AddElement(element, 0);

mxdoc.ActiveView.PartialRefresh(esriViewDrawPhase.esriViewGraphics,
    null, null);
```

Instead of hard-coding the coordinates of the element, it is a good idea to let users clicks determine the coordinates. In other words, this code puts the element wherever she or he clicks. This is where the Tool add-in comes into play. In the next Try It Out, you explore this kind of add-in component.

TRY IT OUT   **Tool for Adding GraphicElements (ToolAddingGraphic.zip)**

1. Add a new add-in component to the CreatingOutputs solution and name the component AddGraphicTool. Select Tool as the type of add-in, set the configuration of the tool as shown in Figure 11-20, and click Finish.

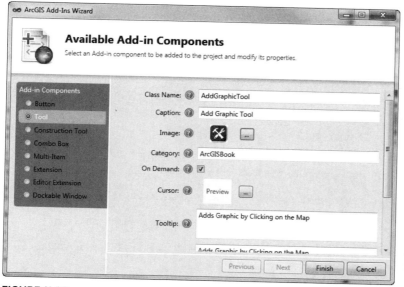

FIGURE 11-20

2. Enter the following using directives at the top of the AddGraphicTool.cs file's code window:

```
using ESRI.ArcGIS.ArcMapUI;
using ESRI.ArcGIS.Geometry;
using ESRI.ArcGIS.Display;
using ESRI.ArcGIS.Carto;
```

3. You are going to write the code for handling the OnMouseDown event. In other words, you want your code to be executed when a user clicks somewhere in the main window of the software application. Because all the events and their handlers are defined in the base class of all tools (ESRI.ArcGIS.Desktop.AddIns.Tool), you have to override the necessary handlers. So write the following code in the AddGraphicTool.cs file inside the definition for the AddGraphicTool class and outside of any method:

```
protected override
```

As soon as you type these two keywords and press the spacebar, you will see the list of all available handlers. Find OnMouseDown in the list as shown in Figure 11-21 and press Enter.

FIGURE 11-21

4. Add the following code to the OnMouseDown() event handler:

```
IMxDocument mxdoc = ArcMap.Application.Document as IMxDocument;
IGraphicsContainer gContiner = mxdoc.FocusMap as IGraphicsContainer;

IDisplayTransformation dispTransformation =
mxdoc.ActiveView.ScreenDisplay.DisplayTransformation;
IPoint point = dispTransformation.ToMapPoint(arg.X, arg.Y);

IRgbColor color = new RgbColorClass();
color.Red = 255; color.Blue = 0; color.Green = 0;

IRgbColor outlineColor = new RgbColorClass();
outlineColor.Red = 0; outlineColor.Blue = 255; outlineColor.Green = 0;

ISimpleMarkerSymbol simpleMarkerSymbol = new SimpleMarkerSymbolClass();
simpleMarkerSymbol.Color = color;
simpleMarkerSymbol.Outline = true;
simpleMarkerSymbol.OutlineSize = 1.5;
simpleMarkerSymbol.OutlineColor = outlineColor;
simpleMarkerSymbol.Size = 9;

if (arg.Button == System.Windows.Forms.MouseButtons.Left)
{
    simpleMarkerSymbol.Style = esriSimpleMarkerStyle.esriSMSDiamond;
}
else if (arg.Button == System.Windows.Forms.MouseButtons.Right)
{
    simpleMarkerSymbol.Style = esriSimpleMarkerStyle.esriSMSSquare;
```

```
}

IElement element = null;
IMarkerElement markerElement = new MarkerElementClass();
markerElement.Symbol = simpleMarkerSymbol;
element = (IElement)markerElement;
element.Geometry = point;

gContiner.AddElement(element, 0);
mxdoc.ActiveView.PartialRefresh(esriViewDrawPhase.esriViewGraphics,
    null, null);
```

5. Place the newly created tool on the Output toolbar by modifying the configuration file.

6. Run the code. In ArcMap, add some data and test the tool. While the Tool is selected, right-clicking on the map results in putting square markers and left-clicking creates diamond markers on the map.

How It Works

The event handler has an input argument that carries all the information about the event. This argument is set by ArcGIS for Desktop applications and contains information such as which button is pressed and the location of users' clicks. In order to put the elements on the map, you need to convert between display units (where the user clicks in the display area of software [the application's main window]) and map units (where the element should be placed). The DisplayTransformation object performs this task for you.

In addition to converting coordinates between map units and display units (device space units), DisplayTransformation can be used to access useful information such as screen resolution and the current spatial reference of the display. The following code can be used for getting the current screen resolution.

```
IDisplayTransformation dispTransformation =
mxdoc.ActiveView.ScreenDisplay.DisplayTransformation;
double screenRes = dispTransformation.Resolution;
```

> **NOTE** Map and PageLayout objects can provide access to the DisplayTransformation object through the IActiveView interface. In other words, IActiveView is implemented by both Map and PageLayout objects. As you saw in the preceding example, the DisplayTransformation object of the map converts the real-world units (map units) and display units and can report the spatial reference of the map. Note that the DisplayTransformation object of PageLayout does not have a spatial reference and performs translation between display units and page units.

Adding FrameElements

As mentioned earlier in this chapter, FrameElements can only be added to a PageLayout and they are generally containers for other objects. MapFrames are containers of layers and each MapFrame can be related to several MapSurroundFrame objects. A MapSurroundFrame is a container of MapSurround objects. A MapSurround object is an object that is related to a specific MapFrame, such as legend, scale bar, and north arrow. In order to display a MapSurround object such as a north arrow in PageLayout, it must be contained in a MapSurroundFrame and be related to a MapFrame.

With four simple steps, you can add all the necessary MapSurround objects, such as legend, north arrow, and scale bars. As an example, write a piece of code to add a simple legend to the PageLayout. The first step is to create or obtain a reference to a MapSurround object. In this step, you have to associate the MapSurround object with a map.

```
//step 1
ILegend legend = new LegendClass_2();
legend.AutoAdd = true;
legend.Title = "Legend of the Map";
legend.Map = mxdoc.FocusMap;
```

MapSurround objects (such as your legend) cannot be added to a PageLayout directly, so you need a MapSurroundFrame instance to frame them.

```
//step 2
IMapSurroundFrame MSFrame = new MapSurroundFrameClass();
MSFrame.MapSurround = legend;
```

As a special kind of element, MapSurroundFrame needs to have a location. As mentioned previously, the location of all elements is defined using the Geometry property of the IElement interface.

```
//step 3
IElement MSElement = MSFrame as IElement;
IEnvelope en = new EnvelopeClass();
en.XMin = 1.5; en.YMin = 1.5;
en.Width = 10; en.Width = 10;
MSElement.Geometry = en as IGeometry;
```

And the final step is to add the legend to the PageLayout using the IGraphicsContainer interface and refreshing the ActiveView.

```
//step 4
IGraphicsContainer gc = mxdoc.PageLayout as IGraphicsContainer;
gc.AddElement(MSElement, 0);
mxdoc.ActiveView.PartialRefresh(esriViewDrawPhase.esriViewGraphics,
    null, null);
```

All kinds of MapSurround subclasses can be added to the PageLayout using these four steps.

In addition to creating MapSurround objects from scratch, it is possible to obtain an existing MapSurround object. In fact, ArcGIS comes with a large number of symbols, colors, color ramps, and elements that can be accessed using the Style Manager window, shown in Figure 11-22. You can find the Style Manager window by selecting the Style Manager item from the Customize menu.

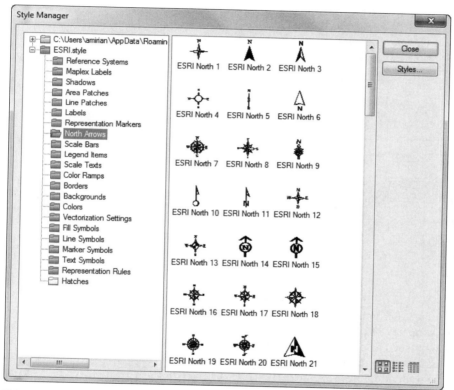

FIGURE 11-22

Expand the ESRI.style node in the Style Manager window to see different classes of styles, such as North Arrows, Scale Bars, and Color Ramps. Each of these style classes contains some style items, such as ESRI North 1. Figure 11-23 illustrates the relationship between classes in different namespaces of ArcObjects that should be used to obtain different style classes.

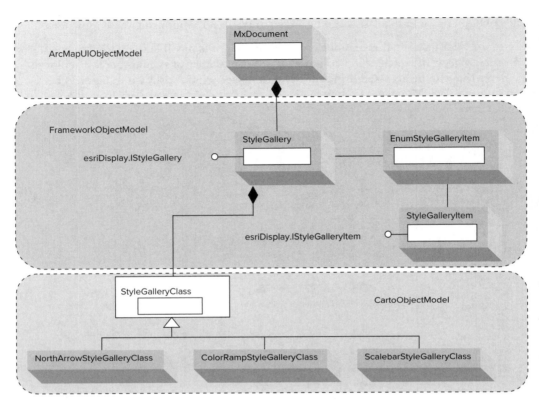

FIGURE 11-23

Each `MxDocument` object is composed of at least one StyleGallery, which is accessible through the `StyleGallery` property of the `IMxDocument` interface. The `StyleGallery` object contains `StyleGalleryClasses` such as north arrows, color ramps, and scale bars. In order to access an individual `StyleGalleryItem`, first an enum of `StyleGalleryItems` should be created. Then using the created enum, an individual `StyleGalleryItem` can be referenced by its name or by its order in the specific `StyleGalleryClass`. Note that the `StyleGalleryItem` is not the actual item. In order to get to the actual item (such as a north arrow), you have to use the `Item` property of the referenced `StyleGalleryItem`.

In order to create an enum of `StyleGalleryItem`, the `get_Items()` method of `StyleGallery` should be called. The following code illustrates the steps necessary to reference an individual north arrow called ESRI North 12:

```
IMxDocument mxdoc = ArcMap.Application.Document as IMxDocument;
IStyleGallery styleGallery = mxdoc.StyleGallery;
          IEnumStyleGalleryItem enumStyleGallery = styleGallery.get_Items
("NorthArrows", "ESRI.STYLE", "Default");
```

```
IStyleGalleryItem northArrowStyle = enumStyleGallery.Next();
while (northArrowStyle != null)
{
    if (northArrowStyle.Name == "ESRI North 12")
    {
        break;
    }
    northArrowStyle = enumStyleGallery.Next();
}
INorthArrow northArrow = northArrowStyle.Item as INorthArrow;
```

In addition to referencing an item by name, it is possible to reference an individual `StyleGalleryItem` by its order in the parent `StyleGalleryClass`. The following code references the fifth scale bar in the `Scale Bars StyleGalleryClass`:

```
IMxDocument mxdoc = ArcMap.Application.Document as IMxDocument;
IStyleGallery styleGallery = mxdoc.StyleGallery;
IEnumStyleGalleryItem enumStyleGallery =
styleGallery.get_Items("Scale Bars", "ESRI.Style", "");

IStyleGalleryItem scalebarStyle = enumStyleGallery.Next();
for (int i = 0; i < 5; i++)
{
    scalebarStyle = enumStyleGallery.Next();
}
IScaleBar scalebar = scalebarStyle.Item as IScaleBar;
```

> **NOTE** The `Item` property of `StyleGalleryItem` is of type `IUnknown`. Since the `StyleGallery` contains many different types of objects (`IColor`, `IColorRamp`, `ISymbol`, and `IScaleBar`), it should provide a generic way to return a specific item without knowing its type. This is why the `Item` property is `IUnknown`. `IUnknown` is the ultimate interface of all COM interfaces, and as a result, it is implemented by all COM objects.

In the last Try It Out of this chapter, you develop two tools to add a north arrow and scale bar to the PageLayout, then put these two tools on a tool palette.

TRY IT OUT | **Tool for Adding GraphicElements (LayoutTools.zip)**

1. Add a new add-in component to the CreatingOutputs solution and name the component **AddNorthArrowTool**. Select Tool as the type of add-in, set the configuration of the tool as shown in Figure 11-24, and click Finish.

FIGURE 11-24

2. Enter the following `using` directives at the top of the AddNorthArrowTool.cs file's code window:

```
using ESRI.ArcGIS.Carto;
using ESRI.ArcGIS.ArcMapUI;
using ESRI.ArcGIS.Geometry;
using ESRI.ArcGIS.Display;
```

3. Create stub code for the `OnMouseDown()` event handler by typing the following keywords outside any method but inside `AddNorthArrowTool.cs`:

```
protected override
```

As soon as you type the above two keywords and press the spacebar, you will see the list of all available handlers. Find OnMouseDown in the list and press Enter:

4. Add the following code to the `OnMouseDown()` event handler.

```
IMxDocument mxdoc = ArcMap.Application.Document as IMxDocument;
IActiveView activeView = mxdoc.PageLayout as IActiveView;
IGraphicsContainer gc = mxdoc.PageLayout as IGraphicsContainer;

IGraphicsContainer graphicsContainer = mxdoc.PageLayout as
    IGraphicsContainer;
graphicsContainer.Reset();

//only one North Arrow should be in a Layout
IElement element = graphicsContainer.Next();
```

```
while (element != null)
{
    if (element is IMapSurroundFrame)
    {
        IMapSurroundFrame MSF = element as IMapSurroundFrame;
        if (MSF.MapSurround is INorthArrow)
        {
            gc.DeleteElement(element);
        }
    }
    element = graphicsContainer.Next();
}

IPoint point = activeView.ScreenDisplay.DisplayTransformation.
    ToMapPoint(arg.X, arg.Y);
IEnvelope envelope = new EnvelopeClass();

envelope.XMin = point.X;
envelope.YMin = point.Y;
envelope.Width = 5;
envelope.Height = 5;

IStyleGallery styleGallery = mxdoc.StyleGallery;
IEnumStyleGalleryItem enumStyleGallery = styleGallery.get_Items("North
    Arrows", "ESRI.STYLE", "Default");

IStyleGalleryItem northArrowStyle = enumStyleGallery.Next();
while (northArrowStyle != null)
{
    if (northArrowStyle.Name == "ESRI North 3")
    {
        break;
    }
    northArrowStyle = enumStyleGallery.Next();
}

INorthArrow northArrow = northArrowStyle.Item as INorthArrow;
northArrow.Map = mxdoc.FocusMap;

IMapSurroundFrame pMSFrame = new MapSurroundFrameClass();
pMSFrame.MapSurround = northArrow;
IElement MSElement = pMSFrame as IElement;

MSElement.Geometry = envelope as IGeometry;

gc.AddElement(MSElement, 0);
mxdoc.ActiveView.PartialRefresh(esriViewDrawPhase.esriViewGraphics,
    null, null);
```

5. Add another add-in component to your project. Name it **AddScalebarTool** and provide the information as displayed in Figure 11-25.

FIGURE 11-25

6. Enter the following using directives at the top of the AddScalebarTool.cs file's code window:

```
using ESRI.ArcGIS.Carto;
using ESRI.ArcGIS.ArcMapUI;
using ESRI.ArcGIS.Geometry;
using ESRI.ArcGIS.Display;
```

7. Create stub code for the OnMouseDown() event handler and enter the following code inside the event handler:

```
IMxDocument mxdoc = ArcMap.Application.Document as IMxDocument;
IActiveView activeView = mxdoc.PageLayout as IActiveView;
IGraphicsContainer gc = mxdoc.PageLayout as IGraphicsContainer;

IGraphicsContainer graphicsContainer = mxdoc.PageLayout as
    IGraphicsContainer;
graphicsContainer.Reset();

//only one scale bar should be in a Layout
IElement element = graphicsContainer.Next();
while (element != null)
{
```

```
        if (element is IMapSurroundFrame)
        {
            IMapSurroundFrame MSF = element as IMapSurroundFrame;
            if (MSF.MapSurround is IScaleBar)
            {
                gc.DeleteElement(element);
            }
        }
        element = graphicsContainer.Next();
    }

    IPoint point = activeView.ScreenDisplay.DisplayTransformation.
        ToMapPoint(arg.X, arg.Y);
    IEnvelope envelope = new EnvelopeClass();

    envelope.XMin = point.X;
    envelope.YMin = point.Y;
    envelope.Width = 5;
    envelope.Height = 5;

    IStyleGallery styleGallery = mxdoc.StyleGallery;
    IEnumStyleGalleryItem enumStyleGallery =
        styleGallery.get_Items("Scale Bars", "ESRI.Style", "");

    IStyleGalleryItem scalebarStyle = enumStyleGallery.Next();
    for (int i = 0; i < 4; i++)
    {
        scalebarStyle = enumStyleGallery.Next();
    }

    IScaleBar scalebar = scalebarStyle.Item as IScaleBar;
    scalebar.Map = mxdoc.FocusMap;

    IMapSurroundFrame pMSFrame = new MapSurroundFrameClass();
    pMSFrame.MapSurround = scalebar;
    IElement MSElement = pMSFrame as IElement;

    MSElement.Geometry = envelope as IGeometry;

    gc.AddElement(MSElement, 0);
    mxdoc.ActiveView.PartialRefresh(esriViewDrawPhase.esriViewGraphics,
        null, null);
```

8. To add a Tool Palette to your project, add a new add-in command container and name it **LayoutToolPalette**. Select Tool Palette as the type of Command Bar and add AddScalebarTool and AddNorthArrowTool to the tool palette, as shown in Figure 11-26.

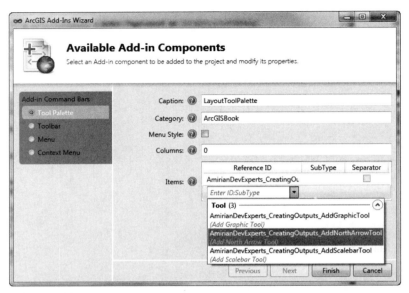

FIGURE 11-26

9. Open the configuration file and notice that a new ToolPalette XML element has been added, as the following XML fragment shows:

```
<ToolPalette id="CreatingOutputs_LayoutToolPalette" caption="LayoutToolPalette"
category="ArcGISBook" isMenuStyle="false" columns="0">
        <Items>
          <Item refID="CreatingOutputs_AddScalebarTool" />
          <Tool refID="CreatingOutputs_AddNorthArrowTool" separator="true" />
        </Items>
    </ToolPalette>
```

The process of adding a tool palette to an existing toolbar is similar to adding a button or a tool to a toolbar. All you need to do is to insert another Item XML element as a child of the Toolbar element and then set the value of the refID attribute as the ID of the ToolPalette element.

10. Run the code, go to Layout view, and test the functionality of the two newly created tools by left-clicking in the Layout view.

How It Works

In this example, you used a tool palette and two tools to place a scale bar and north arrow interactively. Generally, a tool palette is a container for tools and usually is placed on a toolbar. As is true for a toolbar, a tool palette is just an XML fragment. It is defined in a configuration file along with other tools and buttons and it can contain one or more tools (only tools). The order of tools and number of columns in the tool palette can be easily set through modifying the configuration file. You also learned that it is possible to control the number of specific MapSurround objects.

SUMMARY

As mentioned in Chapter 10, making maps is one of the primary tasks of a GIS professional or GIS user. Making flexible labels and displaying them on the map or PageLayout at appropriate scales results in more intuitive and easier-to-understand maps. In addition, MapSurround elements such as legend and north arrow are dynamically related to data in Data Frames.

As you have seen in this chapter, it was an easy task to use an item of the extensive set of symbols, colors, and map elements that are shipped with ArcGIS. As a developer, you can access these items through the StyleGallery CoClass. In this chapter, you learned how to get a MapSurround element from the StyleGallery. It is also a simple task to get another type of item such as ColorRamp from the StyleGallery. This way there is no need to create the needed object from the ground up.

EXERCISES

1. What is the major difference between GraphicElement and FrameElement?

2. What softcopy format can be used to export an ActiveView including attribute data?

3. How can you determine the screen resolution?

You will find the answers to these exercises in this book's appendix.

▶ **WHAT YOU LEARNED IN THIS CHAPTER**

TOPIC	KEY CONCEPTS
Using the Maplex Label Engine	The map (Data Frame) uses a single labeling engine for all FeatureLayers. There are two possible labeling engines in ArcGIS for Desktop applications. The default labeling engine is called the Standard Label Engine. In addition to the Standard Label Engine, it is also possible to take advantage of a more flexible labeling engine, the Esri Maplex Label Engine. In order to use the Esri Maplex Label Engine, you need to change the `AnnotationEngine` property of the `Map` object. In this case, the default labeling engine, which is of type `AnnotateMap`, should be changed to an instance of the `MaplexAnnotateMap` CoClass. In addition, you need to instantiate from an appropriate `AnnotateLabelProperties` subclass, as shown in the following code: ```IAnnotateMap2 annMap = new MaplexAnnotateMapClass();\nmap.AnnotationEngine = annMap as IAnnotateMap;\nIAnnotateLayerProperties annotateLP = new\nMaplexLabelEngineLayerPropertiesClass();```
Difference between Envelope and tagRECT	Both `Envelope` and `tagRECT` represent a box. But `Envelope` is a class while `tagRECT` is a structure. Classes are reference types and reside in the managed heap in memory; structures are value types and are created in the stack part of memory. There is another important difference between the `tagRECT` structure and the `Envelope` class: The direction of the y axis in the `Envelope` coordinate system is the opposite of the y axis of the `tagRECT` coordinate system. The origin of `Envelope`'s coordinate system is at the lower-left point, while the origin of the `tagRECT` coordinate system is the upper-left point of the display.
Real-world, display, and page units	`IDisplayTransformation` is the primary interface for performing translation between real-world (map) display, and page units. The `Map` and `PageLayout` objects can access the `DisplayTransformation` object through the `IActiveView` interface. `IActiveView` is implemented by both `Map` and `PageLayout` objects. The `IDisplayTransformation` object of `Map` converts the real-world units (map units) and display units. In contrast, the `IDisplayTransformation` object of `PageLayout` translates between display units and page units. In summary, the user clicks on the display and based on the type of ActiveView (`Map` or `PageLayout`), `IDisplayTransformation` is able to convert coordinates of the clicked point to `Map` or `PageLayout` units, respectively.

Getting an item from the style gallery

The StyleGallery object contains StyleGalleryClasses such as North Arrows, ColorRamps, and ScaleBars. In order to access an individual style gallery item, first an enum of StyleGalleryItems should be created. Then using the created enum, an individual StyleGalleryItem can be referenced by its name or by its order in the specific StyleGalleryClass. As the final step, the Item property of StyleGalleryItem returns the actual object, as shown in the following code:

```
IStyleGallery styleGallery = mxdoc.StyleGallery;
IEnumStyleGalleryItem enumStyleGallery =
    styleGallery.get_Items("North Arrows", "ESRI.STYLE",
    "Default");

IStyleGalleryItem northArrowStyle =
    enumStyleGallery.Next();
while (northArrowStyle != null)
{
    if (northArrowStyle.Name == "ESRI North 12")
    {
        break;
    }
    northArrowStyle = enumStyleGallery.Next();
}
INorthArrow northArrow = northArrowStyle.Item as
    INorthArrow;
```

12

Geoprocessing with Tools and Models

WHAT YOU WILL LEARN IN THIS CHAPTER:

➤ Getting to know the geoprocessing framework

➤ Discovering system and custom tools

➤ Running system and custom tools

➤ Opening a tool's dialog box

➤ Geoprocessing in the background

WROX.COM CODE DOWNLOADS FOR THIS CHAPTER

The wrox.com code downloads for this chapter can be found at www.wrox.com/remtitle
.cgi?isbn=1118442547 on the Download Code tab. The code is in the Chapter12 folder and
is individually named according to the names throughout the chapter.

Geoprocessing is the bread and butter of any GIS professional. ArcObjects provides a
vast amount of geoprocessing tools that can be chained together using the ModelBuilder
window or Python scripts. These geoprocessing tools are accessible to developers using
the geoprocessing framework. This chapter provides an introduction to geoprocessing in
ArcObjects.

ARCOBJECTS AND THE GEOPROCESSING FRAMEWORK

Geoprocessing is a core and indispensable part of most GIS software. Users of ArcGIS perform
geoprocessing using the geoprocessing tools in the ArcToolbox. In the very first versions of
ArcGIS, the ArcToolbox was a separate application. In recent versions, it is fully integrated

with core ArcGIS for Desktop applications as the ArcToolbox window. The ArcToolbox contains a multitude of tools that can be used to perform both simple and complicated GIS workflows.

Users of ArcGIS for Desktop applications can perform GIS workflows by chaining tools manually or by designing models in the ModelBuilder window or by writing scripts in Python. Behind the scenes, the geoprocessing framework provides tools, the ModelBuilder, and integration with Python to automate tasks. The easiest way to create and run a GIS workflow is to use the ModelBuilder, but Python as an advanced programming language is more powerful and provides more options to execute and publish scripts. The ModelBuilder is a visual designer for designing all kinds of GIS workflows using existing tools in ArcToolbox or custom tools.

In Chapter 9 you learn that developers of ArcObjects can use ArcObjects libraries to write low-level code to perform geoprocessing tasks. Starting at version 9.2, all tools in ArcToolbox and created models in ModelBuilder can be invoked in code without writing low-level ArcObjects code.

As is true for all parts and components of ArcGIS for Desktop applications, the geoprocessing framework is completely written and developed using low-level ArcObjects code. ArcObjects can be used by developers to extend the functionality of existing applications. On the other hand, geoprocessing is a framework to automate tasks and to simplify GIS workflows.

ArcObjects provides low-level interfaces of types to developers and geoprocessing let developers run the tools, models, and scripts at a higher level of abstraction. In ArcObjects, developers have to set required members and call methods of various types, while in the geoprocessing framework all a developer needs to run a tool or model is the tool's or model's parameters.

Consider a black box that is able to perform a single GIS function, such as buffering. When you use ArcObjects, you are inside the black box; on the other hand, when using geoprocessing, you are standing outside of the black box and you don't see what is going on inside the box. The task will be done in both cases, but when using ArcObjects you see and feel a lot more than what can be seen and felt when using geoprocessing. In summary, when using low-level ArcObjects code to perform geoprocessing, you get a higher level of flexibility in terms of error handling capability and control on the running code and you get faster code execution. When using the geoprocessing framework, you can design models quicker, and as a result, it takes less time to write the code.

To sum up, ArcObjects and the geoprocessing framework complement each other. In most cases, they are used together to get the best of both worlds and extend existing applications or create new applications.

RUNNING GEOPROCESSING TOOLS

A large number of prebuilt geoprocessing tools come with ArcGIS for Desktop applications. These tools are called *system tools*.

> **NOTE** In this chapter, geoprocessing tools are often referred to simply as tools.

As mentioned in the preceding section, in addition to system tools, users of ArcGIS can utilize the ModelBuilder or Python to design and create their own *custom tools*.

Both kinds of tools can be executed using a geoprocessor object. But before using a geoprocessor object, you must know the name of the tool, the tool's input and output parameters, and any other required settings. This kind of information can be accessed using a tool's reference page. The best way to access a tool's reference page is to browse for it in ArcGIS Desktop Help. (All tools have such a reference page.)

To get familiar with tool reference pages, take a look at the reference page for the Thiessen Polygons tool. Click on ArcGIS Desktop Help in the Help menu in ArcMap or ArcCatalog. Find the Create Thiessen Polygons tool's reference page by searching for "thiessen polygon" in the Search tab of ArcGIS 10 Help. Figure 12-1 shows the reference page of the Create Thiessen Polygons tool.

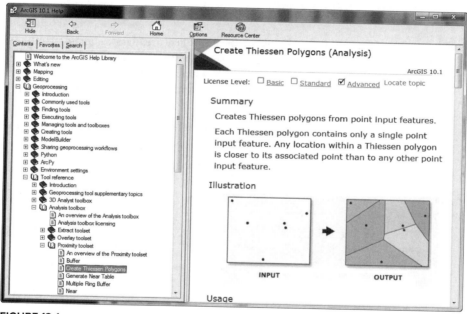

FIGURE 12-1

This page contains all the information needed to run and execute the tool. The license level is specified at the bottom of the page and in ArcGIS 10.1, at the top of the page. It is important to know which tools are available for a certain license level. The most important part of the tool's reference page is the Syntax part and its following table, which indicate all of the tool's parameters as well as the parameters' data types. The Code Sample part of the tool's reference page shows an example of using the tool in the Python scripting language. It is also possible to access the same information online.

In addition, if you right-click on a tool in ArcToolbox and select Item Description... from the context menu, some useful information about using the tool can be found.

Running system or custom tools requires three steps, as follows:

1. Create a geoprocessor object and set its properties.

2. Set the appropriate values for the tool's parameters.

3. Execute a tool using the geoprocessor object's `Execute()` method.

In order to create a geoprocessor object, the `IGeoProcessor2` interface can be used. This interface is defined in the geoprocessing library of ArcObjects and is implemented by the `GeoProcessor` CoClass.

```
IGeoProcessor2 gp = new GeoProcessorClass();
//add the result of geoprocessing as a new layer to Map
gp.AddOutputsToMap = true;
//if output of geoprocessing exists before the execution of tool
//it will be overwritten
gp.OverwriteOutput = true;
```

Assume that you want to create Thiessen polygons for the cities FeatureClass to create proximal zones for all cities. The proximal zones represent full areas where any location inside the zone is closer to its associated city than any other city. Based on the Create Thiessen Polygons reference page, you have to provide at least an input point FeatureLayer and the path to the output FeatureClass.

In order to create and set each parameter, the `IVariantArray` interface of the System library must be used.

```
IVariantArray parameters = new VarArrayClass();
```

Each parameter has to be added to the `IVariantArray` interface in the exact order that is specified on the tool's reference page.

```
//in_features
parameters.Add(@"D:\DataFolder\fileGDB.gdb\cities");
//out_feature_class
parameters.Add(@"D:\DataFolder\fileGDB.gdb\citiesThiessen");
//fields_to_copy(Optional)
parameters.Add("ALL");
```

As it is illustrated on the Create Thiessen Polygons reference page, the third parameter is optional. You can simply not add any value to `IVariantArray` or, as shown in the preceding code, you can provide an appropriate value for the optional parameter. You can skip the optional parameter using an empty string as input to IVariantArray's `Add()` method. For example, look at the reference page of the Buffer tool; you can see that three of the seven available parameters are mandatory. The following code demonstrates how to skip the fourth parameter and specify the fifth parameter:

```
//1-in_features
parameters.Add(@"D:\test.gdb\cities");
//2-out_feature_class
parameters.Add(@"D:\test.gdb\citiesBuffer");
//3-buffer_distance_or_field
parameters.Add("50 kilometers");
//4-line_side(Optional)
parameters.Add("");
//5-line_end_type(Optional)
parameters.Add("ROUND");
//6 &7 there is no need to provide empty string
//for the rest of parameters since you don't want to set them
```

After setting all the required parameters, all you need to run a tool is to call the Execute() method of the geoprocessor object. The Execute() method solicits the name of the tool and its parameters.

```
gp.Execute("CreateThiessenPolygons_analysis", parameters, null);
```

The following code shows the complete code for this example. In order to run the code, you need to add references to the Geoprocessing and System libraries of ArcObjects:

```
IGeoProcessor2 gp = new GeoProcessorClass();
//add the result of geoprocessing as a new layer to Map
gp.AddOutputsToMap = true;
//if output of geoprocessing exists before the execution of tool
//it will be overwritten
gp.OverwriteOutput = true;

IVariantArray parameters = new VarArrayClass();
//in_features
parameters.Add(@"D:\DataFolder\fileGDB.gdb\cities");
//out_feature_class
parameters.Add(@"D:\DataFolder\fileGDB.gdb\citiesThiessen");
//fields_to_copy(Optional)
parameters.Add("ALL");
//or parameters.Add("");
gp.Execute("CreateThiessenPolygons_analysis", parameters, null);
```

The Geoprocessing library of ArcObjects is accessible through the ESRI.ArcGIS.Geoprocessing namespace. This library contains a few hundred types which can be used to run and manage tools and GIS workflows. You learned earlier in this section that IGeoProcessor2 is the main interface of this library and the easiest way to run a geoprocessing tool is to call its Execute() method.

However, using IGeoProcessor2 is not the only approach to run a geoprocessing tool or model. There are some managed assemblies created by Esri to performing geoprocessing in a managed way. A *managed way* means there is a native .NET assembly (the Geoprocessor assembly) that is a wrapper for some types in the Geoprocessing library of ArcObjects, and there are other .NET assemblies for each system toolbox.

These native .NET assemblies provide an even easier way to run a system tool. In general, the procedure for running a tool using the Geoprocessor-managed assembly is the same as running a tool using the Geoprocessing library. You need to add a reference to the Geoprocessor assembly as well as the toolbox assembly that contains the tool (for example, ESRI.ArcGIS.AnalysisTools since the Analysis toolbox contains the Create Thiessen Polygons tool). Then you can initialize the objects as the normal .NET objects. The following code snippet is equivalent to the preceding example:

```
Geoprocessor gp = new Geoprocessor();
gp.AddOutputsToMap = true;
gp.OverwriteOutput = true;

CreateThiessenPolygons createThiessen = new CreateThiessenPolygons();
//in_features
createThiessen.in_features = @"D:\DataFolder\fileGDB.gdb\cities";
//fields_to_copy(Optional)
createThiessen.fields_to_copy = "ALL";
//out_feature_class
createThiessen.out_feature_class = @"D:\DataFolder\fileGDB.gdb\citiesThiessen";

gp.Execute(createThiessen, null);
```

As illustrated in this code, the parameters of a tool are available as members of the tool's instance and there is no need to provide the parameters in any specific order.

> **NOTE** Since Geoprocessor *is a true .NET class, it has a parameterized constructor. In other words, you can use the following line of code to instantiate a* CreateThiessenPolygons *instance.*
>
> ```
> CreateThiessenPolygons createTP = new
> CreateThiessenPolygons("Input", "Output");
> ```

So what approach should be used? In short, both methods are two sides of the same coin. Both approaches provide a high-level execution of tools. In other words, they provide a fast and easy way to create sophisticated GIS workflows.

Specifically in the case of the Geoprocessing library's IGeoProcessor2 interface, the order of parameters must be known before the execution and there is no IntelliSense facility in Visual Studio. On the other hand, the Geoprocessor assembly just provides a handful of members that are needed for execution of a tool. For example, when using the Geoprocessor-managed assembly, if you need to get messages from a tool and get information about the output of a successful execution of a tool, you have to resort to the Geoprocessing library. In the next Try It Out, you explore more features of the geoprocessing framework.

TRY IT OUT   **Multiple Ring Buffer Geoprocessing (MultipleRingBuffer.zip)**

1. Create a new ArcMap Add-in project. Name the solution **GeoprocessingProject**. In the Welcome page of the Add-Ins Wizard, provide the necessary information and then click the Next button. Select Button as the type of add-in, provide the information shown in Figure 12-2, and then click Finish.

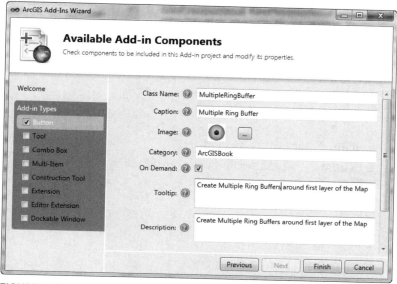

FIGURE 12-2

2. Add ESRI.ArcGIS.Carto, ESRI.ArcGIS.Geoprocessing, and ESRI.ArcGIS.Geodatabase references using the Add ArcGIS Reference window, as shown in Figure 12-3.

3. Add a reference to System.Windows.Forms assembly using the Add Reference window, as shown in Figure 12-4.

FIGURE 12-3

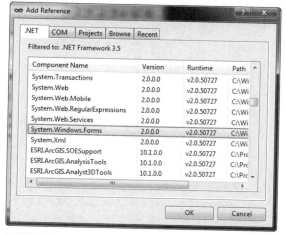

FIGURE 12-4

4. Type the following `using` directives at the top of the `MultipleRingBuffer.cs` file's code window.

```
using ESRI.ArcGIS.ArcMapUI;
using ESRI.ArcGIS.Carto;
using ESRI.ArcGIS.esriSystem;
using ESRI.ArcGIS.Geoprocessing;
using ESRI.ArcGIS.Geodatabase;
using System.Windows.Forms;
```

5. Add the following code to the button's `OnClick()` method:

```
IMxDocument mxdoc = ArcMap.Application.Document as IMxDocument;
IMap map = mxdoc.FocusMap;
if (map.Layer[0] == null)
{ return; }

ILayer layer = map.Layer[0];
IDataset dataset = layer as IDataset;

IGeoProcessor2 gp = new GeoProcessorClass();
gp.AddOutputsToMap = true;
gp.OverwriteOutput = true;

//syntax of the tool from tool's reference page
//MultipleRingBuffer_analysis (Input_Features, Output_Feature_class, Distances,
//{Buffer_Unit}, {Field_Name}, {Dissolve_Option}, {Outside_Polygons_Only})

IVariantArray parameters = new VarArrayClass();
//Input_Features
parameters.Add(layer);
//Output_Feature_class
parameters.Add(dataset.BrowseName + "MRB");
//you have to use ; to separate the distances (multivalue)
parameters.Add("10;50;100");
//{Buffer_Unit}
parameters.Add("kilometers");
//{Field_Name}
parameters.Add("");
//{Dissolve_Option}
parameters.Add("ALL");

gp.Execute("MultipleRingBuffer_analysis", parameters, null);

object severity = null;
MessageBox.Show(gp.GetMessages(ref severity));
```

6. Add a new add-in command container (toolbar) and name it GeoprocessingToolbar. Select Toolbar as the type of Add-in Command Bars and add the reference to the button, as shown in Figure 12-5.

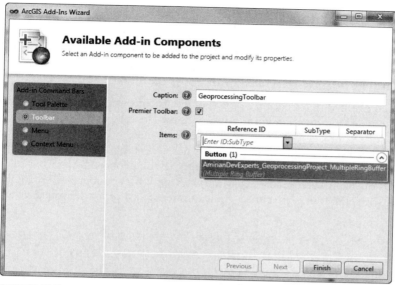

FIGURE 12-5

7. Run the code, add some layers to your map, and press the button. You should see multiple ring buffers around the features after a few seconds and a message box that reports messages about the tool's execution, as shown in Figure 12-6.

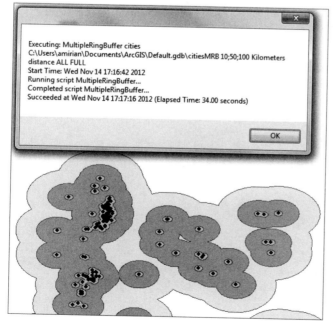

FIGURE 12-6

How It Works

In this Try It Out, you used an object instead of a hard-coded path as an input to the tool. In reality, if a parameter's data type is specified as Feature Layer in the tool's reference page, you can provide any object of one of types `IFeatureClass`, `ILayer`, `IName`, and `IDataset`. `IGeoProcessor2`'s `GetMessages()` method returns all messages generated by the tool's execution.

Calling the `Execute()` method resulted in execution of the tool in a foreground process. This means during execution of the tool, any user interaction with the ArcGIS for Desktop application's user interface will be disabled and the code after the `geoprocessor.Execute()` method cannot be executed until the tool's execution completed successfully or fails. This is not acceptable behavior for geoprocessing in some situations. That is why Esri provides the capability to run geoprocessing tools in a background process since version 10. If you execute the Multiple Ring Buffer tool in the ArcToolbox window, you will notice that while the tool is executing you can interact with the user interface and query data for instance.

NOTE *By default, background geoprocessing is enabled, but you can change this setting using the Geoprocessing Options window, shown in Figure 12-7, which is accessible through the Geoprocessing menu.*

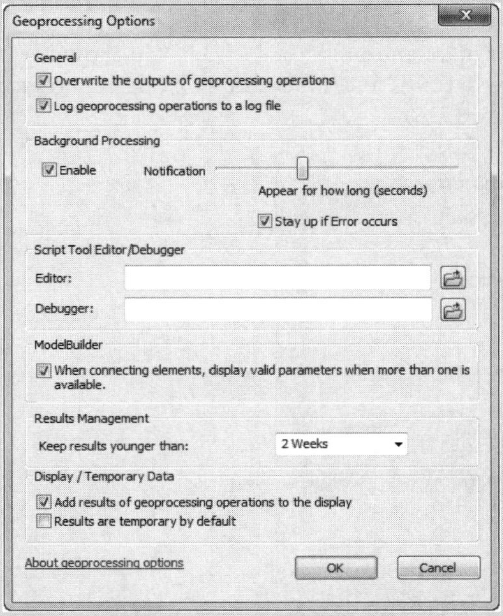

FIGURE 12-7

Another point worth mentioning is that in some situations an ArcMap session crashes after running the Multiple Ring Buffer tool. If your ArcMap crashed after pressing the MultipleRingBuffer button, it is good idea to use another system tool such as buffer.

You learn how to perform geoprocessing in a background process later in this chapter. The following code implements the same logic using the Geoprocessor-managed assembly. To run this code, you have to add references to the ESRI.ArcGIS.Geoprocessor and ESRI.ArcGIS.AnalysisTools assemblies. Note that in order to add these references, you have to use the Add Reference command instead of the Add ArcGIS Reference command in Solution Explorer.

```
IMxDocument mxdoc = ArcMap.Application.Document as IMxDocument;
IMap map = mxdoc.FocusMap;
if (map.Layer[0] == null)
{ return; }

ILayer layer = map.Layer[0];
IDataset dataset = layer as IDataset;

Geoprocessor gp = new Geoprocessor();
gp.AddOutputsToMap = true;
gp.OverwriteOutput = true;

ESRI.ArcGIS.AnalysisTools.
    MultipleRingBuffer multipleRB = new ESRI.ArcGIS.AnalysisTools.
    MultipleRingBuffer();
multipleRB.Buffer_Unit = "Kilometers";
multipleRB.Dissolve_Option = "ALL";
multipleRB.Distances = "10;50;100";
multipleRB.Input_Features = layer;
multipleRB.Output_Feature_class = dataset.BrowseName +
    "MRB";
gp.Execute(multipleRB, null);

object severity = null;
MessageBox.Show(gp.GetMessages(ref severity));
```

Remember to put the following using directives at top of the code window if you want to test the preceding code:

```
using ESRI.ArcGIS.ArcMapUI;
using ESRI.ArcGIS.Carto;
using ESRI.ArcGIS.esriSystem;
using ESRI.ArcGIS.Geoprocessing;
using ESRI.ArcGIS.Geodatabase;
using ESRI.ArcGIS.Geoprocessor;
using ESRI.ArcGIS.AnalysisTools;
```

Running Custom Tools

Custom tools can be created using ModelBuilder or Python scripts. Usually, a custom tool is a chain of system tools in which output of a system tool is an input for another system tool. In addition, a custom tool or model can itself be used in another model. The level of flexibility provided by the geoprocessing framework provides countless opportunities for automating the daily business of a GIS user. As an ArcGIS developer, you can run custom tools in code in the same way that you call the system tools. The only difference is that you have to add the physical path of the toolbox to the geoprocessor object.

In the next Try It Out, you first create a simple custom model and then use a geoprocessor object to run it in a foreground process.

TRY IT OUT **Creating and Running Custom Model (RunningCustomModel.zip)**

1. Run ArcCatalog or ArcMap and right-click a folder connection such as D:\ in the Catalog tree. Select the Toolbox item from the New submenu to create a new toolbox, as shown in Figure 12-8.

2. Name the new toolbox **testToolbox**. Right-click the testToolbox and, as shown in Figure 12-9, select Model from the New submenu to open the ModelBuilder window.

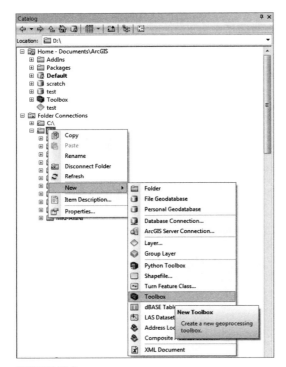

FIGURE 12-8

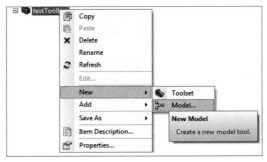

FIGURE 12-9

3. You are going to create a simple model that contains three system tools. The purpose of the model is to select a subset of features of the input FeatureLayer and generate a KMZ file for those features. In this model, the subset of features of the input FeatureLayer falls within 20 kilometers of the features of the selecting FeatureLayer. So you need the Buffer, Select Layer By Location, and Layer To KML system tools. All these tools are supported by all license levels of ArcGIS.

4. From the ArcToolbox window, click on the Buffer tool, drag it to the ModelBuilder window, and then drop it. Two icons for Buffer tools will be displayed. Right-click on the Buffer; from the context menu, select Make Variable ⇨ From Parameter ⇨ Input Features, as shown in Figure 12-10.

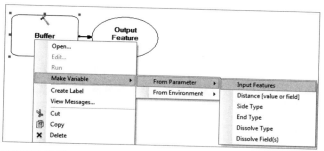

FIGURE 12-10

Next, right-click on the Input Features oval and select the Model Parameter option. Making a model's variable a Model Parameter lets users of the model set its value when running the model. Also rename the input of the Buffer to **BufferFeatures** by right-clicking it and selecting the Rename item.

5. Double-click the Buffer tool and provide 20 Kilometers as the Linear Unit, as in Figure 12-11. This way of providing a value for parameters is different from making them model parameters, and it is more like hard-coding a variable.

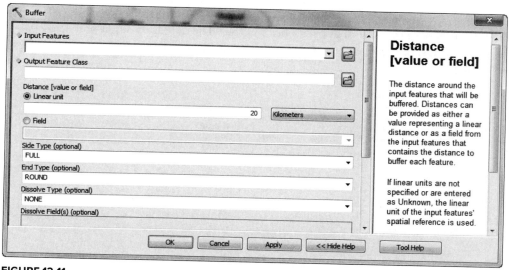

FIGURE 12-11

6. In the Data Management Tools toolbox, expand the Layers and Table Views toolset and then drag and drop the Select Layer By Location tool to your model. Right-click on the Select Layer By Location tool, and from the context menu, select Make Variable ⇨ From Parameter ⇨ Input Feature Layer, as shown in Figure 12-12.

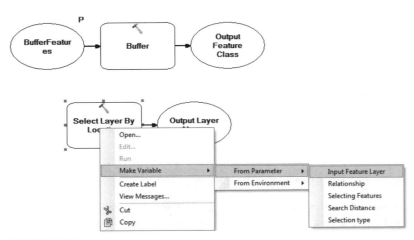

FIGURE 12-12

Then right-click on Input Feature Layer and choose the Model Parameter option.

7. You are going to chain two tools by providing the output of a tool as the input of another tool. Click the connect button (the button with an icon showing two connected squares), then click the output of the Buffer tool (Output FeatureClass), and finally, click the Select Layer By Location tool to provide its input. Because the tool has two inputs, you have to specify using the output of the Buffer tool in the Select Layer By Location tool. The output of Buffer will be used as the selecting features for the Select Layer By Location tool. So select Selecting Features, as shown in Figure 12-13.

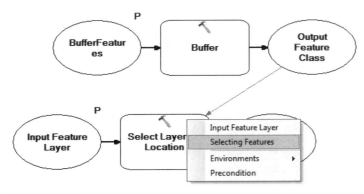

FIGURE 12-13

8. From Conversion Tools, expand the To KML toolset and drag and drop the Layer To KML tool to your model. Rename the output of the Layer To KML tool to **Output KMZ File** and make it a model parameter, as shown in Figure 12-14. Then double-click the Layer To KML tool and provide 2000000 as the Layer Output Scale.

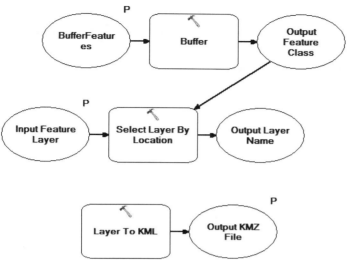

FIGURE 12-14

9. Provide the output of Select Layer By Location as layer input to the Layer To KML tool using the connect button. (See Figure 12-15.)

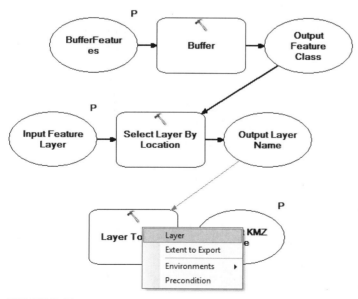

FIGURE 12-15

10. Select Model Properties from the Model Menu, provide descriptive text in the Name and Label textboxes, as shown in Figure 12-16. Then click the OK button, and finally, save and close it.

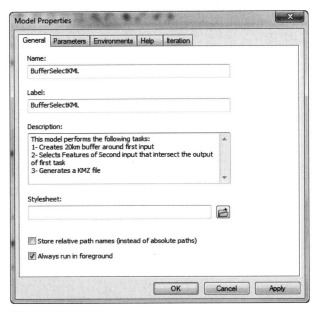

FIGURE 12-16

11. Test the model by double-clicking it in the Catalog tree. Double-clicking the model opens the window of the BufferSelectKML custom tool, as shown in Figure 12-17. Notice that its window is quite similar to the window of system tools.

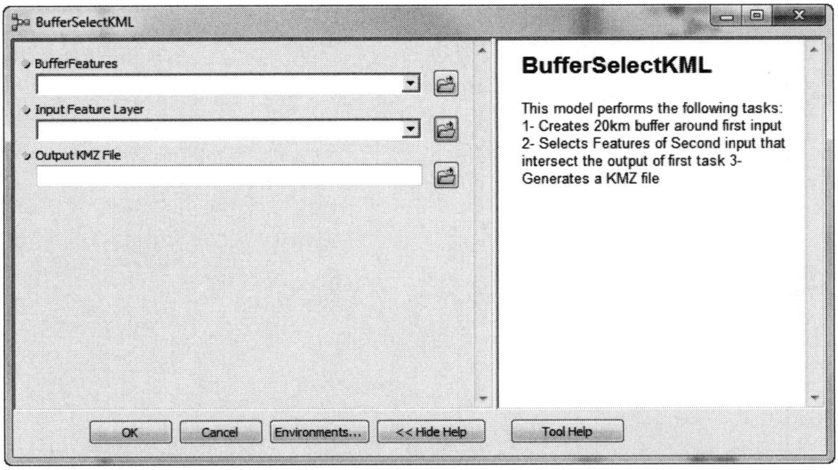

FIGURE 12-17

12. Provide input parameters for the tool. You can use the `us_rivers` or `intrstat` FeatureClasses as the BufferFeatures parameter and cities as the Input Feature Layer. Because you need to provide a FeatureLayer for this parameter, add a feature class to the map to create an in-memory layer or use the saved FeatureLayer and then use it. You have to provide a path for the output KMZ file. After setting all the input parameters, click the OK button to run the custom tool, shown in Figure 12-18.

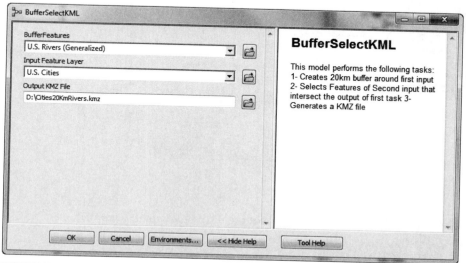

FIGURE 12-18

During the execution of a custom tool, a progress bar reports the status of running of the model. Also, as shown in Figure 12-19, you can see useful information about the execution of system tools as well as custom tools in the Results window.

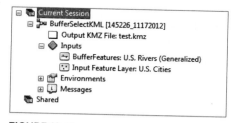

FIGURE 12-19

13. If the custom tool works properly, you can start writing code to use it. If the tool does not work properly, go back to Step 1 and try to solve the issue. Open the GeoprocessingProject solution and add an add-in component to your project. Name it **UsingCustomTool** and provide the configuration for the button, as shown in Figure 12-20, then click Finish.

FIGURE 12-20

14. Add the following using directives at the top of the UsingCustomTool.cs file:

```
using ESRI.ArcGIS.ArcMapUI;
using ESRI.ArcGIS.Carto;
using ESRI.ArcGIS.esriSystem;
using ESRI.ArcGIS.Geoprocessing;
using ESRI.ArcGIS.Geodatabase;
using System.Windows.Forms;
```

15. Enter the following code in the UsingCustomTool class's OnClick() method:

```
IMxDocument mxdoc = ArcMap.Application.Document as IMxDocument;
IMap map = mxdoc.FocusMap;

IGeoProcessor2 gp = new GeoProcessorClass();
gp.AddOutputsToMap = true;
gp.OverwriteOutput = true;

if (map.LayerCount < 2)
{ return; }

gp.AddToolbox(@"D:\testToolbox.tbx");

//syntax of the custom tool
//BufferSelectKML (BufferFeatures, Input_Feature_Layer, Output_KMZ_File)
IVariantArray parameters = new VarArrayClass();
//BufferFeatures (for example us_rivers)
parameters.Add(map.Layer[1]);
```

```
//Input_Feature_Layer (for example cities)
parameters.Add(map.Layer[0]);

//Output_KMZ_File
parameters.Add(@"D:\selectedCities.kmz");

//executing by Name of custom tool
gp.Execute("BufferSelectKML", parameters, null);

object severity = null;
MessageBox.Show(gp.GetMessages(ref severity));
```

16. Add the newly created button to the GeoprocessingToolbar by modifying the configuration file and then test it. Add at least two layers to your map and run the code. The custom model uses the first layer in the Table Of Contents window to perform buffering and the second layer for Select By Location. If you test the code for the cities and us_rivers FeatureClasses, you will get the result shown in Figure 12-21 in Google Earth.

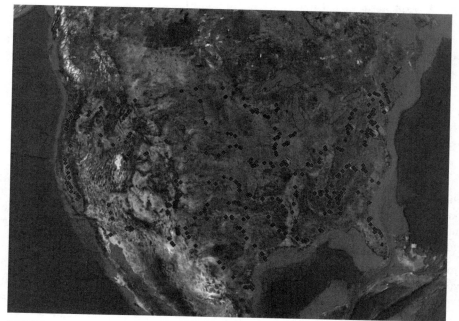

FIGURE 12-21

How It Works

In this example, you created a simple model in ModelBuilder and then called the model in code. As shown in Figure 12-22, the syntax for calling the model can be found by right-clicking the tool in the Catalog tree and selecting the Item Description item.

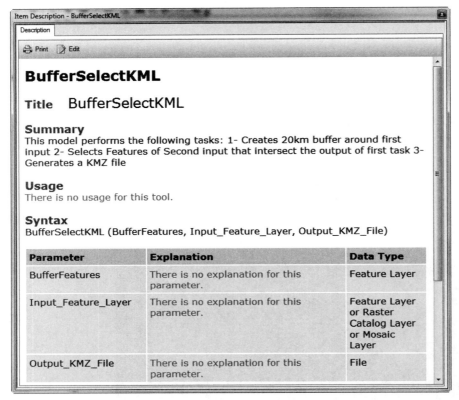

FIGURE 12-22

As mentioned earlier, the name of the tool and the order and data type of all parameters are important. A common mistake made when running custom tools in code is using the model's label instead of the custom tool's name. In this case, the standard exception handling mechanism of .NET (try-catch blocks) is not useful at all.

To run a custom tool in code, you just need the additional step of adding a toolbox to the geoprocessor object. In other words, there is no difference in using the Geoprocessing library or a managed assembly to run a custom model.

OPENING A TOOL'S DIALOG BOX IN CODE

Previous sections explain how to run (execute) a system or custom tool. Executing tools using their dialog box provides a higher level of flexibility for users. For example, in the first Try It Out in this chapter, the user is not able to change the buffer distances or buffer unit. There is a type in the Geoprocessing library with the sole purpose of opening the dialog box of tools. This type and its members are displayed in Figure 12-23.

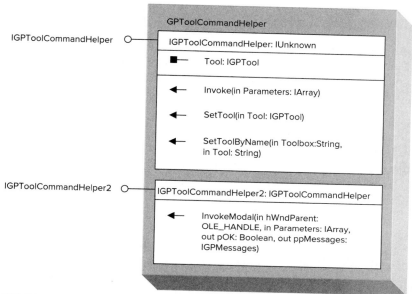

FIGURE 12-23

In order to open a tool's dialog box using the GPToolCommandHelper CoClass, you have to first set the tool using either the SetTool() or SetToolByName() method and then simply call Invoke() or InvokeModal(). The following code snippet illustrates the easiest way to open a tool's dialog box:

```
IGPToolCommandHelper2 commandHelper = new GPToolCommandHelperClass() as
    IGPToolCommandHelper2;
string arcGISinstallationAddress = @"C:\Program Files (x86)\
    ArcGIS\Desktop10.1";
string arctoolboxAddress = @"ArcToolbox\Toolboxes";
string toolbox = "Analysis Tools.tbx";
string completeToolboxAddress = arcGISinstallationAddress + "\\" +
    arctoolboxAddress + "\\" + toolbox;
commandHelper.SetToolByName(completeToolboxAddress,
    "MultipleRingBuffer");
commandHelper.Invoke(null);
```

> **NOTE** In fact, there are two situations where you need the tool's name. The first is when you want to execute the tool using a geoprocessor object, the second when you want to open the tool's dialog box. There is a slight difference between a tool's name in these situations. For example, the Multiple Ring Buffer tool's syntax uses MultipleRingBuffer_analysis as the name of the tool, but as you have seen in the preceding code snippet, you have to use MultipleRingBuffer as the name of tool.
>
> For the first situation, refer to the tool's reference page and see the syntax of the tool. And for second situation, simply right-click the tool and select the Properties item from the context menu.

As you may know, a toolbox can exist in or out of all kinds of geodatabases. In other words, you may have a geodatabase that contains geospatial data (vector, raster, and table) as well as toolboxes.

If the toolbox exists outside of a geodatabase, it can be easily accessed using its location in the file system (as you saw in the preceding code snippet). But in order to access tools inside toolboxes that reside in a geodatabase, you have to resort to one of the very special interfaces of the `Workspace` Abstract Class. In the next Try It Out, you open the dialog box of a custom tool that resides in a file geodatabase.

TRY IT OUT   **Opening a Custom Tool's Dialog Box (OpeningCustomModel DialogBox.zip)**

1. Run ArcCatalog or ArcMap and right-click on a folder connection, such as D:\ in the Catalog tree, and create a new file geodatabase. Name it **testFileGDB**.

2. Right-click the newly created file geodatabase and select the Toolbox item from the New submenu. Name the new toolbox **testToolbox**. Right-click the testToolbox and select Model from the New submenu to open the ModelBuilder window.

3. To simplify this example, drag and drop the Multiple Ring Buffer tool onto the model. Right-click the Multiple Ring Buffer and create three parameters for Input Features, Distances, and Buffer Unit, as shown in Figure 12-24. Then save the model, but don't close the model window.

4. From the Model menu, select Model Properties. Name the model **simpleMultipleRingBuffer** and provide something descriptive for its label, as shown in Figure 12-25.

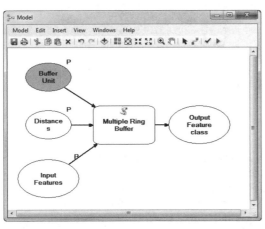

FIGURE 12-24

FIGURE 12-25

5. Open the GeoprocessingProject solution and add a new add-in component to your project. Name it **OpeningDialogBox** and provide the setting as shown in Figure 12-26 for the button, then click Finish.

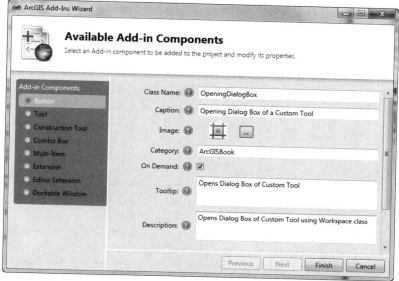

FIGURE 12-26

6. Add references to ESRI.ArcGIS.DataSourcesGDB and ESRI.ArcGIS.GeoprocessingUI. Note that in order to add reference to the GeoprocessingUI assembly you must use Add Reference instead of Add ArcGIS Reference.

7. Enter the following using directives at the top of the OpeningDialogBox.cs file:

```
using ESRI.ArcGIS.Geodatabase;
using ESRI.ArcGIS.Geoprocessing;
using ESRI.ArcGIS.DataSourcesGDB;
using ESRI.ArcGIS.GeoprocessingUI;
```

8. Enter the following code in OnClick() method of UsingCustomTool class:

```
string fileGDBAddress = @"D:\testFileGDB.gdb";
string toolboxName = "testToolbox";
string toolName = "simpleMultipleRingBuffer";

IWorkspaceFactory fWF = new FileGDBWorkspaceFactoryClass();
IWorkspace ws = fWF.OpenFromFile(fileGDBAddress,
    ArcMap.Application.hWnd);
IToolboxWorkspace toolboxWS = ws as IToolboxWorkspace;

//access to the toolbox
IGPToolbox toolbox = toolboxWS.OpenToolbox(toolboxName);
//get the tool or model
IGPTool tool = toolbox.OpenTool(toolName);

IGPToolCommandHelper2 commandHelper = new GPToolCommandHelperClass() as
    IGPToolCommandHelper2;
commandHelper.SetTool(tool);
commandHelper.Invoke(null);
```

9. Add the newly created button to the GeoprocessingToolbar by modifying the configuration file and run your code it. When you press the button in ArcMap, the custom tool's dialog box opens with all the functionality of a normal ArcToolbox dialog box, such as drag and drop layers

How It Works

In this example, you used the `IGPToolbox` and `IGPTool` interfaces to get a reference to an existing tool. Since you have a reference to a tool instead of its address, you used `IGPCommandHelper`'s `SetTool()` method.

WORKSPACE OBJECTS

Put simply, a workspace is a container of geospatial data. A folder containing some geospatial data, a file geodatabase, and an enterprise geodatabase are all examples of workspace objects. In fact, in the ArcObjects world, all kinds of geospatial data are contained in some sort of workspace. As you see in Chapter 7, since there are different types of geospatial data sources and formats, there are different subclasses of the `WorkspaceFactory` class.

As is true for geospatial data, all toolboxes must be stored inside workspaces — but not all types of workspace objects can be used to save toolboxes. In this Try It Out, since you have saved the simple custom tool in a file geodatabase, you need to use `FileGDBWorkspaceFactoryClass` to instantiate a workspace instance.

In summary, a toolbox can be in a folder or in a geodatabase. Consult Table 12-1 to find the appropriate class to get a reference to a tool.

TABLE 12-1: Appropriate CoClasses to Instantiate Workspace Object in Order to Open Dialog Box of a Tool

TOOLBOX SAVED IN	APPROPRIATE COCLASS
Folder or file system	`ToolboxWorkspaceFactory`
Personal geodatabase	`AccessWorkspaceFactory`
File geodatabase	`FileGDBWorkspaceFactory`
Enterprise geodatabase	`SdeWorkspaceFactory`

You see more detail on the `IWorkspace` interface in Chapter 13. In this chapter, you see how to open a tool's dialog box that resides in a folder. ArcObjects often provides several ways to accomplish the same task. The following code uses the `ToolboxWorkspaceFactory` class to open a tool's dialog box in the file system:

```
IGPToolCommandHelper2 commandHelper = new
GPToolCommandHelperClass() as IGPToolCommandHelper2;
string arcGISinstallationAddress = @"C:\Program Files
    (x86)\ArcGIS\Desktop10.1";
string arctoolboxAddress = @"ArcToolbox\Toolboxes";
string toolbox = "Analysis Tools.tbx";
string completeToolboxAddress =
    arcGISinstallationAddress + "\\" + arctoolboxAddress +
    "\\" + toolbox;
IWorkspaceFactory txWSF = new
    ToolboxWorkspaceFactoryClass();
IWorkspace ws = txWSF.OpenFromFile(
arcGISinstallationAddress + "\\" + arctoolboxAddress,
    ArcMap.Application.hWnd);
IToolboxWorkspace toolboxWS = ws as IToolboxWorkspace;

IGPToolbox gpToolbox = toolboxWS.OpenToolbox(toolbox);
IGPTool gpTool = gpToolbox.
    OpenTool("MultipleRingBuffer");

commandHelper.SetTool(gpTool);
commandHelper.Invoke(null);
```

GEOPROCESSING IN THE BACKGROUND

Prior to ArcGIS 10, the only available option to execute geoprocessing tools through ArcToolbox or code was foreground geoprocessing. In other words, the tool is executed in the same process as the main application (such as ArcMap) was executing. As mentioned earlier in this chapter, the Execute() method of a geoprocessor object runs in the foreground. As a result, the next line of code after geoprocessor.Execute() is not executed until the geoprocessing has finished its job.

Since version 10 of ArcGIS, the preferred and default method of geoprocessing is background geoprocessing. With background geoprocessing, users of ArcGIS for Desktop applications can keep on working within applications (such as selecting and querying geospatial data and even executing other geoprocessing tools) while a geoprocessing tool is running in the background. In contrast to foreground geoprocessing, there is another process that handles the background geoprocessing.

If a user wants to run a geoprocessing tool using ArcMap, background geoprocessing can be thought of as another ArcMap session beside the main ArcMap session. In this case, the geoprocessing tool will run in an ArcMap session on the user's computer without opening another window for ArcMap. This additional process (additional ArcMap session) is launched the first time a tool executes in the background and remains until the user exits the main ArcMap session. In this situation, a user of ArcMap will notice a short delay on the first execution of the tool as the background process is started. This delay is not noticed by the user in subsequent executions of the tool.

Developers can execute system and custom tools asynchronously very simply by calling the geoprocessor object's `ExecuteAsync()` method. By calling `ExecuteAsync()`, the tool is submitted to the geoprocessing queue.

As an example, the following code snippet executes the Multiple Ring Buffer system tool in a background process:

```
protected override void OnClick()
        {
            IMxDocument mxdoc = ArcMap.Application.Document as IMxDocument;
            IMap map = mxdoc.FocusMap;
            if (map.Layer[0] == null)
            { return; }

            ILayer layer = map.Layer[0];
            IDataset dataset = layer as IDataset;

            IGeoProcessor2 gp = new GeoProcessorClass();
            gp.AddOutputsToMap = true;
            gp.OverwriteOutput = true;

            //syntax of the tool from tool's reference page
            //MultipleRingBuffer_analysis (Input_Features, Output_Feature_class,
            //Distances,
            //{Buffer_Unit}, {Field_Name}, {Dissolve_Option},
            //{Outside_Polygons_Only})

            IVariantArray parameters = new VarArrayClass();
            //Input_Features
            parameters.Add(layer);
            //Output_Feature_class
            parameters.Add(dataset.BrowseName + "MRB");
            //you have to use ; to separate the distances (multivalue)
            parameters.Add("10;50;100");
            //{Buffer_Unit}
            parameters.Add("kilometers");
            //{Field_Name}
            parameters.Add("");
            //{Dissolve_Option}
            parameters.Add("ALL");
            gp.ExecuteAsync("MultipleRingBuffer_analysis", parameters);
        }
```

For custom tools, you have to be sure that the tool is not configured to always be executed in the foreground. By default, all custom tools are configured to be executed in the foreground. You can change this option simply by right-clicking the tool in the Catalog tree and selecting Properties from the context menu. Then, just make sure the Always run in foreground check box is not checked. (See Figure 12-27.)

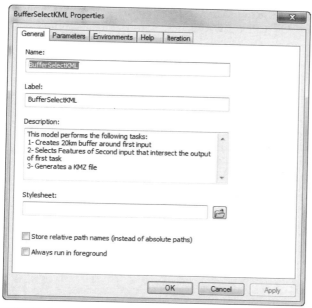

FIGURE 12-27

Note that calling `ExecuteAsync()` without changing the configuration of the custom tool doesn't make it run in a background process. The following code snippet illustrates how to execute a custom tool in a background process:

```
protected override void OnClick()
        {
            IMxDocument mxdoc = ArcMap.Application.Document as IMxDocument;
            IMap map = mxdoc.FocusMap;
            if (map.Layer[0] == null)
            { return; }
            if (map.LayerCount < 2)
            { return; }
            Geoprocessor gp = new Geoprocessor();
            gp.AddOutputsToMap = true;
            gp.OverwriteOutput = true;

            gp.AddToolbox(@"D:\testToolbox.tbx");

            //syntax of the custom tool
            //BufferSelectKML (BufferFeatures, Input_Feature_Layer, Output_KMZ_File)
            IVariantArray parameters = new VarArrayClass();
            //BufferFeatures
            parameters.Add(map.Layer[1]);

            //Input_Feature_Layer
            parameters.Add(map.Layer[0]);
            //Output_KMZ_File
            parameters.Add(@"D:\selectedCities.kmz");
            //executing by Name of custom tool
            gp.ExecuteAsync("BufferSelectKML", parameters);
        }
```

You can find the source code for this example in the `RunningCustomToolInBackground.cs` file in the GeoprocessingProject solution on this book's page on Wrox.com.

> **NOTE** As mentioned previously, by invoking `ExecuteAsync()`, the tool is submitted to the geoprocessing queue. A tool on the geoprocessing queue will not start executing until the method that submitted the tool to the queue has been fully processed. As an example, in the following code, the `OnClick()` method submits `tool1` and `tool3` to the geoprocessing queue, so these geoprocessing processes will not start until after the full execution of `OnClick()`.
>
> ```
> protected override void OnClick()
>     {
>         //code to instantiate geoprocessor object
>         //and configure each geoprocessing tool
>         gp.ExecuteAsync(tool1);
>         gp.Execute(tool2, null);
>         gp.ExecuteAsync(tool3);
>         gp.Execute(tool4,  null);
>         MessageBox.Show("some message");
>
>     }
> ```
>
> The execution of this code is as follows (assuming that all tools finished their jobs successfully):
>
> 1. `tool2` is executed.
> 2. `tool4` is executed.
> 3. `MessageBox` pops up.
> 4. `tool1` is submitted to the geoprocessing queue.
> 5. `tool3` is submitted to the geoprocessing queue.
>
> Tools are executed in a background process in the order in which they were added to the queue.

Only one tool can run in the background; all other submitted tools will be waiting for execution in the queue. Once a tool finishes executing, the next waiting tool will start executing from queue.

An important point in background geoprocessing is that inputs of tools that are going to be submitted to the geoprocessing queue must exist when the tools are submitted to the geoprocessing queue. Otherwise the tools fail to be submitted. With the knowledge of this important point, two cases might happen.

The first case happens when geoprocessing tools are independent of each other. In this case, you can freely submit multiple unrelated geoprocessing tools to the queue to be executed in the background in the same method. By unrelated tools, I mean there is no connection or relationship between input and output parameters of submitted tools. For example, considering the code snippet in the preceding note, `tool1` can be an overlay of two existing feature classes and `tool3` can be a buffer of another existing feature class.

In the second case, when there is a connection or relationship between input and output parameters of tools, you have to consider that carefully. In this case, since all input parameters of all tools must exist prior to the tools' submissions, submitting dependent tools to the geoprocessing queue in the same method is not possible and results in an error. As an example, when `tool1` buffers an existing feature class and the resultant feature class becomes an input in `tool3`'s execution, you cannot submit `tool1` and `tool3` to the geoprocessing queue in the `OnClick()` method.

In this case, there are some approaches you can use to be sure about the existence or creation of input parameters before submitting tools to the geoprocessing queue. The simplest approach is using ModelBuilder to chain various tools. As you see in this chapter, a model can be executed by a geoprocessor object in foreground as well as background processes. Although the model is composed of several tools, it is treated as a single tool by the geoprocessor object; as a result, the existence of any intermediate data will not be validated.

Another more flexible approach is to submit each tool in different method calls after ensuring the completion of execution of previous tool(s). In this approach, the geoprocessor object must listen to the events that are fired by geoprocessing tools after completion of background execution. In the last Try It Out of this chapter, you implement this approach.

TRY IT OUT Opening a Running Dependent Geoprocessing Tool Using a Queue (BackgroundGPUsingQ.zip)

1. Open the GeoprocessingProject solution and add a new add-in component to your project. Name it **BackgroundGPUsingQ**, provide the configuration for the button (shown in Figure 12-28), then click Finish.

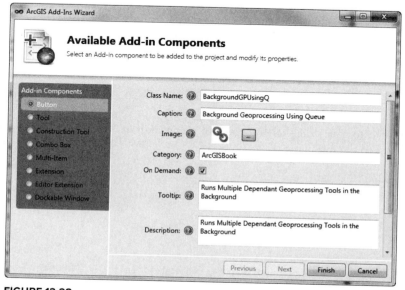

FIGURE 12-28

2. In this example, you are going to determine which areas are more than 50 kilometers away from existing rivers. For the sake of simplicity, this example uses the data from TemplateData.gdb, but feel free to use another data set. Note that in this example TemplateData.gdb is copied to D:\DataFolder and renamed to fileGDB.gdb. Enter the following using directives at the top of the BackgroundGPUsingQ.cs file:

```
using ESRI.ArcGIS.Geoprocessing;
using ESRI.ArcGIS.esriSystem;
using ESRI.ArcGIS.Geoprocessor;
using ESRI.ArcGIS.AnalysisTools;
using System.Windows.Forms;
```

3. You need to declare two module level variables to be accessible by all methods in the BackgroundGPUsingQ class. Enter the following code somewhere in the BackgroundGPUsingQ class outside of any existing method:

```
Geoprocessor geoprocessor = null;
Queue<IGPProcess> gpToolsQ = null;
```

4. Initialize the geoprocessor and queue objects in the constructor of the class.

```
geoprocessor = new Geoprocessor();
gpToolsQ = new Queue<IGPProcess>();
geoprocessor.OverwriteOutput = true;
geoprocessor.AddOutputsToMap = true;
```

In order to add an event handler for the ToolExecuted event of a geoprocessor object, enter += after geoprocessor.ToolExecuted and you will see what is shown in Figure 12-29.

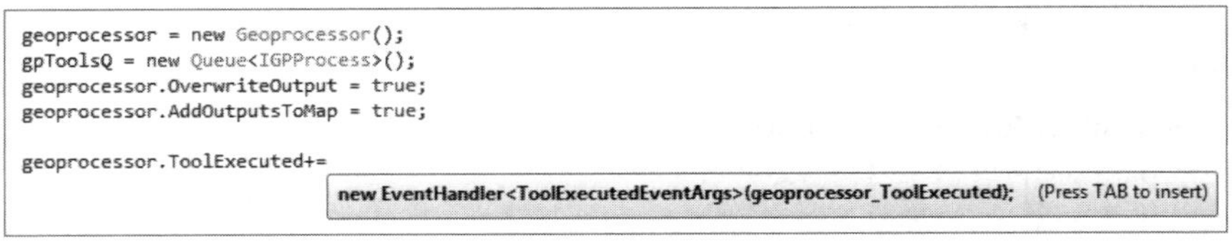

```
geoprocessor = new Geoprocessor();
gpToolsQ = new Queue<IGPProcess>();
geoprocessor.OverwriteOutput = true;
geoprocessor.AddOutputsToMap = true;

geoprocessor.ToolExecuted+=
                    new EventHandler<ToolExecutedEventArgs>(geoprocessor_ToolExecuted);   (Press TAB to insert)
```

FIGURE 12-29

Press the TAB button twice to insert the skeleton code for the event handler. The final class constructor should be similar to the following code:

```
public BackgroundGPUsingQ()
    {
        geoprocessor = new Geoprocessor();
        gpToolsQ = new Queue<IGPProcess>();
        geoprocessor.OverwriteOutput = true;
        geoprocessor.AddOutputsToMap = true;

        geoprocessor.ToolExecuted += new
            EventHandler<ToolExecutedEventArgs>(geoprocessor_ToolExecuted);
    }
```

5. Enter following code in the `OnClick()` method:

```
try
        {
            string copyOfTemplateGDB = @"D:\DataFolder\fileGDB.gdb";
            gpToolsQ.Clear();

            ESRI.ArcGIS.AnalysisTools.Buffer bufferTool = new
                ESRI.ArcGIS.AnalysisTools.Buffer();
            bufferTool.in_features = copyOfTemplateGDB + @"\us_rivers";
            bufferTool.buffer_distance_or_field = "50 Kilometers";
            bufferTool.out_feature_class = copyOfTemplateGDB + @"\bufferRivers";

            Erase eraseTool = new Erase();
            eraseTool.in_features = copyOfTemplateGDB + @"\states";
            eraseTool.erase_features = bufferTool.out_feature_class;
            eraseTool.out_feature_class = copyOfTemplateGDB +
                @"\distantAreasFromRivers";

            gpToolsQ.Enqueue(bufferTool);
            gpToolsQ.Enqueue(eraseTool);

            geoprocessor.ExecuteAsync(gpToolsQ.Dequeue());
        }
        catch (Exception ex)
        {
            MessageBox.Show(ex.Message);
        }
```

6. Clear a line of code inside the event handler that starts with `throw` and write some code to execute tools by using the concept of first-in-first-out. The following is the complete event handler for the `ToolExecuted` event:

```
void geoprocessor_ToolExecuted(object sender, ToolExecutedEventArgs e)
        {
            IGeoProcessorResult2 result = (IGeoProcessorResult2)e.GPResult;
            try
            {
                //the first tool has executed successfully
                if (result.Status == esriJobStatus.esriJobSucceeded)
                {
                    //execute next tool in the queue using background
                    if (gpToolsQ.Count > 0)
                    {
                        geoprocessor.ExecuteAsync(gpToolsQ.Dequeue());
                    }
                }
                //If the background process of a tool fails
                //stop executing next tools in the queue
                else if (result.Status == esriJobStatus.esriJobFailed)
                {
                    string message = result.Process.Tool.Name + " failed, any
                        remaining processes will not be executed.";
```

```
                        gpToolsQ.Clear();
                        MessageBox.Show(message, "Error");
                    }
            }
            catch (Exception ex)
            {
                MessageBox.Show(ex.Message);
            }
        }
```

7. Change the XML configuration file to place the button on the GeoprocessingToolbar and run the code.

How It Works

In this Try It Out, you created a queue object that contains all the tools needed for it to be executed in the background. You added all the tools to the queue object by calling its `Enqueue()` method. Then you called the geoprocessor's `ExecuteAsync()` method to run the first tool in the queue in the background.

Before that, you made the geoprocessor object to listen to events that geoprocessing tools fire. Since you want to execute dependent geoprocessing tools, you need to submit tools to the geoprocessing queue in different methods or different method calls. In this situation, you resorted to the concept of FIFO (First In First Out) to implement this logic.

As mentioned, you called the geoprocessor's `ExecuteAsync()` method in the `OnClick()` method to run the first tool in the queue. When this tool finishes its job, it fires the `ToolExecuted` event. Since you added an event handler for this kind of event, you can use the `IGeoProcessorResult2` interface, which contains valuable information about the status and output of the executed tool.

If the tool completed its job successfully and the queue object contains other tools, you use the `Dequeue()` method of the queue object to offer the next tool to be submitted to the geoprocessing queue.

In summary, all the tools in the queue (except the first one) are submitted to the geoprocessing queue in different calls to the `ToolExecuted` event handler.

> **NOTE** Erase analysis is only available in ArcGIS for Desktop with the ArcInfo license in ArcGIS 10.0 and Advanced in ArcGIS 10.1.

When a geoprocessing tool is executing in the background, the progress bar of ArcGIS for Desktop applications shows what is running. Unfortunately, this new and sometimes confusing marquee style report of running tools doesn't provide the percentage of the completed job. It just shows what geoprocessing tool at the moment is running in the background. If a user clicks on the marquee, she or he will be guided to the Results window, shown in Figure 12-30.

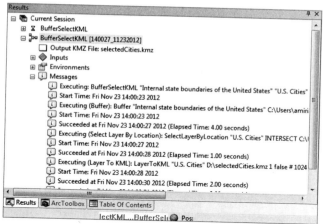

FIGURE 12-30

> **NOTE** *The funny thing about this progress bar is that sometimes, the first time you run a tool in the background in any ArcGIS for Desktop applications session, you won't see the tool's marquee. But after execution of the first tool, you will see the marquee, which reports the running tool.*

Bach Processing

Up to this point in this chapter you have learned how to run geoprocessing tools and models on limited set of data sets in foreground as well as background processes. Sometimes it is necessary to run the same set of geoprocessing tools on large number of data sets and this is where batch processing comes into play.

In order to perform geoprocessing in batch mode, as a user of ArcGIS for Desktop applications you can right-click on the tool in the ArcToolbox window and select the Batch item from context menu. Then you should add all the required input parameters in the batch grid for the first process (since the batch grid includes one process by default). For adding another process (iteration of the same tool or model with the different set of inputs) you should click on the Add Row button and provide the necessary input parameters for the second process and so on.

As a developer, you need to list all kinds of available geospatial data such as feature classes, tables, and raster files to iterate through them and then perform geoprocessing. In order to iterate through a list of available geospatial data of a specific kind, you can use several methods of the `IGeoProcessor2` interface in very flexible manner. For example, suppose that you want to execute the Create Thiessen Polygons tool for all point feature classes that are in the USA feature data set of the `D:\fileGDB.gdb` file geodatabase. The following code snippet illustrate using the `ListFeatureClasses()` method of `IGeoProcessor2` for this task:

```
IGeoProcessor2 gp = new GeoProcessorClass();
gp.SetEnvironmentValue("workspace", @"D:\fileGDB.gdb");
gp.AddOutputsToMap = false;
gp.OverwriteOutput = true;
//List all point feature classes in USA FeatureDataset
IGpEnumList featureClasses = gp.ListFeatureClasses("*", "point", "USA");
string featureClass = featureClasses.Next();
while (string.IsNullOrEmpty(featureClass) == false)
{
    IVariantArray parameters = new VarArrayClass();
    //in_features
    parameters.Add(featureClass);
    //out_feature_class
    parameters.Add(featureClass + "Thiessen");

    //Run in foreground process
    //gp.Execute("CreateThiessenPolygons_analysis", parameters, null);

    //or Run in background process
    gp.ExecuteASync("CreateThiessenPolygons_analysis", parameters);
    featureClass = featureClasses.Next();
}
```

Before using `ListFeatureClasses()` or any other methods of `IGeoProcessor2` that lists available geospatial data, you have to set the workspace environment variable using the `SetEnvironmentValue()` method. After setting the workspace environment variable, the geoprocessor object knows where to find the geospatial data.

The `ListFeatureClasses()` method solicits three inputs. The first input parameter filters out the name of available geospatial data using wild card characters. The second parameter determines the feature type and uses the specific keyword. The third parameter specifies the parent FeatureDataset. Using these three inputs provides a flexible way of listing desired geospatial data.

> **NOTE** In addition to `ListFeatureClasses()`, there are other methods provided by `IGeoProcessor2` interface with almost same set of input parameters to list geospatial data as well as toolboxes and tools. These methods are called list methods.

The return value of these methods is of type `IGpEnumList`. As illustrated in preceding code snippet, the `Next()` method of the `IGpEnumList` is a string. Based on the method used for instantiating `IGpEnumList`, the string points to the name of different things. For example, if `IGpEnumList` is created as a result of invoking the `ListTables()` method, the `Next()` method will return name of available tables.

Each list method has different set of keywords (such as "point" for `ListFeatureClasses()`) that can be used to confine the result. Consult the online ArcGIS Resource Center to find out more about list methods.

Can I Manage the Execution of Geoprocessing Tools?

Throughout this chapter, you see how to manage the execution of a geoprocessing tool in background or foreground processes. There are some situations in which developers haven't enough control on execution of a tool in background or foreground processes. On the other hand, users of ArcGIS for Desktop applications cannot perform certain tasks with data processed in background. Some of the most important situations are listed below. Consult the ArcGIS online help for complete descriptions of these situations.

➤ **Background geoprocessing before edit session:** Users cannot start an edit session while a geoprocessing tool is executing in the background or there are pending background processes. This means all the geoprocessing tools that have been submitted to the geoprocessing queue must be executed or canceled to begin an edit session.

➤ **Edit session before background geoprocessing:** When users edit data, all geoprocessing tools (accessed using ArcToolbox) will be executed in a foreground process even if background processing is enabled. In this case, calling the geoprocessor object's `ExecuteAsync()` method results in an error. The easiest approach to work around this issue is to warn the user to save his or her edits and perform Stop Editing, as illustrated in the following code snippet:

```
UID uid = new UIDClass();
uid.Value = "esriEditor.Editor";
IEditor editor = ArcMap.Application.FindExtensionByCLSID(uid) as IEditor;

//Check to see if an edit session has already been started
if (editor.EditState == esriEditState.esriStateEditing)
{
    MessageBox.Show("Stop your edit and try again", "STOP!");
    return;
}

//code to initialize geoprocessor
//...
```

In order to run the preceding code, add a reference to ESRI.ArcGIS.Editor.

➤ **Working with personal geodatabases with 64-bit background geoprocessing:** With the release of service pack 1 of ArcGIS for Desktop, 64-bit background geoprocessing became available to users. This new framework needs 64-bit client libraries to make connections to data sources. On the other hand, personal geodatabases are implemented using Microsoft JET Database Engine, which is natively 32-bit. Therefore, 64-bit background geoprocessing cannot connect to a personal geodatabase and use its containing data sets as input or output. This means if you install service pack 1 of ArcGIS, you will not be able to use a personal geodatabase in background geoprocessing. But this doesn't mean you have to forget the personal geodatabase format. Since ArcGIS for Desktop applications are 32-bit applications, they communicate with each data source using 32-bit libraries and they can use data sets inside a personal geodatabase. In this case, if your GIS workflows contain various data sets with a personal geodatabase format, you can run the geoprocessing tools in a foreground process or uninstall the 64-bit background geoprocessing. The normal 32-bit background geoprocessing will return after removing 64-bit background geoprocessing.

SUMMARY

The geoprocessing framework is an indispensable part of ArcObjects. The fundamental purpose of geoprocessing in ArcObjects is to provide an easier way to create tools and models to automate tasks.

Covering all aspects of geoprocessing in ArcObjects can take a whole book, and explaining all aspects of geoprocessing using ModelBuilder or Python needs another book, so this chapter is just an introduction to the topic. Remember that geoprocessing is the bread and butter of every GIS professional and you need to know the nuts and bolts of this framework. If you master the geoprocessing framework, you can perform many of the needed tasks of a GIS developer with less code and in a shorter time. It is one of the ways that developers can get things done quickly.

EXERCISES

1. What types in ArcObjects are used to handle the parameters of geoprocessing tools?

2. In order to run custom geoprocessing tools, first the toolbox containing the custom tools must be added to the geoprocessor object. How can custom toolboxes be added to a geoprocessor object?

3. How can you make use of background geoprocessing when your tools are irrelevant to each other? In other words, there is no connection between the input and output parameters of tools.

4. Is it possible to start an edit session when there are one or more geoprocessing tools running?

You will find the answers to these exercises in this book's appendix.

▶ **WHAT YOU LEARNED IN THIS CHAPTER**

TOPIC	KEY CONCEPTS
Geoprocessor object	Starting at version 9.2, all tools in ArcToolbox and created models in ModelBuilder can be invoked in code without writing low-level ArcObjects code using a geoprocessor object. This object can be created using the `IGeoprocessor2` interface of the ArcObjects Geoprocessing library as well as using the Geoprocessor-managed assembly.
`geoprocessor.Execute()` **method**	The `Execute()` method solicits for the geoprocessing tool, which is going to be executed as well as the parameters needed for the execution of the tool.
	Calling the `Execute()` method results in execution of the tool in a foreground process. This means that during execution of the tool, any interaction of the user with the user interface of ArcGIS for Desktop applications will be disabled and the code after the `geoprocessor.Execute()` method cannot be executed until the tool's execution completes successfully or fails.
Opening a tool's dialog box	There is a type in the Geoprocessing library of ArcObjects with the sole purpose of opening the dialog box of tools: the `GPToolCommandHelper` CoClass. In order to open a tool's dialog box using this class, you have to first get a reference to a tool, then set the tool using either the `SetTool()` or `SetToolByName()` method and finally call the `Invoke()` or `InvokeModal()` method.
Background geoprocessing	Since ArcGIS version 10, the preferred and default method of geoprocessing is background geoprocessing. With background geoprocessing, ArcGIS for Desktop applications users can keep working within applications while a geoprocessing tool is running in the background. In contrast to foreground geoprocessing, there is another Windows process that handles the background geoprocessing.
64-bit background geoprocessing and personal geodatabases	With release of ArcGIS for Desktop service pack 1, 64-bit background geoprocessing became available to users. This 64-bit background geoprocessing needs 64-bit client libraries to connect to data sources. Personal geodatabases are implemented using Microsoft JET Database Engine, which is natively 32-bit. Therefore, 64-bit background geoprocessing cannot connect to a personal geodatabase and use its containing data sets as input or output.

13

Feature Data Management

WHAT YOU WILL LEARN IN THIS CHAPTER:

- ➤ Using GUIDs to make the most of customization
- ➤ Creating new geodatabases
- ➤ Specifying spatial reference systems
- ➤ Creating FeatureClasses and FeatureDatasets
- ➤ Inserting new features using insert and search cursors
- ➤ Modifying features using search and update cursors

WROX.COM CODE DOWNLOADS FOR THIS CHAPTER

The wrox.com code downloads for this chapter can be found at www.wrox.com/remtitle .cgi?isbn=1118442547 on the Download Code tab. The code is in the Chapter13 folder and is individually named according to the names throughout the chapter.

This chapter describes common techniques and methods for working with vector geospatial data using the geodatabase model. The geodatabase model provides straightforward and well-designed types for most supported data sources in ArcGIS. You can perform almost all the operations outlined in this chapter using the geoprocessing framework (see Chapter 12). But you gain a lot more flexibility and higher performance when using the geodatabase model directly. This chapter starts with using GUIDs in ArcObjects, which may seem strange at first. But you will see the use of GUIDs in all aspects of ArcObjects programming, including data management and what role it plays.

USE OF GUID IN ARCOBJECTS

As stated several times in this book, ArcObjects is based on Microsoft COM technology. In ArcObjects, any type (such as interfaces and CoClasses) can be accessed through its Global Unique Identifier, or GUID. The GUID for classes is called CLSID, and the GUID for interfaces is called interface ID (IID). A ProgID is friendly text replacement for a CLSID.

You can see the GUIDs of all the types in ArcObjects using ILSpy or .NET Reflector. Figure 13-1 illustrates the GUID of `PointClass` in ILSpy.

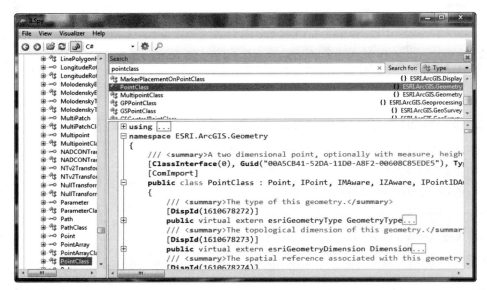

FIGURE 13-1

You can use a type's GUID to create a new instance of that type. The following code snippet creates a new instance of `PointClass`. In this case, you use the `Activator` type in the `System` namespace to instantiate the specified type using a GUID.

```
Guid pointClassGUID = new Guid("00A5CB41-52DA-11D0-A8F2-00608C85EDE5");
Type PointClassType = Type.GetTypeFromCLSID(pointClassGUID);
IPoint newPoint = Activator.CreateInstance(PointClassType) as IPoint;
//alternative to the following line of code
//IPoint newpoint = new PointClass();
```

In most cases in ArcObjects, you can use the simple instantiation approach using the `new` keyword. But you have to resort to this unusual way of instantiation in certain situations, which you see in the next section.

In addition to instantiation, you can use the GUID to access or reference an existing instance of the objects. This way, you can easily use existing commands, menus, and extensions of ArcGIS for Desktop applications.

In Chapter 12, you learned how to open a dialog box of an existing geoprocessing tool using the following code:

```
string fileGDBAddress = @"D:\testFileGDB.gdb";
string toolboxName = "testToolbox";
string toolName = "simpleMultipleRingBuffer";

IWorkspaceFactory fWF = new FileGDBWorkspaceFactoryClass();
IWorkspace ws = fWF.OpenFromFile(fileGDBAddress, ArcMap.Application.hWnd);
IToolboxWorkspace toolboxWS = ws as IToolboxWorkspace;

//access to the toolbox
IGPToolbox toolbox = toolboxWS.OpenToolbox(toolboxName);
//get the tool or model
IGPTool tool = toolbox.OpenTool(toolName);

IGPToolCommandHelper2 commandHelper = new GPToolCommandHelperClass() as
IGPToolCommandHelper2;
commandHelper.SetTool(tool);
commandHelper.Invoke(null);
```

As an alternative solution you can use the ArcToolbox extension for the same purpose as using the ProgID of ArcToolboxExtensionClass.

```
string fileGDBAddress = @"D:\testFileGDB.gdb";
string toolboxName = "testToolbox";
string toolName = "simpleMultipleRingBuffer";

IWorkspaceFactory fWF = new FileGDBWorkspaceFactoryClass();
IWorkspace ws = fWF.OpenFromFile(fileGDBAddress, ArcMap.Application.hWnd);
IToolboxWorkspace toolboxWS = ws as IToolboxWorkspace;

//access to the toolbox
IGPToolbox toolbox = toolboxWS.OpenToolbox(toolboxName);
//get the tool or model
IGPTool tool = toolbox.OpenTool(toolName);
IArcToolboxExtension arcToolboxEx = ArcMap.Application.
FindExtensionByName("esriGeoprocessingUI.ArcToolboxExtension") as
IArcToolboxExtension;
arcToolboxEx.ArcToolbox.InvokeTool(0, tool, null, true);
```

You can search the topics Names and IDs in ArcObjects Help for .NET to see the GUID of all commands and extensions in all ArcGIS for Desktop applications. Also you can use the GUID of commands and tools of ArcGIS for Desktop applications without writing any code. The following XML fragment defines a toolbar with a tool (Select By Circle) and a command (Clear Selected Features).

```
<Toolbars>
      <Toolbar id="AmirianDevExpert_SimpleToolbar" caption="Sample Toolbar"
  showInitially="true">
         <Items>
            <Button refID="{91A04425-46F5-49B4-847B-7ED004073491}"
  separator="true"/>
            <Button refID ="{37C833F3-DBFD-11D1-AA7E-00C04FA37860}"/>
         </Items>
      </Toolbar>
   </Toolbars>
```

As you see with using just the GUID of commands, you can easily customize the user interface of ArcGIS for Desktop applications. In addition, you can also execute the commands using the `ICommandBars` interface, which is defined in the `esriSystem` namespace. The following code snippet references ArcMap's Clear Selected Features command and then clears all selected features in the active data frame:

```
ICommandBars commandBars = ArcMap.Application.Document.CommandBars;
UID clearSelectedFeaturesUID = new ESRI.ArcGIS.esriSystem.UIDClass();
clearSelectedFeaturesUID.Value = "{37C833F3-DBFD-11D1-AA7E-00C04FA37860}";
ICommandItem commandItem = commandBars.Find(clearSelectedFeaturesUID,
false, false);

if (commandItem != null)
{
    commandItem.Execute();
}
```

WORKING WITH THE GEODATABASE MODEL

The ArcGIS platform works with geospatial data through the geodatabase model. The geodatabase model consists of several ArcObjects libraries that provide a common programming model for all supported data sources in ArcGIS.

Primary interfaces for working with geospatial data using the geodatabase model are `IWorkspaceFactory` and `IWorkspace`. The `IWorkspaceFactory` interface is implemented by the `WorkspaceFactory` Abstract Class. Based on the type and format of geospatial data, there are different subclasses of `WorkspaceFactory` CoClasses that developers can use to work with diverse types of geospatial data.

As opposed to most other objects in ArcObjects, all subclasses of `WorkspaceFactory` are singleton objects. Singleton objects are objects which have only one instance. In other words, any call to the constructor of a singleton object (using the `new` keyword) will return a reference to an existing object. After instantiation, they are available to all objects in the application. Using singleton COM objects in a similar way to normal objects in .NET might result in unexpected errors. For this reason, using ArcObjects singleton objects needs careful memory management. In ArcObjects programming, the `System.Activator` class must be used to instantiate, and the `System.Runtime.InteropServices.Marshal` or `ESRI.ArcGIS.ADF.ComReleaser` classes should be used for releasing the references of singleton objects. Because of this, you need to know the GUID of the singleton object to be able to use the `Activator` class.

> **NOTE** You can find the ProgID of all ArcObjects singleton objects in the "Interacting with singleton objects" topic in the ArcObjects Help for .NET.

Figure 13-2 shows the primary types for working with geodatabases.

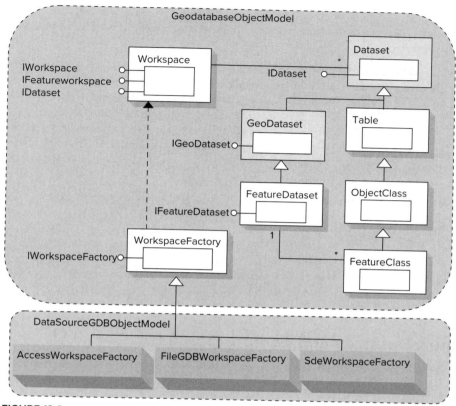

FIGURE 13-2

Creating Geodatabases

In order to create a brand new geodatabase, you first need to create an instance of the appropriate WorkspaceFactory subclass using the System.Activator class and then call IWorkspaceFactory's Create() method. The following code uses the GUID or ProgID of the FileGDBWorkspaceFactory CoClass to create a new file geodatabase:

```
Guid fgdbGUID = new Guid("71FE75F0-EA0C-4406-873E-B7D53748AE7E");
Type factoryType = Type.GetTypeFromCLSID(fgdbGUID);

//alternatively
//Type factoryType = Type.
//GetTypeFromProgID("esriDataSourcesGDB.FileGDBWorkspaceFactory");

IWorkspaceFactory wsF = Activator.CreateInstance(factoryType) as
IWorkspaceFactory;
wsF.Create(path, fileGDBName, null, ArcMap.Application.hWnd);
```

As the name suggests, the `Create()` method builds a new file geodatabase in the specified path and with the supplied name. This method returns the `IWorkspaceName` interface, which can be used to get the `IWorkspace` interface.

Because there is no need for the `wsF` variable (an instance of `FileGDBWorkspaceFactory`) at this point, you have to release any reference to this singleton object. In this case, you can use the `ComReleaser` or `Marshal` class. The `ComReleaser` class is defined in the `ESRI.ArcGIS.ADF` namespace, but in order to use it you have to add a reference to the `ESRI.ArcGIS.ADF.Connection.Local` assembly. Internally, this class uses the `Marshal` class to release any reference to COM objects (even after the references go out of scope, such as at the end of the method that uses the singleton object). The `Marshal` class is defined in the `System.Runtime.InteropServices` namespace. The following code illustrates both methods:

```
//release all the references to singleton object (WorkspaceFactory)
ESRI.ArcGIS.ADF.ComReleaser.ReleaseCOMObject(wsF);
//alternatively
int refsLeft = 0;
do
{
    refsLeft = System.Runtime.InteropServices.Marshal.ReleaseComObject(wsF);
}
while (refsLeft > 0);
```

Creating FeatureDatasets and FeatureClasses

In order to create FeatureDatasets, FeatureClasses, and tables, you can use the `IFeatureWorkspace` interface. This interface is implemented by the `Workspace` class (refer to Figure 13-2). But in order to use `IFeatureWorkspace`, you have to use `IWorkspaceFactory` to create or get a reference to an existing workspace.

> **NOTE** Chapter 7 explained the topic of creating tables using the IFeatureWorkspace interface. The procedure for creating tables and FeatureClasses is similar except for the need to use a spatial reference system for creating FeatureClasses.

As mentioned in the previous section, the `IWorkspaceFactory`'s `Create()` method returns an `IWorkspaceName` object. You can use the `IWorkspaceName` object to get to the created `Workspace` object using the `Open()` method of its `IName` interface. The following code illustrates the necessary steps for creating a new geodatabase and treating it as a `Workspace`. (For more information on `Name` objects, read the last pages of Chapter 7.)

```
IWorkspaceName wsName = wsF.Create(path, fileGDBName, null,
ArcMap.Application.hWnd);
IName nameObj = wsName as IName;
IWorkspace ws = nameObj.Open() as IWorkspace;
```

For existing data sources such as geodatabases, you can use `IWorkspaceFactory`'s `Open()` or `OpenFromFile()` method to connect to remote or local workspaces, respectively.

```
IWorkspace ws = wsF.OpenFromFile(fileGDBAddress, ArcMap.Application.hWnd);
```

NOTE *Usually,* `IWorkspaceFactory`'s `Open()` *method is used to connect to ArcSDE geodatabases, as shown in the following code:*

```
//for ArcSDE Geodatabase
Guid sdebGUID = new
Guid("D9B4FA40-D6D9-11D1-AA81-00C04FA33A15");

Type factoryType = Type.GetTypeFromCLSID(sdebGUID);
IWorkspaceFactory wsF = Activator.
CreateInstance(factoryType) as IWorkspaceFactory;

IPropertySet pSet = new PropertySetClass();
//name of server
pSet.SetProperty("Server", "gisServer");
//port
pSet.SetProperty("Instance", "5151");
//name of Database
pSet.SetProperty("Database", "MunicipalityGDB");
//name of user connecting to DB
pSet.SetProperty("User", "sde");
//password of the user
pSet.SetProperty("Password", "@Keep#Moving_Forward");
//version of the geodatabase
pSet.SetProperty("Version", "sde.Default");

IWorkspace ws = wsF.Open(pSet, ArcMap.Application.hWnd);
```

In addition to remote geodatabases, `IWorkspaceFactory's Open()` *method can be used for opening local geodatabases. In this case, you need to provide just the* `Database` *parameter. See the following code:*

```
IPropertySet pSet = new PropertySetClass();
//path of Database
pSet.SetProperty("Database",
@"D:\DataFolder\testGDB.gdb");

IWorkspace ws = wsF.Open(pSet, ArcMap.Application.hWnd);
```

To create FeatureDatasets and stand-alone FeatureClasses (FeatureClasses not residing in any FeatureDataset), you need to specify a spatial reference system object. To do so, you have to use the `ISpatialReferenceFactory` interface, which is implemented by the `SpatialReferenceEnvironment` CoClass. This interface has a number of methods for specifying a spatial reference system.

The ArcObjects `Geometry` namespace contains several enumerations that can be used to specify the Well Known ID (WKID) of many available spatial reference systems in ArcGIS. The following code illustrates the simplest way to specify a spatial reference system:

```
ISpatialReferenceFactory spatialReferenceFactory = new
SpatialReferenceEnvironmentClass();
int coordinateSystemID = (int)esriSRGeoCSType.esriSRGeoCS_WGS1984;

ISpatialReference srs = spatialReferenceFactory.
CreateGeographicCoordinateSystem(coordinateSystemID);
```

It also is possible to directly use the EPSG code for the known spatial references.

```
//for WGS 84 EPSG 4326
ISpatialReference srs = spatialReferenceFactory.
CreateGeographicCoordinateSystem(4326);
```

ArcGIS contains many predefined and ready-to-use spatial reference objects that can be accessed using enumerations such as `esriSRGeoCSType` and `esriSRProjCSType`. In a case in which you cannot find your desired spatial reference system, you can define the parameters of your spatial reference system in a `*.prj` file and use the `CreateESRISpatialReferenceFromPRJFile()` method of the `ISpatialReferenceFactory` interface.

```
ISpatialReferenceFactory spatialReferenceFactory = new
SpatialReferenceEnvironmentClass();
ISpatialReference srs = spatialReferenceFactory.
CreateESRISpatialReferenceFromPRJFile(@"D:\DataFolder\
higherResolutionWGS84.prj");
```

With `Workspace` and a spatial reference system, you can easily create a FeatureDataset using `IFeatureWorkspace`'s `CreateFeatureDataset()` method.

```
//suppose that there is an existing file geodatabase
IWorkspace ws = wsF.OpenFromFile(fileGDBAddress, ArcMap.Application.hWnd);
IFeatureWorkspace fws = ws as IFeatureWorkspace;
IFeatureDataset fds = fws.CreateFeatureDataset(featureDatasetName, srs);
```

To create a FeatureClass inside an existing FeatureDataset, there is no need to specify a spatial reference system; the spatial reference system will be inherited from the FeatureDataset. But to create stand-alone FeatureClasses, you have to specify the spatial reference system for the field that stores the geometry of features. The next Try It Out shows how to create a file geodatabase and two FeatureClasses inside and outside a FeatureDataset.

TRY IT OUT **Creating a FileGeodatabase and FeatureClasses (SchemaCreation.zip)**

1. Create a new ArcMap Add-in project. Name the solution FeatureDataManagement. On the Add-Ins Wizard's Welcome page, provide the necessary information and click Next. Select Button as the type of add-in, provide the information as shown in Figure 13-3, and click Finish.

FIGURE 13-3

2. Because you want to add various functionalities to this add-in, you need a way to share parameters (such as the address of a file geodatabase) between different classes in your add-in. The easiest way is to use a static class and static members. Add a new class to your add-in project by right-clicking on your project in the Solution Explorer window and selecting Class from the New Item submenu. Name the newly added class `util`. Then add six static variables that can be accessed from anywhere in your add-in project. Figure 13-4 shows the entire `util` class (feel free to change the hard-coded values).

```
util.cs* ×  Config.esriaddinx    Object Browser
FeatureDataManagement.util                              xmlWorkspaceDocumentDS
    1  using System;
    2  using System.Collections.Generic;
    3  using System.Linq;
    4  using System.Text;
    5
    6  namespace FeatureDataManagement
    7  {
    8      public static class util
    9      {
   10          public static string path = @"D:\DataFolder";
   11          public static string fileGDBName = "testFileGDB.gdb";
   12          public static string featureDatasetName = "pointFeatureClasses";
   13          public static string featureClassName = "majorCities";
   14          public static string xmlWorkspaceDocument = "FullGDB.xml";
   15          public static string xmlWorkspaceDocumentDS = "DatasetGDB.xml";
   16      }
   17  }
```

FIGURE 13-4

3. Add ESRI.ArcGIS.Geodatabase, ESRI.ArcGIS.DataSourcesGDB, and ESRI.ArcGIS.Geometry references to your project. In addition, add a reference to the System.Windows.Forms assembly (using the Add Reference command) and type the following `using` directives at the top of the `CreatingFileGeodatabase.cs` file's code window:

```
using System.Windows.Forms;
using ESRI.ArcGIS.esriSystem;
using ESRI.ArcGIS.Geodatabase;
using ESRI.ArcGIS.DataSourcesGDB;
using ESRI.ArcGIS.Geometry;
```

4. Add the following code to the button's `OnClick()` method to create the new file geodatabase. Note that all the string parameters, such as the path and name of the file geodatabase, are acquired from the static `util` class.

```
try
        {
            string path = util.path;
            string fileGDBName = util.fileGDBName;

            if (System.IO.Directory.Exists(path + "\\" + fileGDBName))
            {
                MessageBox.Show("there is a file geodatabase with the same path
                and name");
                return;
            }

            //for file Geodatabase
            Guid fgdbGUID = new Guid("71FE75F0-EA0C-4406-873E-B7D53748AE7E");
            Type factoryType = Type.GetTypeFromCLSID(fgdbGUID);

            IWorkspaceFactory wsF = Activator.CreateInstance(factoryType) as
            IWorkspaceFactory;
            wsF.Create(path, fileGDBName, null, ArcMap.Application.hWnd);
            MessageBox.Show(fileGDBName + " created successsfully");

            //releasing all the references to singleton COM objects
            int refsLeft = 0;
            do
            {
                refsLeft = System.Runtime.InteropServices.Marshal.
                ReleaseComObject(wsF);
            }
            while (refsLeft > 0);
        }
        catch (Exception ex)
        {
            MessageBox.Show(ex.Message);
        }
```

5. Add a new add-in command container and name it **FeatureDataManagementToolbar** (remember the procedures for adding a command container, such as a toolbar, for ArcGIS 10.0 and 10.1 are slightly different). Select Toolbar as the type of Add-in Command Bars, and add the reference to the newly created button. Run the code and press the button within the ArcMap interface.

6. Add another add-in component to your project and name it **StandaloneFC**. Select Button as the type of add-in, provide the settings displayed in Figure 13-5, and click Finish.

FIGURE 13-5

7. Add the following using directives at the top of the StandaloneFC.cs file:

```
using System.Windows.Forms;
using ESRI.ArcGIS.esriSystem;
using ESRI.ArcGIS.Geodatabase;
using ESRI.ArcGIS.DataSourcesGDB;
using ESRI.ArcGIS.Geometry;
```

8. Add the following code in the OnClick() method of StandaloneFC.cs to create a point FeatureClass in the WGS84 spatial reference system:

```
try
{
    Type factoryType = Type.GetTypeFromProgID("esriDataSourcesGDB.
    FileGDBWorkspaceFactory");
    IWorkspaceFactory wsF = Activator.CreateInstance(factoryType) as
    IWorkspaceFactory;
    string fileGDBAddress = util.path + "\\" + util.fileGDBName;
    string fcName = util.featureClassName;
    //check the existence of the file geodatabase
    if (!System.IO.Directory.Exists(fileGDBAddress))
    {
        MessageBox.Show("there isn't a file geodatabase with the
        specified path and name");
        return;
```

```
}
IWorkspace ws = wsF.OpenFromFile(fileGDBAddress, ArcMap.Application.
hWnd);
IFeatureWorkspace fws = ws as IFeatureWorkspace;
//check the existence of the FeatureClass
IWorkspace2 ws2 = fws as IWorkspace2;
if (ws2.get_NameExists(esriDatasetType.esriDTFeatureClass, fcName)
== true)
{
    MessageBox.Show(string.Format("The {0} FeatureClass already
    exists in the {1} file geodatabase", fcName, util.fileGDBName));
    return;
}

//create fields
IFieldsEdit fields = new FieldsClass();

IFieldEdit field = new FieldClass();
field.Name_2 = "ObjectID";
field.Type_2 = esriFieldType.esriFieldTypeOID;
fields.AddField(field);

// Create a geometry definition (and spatial reference) for the
//feature class.
IGeometryDefEdit geometryDefEdit = new GeometryDefClass();
geometryDefEdit.GeometryType_2 = esriGeometryType.esriGeometryPoint;
ISpatialReferenceFactory spatialReferenceFactory = new
SpatialReferenceEnvironmentClass();
int coordinateSystemID = (int)esriSRGeoCSType.esriSRGeoCS_WGS1984;
ISpatialReference spatialReference = spatialReferenceFactory.
CreateGeographicCoordinateSystem(coordinateSystemID);
geometryDefEdit.SpatialReference_2 = spatialReference;

field = new FieldClass();
field.Name_2 = "Shape";
field.Type_2 = esriFieldType.esriFieldTypeGeometry;
field.GeometryDef_2 = geometryDefEdit as IGeometryDef;
fields.AddField(field);

field = new FieldClass();
field.Name_2 = "Name";
field.Type_2 = esriFieldType.esriFieldTypeString;
fields.AddField(field);

field = new FieldClass();
field.Name_2 = "Population";
field.Type_2 = esriFieldType.esriFieldTypeInteger;
fields.AddField(field);

field = new FieldClass();
field.Name_2 = "Area";
field.Type_2 = esriFieldType.esriFieldTypeDouble;
fields.AddField(field);

IFeatureClass fc = fws.CreateFeatureClass(fcName, fields, null,
```

```
null, esriFeatureType.esriFTSimple, "Shape", null);
MessageBox.Show(fcName + " created successsfully");
//release all the references to singleton COM object
//(WorkspaceFactory)
int refsLeft = 0;
do
{
    refsLeft = System.Runtime.InteropServices.Marshal.
    ReleaseComObject(wsF);
}
while (refsLeft > 0);
}
catch (Exception ex)
{
    MessageBox.Show(ex.Message);
}
```

9. Add another add-in component to your project and name it **CreatingFDS**. Select Button as the type of add-in, provide the settings shown in Figure 13-6, and click Finish.

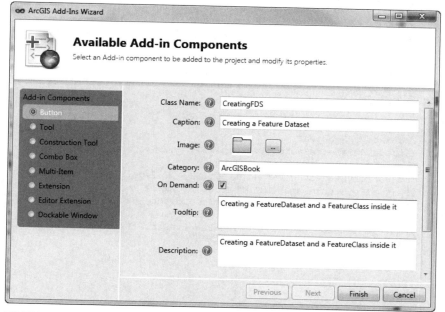

FIGURE 13-6

10. Add the following using directives at the top of the CreatingFDS.cs file's code window:

```
using System.Windows.Forms;
using ESRI.ArcGIS.esriSystem;
using ESRI.ArcGIS.Geodatabase;
using ESRI.ArcGIS.DataSourcesGDB;
using ESRI.ArcGIS.Geometry;
```

11. Enter the following code in the `OnClick()` method of `CreatingFDS.cs` to create a FeatureDataset and a FeatureClass inside it:

```
try
{
    Type factoryType = Type.GetTypeFromProgID("esriDataSourcesGDB.
    FileGDBWorkspaceFactory");
    IWorkspaceFactory wsF = Activator.CreateInstance(factoryType) as
    IWorkspaceFactory;
    string fileGDBAddress = util.path + "\\" + util.fileGDBName;
    string fdsName = util.featureDatasetName;
    //check the existence of the file geodatabase
    if (!System.IO.Directory.Exists(fileGDBAddress))
    {
        MessageBox.Show("there isn't a file geodatabase with the
        specified path and name");
        return;
    }

    IFeatureWorkspace fws = wsF.OpenFromFile(fileGDBAddress, ArcMap.
    Application.hWnd) as IFeatureWorkspace;
    //check the existence of FeatureDataset
    IWorkspace2 ws = fws as IWorkspace2;
    if (ws.get_NameExists(esriDatasetType.esriDTFeatureDataset,
    fdsName) == true)
    {
        MessageBox.Show(string.Format("The {0} FeatureDataset already
        exists in the {1} file geodatabase", fdsName, util.fileGDBName));
        return;
    }

    //create SRS object
    ISpatialReferenceFactory spatialReferenceFactory = new
    SpatialReferenceEnvironmentClass();
    int coordinateSystemID = (int)esriSRGeoCSType.esriSRGeoCS_WGS1984;
    ISpatialReference spatialReference = spatialReferenceFactory.
    CreateGeographicCoordinateSystem(coordinateSystemID);
    //creating FeatureDataset
    IFeatureDataset fds = fws.CreateFeatureDataset(fdsName,
    spatialReference);

    //Creating FeatureClass
    IFieldsEdit fields = new FieldsClass();
    fields.FieldCount_2 = 5;

    IFieldEdit field = new FieldClass();
    field.Name_2 = "ObjectID";
    field.Type_2 = esriFieldType.esriFieldTypeOID;
    fields.Field_2[0] = field;

    //there is no need to set the spatial reference for FeatureClasses
    //inside a FeatureDataset
    //since the spatial reference system is inherited from the parent
    //FeatureDataset
    IGeometryDefEdit geometryDef = new GeometryDefClass();
```

```
geometryDef.GeometryType_2 = esriGeometryType.esriGeometryPoint;

field = new FieldClass();
field.Name_2 = "Shape";
field.Type_2 = esriFieldType.esriFieldTypeGeometry;
field.GeometryDef_2 = geometryDef;
fields.Field_2[1] = field;

field = new FieldClass();
field.Name_2 = "Name";
field.Type_2 = esriFieldType.esriFieldTypeString;
fields.Field_2[2] = field;

field = new FieldClass();
field.Name_2 = "Population";
field.Type_2 = esriFieldType.esriFieldTypeInteger;
fields.Field_2[3] = field;

field = new FieldClass();
field.Name_2 = "Area";
field.Type_2 = esriFieldType.esriFieldTypeDouble;
fields.Field_2[4] = field;

fds.CreateFeatureClass(util.featureClassName + "2", fields, null,
null, esriFeatureType.esriFTSimple, "Shape", null);

int refsLeft = 0;
do
{
    refsLeft = System.Runtime.InteropServices.Marshal.
    ReleaseComObject(wsF);
}
while (refsLeft > 0);
}
catch (Exception ex)
{

    MessageBox.Show(ex.Message);
}
```

12. Modify the add-in configuration file to place all the buttons on the toolbar. Then run your code and test it in ArcMap.

How It Works

In this example, you used static classes for sharing functionality between different add-in components. Static classes and static class members are used to create data members and methods that can be accessed without creating an instance of the class.

Every FeatureClass in a geodatabase must have an ID and a geometry field. You explored the use of the IGeometryDefinition interface for setting a spatial reference system and the type of geometry for FeatureClasses and as a result for the definition of a geometry field. Also, as you have witnessed you can check for the existence of any dataset in a Workspace using the IWorkspace2 interface.

WORKING WITH FEATURES

Features can be created and accessed directly from FeatureClasses. In other words, FeatureClasses (through the `IFeatureClass` interface) have methods such as `CreateFeature()` and `GetFeature()` to access and modify features. In addition, a feature can call the `Delete()` method on the `IRow` interface to remove itself from the FeatureClass where it is stored. But using these methods is not efficient in certain situations. The following sections describe some solutions that can be used efficiently when working with features.

Creating New Features

In general, new features can be created using two approaches. In the first approach, a feature is created as a result of calling `IFeatureClass`'s `CreateFeature()` method. Then after assigning geometry and other attributes to the feature, you must call the `Store()` method on the `IFeature` interface to insert the new feature into a geodatabase. The following code snippet creates a new feature and sets one of its attribute values and its geometry:

```
//featureClass variable is an instance of IFeatureClass
IFeature newFeature = featureClass.CreateFeature();
newFeature.Value[indexOfAField] ="someValue";
newFeature.Shape = Polygon;
newFeature.Store();
```

The second approach for creating features is to use insert cursors and the `IFeatureBuffer` interface. In this case, a new FeatureBuffer and an insert cursor are created using the IFeatureClass's `CreateFeatureBuffer()` and `Insert()` methods, respectively. The `Shape` property must be used to set the geometry of the FeatureBuffer, and the `set_Value()` method has to be used to set the value for fields.

```
//featureClass variable is an instance of IFeatureClass
IFeatureBuffer newFeatureBuffer = featureClass.CreateFeatureBuffer();
IFeatureCursor fCursor = featureClass.Insert(false);
newFeatureBuffer.set_Value(indexOfAField, "someValue");
fCursor.InsertFeature(newFeatureBuffer);
fCursor.Flush();
```

The `Insert()` method of the `IFeatureClass` takes a boolean value that indicates the buffering capability of the cursor. This capability can be used only during an edit session. Using buffering makes it possible to store new features on the client side (cursor object) and load them in a bulk mode to the server (geodatabase). This characteristic results in higher performance in comparison with non-buffering insert cursors. Using the insert cursor's `Flush()` method results in pushing a new feature to the geodatabase. If a call to the `Flush()` method is missed, the cursor pushes all the features before the cursor is destroyed (goes out of scope or the application releases any references to the cursor).

To sum up, an insert cursor provides a faster way of inserting a huge amount of features in simple FeatureClasses. But when FeatureClasses implement custom behavior, such as participation in topologies and geometric networks or custom class extensions, using an insert cursor doesn't provide significant benefits. The real advantage of insert cursors can be obtained using buffering.

With buffering enabled for an insert cursor, calling `InsertFeature()` doesn't push the feature to the geodatabase. Rather, it pushes the feature into the specific area in memory, which is called the *buffer*. Features will remain in the buffer till the cursor's `Flush()` method is called or the buffer reaches its maximum capacity. Then all features in the buffer are written to the geodatabase. This way of bulk loading outperforms using the first approach of inserting new features. The next Try It Out illustrates the use of an insert cursor. Note that buffering can be enabled during an edit session.

TRY IT OUT   **Inserting New Features (NewFeatures.zip)**

1. Add a class to the FeatureDataManagement add-in solution. Name it **City** and define members as shown in the following code:

```
class City
    {
        //properties
        public string Name
        { get; set; }

        public long Population
        { get; set; }

        public decimal Area
        { get; set; }

        public double X
        { get; set; }

        public double Y
        { get; set; }

        public City(string name, long population, decimal area, double x, double y)
        {
            this.Name = name;
            this.Population = population;
            this.Area = area;
            this.X = x;
            this.Y = y;
        }
    }
```

2. Add a new add-in component to your solution. Name it **InsertNewFeatures**, select Button as the type of add-in, provide the information as shown in Figure 13-7, and click Finish.

FIGURE 13-7

3. Add references to ESRI.ArcGIS.Carto, ESRI.ArcGIS.Display, and ESRI.ArcGIS.Editor, and add the following `using` directives at the top of the `InsertNewFeatures.cs.` file's code window:

```
using ESRI.ArcGIS.Geodatabase;
using ESRI.ArcGIS.DataSourcesGDB;
using ESRI.ArcGIS.esriSystem;
using ESRI.ArcGIS.Geometry;
using System.Windows.Forms;
using ESRI.ArcGIS.Editor;
using ESRI.ArcGIS.Carto;
using ESRI.ArcGIS.ArcMapUI;
```

4. You need to get to the FeatureClass in order to insert new features in it. So add the following code in the `InsertNewFeatures` class's `OnClick()` method:

```
Type factoryType = Type.GetTypeFromProgID("esriDataSourcesGDB.
FileGDBWorkspaceFactory");
IWorkspaceFactory wsF = Activator.CreateInstance(factoryType) as
IWorkspaceFactory;
string fileGDBAddress = util.path + "\\" + util.fileGDBName;
string fcName = util.featureClassName;
//check the existence of the file geodatabase
if (!System.IO.Directory.Exists(fileGDBAddress))
{
    MessageBox.Show("there isn't a file geodatabase with the
    specified path and name");
    return;
}
IWorkspace ws = wsF.OpenFromFile(fileGDBAddress, ArcMap.Application.
hWnd);
```

```
IFeatureWorkspace fws = ws as IFeatureWorkspace;
IWorkspace2 ws2 = fws as IWorkspace2;
if (ws2.get_NameExists(esriDatasetType.esriDTFeatureClass, fcName)
== false)
{
    MessageBox.Show(string.Format("The {0} FeatureClass doesn't
    exist in the {1} file geodatabase", fcName, util.fileGDBName));
    return;
}

//get the FeatureClass
IFeatureClass fc = fws.OpenFeatureClass(fcName);
```

5. After getting a reference to the FeatureClass, you need some sample data. Add the following code:

```
//create list of major cities
List<City> cities = new List<City>();
cities.Add(new City("New York", 16500000, 1210, -74.0999, 40.7500));
cities.Add(new City("Tokyo", 23650000, 2187, 139.8092, 35.6830));
cities.Add(new City("Berlin", 5100000, 892, 13.3276, 52.5163));
cities.Add(new City("Paris", 10000000, 105, 2.4328, 48.8815));
```

6. In order to create a buffering insert cursor, you need to use the Editor extension and invoke the `StartEditing()` method of the `IEditor3` interface. The `StartEditing()` method requests the `IWorkspace` input parameter. This shows that only one `Workspace` can be edited at a time. Also, the FeatureLayer from the specified `Workspace` must be in the active data frame; otherwise, the call to `StartEditing()` will result in an error. So enter the following code to create a FeatureLayer, and add it to the active data frame:

```
IFeatureLayer fl = new FeatureLayerClass();
fl.Name = fcName;
fl.FeatureClass = fc;
IMxDocument mxdoc = ArcMap.Application.Document as IMxDocument;
IMap map = mxdoc.FocusMap;
map.AddLayer(fl);
```

7. The rest of the code accesses the Editor extension, creates a buffering insert cursor, and finally pushes all the buffered features into the geodatabase.

```
int idxName = fc.Fields.FindField("Name");
int idxPop = fc.Fields.FindField("Population");
int idxArea = fc.Fields.FindField("Area");

if (idxName < 0 || idxArea < 0 || idxPop < 0)
{ return; }
UID editorExtension = new UIDClass();
editorExtension.Value = "esriEditor.Editor";
IEditor3 editor = ArcMap.Application.
FindExtensionByCLSID(editorExtension) as IEditor3;
editor.StartEditing(ws);

IFeatureBuffer cityBuffer = fc.CreateFeatureBuffer();
//Buffering can only be used during an edit session.
IFeatureCursor fCursor = fc.Insert(true);
foreach (City ct in cities)
```

```
    {
        IPoint point = new PointClass();
        point.X = ct.X;
        point.Y = ct.Y;
        cityBuffer.Shape = point;

        cityBuffer.set_Value(idxName, ct.Name);
        cityBuffer.set_Value(idxPop, ct.Population);
        cityBuffer.set_Value(idxArea, ct.Area);
        IRowSubtypes cityST = cityBuffer as IRowSubtypes;
        cityST.InitDefaultValues();
        fCursor.InsertFeature(cityBuffer);
    }

    fCursor.Flush();
    editor.StopEditing(true);
    MessageBox.Show("All features inserted successfully");
    System.Runtime.InteropServices.Marshal.ReleaseComObject(fCursor);

    int refsLeft = 0;
    do
    {
        refsLeft = System.Runtime.InteropServices.Marshal.
        ReleaseComObject(wsF);
    }
    while (refsLeft > 0);
    mxdoc.ActiveView.Refresh();
```

8. Add the button to the toolbar and enjoy it (run your code and test it in ArcMap).

How It Works

In this example, you used the insert cursor during an edit session to insert new features. When creating new features in ArcGIS for Desktop applications, the default values and subtypes are automatically set. When features are created in code, the default values and subtypes are not set automatically. In other words, a call to the `CreateFeature()` or `CreateFeatureBuffer()` method doesn't set the default value for fields that have them. At this point, the `IRowSubtypes` interface comes into play. The `IRowSubtypes` interface is the primary interface for working with default values and subtypes for any dataset that supports them. The `InitDefaultValues()` method populates fields with the specified default values and subtypes at the time features are created.

Modifying Existing Features

In general, you can modify existing features in one of two ways. The first way is to use the `Store()` and `Delete()` methods, which are implemented by the `IRow` interface. In other words, the feature itself performs the update or delete. The following code illustrates updating features using a search cursor:

```
//featureClass variable is an instance of IFeatureClass
int idxName = featureClass.Fields.FindField("Name");

IQueryFilter qF = new QueryFilterClass();
```

```
        qF.WhereClause = "\"Name\" <> \'New York\'";

        IFeatureCursor fCursor = featureClass.Search(qF, false);
        IFeature city = fCursor.NextFeature();
        while (city != null)
        {
            city.Value[idxName] = "New " + city.Value[idxName];
            city.Store();
            city = fCursor.NextFeature();
        }
```

The following code demonstrates the use of the `Delete()` method with a search cursor:

```
        IQueryFilter qF = new QueryFilterClass();
        qF.WhereClause = "\"Name\" <> \'New York\'";

        IFeatureCursor fCursor = featureClass.Search(qF, false);
        IFeature city = fCursor.NextFeature();
        while (city != null)
        {
            city.Delete();
            //there is no need to call Store() after delete
            city = fCursor.NextFeature();
        }
```

When using search cursors to update or delete features, the recycling parameter must always be set to `false`.

The second way to modify features is by using an update cursor. The update cursors can use recycling when there is no need to update more than one feature at once. This kind of cursor provides better performance in comparison with a non-recycling search cursor.

```
        //featureClass variable is an instance of IFeatureClass
        IQueryFilter qF = new QueryFilterClass();
        qF.WhereClause = "\"Name\" <> \'New York\'";
        IFeatureCursor fCursor = featureClass.Update(qF, true);
        IFeature city = fCursor.NextFeature();
        while (city != null)
        {
            city.set_Value(idxName, "New " + city.Value[idxName]);
            fCursor.UpdateFeature(city);
            city = fCursor.NextFeature();
        }
```

For deleting features, update cursors provide the `DeleteFeature()` method. But the most efficient method for deleting a huge amount of features in files or personal geodatabases is to use the `DeleteSearchedRows()` method, which is defined by the `ITable` interface. But when a FeatureClass is in an ArcSDE geodatabase, the most efficient method for deleting numerous features is to use a search cursor.

```
        //featureClass variable is an instance of IFeatureClass
        IQueryFilter qF = new QueryFilterClass();
        qF.WhereClause = "\"Name\" <> \'New York\'";
        ITable table = feeatureClass as ITable;
        table.DeleteSearchedRows(qF);
```

In the next Try It Out, you create a domain, assign it to a field, and then update features.

TRY IT OUT   Modifying Existing Features (ModifyFeatures.zip)

1. Add a new add-in component to your solution. Name it **ModifyFeatures**, select Button as the type of add-in, provide the information as shown in Figure 13-8, and click Finish.

FIGURE 13-8

2. Enter the following using directives at the top of the ModifyFeature.cs. file's code window:

```
using ESRI.ArcGIS.Geodatabase;
using ESRI.ArcGIS.DataSourcesGDB;
using System.Windows.Forms;
```

3. Add the following code to the ModifyFeatures class's OnClick() method:

```
try
        {
            //creating a domain
            Type factoryType = Type.GetTypeFromProgID("esriDataSourcesGDB.
            FileGDBWorkspaceFactory");
            IWorkspaceFactory wsF = Activator.CreateInstance(factoryType) as
            IWorkspaceFactory;
            string fileGDBAddress = util.path + "\\" + util.fileGDBName;
            if (!System.IO.Directory.Exists(fileGDBAddress))
            {
                MessageBox.Show("there isn't a file geodatabase with the
                specified path and name");
                return;
            }
            //define CodedValue Domain
            ICodedValueDomain codedDomain = new CodedValueDomainClass();
            codedDomain.AddCode(1, "Is Capital");
```

```csharp
                codedDomain.AddCode(0, "Is not Capital");
                IDomain capitalDomain = codedDomain as IDomain;
                capitalDomain.Name = "CapitalDomain";
                capitalDomain.FieldType = esriFieldType.esriFieldTypeSmallInteger;
                capitalDomain.SplitPolicy = esriSplitPolicyType.esriSPTDuplicate;
                capitalDomain.MergePolicy = esriMergePolicyType.esriMPTAreaWeighted;

                //add domain to geodatabase
                IWorkspace ws = wsF.OpenFromFile(fileGDBAddress, ArcMap.Application.
                hWnd);
                IWorkspaceDomains2 wsD = ws as IWorkspaceDomains2;
                wsD.AddDomain(capitalDomain);

                //add field and assign domain
                IFeatureWorkspace fws = ws as IFeatureWorkspace;
                IFeatureClass fc = fws.OpenFeatureClass(util.featureClassName);

                //create a new field
                IFieldEdit2 field = new FieldClass();
                field.Name_2 = "status";
                field.Type_2 = esriFieldType.esriFieldTypeSmallInteger;
                field.DefaultValue_2 = 0;
                field.Domain_2 = capitalDomain;
                fc.AddField(field);

                //update features
                int idxStatus = fc.Fields.FindField("status");
                IQueryFilter qF = new QueryFilterClass();
                qF.WhereClause = "\"Name\" <> \'New York\'";

                IFeatureCursor fCursor = fc.Update(qF, true);
                IFeature city = fCursor.NextFeature();
                while (city != null)
                {
                    city.set_Value(idxStatus, 1);
                    fCursor.UpdateFeature(city);
                    city = fCursor.NextFeature();
                }
                //release cursor
                System.Runtime.InteropServices.Marshal.ReleaseComObject(fCursor);

                //release all the references to singleton object (WorkspaceFactory)
                int refsLeft = 0;
                do
                {
                    refsLeft = System.Runtime.InteropServices.Marshal.
                    ReleaseComObject(wsF);
                }
                while (refsLeft > 0);
            }
            catch (Exception ex)
            {
                MessageBox.Show(ex.Message);
            }
```

4. Add the button to the toolbar and test its functionality.

How It Works

Because domains are defined at the `Workspace` level, they can be used by various fields in different FeatureClasses or tables. You can add or delete domains using the `IWorkspaceDomains` interface, which is implemented by the `Workspace` class.

SUMMARY

This chapter explains some basic but common topics of vector geospatial data management. The ArcGIS platform supports many formats, but geodatabase is ArcGIS's native format. Besides being the native format for handling geospatial data, the geodatabase is the common model for working with all types of geospatial data. Whether your geospatial data is a simple CAD drawing or a complex FeatureClass with custom behavior in an ArcSDE geodatabase, all of them are treated using the geodatabase model in ArcObjects. This characteristic indicates the extensibility and high quality of ArcObjects. The next and final chapter of the book is devoted to deployment.

EXERCISES

1. What is the best method for deleting a huge number of features?

2. Which is faster for updating geospatial data: a non-recycling search cursor or a recycling update cursor?

3. How it is possible to get a reference to supported spatial reference systems in ArcGIS through ArcObjects?

You will find the answers to these exercises in this book's appendix.

▶ WHAT YOU LEARNED IN THIS CHAPTER

TOPIC	KEY CONCEPTS
Primary interfaces for working with geospatial data	The primary interfaces for working with geospatial data using the geodatabase model are `IWorkspaceFactory` and `IWorkspace`. The `IWorkspaceFactory` interface is implemented by the `WorkspaceFactory` Abstract Class. Based on the type and format of geospatial data, there are different subclasses of `WorkspaceFactory` CoClasses that developers can use to work with diverse types of geospatial data. The `IWorkspace` interface is implemented by the `Workspace` class. `Workspace` is a container of geospatial and non-geospatial data and elements. A folder containing shapefiles, a folder containing a toolbox, a file geodatabase, and an ArcSDE geodatabase are all `Workspace` objects.
Singleton objects in ArcObjects	Singleton objects are objects which have only one instance. In other words, any call to a constructor of a singleton object (using the `new` keyword) will return a reference to an existing object. After instantiation, they are available to all objects in the application. Using singleton COM objects in the similar way to normal objects in .NET might result in unexpected errors. For this reason, using ArcObjects singleton objects requires careful memory management. In ArcObjects programming, the `System.Activator` class must be used to instantiate, and the `System.Runtime.InteropServices.Marshal` or `ESRI.ArcGIS.ADF.ComReleaser` classes should be used for releasing the references of singleton objects. For this reason, you need to know the GUID of the singleton object to be able to use the `Activator` class. All subclasses of `WorkspaceFactory` are singleton objects.
Buffering insert cursors	With buffering enabled for an insert cursor, calling the `InsertFeature()` method of an insert cursor doesn't push the feature to the geodatabase. Rather, it pushes the feature into the buffer. Features will remain in the buffer till the cursor's `Flush()` method is called or the buffer reaches its maximum capacity. Then all features in the buffer are written to the geodatabase. This method of bulk loading outperforms using the approach of inserting new features using `CreateFeature()` and `Store()` methods.
Recycling update cursors	There are two ways of modifying existing features: use of search cursors and use of update cursors. The search cursor can use recycling in a search operation, but when using search cursors for update or delete operations, the recycling parameter must always be set to `false` (a non-recycling search cursor). Update cursors can use recycling when there is no need to update more than one feature at once. This kind of cursor (a recycling update cursor) provides better performance in comparison with non-recycling search cursors.

14

Advanced Topics in ArcObjects Programming and Deployment

WHAT YOU WILL LEARN IN THIS CHAPTER:

➤ Wiring ArcObjects events

➤ Creating application extensions

➤ Sharing state and functionality between components

➤ Desktop Add-Ins deployment

➤ Custom component deployment

➤ Custom actions with custom component deployment

WROX.COM CODE DOWNLOADS FOR THIS CHAPTER

The wrox.com code downloads for this chapter can be found at www.wrox.com/remtitle .cgi?isbn=1118442547 on the Download Code tab. The code is in the Chapter14 folder and is individually named according to the names throughout the chapter.

Congratulations! The fact that you're reading this chapter probably means you now have a solid understanding of ArcObjects programming. The next step in ArcGIS for Desktop applications development is to release your Desktop Add-In or custom component to your target audience.

Desktop Add-Ins and custom components have two distinct models for deployment. In this chapter, you learn how to deploy your customization using both models. In addition to deployment, this chapter deals with sharing state and functionality as well as developing application extensions.

SHARING STATE AND FUNCTIONALITY BETWEEN COMPONENTS

Almost every ArcObjects project (add-in or custom component) needs inter-component communication for changing state or calling methods of other components in the project. As an example, suppose you have two buttons (btn1 and btn2) and a combo box (cbo) in your add-in project and you want to populate the combo box with every click of the first button (btn1). ComboBox provides an Add() method to add items; however, this method is defined as protected (with the protected access modifier) in the add-in framework, so it is not possible for Button to call this method directly. No protected member of an add-in component (even add-in components of the same type, such as two combo boxes) can be accessed outside of that component.

> **NOTE** Access modifier keywords (like public, private, and protected) are discussed in the "Object-Oriented Programming in Action" section of Chapter 3.

The solution is to use the static members inside ArcObjects components. In Chapter 13, you use static members to share state. So the first step to enable inter-component communication in this example is to define a static member of type cbo inside the cbo class, which is initialized in the class's constructor. Then the Add() method is wrapped using a static method that can be called from other components in the same add-in project. Ponder the following code, which illustrates this process in action:

```
public class cbo : ESRI.ArcGIS.Desktop.AddIns.ComboBox
    {
        //private static member
        private static cbo s_comboBox;

        //constructor
        public cbo()
        {
            s_comboBox = this;
        }
        //static method (wrapper method)
        internal static void AddItem(string caption)
        {
            s_comboBox.Add(caption);
        }

    }
```

Because the AddItem() method is defined using the internal access modifier keyword, it is accessible by all classes in the Add-In project. As a result, the btn1 class can easily use this method.

```
public class btn1 : ESRI.ArcGIS.Desktop.AddIns.Button
    {
        public btn1()
        {
```

```
        }

        public override void OnClick()
        {
            cbo.AddItem(DateTime.Now.ToLongTimeString());
        }
    }
```

Also, if you want to access properties of other components in the Add-In project, you can easily create a *getter* method (also known as an *accessor* method) for the desired property. For example, if you want to see which item is selected in the previous combo box, you can define another static member and another static method that returns the defined static variable. The value for this variable must be set in the appropriate method based on the type of the Add-In component. The following code illustrates this process for the combo box:

```
public class cbo : ESRI.ArcGIS.Desktop.AddIns.ComboBox
    {
        //private static
        private static cbo s_comboBox;

        private static string s_selectedTime;

        //constructor
        public cbo()
        {
            s_comboBox = this;
        }

        internal static void AddItem(string caption)
        {
            s_comboBox.Add(caption);
        }
        protected override void OnSelChange(int cookie)
        {
            //if user selects nothing
            if (cookie == -1)
            { return; }
            //since Add-In types are singleton, this and s_cbo point to the same
            //thing
            //get selected item (caption)
            s_selectedField = this.GetItem(cookie).Caption;
        }

        //getter (accessor) method
        internal static string GetSelectedTime()
        {
            return s_selectedTime;
        }
    }
```

In a similar manner, you can use this getter (or accessor) method in other components in your Add-In project, as shown in the following code:

```
public class btn2 : ESRI.ArcGIS.Desktop.AddIns.Button
    {
        public btn2()
        {
        }

        public override void OnClick()
        {
            MessageBox.Show(cbo.GetSelectedTime());
        }
    }
```

This powerful and straightforward way of inter-component communication can be used in Add-In as well as custom component development.

> **NOTE** The Add-In framework provides an even easier way to access a specific component in an Add-In project. When you develop add-ins, you can use the static `AddIn.FromID()` method to get a reference to an existing instance of a component within your Add-In project. The following code gets a reference to the combo box's members without defining any static member. In order to use this code snippet, you must enter the `using ESRI.ArcGIS.Desktop.AddIns` directive at the top of your class file.

```
public class btn1 : ESRI.ArcGIS.Desktop.AddIns.Button
    {
        public btn1()
        {
        }

        public override void OnClick()
        {
            var theCombobox = AddIn.FromID<cbo>(ThisAddIn.IDs.cbo);
            theCombobox.AddItem(DateTime.Now.ToLongTimeString());
        }
    }
```

EVENT HANDLING IN ARCOBJECTS

ArcGIS for Desktop applications are Windows applications; as a result, they are event-driven. As you might remember, events are actions initiated by either a user or the system. In the .NET Framework, a special type is used for communication between event-sender and event-receiver delegates.

The delegate holds a reference to a method. The method is an event handler and implements logic for responding to the initiated action. For this reason, the method must have the signature defined by the event.

Up to this point in this book, all the events are fired directly by the user by clicking a button, for example. Events can be fired by ArcObjects, too; for example, when a user adds layers to the active Data Frame, the AddItem event is fired by the Map object.

Event handling in ArcObjects is simple. First you have to get a reference to an instance of an object that implements a certain event interface. Then you create an event handler method and register the method with the object that raises the event. This process is called *event wiring*. The signatures of events are defined in event interfaces. All the members of the event interfaces are of type event. For this reason, other objects are needed in order to handle events that are notified using event interfaces.

> **NOTE** *Event interfaces are denoted by filled lollipops in object model diagrams. They are also known as outbound interfaces. Because they have an* Events *suffix (for example,* IActiveViewEvents*), you can easily find them in object model diagrams. Note that in .NET they are suffixed with* _Event *(*IActiveViewEvents_Event*). Another important tip is that they are hidden in Visual Studio. In other words, outbound interfaces in .NET (such as* IActiveViewEvents_Event*) are not displayed when you code in Visual Studio, but you can use them in C# or VB.*

Suppose that you want to develop a combo box that shows all the FeatureLayers in the active Data Frame. In addition, you want the combo box to automatically update itself based on the addition or removal of layers in the Data Frame. In this case, you have to resort to the ItemAdded and ItemDeleted events of the IActiveViewEvents_Event interface. This interface is implemented by a Map object. So you use the Map object to get a reference to IActiveViewEvents_Event and implement two event handlers. Since you need this functionality from the beginning of the combo box's lifetime, you have to put the event wiring logic in the combo box's constructor. The following code illustrates this procedure:

```
public class cboFeatureLayers : ESRI.ArcGIS.Desktop.AddIns.ComboBox
    {
        IMxDocument mxdoc;
        IMap map;

        //constructor of combobox
        public cboFeatureLayer()
        {
            mxdoc = ArcMap.Application.Document as IMxDocument;
            map = mxdoc.FocusMap;
            //get a reference to an object that implements specific event interface
            IActiveViewEvents_Event avEvent = map as IActiveViewEvents_Event;
            //register and insert event handlers with appropriate events
            avEvent.ItemAdded += new
            IActiveViewEvents_ItemAddedEventHandler(LayerAdded);
            avEvent.ItemDeleted += new
            IActiveViewEvents_ItemDeletedEventHandler(LayerDeleted);
        }

        protected override void OnSelChange(int cookie)
```

```
        {
        }
        protected override void OnUpdate()
        {
        }

        //event handlers
        void LayerAdded(object item)
        {
                this.Clear();
                for (int i = 0; i < map.LayerCount; i++)
                {
                    if (map.Layer[i] is IFeatureLayer)
                    {
                        this.Add(map.Layer[i].Name);
                    }
                }
        }
        void LayerDeleted(object item)
        {
                this.Clear();
                for (int i = 0; i < map.LayerCount; i++)
                {
                    if (map.Layer[i] is IFeatureLayer)
                    {
                        this.Add(map.Layer[i].Name);
                    }
                }
        }

    }
```

As you can see from this code, the signature and logic of both event handlers are the same, so you can specify a single method to handle both events. Ponder the following code, which illustrates the updated constructor method of the preceding code:

```
        //constructor of combobox
        public cboFeatureLayer()
        {
            mxdoc = ArcMap.Application.Document as IMxDocument;
            map = mxdoc.FocusMap;
            //get a reference to an object that implements specific event interface
            IActiveViewEvents_Event avEvent = map as IActiveViewEvents_Event;
            //register event handlers with appropriate events
            avEvent.ItemAdded += new
            IActiveViewEvents_ItemAddedEventHandler(LayerAdded);
            avEvent.ItemDeleted += new
            IActiveViewEvents_ItemDeletedEventHandler(LayerAdded);
        }
```

You can find the source code for this example in the ListenerCombobox.zip file in the download files for this chapter on Wrox.com.

> **NOTE** *Usually different classes that implement an event interface fire the same event in different situations. For example, many CoClasses such as* Map, PageLayout, MapFrame, *and* Legend *implement the* IActiveViewEvents_Event *interface. As you have seen, the* Map *CoClass fires the* ItemAdded *event when a layer is added to a map. The* PageLayout *CoClass fires* ItemAdded *when a legend, MapFrame, and graphics are added to the page layout. In addition, implementation of an event interface does not mean that all events of the event interface must be fired by a class. As another example, the* Map *CoClass implements the* IActiveViewEvents_Event *interface but it doesn't fire the* FocusMapChanged *event.*

APPLICATION EXTENSION

To this point in this chapter, you have seen how to share state between various components in an Add-In project as well as handling ArcObjects events. You can handle various events in different components in an add-in. However, this makes your code less maintainable because at some point you need to duplicate your written code in another component. Even worse, in some situations you need to reengineer the whole project just to make sure your add-in or custom component works in the desired manner. To avoid these pitfalls, you can use *application extensions* (*extensions* for short).

The ArcGIS platform has, in addition to the core products, lots of extensions to provide additional capabilities that can be evaluated freely or purchased. For example, ArcGIS 3D Analyst is a valuable extension for visualizing, analyzing, and managing three-dimensional geospatial data. ArcGIS for Desktop application users can enable or disable available extensions in the Extensions window by selecting Customize ➪ Extensions.

ArcObjects developers can develop application extensions and add them to the Extensions window. Extensions are special types of components with the sole purpose of managing other types of components in an add-in or custom component project. Extensions provide a central point of coordination — through extensions it is possible to handle application events in just one place and manage the state of all other components in an ArcObjects add-in or custom component project.

> **NOTE** *Always develop your add-in or custom component project with extensibility and future development in mind. To make this happen, always use an extension component in your project to manage and coordinate other types of components. With little effort, you will end up with a more prestigious and well-designed add-in or custom component.*
>
> *Extensions are not limited to Desktop Add-Ins. You can create application extensions using the custom component model of ArcObjects development (extending ArcObjects templates).*

In the following Try It Out, you learn how to manage and coordinate three add-in components using an extension to create a simple extension. This extension provides a toolbar with two combo boxes and a button. The first combo box displays all the FeatureLayers in the active Data Frame. Using this combo box, a user can select a FeatureLayer. The second combo box displays numerical fields of the selected FeatureLayer. Clicking the button creates a bar chart of the selected field.

TRY IT OUT   **Creating a Simple Application Extension (SimpleAppExtension.zip)**

1. Create a new ArcMap Add-In project. Name the solution **SimpleAppExtension**. In the Add-Ins Wizard, provide the necessary information in the Welcome page, and then click the Next button. Select Extension as the type of add-in, provide the information shown in Figure 14-1, and click Finish. Make sure that you check the Show in Extension Manager check box.

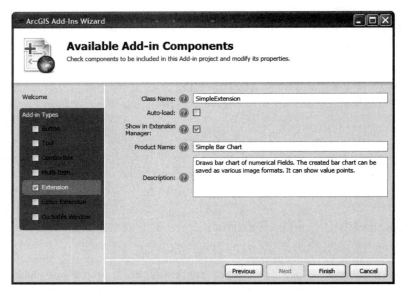

FIGURE 14-1

2. Add a new Add-In component to your project. Name it **cboFields** and choose ComboBox as the type of Add-In component. Configure the combo box as illustrated in Figure 14-2. Click the Finish button. This combo box will hold the names of numerical fields.

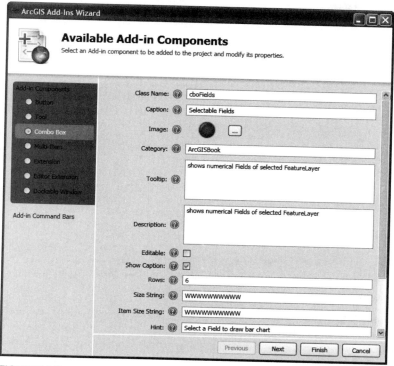

FIGURE 14-2

3. Since you need to access the functionality of this combo box from other components in this Add-In project, you have to use the techniques described in previous sections of this chapter. In summary, you need to find out which item (name of a field) in this combo box the user selects. In addition, this combo box must provide the means for adding and clearing items. The following code illustrates the implementation of the cboFields.cs class:

```
public class cboFields : ESRI.ArcGIS.Desktop.AddIns.ComboBox
    {
        private static cboFields s_cboFields;
        private static string s_selectedField;

        public cboFields()
        {
            s_cboFields = this;
        }
        //override methods
        protected override void OnUpdate()
        {
            //the state of this Add-In component must be controlled by the extension
        }
        protected override void OnSelChange(int cookie)
        {
            //if user selects nothing
            if (cookie < 0)
            { return; }
```

```
            s_selectedField = this.GetItem(cookie).Caption;
        }

        //for sharing functionality
        internal static string GetSelectedField()
        {
            return s_selectedField;
        }

        internal static void ClearAllItems()
        {
            s_selectedField = null;
            s_cboFields.Clear();
        }

        internal static void AddItem(string fieldName)
        {
            s_cboFields.Add(fieldName);
        }
    }
}
```

Note that the state of this component, along with other components, must be managed in an extension class. You do this in later steps of this Try It Out.

4. Add a new Add-In component to your project. Name it **cboFeatureLayers** and choose ComboBox as the type of Add-In component. Configure the combo box as illustrated in Figure 14-3. Click the Finish button. This combo box will hold the names of FeatureLayers in the active Data Frame.

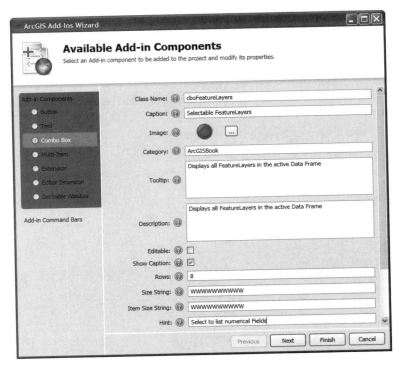

FIGURE 14-3

5. For this combo box, you need to determine which item (name of a FeatureLayer) in this combo box is selected by the user. In addition, this combo box must provide the means for adding and clearing items. More importantly, when a user clicks on any item (name of a FeatureLayer) the numerical fields of the selected FeatureLayer must be added to the cboFields combo box. So add a reference to ESRI.ArcGIS.Carto and ESRI.ArcGIS.Geodatabase using the Add ArcGIS Reference command inside the Solution Explorer window, and then type the following using directives at the top of cboFeatureLayers.cs:

```
using ESRI.ArcGIS.Carto;
using ESRI.ArcGIS.Geodatabase;
using ESRI.ArcGIS.ArcMapUI;
```

The following code illustrates the implementation of the cboFeatureLayers.cs class:

```
public class cboFeatureLayers : ESRI.ArcGIS.Desktop.AddIns.ComboBox
    {
        private static cboFeatureLayers s_cboFeatureLayers;
        private static string s_selectedFeatureLayer;

        public cboFeatureLayers()
        {
            s_cboFeatureLayers = this;
        }

        protected override void OnUpdate()
        {
            //the state of this Add-In component must be controlled by the extension
        }

        protected override void OnSelChange(int cookie)
        {
            if (cookie < 0)
            { return; }
            s_selectedFeatureLayer = this.GetItem(cookie).Caption;

            //populate  cboFields
            cboFields.ClearAllItems();
            IMxDocument mxdoc = ArcMap.Document as IMxDocument;
            IMap map = mxdoc.FocusMap;

            for (int i = 0; i < map.LayerCount; i++)
            {
                if (map.Layer[i] is IFeatureLayer &&
                map.Layer[i].Name == s_selectedFeatureLayer)
                {
                    IFeatureClass fClass = ((map.Layer[i]) as
                    IFeatureLayer).FeatureClass;
                    for (int j = 0; j < fClass.Fields.FieldCount; j++)
                    {
                        switch (fClass.Fields.Field[j].Type)
                        {
                            case esriFieldType.esriFieldTypeDouble:
                            case esriFieldType.esriFieldTypeInteger:
                            case esriFieldType.esriFieldTypeSingle:
                            case esriFieldType.esriFieldTypeSmallInteger:
```

```
                                     cboFields.AddItem(fClass.Fields.Field[j].Name);
                                     break;
                                 }
                             }
                             //since selected featureLayer is found there is no need to
                             //continue
                             break;
                         }
                     }
             }

             //for sharing functionality
             internal static string GetSelectedFeatureLayer()
             {
                 return s_selectedFeatureLayer;
             }

             internal static void ClearAllItems()
             {
                 s_selectedFeatureLayer = null;
                 s_cboFeatureLayers.Clear();
             }

             internal static void AddItem(string featureLayerName)
             {
                 s_cboFeatureLayers.Add(featureLayerName);
             }
         }
```

As you might have guessed, wiring events for adding or removing FeatureLayers to an active Data Frame will be implemented in an extension class.

6. Go to the extension class file (SimpleExtension.cs) and type the following using directives at the top of the code file:

```
using ESRI.ArcGIS.esriSystem;
using ESRI.ArcGIS.Carto;
using ESRI.ArcGIS.Desktop.AddIns;
using ESRI.ArcGIS.ArcMapUI;
```

Then delete all methods inside SimpleExtension except its empty constructor.

Your extension class should be similar to the following code snippet:

```
public class SimpleExtension : ESRI.ArcGIS.Desktop.AddIns.Extension
    {
        public SimpleExtension()
        {
        }
    }
```

7. You are going to use this extension as a central point to coordinate the state of other components in your Add-In project. So you need a static variable of type SimpleExtension to get the state of the extension.

You also want to handle ItemAdded and ItemDeleted events, which are defined on the IActiveViewEvents_Event interface. This interface is implemented by the Map class. So you need a variable of type IMap that can be accessed inside the SimpleExtension class. Add the following lines of code to the SimpleExtension class at the top of the class block and outside any method:

```
private IMap map;
private static SimpleExtension s_extension;
```

8. A few blocks of code must be called by other methods in the extension. For the purpose of reusability, you can group them into some helper methods. Enter the following methods in your SimpleExtension class:

```
// helper methods
private void InitializeExtension()
{
    if (s_extension == null || this.State != ExtensionState.Enabled)
    { return; }

    // event wiring (registering and attaching event handlers to events)
    IMxDocument mxdoc = ArcMap.Document as IMxDocument;
    map = mxdoc.FocusMap;
    IActiveViewEvents_Event activeviewEvents = map as
    IActiveViewEvents_Event;
    activeviewEvents.ItemAdded += new
    IActiveViewEvents_ItemAddedEventHandler(LayerAddedOrDeleted);
    activeviewEvents.ItemDeleted += new
    IActiveViewEvents_ItemDeletedEventHandler(LayerAddedOrDeleted);

    FillcboFeatureLayers();
}
private void LayerAddedOrDeleted(object Item)
{
    map = ArcMap.Document.FocusMap;
    FillcboFeatureLayers();
}
private void FillcboFeatureLayers()
{
    cboFields.ClearAllItems();
    cboFeatureLayers.ClearAllItems();

    // Loop through the layers in the map and add the layer's name to the
    //combo box.
    for (int i = 0; i < map.LayerCount; i++)
    {
        if (map.Layer[i] is IFeatureLayer)
        {
            cboFeatureLayers.AddItem(map.Layer[i].Name);
        }
    }
}
private void UnInitializeExtension()
{
    if (s_extension == null)
        return;

    // Detach event handlers
```

```
IActiveViewEvents_Event activeviewEvents = map as
IActiveViewEvents_Event;
activeviewEvents.ItemAdded -= LayerAddedOrDeleted;
activeviewEvents.ItemDeleted -= LayerAddedOrDeleted;
activeviewEvents = null;

cboFields.ClearAllItems();
cboFeatureLayers.ClearAllItems();
}
```

9. At this point, you have grouped most of the logic of your extension in the preceding helper methods. So you invoke these helper methods in the methods that are actually called by ArcObjects and users when certain methods such as OnStartup() and OnShutDown() are called.

First you are going to implement the OnStartup() method of your extension. Inside the SimpleExtension class and outside any method, type **protected override** followed by a space and you will see that Visual Studio displays all methods that can be overridden. Nearly at the end of the list, select OnStartup() and press Enter. The OnStartup() method is the place where you must initialize your extension and wire it to any desired event. This method is called by ArcObjects when the extension is loaded. Enter the following code snippet that illustrates the OnStartup() method:

```
protected override void OnStartup()
        {
             s_extension = this;
             InitializeExtension();
        }
```

10. In contrast to OnStartup(), OnShutdown() is called when the extension is unloaded by ArcObjects. This situation usually happens when a user closes any of the ArcGIS for Desktop applications. So OnShutdown() is the place for cleanup. Enter the following code in the SimpleExtension class:

```
protected override void OnShutdown()
        {
             UnInitializeExtension();
             map = null;
             s_extension = null;
             base.OnShutdown();
        }
```

11. Because your extension is displayed in the Extension Manager window, you have to provide implementation for two other methods that are called by ArcObjects when users toggle the extension in the Extension Manager window. Add the following methods in the SimpleExtension class:

```
    protected override bool OnSetState(ExtensionState state)
        {
             this.State = state;
             if (state == ExtensionState.Enabled)
             {
                 InitializeExtension();
             }
             else
             {
```

```
            UnInitializeExtension();
        }
        return true;
    }

    protected override ExtensionState OnGetState()
    {
        return this.State;
    }
```

In addition to toggling the extension in the Extension Manager window, when the extension is loaded, `OnSetState()` will be called by ArcObjects. Note that regardless of the value of the state parameter, the `OnSetState()` method should always return `true`. If it returns `false`, the extension will be locked and it cannot be activated or deactivated.

12. It is time to create methods for coordination of the state of other components in this Add-In project. Because your Add-In extension is a simple one, you just need to provide code for enabling or disabling the other components. Add the following methods at the end of your extension class (`SimpleExtension.cs`):

```
//static method
//for managing and coordinating the state of other components
internal static bool IsExtensionEnabled()
{
    if (s_extension == null)
    {
        GetTheExtension();
    }

    if (s_extension == null)
    {
        return false;
    }

    if (s_extension.State == ExtensionState.Enabled)
    {
        return true;
    }
    else
    {
        return false;
    }
}

private static SimpleExtension GetTheExtension()
{
    // Call FindExtension method to create the s_extension
    // if the extension has been checked in the Extensions window

    UID extensionID = new UIDClass();
    extensionID.Value = ThisAddIn.IDs.SimpleExtension;
    ArcMap.Application.FindExtensionByCLSID(extensionID);
    return s_extension;
}
```

When the extension is enabled beforehand in ArcMap, s_extension is null (because OnStartup() is not called). If you start ArcMap, the extension is not loaded even if it was enabled in the Extension Manager window. In this case, the extension is loaded when you enable its toolbar or you open the Extension Manager window. This way, the start-up time for ArcGIS for Desktop applications is reduced significantly. The extensions that load only when they are needed are called Just-In-Time (JIT) extensions.

The FindExtensionByCLSID() function can load all the extensions available in ArcGIS for Desktop applications (standard and JIT extensions). So you use the FindExtensionByCLSID() method to access the State property of the s_extension variable.

13. You will use the IsExtensionEnabled() method of the SimpleExtension class to manage the state of other components in your Add-In project. So change the OnUpdate() methods of the two combo boxes to match the following code:

```
protected override void OnUpdate()
{
    //the state of this Add-In component must be controlled by the extension
    this.Enabled = SimpleExtension.IsExtensionEnabled();
}
```

14. Add another Add-In component to your project. Name it **CreateBarChart** and select Button as the type of component. Configure the button as shown in Figure 14-4 and click Finish.

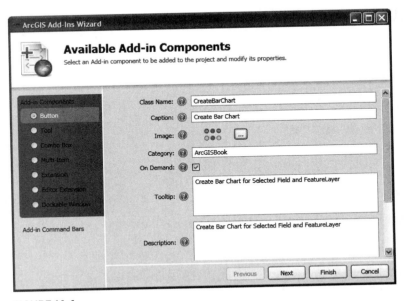

FIGURE 14-4

15. At the moment, you can only implement the button's OnUpdate() method. In fact, all the components in this Add-In project have the same implementation for this method. So enter the following code in CreateBarChart.cs to synchronize the state of the button with the state of the extension:

```
protected override void OnUpdate()
    {
        this.Enabled = SimpleExtension.IsExtensionEnabled();        }
```

You are going to implement the button's `OnClick()` method later in this Try It Out.

16. Add an Add-In component container. Name it **SimpleExtensionToolbar** and select Toolbar as the type of command container. Change the settings of the toolbar to match Figure 14-5.

At this point, you have a chance to test the functionality of the extension. So run the code and add some feature layers to your map. You should see the extension (SimpleExtension) in the Extensions window. Remember that it is not finished yet and you have to provide logic to create the bar chart and implement the button's `OnClick()` event.

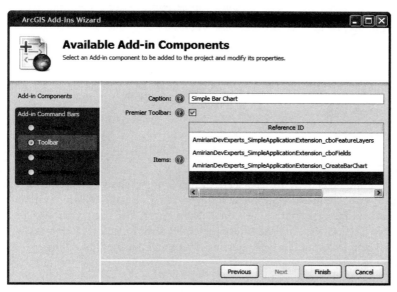

FIGURE 14-5

17. In order to create a bar chart for the selected field, you are going to use the ZedGraph component. ZedGraph is an open source .NET control for creating flexible charts and graphs. You can download it freely from `http://sourceforge.net/projects/zedgraph`. After downloading it, add a reference to `ZedGraph.dll` using the Add Reference command in the Solution Explorer window. This time use the Browse tab to find the ZedGraph assembly.

18. You need to add the ZedGraph control to your Toolbox dockable window in Visual Studio. Right-click somewhere in the Toolbox dockable window and select Choose Items from the context menu. As shown in Figure 14-6, in the Choose Toolbox Items window under the .NET Framework Components tab, click the Browse button to point to the `.dll` file you have downloaded for ZedGraph. By doing this, you have added ZedGraph to the list of components that can be used in Visual Studio. To add ZedGraph as a control (that can be used in Windows Forms projects) you need to find the ZedGraphControl item (under the .NET Framework Components tab), check the check box next to it, and then click OK. The ZedGraphControl is added to the Visual Studio Toolbox.

19. Add a Windows Form to your project and name it **frmBarchart**. Double-click the ZedGraphControl to add an instance of it to frmBarchart. In the Properties window, rename it to **zgc**. There is no need to set its location and size; the control will be configured in code. In the Solution Explorer window, double-click

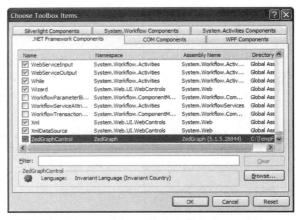

FIGURE 14-6

on frmBarchart to open it in the designer. Type the following using directives at the top of the frmBarchart.cs file:

```
using ZedGraph;
using ESRI.ArcGIS.Geodatabase;
using ESRI.ArcGIS.Carto;
using ESRI.ArcGIS.Desktop;
using ESRI.ArcGIS.ArcMapUI;
using ESRI.ArcGIS.esriSystem;
```

20. This form will have two public properties for the selected field and selected FeatureLayer. Based on the values of these properties, a FeatureCursor will populate two arrays of values and names for all features in the FeatureClass associated with the FeatureLayer. Use the primary display field of FeatureLayer for the feature names. Add the following code in the frmBarchart class — it contains public properties and three methods for getting data and creating a bar chart:

```
public string ValueFieldName { get; set; }
        public string FeatureLayerName { set; get; }



        private void chartFormResize()
        {
            zgc.Location = new Point(10, 10);
            zgc.Size = new Size(ClientRectangle.Width - 20,
            ClientRectangle.Height - 20);
        }
        private void CreateBarchart(ZedGraphControl zgc)
        {
            GraphPane pane = zgc.GraphPane;
            pane.Fill = new Fill(Color.MistyRose);
            pane.Title.Text = string.Format("Bar Chart for {0} Field of {1}",
            this.ValueFieldName, this.FeatureLayerName);
            pane.XAxis.Title.Text = "Features";
            pane.YAxis.Title.Text = "Values for " + this.ValueFieldName;
```

```
            pane.XAxis.Type = AxisType.Text;

            string[] nameOfFeatures = null;
            double[] valuesOfFeatures = null;
            FillDataArrays(out nameOfFeatures, out valuesOfFeatures);

            BarItem bar = pane.AddBar(this.ValueFieldName, null, valuesOfFeatures,
            Color.Red);
            pane.XAxis.Scale.TextLabels = nameOfFeatures;
            pane.XAxis.MajorGrid.IsVisible = true;
            pane.XAxis.MajorGrid.PenWidth = 2f;
            pane.YAxis.MajorGrid.IsVisible = true;

            pane.Legend.IsVisible = false;
            pane.Chart.Fill = new Fill(Color.White, Color.Blue, 45f);
            //draw the chart
            zgc.AxisChange();
        }
        private void FillDataArrays(out string[] nameOfFeatures, out double[]
    valuesOfFeatures)
        {
            try
            {
                IMxDocument mxdoc = ArcMap.Application.Document as IMxDocument;
                IMap map = mxdoc.FocusMap;
                IFeatureLayer fLayer = null;
                for (int j = 0; j < map.LayerCount; j++)
                {
                    if (map.Layer[j].Name == this.FeatureLayerName && map.Layer[j]
                    is IFeatureLayer)
                    {
                        fLayer = map.Layer[j] as IFeatureLayer;
                        break;
                    }
                }
                if (fLayer == null)
                {
                    nameOfFeatures = null; valuesOfFeatures = null;
                    return;

                }

                IFeatureClass fClass = fLayer.FeatureClass;
                int idxNameField = fClass.Fields.FindField(fLayer.DisplayField);
                int idxValueField = fClass.Fields.FindField(this.ValueFieldName);

                int numberOfFeatures = fClass.FeatureCount(null);
                nameOfFeatures = new string[numberOfFeatures];
                valuesOfFeatures = new double[numberOfFeatures];

                IFeatureCursor fCursor = fClass.Search(null, true);
                IFeature feature = fCursor.NextFeature();
                int i = 0;
                while (feature != null)
                {
```

```
                    if (feature.Value[idxNameField] != null)
                    {
                        nameOfFeatures[i] = Convert.ToString(feature.
                        Value[idxNameField]);
                    }
                    else
                    {
                        nameOfFeatures[i] = "";
                    }

                    if (feature.Value[idxValueField] != null)
                    {
                        valuesOfFeatures[i] = Convert.ToDouble(feature.
                        Value[idxValueField]);
                    }
                    else
                    {
                        valuesOfFeatures[i] = 0;
                    }

                    i++;
                    feature = fCursor.NextFeature();
                }
                //releasing the Cursor object
                System.Runtime.InteropServices.Marshal.ReleaseComObject(fCursor);
            }
            catch (Exception ex)
            {
                nameOfFeatures = null; valuesOfFeatures = null;
                MessageBox.Show(ex.Message);
            }
        }
```

21. Double-click on the form to make Visual Studio create the stub code for the Load event handler and call the CreateBarchart() and chartFormResize() methods in this event handler.

```
        private void frmBarchart_Load(object sender, EventArgs e)
        {
            CreateBarchart(zgc);
            chartFormResize();
        }
```

22. Next, handle the resize event of frmBarchart. Go to the Design window. From the list of events in the Properties window, double-click the Resize event, and type the following code as the handler for this event:

```
    private void frmBarchart_Resize(object sender, EventArgs e)
        {
            chartFormResize();
        }
```

> **NOTE** By default, the Properties window displays a list of the properties of the selected object, such as a Windows Form. If you want access to the list of events, you need to press the Events button in the Properties window.

23. The final step in building this add-in is to provide logic for the button's `OnClick()` method. Go to the `CreateBarchart.cs` class file and implement the `OnClick()` method to match the following code:

```
protected override void OnClick()
        {
            frmBarchart chartForm = new frmBarchart();
            chartForm.FeatureLayerName = cboFeatureLayers.
            GetSelectedFeatureLayer();
            chartForm.ValueFieldName = cboFields.
            GetSelectedField();
            if (chartForm.ValueFieldName == null || chartForm.
            FeatureLayerName == null)
            {
                string errorMsg = "Please select a FeatureLayer
                and a Field";
                System.Windows.Forms.MessageBox.Show(errorMsg);
                return;
            }

            chartForm.ShowDialog();
        }
```

24. Run your project. In ArcMap, select Extensions from the Customize menu. You can see your simple extension (Simple Bar Chart) listed in the available extensions. If it is not enabled, enable it by checking its check box in the Extensions window. See Figure 14-7.

25. Again from the Customize menu, select the Toolbars item and find and display the Simple Bar Chart toolbar. Add some layers to your active Data Frame and test the functionality of this simple extension. You should get something like Figure 14-8 if you use the `States` feature class of `TemplateData.gdb` and the POP 2000 field.

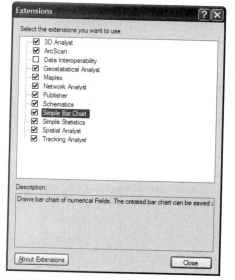

FIGURE 14-7

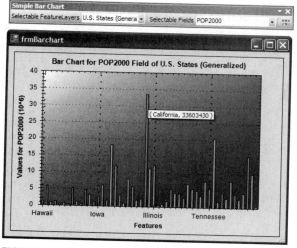

FIGURE 14-8

How It Works

This is the longest Try It Out in this book, and the most complete one. Since you don't check the Auto-load check box when you add the extension, your extension is a JIT extension (refer to Figure 14-1). You can also change or see this attribute in the XML configuration file of the add-in (Config.esriaddinx). The type of extension is controlled by the autoLoad attribute in the Extension element in the configuration file. If the value of the autoLoad attribute is true, the extension will be a standard extension, meaning that the extension is loaded when an ArcGIS for Desktop application starts and unloaded when the application closes. The following XML fragment illustrates a JIT extension:

```
<Extension id="AmirianDevExperts_SimpleApplicationExtension_
SimpleExtension" class="SimpleExtension" productName="Simple Bar
Chart" showInExtensionDialog="true" autoLoad="false">
```

The default value for the autoLoad attribute is false; for this reason, if you uncheck the Auto-load check box in the ArcGIS Add-Ins Wizard, this attribute doesn't appear in the Extension element in the configuration file. JIT extensions need more code to handle the state of the extension, but they provide faster startup performance in comparison with standard extensions.

ADD-IN DEPLOYMENT

As mentioned in Chapter 2, developing and customizing ArcGIS for Desktop applications using the Add-In model provides some advantages when compared with other methods of developing and extending ArcGIS for Desktop applications. One of the most important advantages of the Add-In model is its deployment approach. In fact, deployment of an add-in is almost the same as distributing any type of ordinary file (such as an *.mp3 file) and includes copying and pasting the file without the need for administrative privileges or alteration of the system registry.

Preparing for Release

Before copying and pasting the add-in, you need to prepare it for release. Up to this point in the development phase, you needed the debug capability of Visual Studio. Now, because you are going to release your add-in to its users, you are in deployment phase and there is no need for the debug capability. The only step required for preparing your add-in is changing the configuration of the Add-In solution from Debug to Release.

Look at the contents of the Add-In's Visual Studio solution bin folder (for example, D:\SimpleAddinExtension\SimpleAddinExtension\bin). You will find two other folders: Debug and Release. These two folders are created by Visual Studio for Debug and Release modes, respectively. Take a look inside the Release folder and you will see that the folder is empty because the active configuration of all types of solutions and projects (including Desktop Add-In) is Debug by default. For this reason, each time you run your code, Visual Studio will build an add-in inside the Debug folder of your add-in's bin folder. Look at the contents of the Debug folder to meet your add-in.

To change the configuration of your Add-In solution, change the configuration of your solution from Debug to Release using the Solution Configurations combo box in the Standard toolbar of Visual Studio, as shown in Figure 14-9.

FIGURE 14-9

Alternatively, you can right-click on your Add-In solution in the Solution Explorer window and choose Properties. In the Solution Property Pages, if you click on Configuration Properties ➪ Configuration node in the left pane, as shown in Figure 14-10, you can change the configuration of the solution.

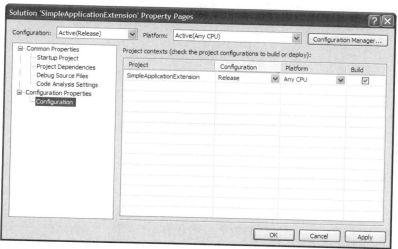

FIGURE 14-10

After changing the Solution Configuration from Debug to Release, press F6 or select Build Solution from the Build menu to create the output of your solution (the Add-In file with an .esriAddIn extension).

Since the Visual Studio in Release mode removes all the debug symbols from code and performs some code optimizations, if you build the add-in solution in Release mode, the output add-in (in the Release folder) is smaller than the same add-in in Debug mode.

NOTE *In addition to solutions, projects have configurations that can be Debug or Release. Note that if you have set the configuration of your solution to Debug, changing the configuration mode of a project from Debug to Release doesn't build your add-in in the Release folder, but the reverse is not true. In other words, solutions have control of the configuration mode of all containing projects. For this reason, you need just to change the configuration mode of the solution when preparing it for release. You can see the configuration of projects in the Build tab of the project's Property page (see Figure 14-11).*

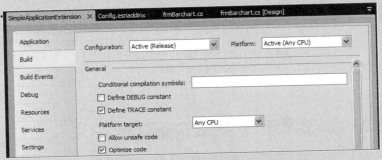

FIGURE 14-11

After changing the project configuration to Release, the debugging capability of Visual Studio is no longer available, even if you have some breakpoints in your code and execution of the code reaches those breakpoints.

Add-In File Structure

Your add-in is a file with the `.esriAddIn` file extension. This single file is a zipped folder that contains all your Add-In components and resources. Change the file extension of your add-in to `.zip` and you will see the actual contents of the add-in. Most add-ins contain two folders (Images and Install) and at least one `Config.xml` file. The `Config.xml` file contains add-in metadata and its content is exactly the same as the `Config.esriaddinx` file you have worked with in Visual Studio. In fact, `Config.esriaddinx` is renamed to `Config.xml` during the Build process.

The images of your Add-In components are stored as `.png` files inside the Images folder. The Install folder contains your Add-In assembly (as a `.dll` file). Other resources are also copied to the Install folder of your add-in if you have used them. For example, in the case of SimpleApplicationExtension, the Install folder of the add-in includes `SimpleApplicationExtension.dll` and `ZedGraph.dll`. All other folders inside the Install folder contain satellite assemblies for ZedGraph.

> **NOTE** *Satellite assemblies are resources for different languages and locales. They contain localized resources and are loaded by the .NET Framework. The .NET Framework will locate and load a suitable satellite assembly that matches the culture and locale of the user. For more information on localization in the .NET Framework, consult the .NET documentation.*

Distributing and Installing an Add-In

One nice feature of Add-Ins is that in order to distribute them, there is no need to build a setup or installation package for them. When you want to share your developed add-in, all you need to do is copy it to media like a USB flash drive, e-mail it, or even upload it to a website.

On the user's machine, to make the Add-In files discoverable by ArcGIS for Desktop applications, he or she needs to put them in well-known folders. In other words, Add-In files are automatically discovered and loaded by ArcGIS for Desktop applications from well-known folders and plugged into the desktop applications at runtime.

By default, based on a user's operating system, a user has the following local well-known folder:

➤ **Windows 7 and Vista:** `<Windows Installation Drive>:\Users\<your user name>\Documents\ArcGIS\AddIns\Desktop10.x`

➤ **Windows XP:** `<Windows Installation Drive>:\Document and Settings\<your user name>\My Documents\ArcGIS\AddIns\Desktop10.x`

In addition to the default local well-known folder, the user can specify other folders as well-known folders on his or her machine using the Add-In Manager window in ArcMap. To open the Add-In Manager window, select Customize ➪ Add-In Manager.

Besides the local well-known folders, the user can also specify any shared folder in a network as a shared well-known folder. By doing this, the add-in in the shared well-known folder can be used by anyone who has access to that folder through the network.

To install an add-in, copy it to a well-known folder. This can be done manually or automatically by using the Esri ArcGIS Add-In Installation utility. For the manual approach, users can simply copy and paste the Add-In file into a well-known folder. Figure 14-12 displays the ListenerComboBox.esriAddIn, which is copied to the default local well-known folder. When you manually copy and paste add-ins, if two or more add-ins have the same name, a name conflict will occur.

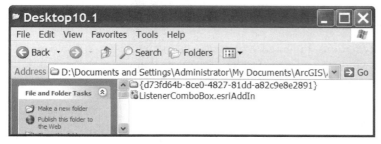

FIGURE 14-12

If a user double-clicks the Add-In file, the Esri ArcGIS Add-In Installation utility pops up, gets the metadata of the add-in, and displays this information to the user. This information can be used by users or organizations for making decisions about the installation and usage of the add-in. If the user decides to install the add-in, the Esri ArcGIS Add-In Installation utility creates a subfolder under the default well-known folder of the user's machine and then copies the add-in into the subfolder. The name of the subfolder is the GUID of the add-in which is defined as the content of the `AddInID` element inside the configuration file, shown in the following code:

```
<Name>SimpleApplicationExtension</Name>
  <AddInID>{ea68dcf0-8ea8-4e87-8e8d-f168f786ed22}</AddInID>
```

Figure 14-13 displays the default well-known folder after installation of the SimpleApplicationExtension Add-In.

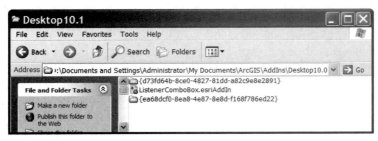

FIGURE 14-13

Creating a subfolder named with the Add-In's GUID prevents naming conflicts. Always use the Esri ArcGIS Add-In Installation utility to install the add-ins.

As mentioned previously, it is possible to specify a shared folder on the network as a local well-known folder using the Add-In Manager window. Using a network shared well-known folder is a better approach for distributing add-ins for multiple users within an organization. In this case, add-ins are loaded when the ArcGIS for Desktop applications of the users run; if a newer version of an add-in is needed, one can easily overwrite the existing version in a shared well-known folder. Next time, when the users restart ArcGIS for Desktop applications, they can make use of the newer version.

As stated in the beginning of this section, deployment of an add-in includes copying and pasting the file without the need for administrative privileges or alteration of the system registry. This doesn't mean that administrators don't have enough control of using add-ins. In fact, the system administrator can restrict usage of add-ins.

There are three different security options, ranging from most secure to least secure, for loading add-ins in the Add-In Manager window, under the Options tab. Note that the user can change these options freely. The administrator can restrict the setting made by a user through the system registry. Log into the system as an administrator to change the Windows Registry. Then find the `BlockAddIns` value. This value is located inside HKEY_LOCAL_MACHINE\SOFTWARE\ESRI\ Desktop10.x\Settings for 32-bit Windows machines and inside HKEY_LOCAL_MACHINE\ SOFTWARE\Wow6432Node\ESRI\Desktop10.x\Settings for 64-bit Windows machines. Figure 14-14 displays the `BlockAddIns` value for 64-bit Windows machines.

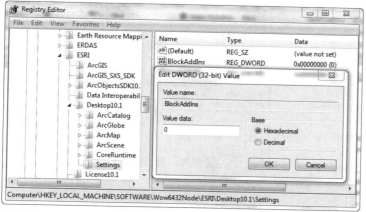

FIGURE 14-14

The administrator can set the value of `BlockAddIns` to one of the values shown in Table 14-1.

TABLE 14-1: Values of BlockAddIns Key

VALUE	PURPOSE
0	Load all add-ins (least secure option)
1	Load digitally signed add-ins
2	Load just Esri add-ins
3	Load Esri add-ins (just like value 2) and load add-ins from the administrator folders
4	Do not load any add-in at all

Note that the user can only use the Add-In Manager window to change the security to something *more* secure than the setting made by the administrator. By default, the data of the `BlockAddIns` value is 0. As a result, the user can change the security of the add-in to any level. Suppose that the administrator changes the data of `BlockAddIns` to 2. At this setting, ArcGIS for Desktop applications just loads Esri add-ins and there is nothing to be changed in the Options tab of the Add-In Manager window. In other words, the other two options in the Add-In Manager window are disabled (see Figure 14-15).

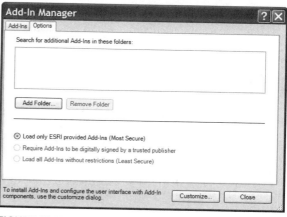

FIGURE 14-15

If `BlockAddIns` is set to 3, add-ins can be loaded if they were published by Esri or they are inside the administrator folders. The administrator folders are ordinary folders that contain add-ins and are defined in the registry using the `AddInFolders` key under the `Settings` key. To specify an administrator folder, go to the system registry and, based on your Windows operating system version, find the `Settings` subkey. Right-click the `Settings` key and from the context menu, select New ⇨ Key to insert a key beneath the

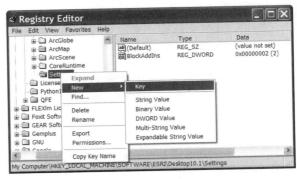

FIGURE 14-16

`Settings` key. Rename the new key to **AddInFolders**. Figure 14-16 illustrates this procedure for creating an AddInFolders key in 32-bit Windows.

With AddInFolders selected in the left pane, right-click in the right pane and insert New ⇨ String Value. Double-click the string value and enter the physical address of the folder. You can add as many administrator folders as you need. Administrator folders make it easier to control the security of add-ins.

CUSTOM COMPONENT DEPLOYMENT

One of the most important features of custom component development is flexibility in deployment. In fact, deployment of a custom component is almost the same as distributing and installing any type of software and includes creating setup packages, registering components, creating folders, and so forth on the host machine. For this reason, installing a custom component needs administrative privileges and modification of the system registry.

Fortunately, most of the registration and modification can be done using software tools designed for creating software packages and installers such as InstallShield, Smart Install Maker, and the Setup project template in Visual Studio. In the following Try It Out, first you create a very simple custom component, and then you learn to create and customize a setup project for custom components.

TRY IT OUT   Creating a Very Simple Custom Component
(VerySimpleCustomComponent.zip)

1. Create a new ArcMap Class Library project (from the left pane, select ArcGIS ⇨ Extending ArcObjects). Name the solution **VerySimpleCustomComponent**. In the ArcGIS Project Wizard, add references to ESRI.ArcGIS.Carto and ESRI.ArcGIS.ArcMapUI, and then click Finish.

2. Delete the `Class1.cs` file, right-click on your project in the Solution Explorer window, and choose New Item from the Add submenu. In the left pane of the Add New Item window, expand the ArcGIS node and select Extending ArcObjects. Select Base Command and name it **RemoveSelectedLayer**. Click the Add button. In the ArcGIS New Item Wizard Options, select Desktop ArcMap Command (as shown in Figure 14-17), and then click OK.

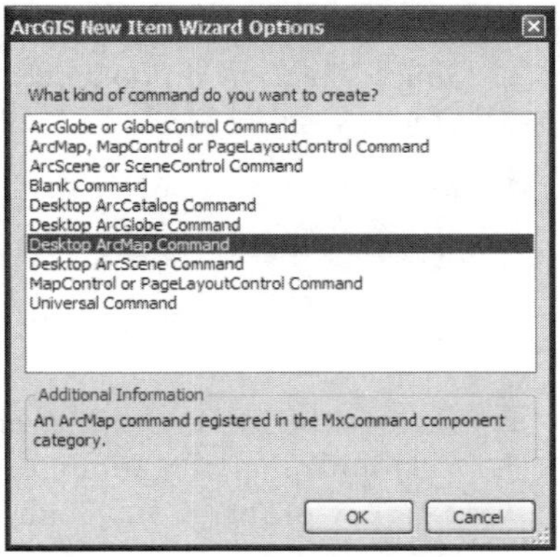

3. Add the following using directive at the top of the RemoveSelectedLayer.cs file:

```
using ESRI.ArcGIS.Carto;
```

Then modify the class constructor to match the following code snippet:

```
public RemoveSelectedLayer()
        {
        base.m_category = "ArcGISBook";
        base.m_caption = "Removes the Selected FeatureLayer";
        base.m_message = "Removes the selected FeatureLayer in TOC";
        base.m_toolTip = "Removes the selected FeatureLayer in TOC";
        base.m_name = "RemovesFeatureLayerinTOC_SimpleCustomComponent";

        try
        {
            string bitmapResourceName = GetType().Name + ".bmp";
            base.m_bitmap = new Bitmap(GetType(), bitmapResourceName);
        }
        catch (Exception ex)
        {
            System.Diagnostics.Trace.WriteLine(ex.Message, "Invalid Bitmap");
        }
    }
```

FIGURE 14-17

4. Add a few lines of code in the OnClick() method to remove the selected item (which will be null if no item is selected) from the Table Of Contents in ArcMap if it is of type IFeatureLayer in the OnClick() method.

```
public override void OnClick()
        {
        IMxDocument mxdoc = m_application.Document as IMxDocument;
        IActiveView activeView = mxdoc.ActiveView;
        IMap map = mxdoc.FocusMap;
        IContentsView contentsView = mxdoc.CurrentContentsView;
        object selectedItem = contentsView.SelectedItem;

        if (selectedItem is IFeatureLayer)
        {
            map.DeleteLayer(selectedItem as ILayer);
            activeView.Refresh();
            contentsView.Refresh(null);
        }
    }
```

5. Add a new item to your project, select Base Toolbar as the type of component, and name it SimpleCustomComponentToolbar. Then click the Add button. In the ArcGIS New Item Wizard Options, select Desktop ArcMap as shown in Figure 14-18, and click OK.

6. Modify the constructor of the toolbar to place the button as shown in the following code snippet:

```
public CustomComponentToolbar()
        {
            AddItem("VerySimpleCustomComponent.RemoveSelectedLayer");
        }
```

7. Change the caption of the toolbar to CustomComponentToolbar. For this task, you can find the Caption property and change its value. Press F5 to run and test your code.

How It Works

In this Try It Out, you created a very simple custom component. This custom component can be added to any toolbar or menu of ArcMap using the Customize window. In other words, since the RemoveSelectedLayer command is registered in the MxCommands category, it can be used in ArcMap. You can find all the available categories using the ArcGIS Component Category Registrar window. From the Project menu, select Add Component Category. As you can see in Figure 14-19, the command (RemoveSelectedLayer) is registered in the MxCommands category. As a result, the mentioned command will be shown in the Customize dialog box of the ArcMap.

FIGURE 14-18

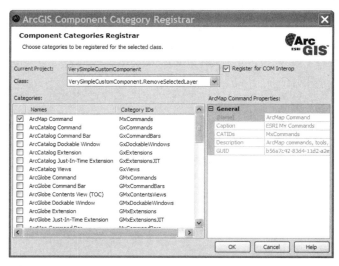

FIGURE 14-19

If the custom component works in its designed way, change the solution configuration to Release and rebuild it.

Creating an Installer for a Custom Component

Usually software tools that make installers and packages are used to create an .msi (Microsoft Installer) file for a custom component. In order to create an .msi file, use the Setup and Deployment template. In the next Try It Out, you learn the typical procedure for creating an installer package for a custom component.

Creating an Installation Package for Very Simple Custom Component (InstallationVerySimpleCustomComponent.zip)

1. Open your solution (VerySimpleCustomComponent.sln), then in the Solution Explorer window, right-click on the solution and choose New Project from the Add submenu.

2. Expand Other Project Types and select Visual Studio Installer from the Setup and Deployment node. Then select Setup Project and name it **SimpleSetup**, as shown in Figure 14-20. Click OK.

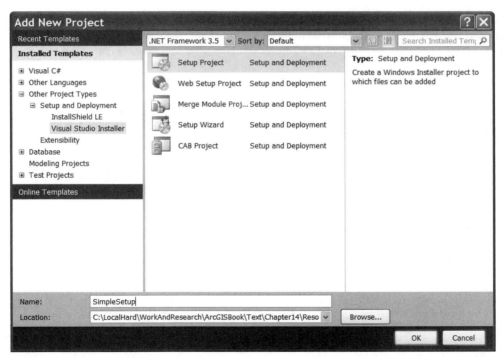

FIGURE 14-20

3. With the SimpleSetup project selected in Solution Explorer, click the File System Editor button at the top of the Solution Explorer window, as shown in Figure 14-21, to display the file system on the target machine.

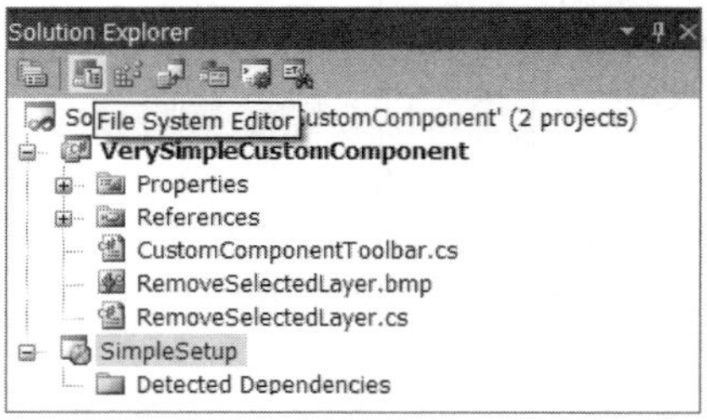

4. Right-click on the Application Folder node and choose Project Output from the Add submenu. Next, select the primary output of the VerySimpleCustomComponent, and then press OK.

FIGURE 14-21

5. At this moment, Visual Studio checks the dependencies of VerySimpleCustomComponent.dll (the primary output) and adds all the needed .dll files to the Application folder on the target machine. Because this custom component will be used inside ArcGIS for Desktop applications, all added Esri assemblies and binary files were installed on the target machine previously. For this reason, you don't need them at all. In addition, distribution of Esri assemblies and binaries is not in line with copyright law and violates the Esri license agreement. So select all Esri assemblies, and from the Properties window, select Exclude to remove them from the setup project (that is, change Exclude from False to True).

6. The final step in packaging a custom component is to register it on the target machine. Those familiar with COM or .NET registration are familiar with RegSvr32.exe or RegAsm.exe for registration of a .dll file. Prior to version 10.0 of ArcGIS, Esri followed the same model of registration, but starting with ArcGIS 10.0, all custom components must be registered using the ESRIRegAsm.exe utility. Your setup package must use this utility to register custom components.

How can you find the ESRIRegAsm.exe utility on the target machine? Look in your registry for the subkey ArcGIS (HKEY_ LOCAL_MACHINE\SOFTWARE\ESRI\ArcGIS for 32-bit Windows and HKEY_LOCAL_ MACHINE\SOFTWARE\Wow6432Node\ESRI\ ArcGIS for 64-bit Windows). It has a value of InstallDir and string data of the folder which contains ESRIRegAsm .exe along with other utilities that ship with ArcGIS. Figure 14-22 illustrates this subkey in the system registry of a 32-bit Windows machine.

FIGURE 14-22

So, for example on your book author's computer, the complete path of the utility will be: D:\Program Files\Common Files\ArcGIS\bin\ESRIRegAsm.exe.

> **NOTE** Based on the type of operating system (64-bit or 32-bit), you will find this subkey in a slightly different path. The registry also contains a lot of other useful information that can be used in ArcObjects programming.

7. For registering custom components at install time, you need to use a special type of Visual Studio class. Right-click your VerySimpleCustomComponent project and select New Item from the Add submenu. Expand Visual C# Items, then select the General node. Find Installer Class in the middle pane, name it **InstallCustomComponent.cs** as shown in Figure 14-23, and click the Add button.

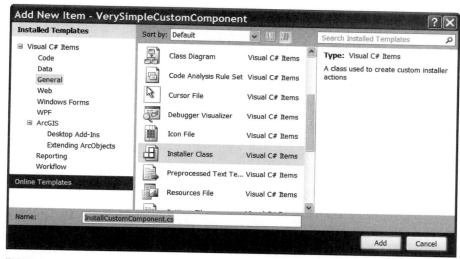

FIGURE 14-23

8. When the Installer class is added to the project, select it in the Solution Explorer window and press F7 to go to code view. Alternatively, you can click on the "Click here to switch to code view" link to go to code view.

9. Add the following using directives at the top of the Installer class:

```
using System.Diagnostics;
using Microsoft.Win32;
```

In this class, you are going to define what methods will handle events such as install and uninstall. So type **public override** and a space in the Installer class to display a list of methods that can be overridden. Select Install and then click the Enter button. Override the Uninstall method for the Installer class too. In both methods you will find the path to the ESRIRegAsm .exe utility. Register or unregister it on the target machine using the appropriate switches as shown in the following code. The following code registers and unregisters your component on 32-bit and 64-bit Windows systems:

```
public override void Install(IDictionary stateSaver)
    {
        base.Install(stateSaver);
        //based on 64 or 32 bit it is different
        string processorArchitecture = Environment.
        GetEnvironmentVariable("PROCESSOR_ARCHITEW6432");
```

```csharp
    bool Is64bit = !string.
    IsNullOrEmpty(processorArchitecture);

    string EsriRegAsm = null;
    //find the folder containing ESRIRegAsm.exe
    string utilityInstallationPath = null;
    if (Is64bit)
    {
        RegistryKey regkey = Registry.LocalMachine.
        OpenSubKey(@"SOFTWARE\Wow6432Node\ESRI\ArcGIS");
        utilityInstallationPath = regkey.
        GetValue("InstallDir").ToString();
        regkey.Close();
    }
    else
    {
        RegistryKey regkey = Registry.LocalMachine.
        OpenSubKey(@"SOFTWARE\ESRI\ArcGIS");
        utilityInstallationPath = regkey.
        GetValue("InstallDir").ToString();
        regkey.Close();
    }
    EsriRegAsm = utilityInstallationPath +
    @"bin\ESRIRegAsm.exe";

    //get from custom action
    string nameOfDll = "VerySimpleCustomComponent.dll";
    string installationFolder = this.Context.
    Parameters["installationDir"];
    string fullPathOfDll = installationFolder + nameOfDll;

    string switches = " /p:Desktop /s";
    string args = "\"" + fullPathOfDll + "\"" + switches;

    //execute using Process class
    int exitCode = ExecuteCommand(EsriRegAsm, args, 10000);
}

public override void Uninstall(IDictionary savedState)
{
    base.Uninstall(savedState);

    //based on 64 or 32 bit it is different
    string processorArchitecture = Environment.
    GetEnvironmentVariable("PROCESSOR_ARCHITEW6432");
    bool Is64bit = !string.
    IsNullOrEmpty(processorArchitecture);

    string EsriRegAsm = null;
    //find the folder containing ESRIRegAsm.exe
    string utilityInstallationPath = null;
    if (Is64bit)
    {
```

```
        RegistryKey regkey = Registry.LocalMachine.
        OpenSubKey(@"SOFTWARE\Wow6432Node\ESRI\ArcGIS");
        utilityInstallationPath = regkey.
        GetValue("InstallDir").ToString();
        regkey.Close();
    }
    else
    {
        RegistryKey regkey = Registry.LocalMachine.
        OpenSubKey(@"SOFTWARE\ESRI\ArcGIS");
        utilityInstallationPath = regkey.
        GetValue("InstallDir").ToString();
        regkey.Close();
    }
    EsriRegAsm = utilityInstallationPath +
    @"bin\ESRIRegAsm.exe";

    string installationFolder = this.Context.
    Parameters["installationDir"];
    string nameOfDll = "VerySimpleCustomComponent.dll";
    string fullPathOfDll = installationFolder + nameOfDll;
    string switches = " /p:Desktop /u /s";

    string args = "\"" + fullPathOfDll + "\"" + switches;

    //execute using Process class
    int exitCode = ExecuteCommand(EsriRegAsm, args, 10000);
}

public static int ExecuteCommand(string exe, string
arguments, int Timeout)
{
    ProcessStartInfo ProcessInfo = new
    ProcessStartInfo(exe, arguments);
    ProcessInfo.CreateNoWindow = true;
    ProcessInfo.UseShellExecute = false;
    ProcessInfo.ErrorDialog = true;
    //execute the Process
    Process Process = Process.Start(ProcessInfo);
    Process.WaitForExit(Timeout);

    int ExitCode = Process.ExitCode;
    Process.Close();
    return ExitCode;
}
```

You can access the installation path of a custom component on the target machine using the `Context.Parameters["installationDir"];` parameter. You see where to set this parameter shortly. Now build your VerySimpleCustomComponent project.

10. In the Solution Explorer window, while you have selected the Setup project, click the Custom Actions Editor button at the top of the Solution Explorer window. Right-click on the Install node and select Add Custom Action. The Select Item in the Project window appears. Go to Application Folder and select Primary output from VerySimpleCustomComponent (Active). Add the same custom action to your Uninstall node. Your Custom Actions window should be similar to Figure 14-24.

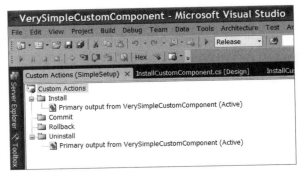

FIGURE 14-24

11. In order to get the installation path of the custom component, select Primary output from VerySimpleCustomComponent(Active) below the Install Custom Action, and in the Properties window enter **/installationDir="[TARGETDIR]\"** as shown in Figure 14-25.

12. Set the same CustomActionData for the Uninstall Custom Action. Build your solution, then build your setup project and test it by right-clicking the setup project (SimpleSetup) in Solution Explorer and selecting Install from the context menu.

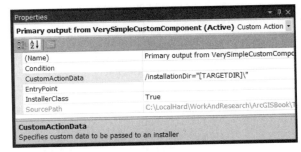

FIGURE 14-25

How It Works

Because the VerySimpleCustomComponent project contains an Installer class, you could specify it as the source of a custom action. In this Try It Out, you used custom actions to register custom components using `ESRIRegAsm.exe`. This utility has different switches that should be used for different purposes — for example, `/p:Desktop` is for the ArcGIS product, `/u` for unregister, and `/s` for silent mode.

In addition, based on your operating system (32- or 64-bit), the path of a utility which can be accessed using a value in registry is different. In this Try It Out, you used the `PROCESSOR_ARCHITEW6432` environment variable to find the type of operating system of the target machine. If you set the target platform of your development to be .NET Framework 4.0, you could use the static property `Environment.Is64BitOperatingSystem` for the same purpose.

SUMMARY

Through the techniques you learned in this chapter, you know how to share state and functionality in ArcObjects programming. Another important topic was wiring events in ArcObjects. You also saw two different models of deployment under the hood of ArcObjects in this chapter. Through these two different models of deployment, it is possible for you to distribute and publish your custom component or add-in. Hopefully, distributing your custom component or add-in enables you to sell a lot of copies and thus make some money!

Though this book mainly focuses on ArcMap and ArcCatalog, all other applications in the ArcGIS for Desktop suite share a similar architecture based on ArcObjects. Through the skills you gained in this book, you can put your knowledge of ArcObjects to work to make all sorts of .NET-based customizations in ArcGIS for Desktop applications. Good luck with your future ArcObjects projects.

EXERCISES

1. What are outbound interfaces?

2. Which utility must be used to register and unregister custom components in version 10.0 and later of ArcGIS?

3. How you can access the installation address of your custom component?

You will find the answers to these exercises in this book's appendix.

▶ WHAT YOU LEARNED IN THIS CHAPTER

TOPIC	KEY CONCEPTS
Sharing state and functionality between components	In order to enable inter-component communication, you can use the static members inside ArcObjects components. So the first step is to define a static member of type `class` inside that class, which is initialized in the constructor. Then you add static methods and properties to perform actions on the static member.
Implementation of event interfaces	Usually, different classes that implement an event interface fire the same event in different circumstances. For example, many CoClasses, such as `Map`, `PageLayout`, and `Legend`, implement the `IActiveViewEvents_Event` outbound interface. The `Map` CoClass fires the `ItemAdded` event when a layer is added to a map. The `PageLayout` CoClass fires `ItemAdded` when a legend, MapFrame, and graphics are added to the page layout. In addition, implementation of an event interface does not mean that all events of the event interface must be fired by a class. As another example, the `Map` CoClass implements the `IActiveViewEvents_Event` interface, but it doesn't fire the `FocusMapChanged` event (which is a member of the `IActiveViewEvents_Event` interface).
Application extensions	Application extensions (or extensions for short) are a special type of component with the sole purpose of management of other types of components in an add-in or custom component project. The extensions provide a central point of coordination. Through extensions, it is possible to handle application events in just one place and manage the state of all other components of the ArcObjects project.
Add-in deployment	In order to deploy an add-in, you need just one step: Build the add-in project using Release configuration.
Custom component deployment	In order to deploy a custom component, you need the following steps: 1. Build the custom component project using Release configuration. 2. Create the setup project. 3. Add an Installer class for registering the custom component with `ESRIRegAsm.exe`.

Answers to Chapter Exercises

CHAPTER 1

Exercise 1 Solution

WFS enables platform-independent querying and retrieval of geospatial data over the web. Unlike WMS, which returns an image of geospatial data for display purposes, WFS retrieves encoded features that can be edited and spatially analyzed.

Exercise 2 Solution

File geodatabase provides the fastest possible performance among the three formats. In addition, it needs less disk space for storing geospatial data.

Exercise 3 Solution

Viewer, virtual globe, and professional.

CHAPTER 2

Exercise 1 Solution

The best way to create and automate geoprocessing workflows is using Python and ArcPy. However, the real strength and power of Python and ArcPy is executing long and advanced workflows.

Exercise 2 Solution

Desktop Add-Ins provide a declarative model for configuration.

Exercise 3 Solution

The full flexibility can be achieved using ArcObjects SDK (extending ArcObjects). In fact, it is possible to really extend ArcObjects by implementing and extending interfaces, which cannot be done using other methods of ArcGIS customization.

Exercise 4 Solution

Sharing customizations (such as newly created toolbars and commands) in the ArcObjects SDK (Extending ArcObjects) requires creating an installation package. As a result, like any installation it needs administrative permission. All the other models of development of ArcGIS for Desktop applications don't need operating system administrator privileges.

CHAPTER 3

Exercise 1 Solution

The `float` and `double` data types have rounding errors. Because the `decimal` data type holds a larger number of significant digits than either the `float` or the `double` data types and it is not subject to rounding errors, it is best suited for scientific calculations inside C#.

Exercise 2 Solution

The `System.Int32` or C# `int` data type provides the fastest possible performance for numeric calculations.

Exercise 3 Solution

Generally, XAML (eXtensible Application Markup Language) is used to define the user interface of WPF applications. It is based on XML and because it is completely declarative, it enables the developer or designer of the user interface to describe the look and feel of the application without any programming.

Exercise 4 Solution

To provide descriptive help about the purpose, parameters, and return value (if any) of methods, you can use XML comments or documentation comments. In order to use the XML or documentation comments, you need to type three slashes (///) before the method declaration to insert XML tags for any methods. Then you should provide a description for every tag.

CHAPTER 4

Exercise 1 Solution

Method overloading and method overriding are part of the polymorphism principle. In addition, operator overloading can be considered as another aspect of polymorphism.

Exercise 2 Solution

The `System.String` or C# `string` data type is a class. In other words, it is a reference type. In reference types, an assignment operator is used to copy the reference of an object, not the contents of that object. But for the `string` type the mentioned operator is overloaded to provide value copying functionality.

Exercise 3 Solution

The exception handling block in .NET consists of three related blocks: `try`, `catch`, and `finally`. The `finally` block is optional. Code inside the `finally` block is executed whether the exception occurs or not. This allows you to perform cleanup procedures, such as closing a stream, database connection, or releasing any unmanaged resources.

Exercise 4 Solution

`ArrayList` objects are not strongly typed, meaning that you can add any data type to a single `ArrayList` object. The flexible nature of the `ArrayList` class causes many issues when you want to evaluate data from an `ArrayList`. When data is added to the `ArrayList`, it is cast to a generic `System.Object` type. In order to use items inside an `ArrayList`, you have to cast elements inside the `ArrayList` back to their proper data type. This is called boxing and unboxing, which reduces performance.

CHAPTER 5

Exercise 1 Solution

There are three types of classes: Abstract Class, Class, and CoClass. Abstract Classes cannot be instantiated and used for organizing common states and behaviors. Unlike Abstract Classes, Classes can have instances. The instances of Classes must be created by other classes (which can be Classes or CoClasses). The third type of classes includes concrete classes or CoClasses that can have instances. Unlike Classes, instances of CoClasses can be created using the new keyword.

Exercise 2 Solution

Type inheritance is a relationship between parent and child classes. In type inheritance, all the interfaces of a parent class are inherited by child classes.

Exercise 3 Solution

In interface inheritance, all the members of a parent interface are inherited by the child interfaces.

Exercise 4 Solution

The main entry points to ArcObjects development are the `Application` or `m_application` preset and public variables in Visual Studio Desktop Add-Ins and Extending ArcObjects project templates, respectively.

CHAPTER 6

Exercise 1 Solution

Inside .NET, any container class, such as collections and arrays, that implements the IEnumerable or IEnumerator interfaces can provide the capability to iterate through its members using a foreach construct. Since neither the IEnumerable nor the IEnumerator interface is implemented for collections and container classes inside ArcObjects, use of a foreach construct for ArcObjects is impossible (without using some advanced features of .NET such as extension methods).

Exercise 2 Solution

By using the LayerCount property, only the first level layers in the Table Of Contents window can be accessed. On the other hand, by using the Layers property you can access all layers in the table of contents. Although it is possible to use recursive coding to iterate through all layers inside a map using the LayerCount property, it is always more efficient and safer to use the Layers property and IEnumLayer object to iterate through all layers.

Exercise 3 Solution

In previous versions of ArcObjects, IFeatureLayer was the main interface for working with vector-based datasets like shapefiles. Via the FeatureClass property of that interface, actual geospatial data can be accessed. In the current version of ArcObjects, the IFeatureLayer interface is superseded by IFeatureLayer2. As a result, the IFeatureLayer2 interface is the main interface for working with vector-based datasets.

Exercise 4 Solution

Through the IDocumentInfo2 interface, some metadata like author, description, and keywords can be saved in *.mxd files. For *.lyr files, the ILayerGeneralProperties interface has to be used for providing lightweight metadata.

Exercise 5 Solution

To access all maps inside an MxDocument instance, the Maps property of the IMxDocument interface must be used. As the name suggests, this property behaves like a collection and provides members for iterating through each map.

To get to the active Data Frame (FocusMap), the IActiveView interface of the Map CoClass should be used. The aforementioned interface provides the IsActive() method, which returns a bool value indicating whether a Map instance has focus (the Data Frame is activated) or not.

CHAPTER 7

Exercise 1 Solution

The IFeatureWorkspace interface of the Workspace Class must be used in order to create a FeatureDataset in all kinds of geodatabases. The FeatureDatasetName CoClass can be used for the same purpose.

Exercise 2 Solution

Data stored in the string variable contains comma-separated values of all fields. Definitely incorrect! As mentioned in Chapter 6, no .NET interfaces that support a `foreach` construct for collections (`IEnumerable` and `IEnumerator` interfaces) are implemented for collections inside ArcObjects. For this reason, the code won't compile.

Exercise 3 Solution

The `showInitially` attribute determines whether or not a toolbar is shown automatically the first time after installation. Using the ArcGIS Add-Ins Wizard, if you select the Premier Toolbar check box, the `showInitially` attribute will set to `true`.

CHAPTER 8

Exercise 1 Solution

Search cursors are used to return a subset of records for some read-only purposes, such as calculating a statistic or getting a count of records. Search `Cursor` objects are created using the `Search()` method of the `SelectionSet`, `FeatureClass`, and `Table` Classes.

Exercise 2 Solution

The `Field` and `Cursor` properties must be set. After setting the `Field` and `Cursor` properties, statistics of the specified field can be accessed through the `Statistics` property, which is of type `IStatisticsResults` interface.

Exercise 3 Solution

The `UID` CoClass is usually used for referencing the GUID of interfaces and CoClasses in ArcObjects as well as all your development in the ArcObjects system. For example, you can get to the Dockable add-in called `myDockableWin` using the following code:

```
UID dockableWinUID = new UIDClass();
dockableWinUID.Value = ThisAddIn.IDs.myDockableWin;
```

Exercise 4 Solution

The following method performs the switch selection for the cities FeatureLayer. It simply gets the current selected features and then uses the `Combine()` method to perform switch selection.

```
private void PerformSwitchSelection()
    {
        IMxDocument mxdoc = ArcMap.Application.Document as IMxDocument;
        IMap map = mxdoc.FocusMap;
        IEnumLayer enumLayer = map.Layers;
        ILayer layer = enumLayer.Next();
        IFeatureLayer FL = null;
        while (layer != null)
        {
```

```
        if (layer is IFeatureLayer && layer.Name == "cities")
        {
            FL = layer as IFeatureLayer;
            break;
        }
        layer = enumLayer.Next();
    }

    if (FL == null)
    { return; }

    IFeatureSelection fSelection = FL as IFeatureSelection;
    ISelectionSet selectedFeatures = fSelection.SelectionSet;
    ISelectionSet allFeatures = FL.FeatureClass.Select(null,
    esriSelectionType.esriSelectionTypeIDSet, esriSelectionOption.
    esriSelectionOptionNormal, null);

    ISelectionSet switchSelection = null;

    allFeatures.Combine(selectedFeatures,
    esriSetOperation.esriSetSymDifference, out switchSelection);

    fSelection.SelectionSet = switchSelection;
    mxdoc.ActiveView.Refresh();
}
```

CHAPTER 9

Exercise 1 Solution

If set to true, the showInitially attribute of a specific toolbar causes the toolbar to be displayed automatically the first time after installation of the add-in.

```
<Toolbar id="Amirian,_DevExperts_GeometrySolution_GeometryToolbar"
 caption="GeometryToolbar" showInitially="true">
```

Exercise 2 Solution

The IRelationalOperator interface has several methods for examining the relationship between two geometries. They return a boolean value indicating whether or not the desired relationship exists. Contains(), Crosses(), Disjoint(), Equal(), Overlaps(), Touches(), and Within() are some useful methods of the IRelationalOperator interface.

Exercise 3 Solution

In order to retain the geometry of all features in memory as separate objects, you need to use a non-recycling cursor.

CHAPTER 10

Exercise 1 Solution

There is no default renderer for raster data. Based on the type of data in a raster dataset, ArcObjects automatically determines the best renderer and uses that RasterRenderer to display the raster dataset. For example, if a multiband satellite image is added to ArcMap, it uses `RasterRGBRenderer` to display it as an RGB composite, and if a Digital Elevation Model (DEM) is added to ArcMap, it uses `RasterStretchColorRampRenderer` to display it.

Exercise 2 Solution

The `IGeoFeatureLayer` interface is used for assigning a FeatureRenderer to a FeatureLayer. More specifically, this interface has a `Renderer` property that is used to assign a FeatureRenderer to a FeatureLayer.

Exercise 3 Solution

In order to perform classification of a numeric field, first of all the histogram of the field is needed. In this case, `IHistogram` and `ITableHistogram` provide histogram data that include values and frequencies.

The next step is to create an appropriate `Classify` instance and call its `Classify()` method to create appropriate break points based on the data and its method of classification. Four methods of classification correspond to four `Classify` subclasses.

Exercise 4 Solution

The `ScaleDependentRenderer` is available only to ArcObjects developers. Put simply, this type of FeatureRenderer is an ordered collection of other types of FeatureRenderers. Users of ArcGIS for Desktop applications could create multiple FeatureLayers and set the maximum and minimum scales for them to provide what can be achieved through code and the `ScaleDependentRenderer`.

CHAPTER 11

Exercise 1 Solution

There are two categories of elements: GraphicElements and FrameElements. GraphicElements are elements which can be added to both maps and PageLayouts and are not related to a map's content. In contrast to GraphicElements, FrameElements can be added only to PageLayouts and depend upon a map's content. In other words, FrameElements will dynamically change as the contents or properties of the map (Data View) change.

Exercise 2 Solution

The PDF export interface (in the `ExportPDF` CoClass) is able to create PDF files which contain geospatial (attributes as well as location) information. Using the `IExportPDF2` interface makes it possible to include geospatial information in the exported file. In addition, in order to implement security for a PDF file, you can set user and master passwords using the `IExportPDFPasswordSecurity` interface.

Exercise 3 Solution

In order to determine the screen resolution, you can use the `Resolution` property of the `IDisplayTransformation` interface. See the following code:

```
IDisplayTransformation dispTransformation = mxdoc.ActiveView.ScreenDisplay.
DisplayTransformation;
double screenResolution= dispTransformation.Resolution;
```

In addition, you can use the .NET specific method for determining the screen resolution. The following code demonstrates how to get the screen resolution in both X and Y directions:

```
System.Windows.Forms.Form myForm = new System.Windows.Forms.Form();
System.Drawing.Graphics myGraphic = myForm.CreateGraphics();
double screenResolutionX = myGraphic.DpiX;
double screenResolutionY = myGraphic.DpiY;
```

Note that in order to use the .NET–specific method, a reference to `System.Windows.Forms` is needed.

CHAPTER 12

Exercise 1 Solution

The `VarArray` CoClass through the `IVariantArray` interface is used to handle parameters for geoprocessing tools. These types are defined in the System library of ArcObjects.

Exercise 2 Solution

The toolboxes can be saved in a folder or in any kind of geodatabase. In order to add a toolbox to a geoprocessor object, when the toolbox is saved in a folder, you can simply call the `geoprocessor .AddToolbox()` method.

```
IGeoProcessor2 gp = new GeoProcessorClass();
string fileSystemAddressOfToolbox = @"D:\testToolbox.tbx";
gp.AddToolbox(fileSystemAddressOfToolbox);
// configuring the parameters
//...
gp.Execute("BufferSelectKML", parameters, null);
```

You can get the same result using the alternative approach through the `ToolboxWorkspaceFactory` CoClass.

```
IWorkspaceFactory txWSF = new ToolboxWorkspaceFactoryClass();
IWorkspace ws = txWSF.OpenFromFile(
arcGISinstallationAddress + "\\" + arctoolboxAddress, ArcMap.
Application.hWnd);
IToolboxWorkspace toolboxWS = ws as IToolboxWorkspace;
```

```
IGPToolbox gpToolbox = toolboxWS.OpenToolbox(toolbox);
IGPTool gpTool = gpToolbox.OpenTool("MultipleRingBuffer");

IGeoProcessor2 gp = new GeoProcessorClass();
gp.AddOutputsToMap = true;
gp.OverwriteOutput = true;
// configuring the parameters
//...

gp.Execute(gpTool.Name, parameters, null);
```

As is true for tools in folders, you can access the tools inside a geodatabase using the
IToolboxWorkspace interface. The following code snippet illustrates how to execute a tool inside a
file geodatabase:

```
string fileGDBAddress = @"D:\testFileGDB.gdb";
string toolboxName = "testToolbox";
string toolName = "simpleMultipleRingBuffer";

IWorkspaceFactory fWF = new FileGDBWorkspaceFactoryClass();
IWorkspace ws = fWF.OpenFromFile(fileGDBAddress, ArcMap.
Application.hWnd);
IToolboxWorkspace toolboxWS = ws as IToolboxWorkspace;

//access to the toolbox
IGPToolbox toolbox = toolboxWS.OpenToolbox(toolboxName);
//get the tool or model
IGPTool tool = toolbox.OpenTool(toolName);
// configuring the parameters
//...

gp.Execute(gpTool.Name, parameters, null);
```

Exercise 3 Solution

When there is no connection between the input and output parameters of tools and you want to
execute tools in the background, you need to submit the tools to the geoprocessing queue using the
geoprocessor.ExecuteAsync() method. In this case, you can freely submit multiple unrelated
geoprocessing tools to the queue to be executed in the background in the same method. Note that,
since all custom tools are configured to be executed in the foreground by default, you have to change
this behavior prior to submitting them to the geoprocessing queue.

Exercise 4 Solution

If tools are running in the foreground, then there is only one tool running, which disables any interaction of the user with the user interface of ArcGIS for Desktop applications. In this case, there will
be no chance of starting an edit session.

If tools are running in the background process, then there is only one tool running and other tools
are waiting in the geoprocessing queue for their execution turn. In this case, while users can interact
with the user interface of ArcGIS for Desktop applications, they cannot start an edit session. This
means all the geoprocessing tools that have been submitted to the geoprocessing queue must be
executed completely or cancelled in order to begin an edit session.

CHAPTER 13

Exercise 1 Solution

The most efficient method for deleting a huge number of features in a file or personal geodatabase is to use the `DeleteSearchedRows()` method, which is defined by the `ITable` interface.

```
//featureClass variable is an instance of IFeatureClass
IQueryFilter qF = new QueryFilterClass();
qF.WhereClause = "\"Name\" <> \'New York\'";
ITable table = featureClass as ITable;
table.DeleteSearchedRows(qF);
```

But when a FeatureClass is in an ArcSDE geodatabase, the most efficient method for deleting numerous features is using a search cursor.

Exercise 2 Solution

When using the search cursor to modify features, the recycling parameter must always be set to `false`. Quite in contrast, the update cursors can use recycling when there is no need to update more than one feature at once. This kind of cursor provides better performance in comparison with a non-recycling search cursor.

Exercise 3 Solution

The ArcObjects `Geometry` namespace contains several enumerations that can be used to specify the Well Known ID (WKID) of many available spatial reference systems in ArcGIS. The WKID of spatial reference systems is defined by a standardization organization such as the European Petroleum Survey Group (EPSG). It is possible to directly use the EPSG code for the known spatial references.

```
//for WGS 84 EPSG 4326
ISpatialReference srs = spatialReferenceFactory.
CreateGeographicCoordinateSystem(4326);
```

Alternatively, you can use these enumerations in the ArcObjects `Geometry` namespace to access the desired spatial reference system.

```
ISpatialReferenceFactory spatialReferenceFactory = new
SpatialReferenceEnvironmentClass();
int coordinateSystemID = (int)esriSRGeoCSType.esriSRGeoCS_WGS1984;

ISpatialReference srs = spatialReferenceFactory.
CreateGeographicCoordinateSystem(coordinateSystemID);
```

CHAPTER 14

Exercise 1 Solution

The outbound interfaces (also known as *event interfaces*) are a special type of interface where all members are of type event. For this reason, other objects are needed in order to handle events that are notified using event interfaces. Also they are hidden in the Visual Studio IDE. In other words, outbound interfaces in .NET (such as `IActiveViewEvents_Event`) are not displayed when you are coding in Visual Studio, but you can use them in C# or VB. They are mainly used for event wiring in ArcObjects programming.

Exercise 2 Solution

Starting with ArcGIS 10.0, all custom components must be registered using the `ESRIRegAsm.exe` utility. Your setup package must use this utility to register custom components. The `ESRIRegAsm.exe` utility ships with ArcGIS for Desktop applications. The default installation path of ESRIRegAsm.exe on 32-bit Windows operating systems is as follows:

```
<Windows Installation Drive >:\Program Files\Common Files\ArcGIS\bin\
ESRIRegAsm.exe
```

and on 64-bit Windows:

```
<Windows Installation Drive >:\Program Files (x86)\Common Files\ArcGIS\bin\
ESRIRegAsm.exe
```

Exercise 3 Solution

Using Custom Action Data, it is possible to keep track of the installation address of a custom component on the target machine. For this purpose, you need to add the following Custom Action Data to the Install and Uninstall actions:

```
/installationDir=" [TARGETDIR]\"
```

Then in the Installer class, you can access the installation address using this code snippet:

```
this.Context.Parameters["installationDir"];
```

INDEX

N

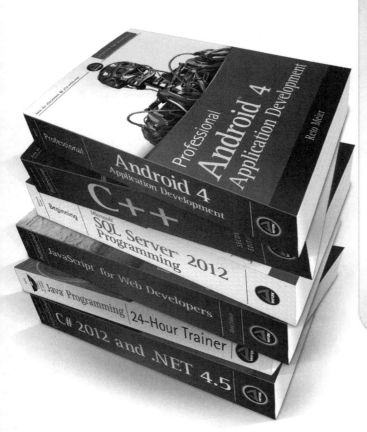